JIM JARMUSCH

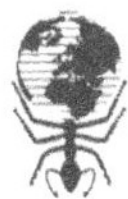

Jim Jarmusch

music,
words
and
noise

sara piazza

REAKTION BOOKS

Published by Reaktion Books Ltd
Unit 32, Waterside
44–48 Wharf Road
London N1 7UX, UK
www.reaktionbooks.co.uk

First published 2015
Transferred to digital printing 2022

Printed and bound in Great Britain by
CPI Group (UK) Ltd, Croydon CR0 4YY

A catalogue record for this book is available from the British Library
ISBN 978 1 78023 441 0

Contents

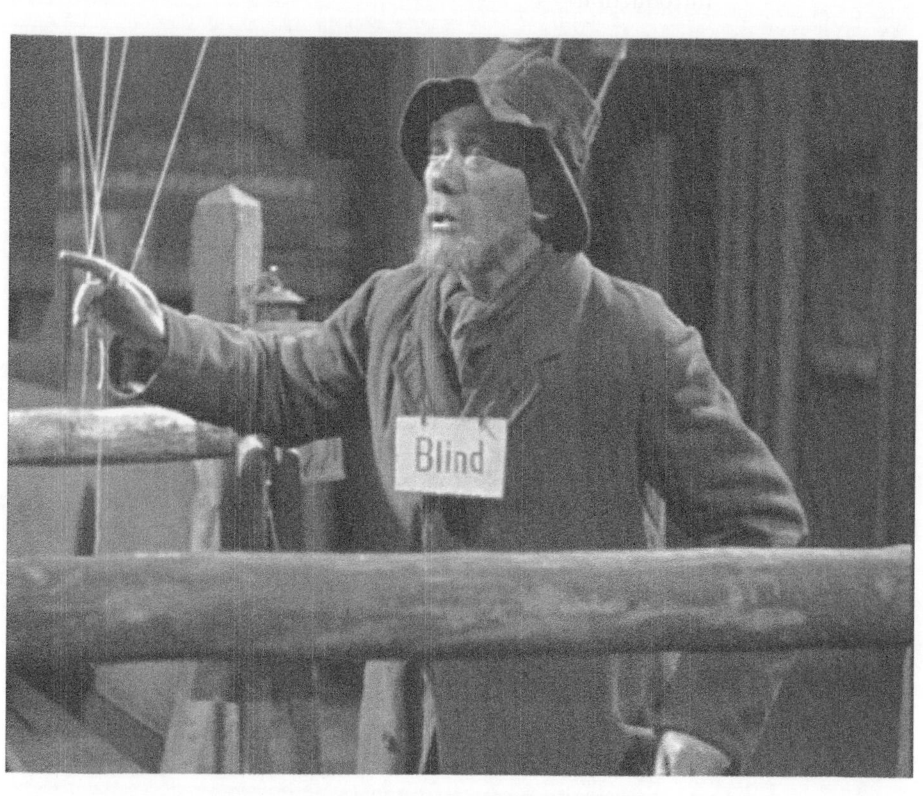
Blind

t is these three invisible mainstays that will bolster my journey
he cinema of Jim Jarmusch, whose career kicked off roughly 50
after the release of Lang's film and in New York, at that time an
d-city' very similar to West Berlin. According to Jarmusch:

erlin is an incredible city. It seems to be very similar to New
ork in terms of tension and atmosphere, but for very different
asons. Like being a walled-in island, torn in half, with the
nstant military presence.[1]

7 he lived in Berlin for almost a year and his reference to the mili-
resence naturally alludes to the atmosphere of a city that at the
as still cut in two by 43 km of brick and barbed wire.[2] In the New
f 1981, the date of Jarmusch's statement about Berlin, bricks
rbed wire played an integral part in the topography of some of
y's neighbourhoods, Manhattan's Lower East Side in particu-
it was more about ruined buildings, crumbling walls and earthen
t were semi-abandoned and fenced off. In this scenario, Jarmusch
first full-length feature, *Permanent Vacation* (1980), shot as his
tion thesis film for NYU Graduate Film School, which, however,
rned down by the commission at the time. To produce the film
ch used his scholarship money – the Louis B. Mayer fellowship
had been sent directly to him instead of to the School.[3] This
alludes to a trait of Jarmusch's method of working that would
e in the decades to come: all the phases of film finance are hand-
ctly by him and not delegated to intermediaries, because
hip of the work – in other words the negative – must be the
's, as both the work's creative and financial point of reference.
e role of the producer is comparable to that of a collaborator
ders the actual shooting of the film materially possible but
t dictate conditions or influence the creative process. This
of working – often associated with the nebulous and versa-
on of 'indie', or independent, a label that Jarmusch, willingly
carries with him everywhere – naturally involves risks. The
k is of taking for ever to complete a project or, in the worst case,
finishing it. Having made eleven feature films since 1980,[4] and
g a four-year absence from cinemas, Jarmusch still manages to
his with irony, as demonstrated by his opening response at
Cannes Film Festival press conference for the world premiere

Introduction

In the spring of 1931 – just four years after the
Talkies – a German film made history by, among
in an undisputable manner the expressive and nar
visible on the screen: Fritz Lang's *M*. Apart fro
Peter Lorre in the role of child killer Hans Becker
memory of those who have seen the film is witho
that Beckert whistles to his little victims before
them. 'In the Hall of the Mountain King' was
Grieg for Henrik Ibsen's *Peer Gynt* and today i
scended the theatre by entering into everyday
said, thanks to the telephone companies aroun
it as a standard ringing tone. In *M* it is this melo
and it is a detail of no small consequence that
report the killer is an elderly, itinerant vendor
small but eloquent sign hanging from the old
to be 'Blind', an adjective that works in both
– alluding perhaps to the use of the written w
cards of silent cinema – clears up any misund
far more than sight, that demonstrates itself t
the disturbing story told by Lang in his first sou
is a simple whistle.

The apparently banal act of whistling is
plex than it might seem due to containing me
word – and finally an acoustic signal, and s
sound material all three fundamental acoust
non-visible sphere on film: MUSIC, WORDS a

The blind vendor,
M, dir. Fritz Lang
(1931).

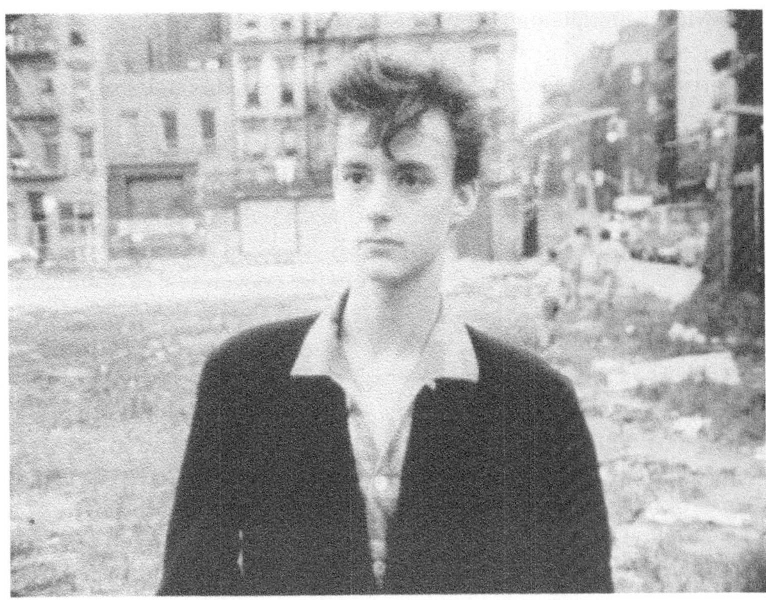

of his most recent film, the long-awaited *Only Lovers Left Alive*. When asked what made him decide to shoot a vampire movie, Jarmusch wryly replied that he had heard about the possibility of earning great sums of money with this type of film. On a more serious note, he added that he had wanted to direct a love story with vampires for seven years, which was roughly the amount of time it took to complete the financing for the film. Not even Jarmusch's consolidated reputation as an 'indie icon' – earned over the course of a 30-year career far from the commercial temptations of Hollywood and studded with films like *Stranger Than Paradise* (1984), *Down By Law* (1986) and *Dead Man* (1995), considered by many as milestones in independent cinema, and fundamental references for generations of younger filmmakers – was enough to conjure up a budget of about $7 million in a short time.[5] And as my acoustic journey through Jarmusch's cinema does not adhere to a chronological order, but instead explores the three sound mainstays of audio-vision – Music, Words and Noise – this is the right place for a brief panorama on certain moments of that 30-year career before I move on to illustrate the structure of the book.

Following its initial film-school 'mishaps', *Permanent Vacation* attracted the attention of the critics: it was awarded the Josef von Sternberg Award at the 1980 Mannheim Film Week in Germany, and in February 1981 it was shown at the young cinema 'Forum' section of the Berlinale. Despite these early successes, the film was not released commercially. The year 1982 saw the start of the long production journey of *Stranger Than Paradise*, the film that consolidated Jarmusch's place as an independent filmmaker on the international scene. Released in its definitive three-episode version only in 1984, it was initially conceived as a 30-minute short entitled *The New World*, about a Hungarian teenager who comes to New York from Budapest. In the feature-length version, the journey continues to Cleveland and then Florida. An outsider's perspective on America, on its cultural melting pot and its interior and exterior land-scapes, is a theme that Jarmusch would continue to develop over the course of the years. The European success of *Stranger Than Paradise*, winner of the prestigious Caméra d'Or for the best debut film at the 1984 Cannes Film Festival, certainly made it a lot easier and faster to produce the next picture, *Down By Law* (1986), in which, other than John Lurie, who had already starred in *Stranger Than Paradise* with Eszter Balint and Richard Edson, two of Jarmusch's close friends and collaborators – Roberto Benigni and Tom Waits – played leading roles. *Down By Law* also sanctioned the start of a long partnership with the Dutch director of photography (and Wim Wenders's regular associate) Robby Müller, confirming another fundamental characteristic of Jarmusch's modus operandi: surround yourself with familiar faces, especially with regard to the crew. Müller is a good example, as are editor Jay Rabinowitz and soundman Drew Kunin, both Jarmusch's frequent collaborators.

In *Down By Law*, the adventures of the three friends/enemies Jack, Zack and Bob, accidental cellmates and equally accidental fellow escapees through the swamps of Louisiana's bayous, gave Jarmusch the opportunity to continue not only exploring the image of America, its literary and musical culture, but also its film genres: the prison or escape movie, gangster movie, road movie, western, samurai, noir, romantic comedy, episodic film, vampire story – all labels that, possibly also combining more than one, may be affixed to Jarmusch's films. And yet I believe this labelling would be a mistake or at least an excessive simplification. Genre in Jarmusch's cinema is a pretext, scaffolding that does not necessarily conceal a structure as one might expect. The ingredients are there, but the recipe has a different, unexpected flavour.

Introduction

In the spring of 1931 – just four years after the official advent of the Talkies – a German film made history by, among other things, showing in an undisputable manner the expressive and narrative power of the invisible on the screen: Fritz Lang's *M*. Apart from the bulging eyes of Peter Lorre in the role of child killer Hans Beckert, what also strikes the memory of those who have seen the film is without a doubt the melody that Beckert whistles to his little victims before abducting and killing them. 'In the Hall of the Mountain King' was composed by Edvard Grieg for Henrik Ibsen's *Peer Gynt* and today its popularity has transcended the theatre by entering into everyday life – partly, it must be said, thanks to the telephone companies around the world often using it as a standard ringing tone. In *M* it is this melody that betrays Beckert, and it is a detail of no small consequence that the one to discover and report the killer is an elderly, itinerant vendor who has lost his sight. A small but eloquent sign hanging from the old man's neck declares him to be 'Blind', an adjective that works in both German and English and – alluding perhaps to the use of the written word so typical to the title cards of silent cinema – clears up any misunderstanding: it is hearing, far more than sight, that demonstrates itself to be the decisive sense in the disturbing story told by Lang in his first sound film, the key to which is a simple whistle.

The blind vendor, M, dir. Fritz Lang (1931).

The apparently banal act of whistling is in reality far more complex than it might seem due to containing melody, voice – a vehicle for word – and finally an acoustic signal, and so synthesizing in a single sound material all three fundamental acoustic layers that make up the non-visible sphere on film: MUSIC, WORDS and NOISE.

It is these three invisible mainstays that will bolster my journey into the cinema of Jim Jarmusch, whose career kicked off roughly 50 years after the release of Lang's film and in New York, at that time an 'island-city' very similar to West Berlin. According to Jarmusch:

> Berlin is an incredible city. It seems to be very similar to New York in terms of tension and atmosphere, but for very different reasons. Like being a walled-in island, torn in half, with the constant military presence.[1]

In 1987 he lived in Berlin for almost a year and his reference to the military presence naturally alludes to the atmosphere of a city that at the time was still cut in two by 43 km of brick and barbed wire.[2] In the New York of 1981, the date of Jarmusch's statement about Berlin, bricks and barbed wire played an integral part in the topography of some of the city's neighbourhoods, Manhattan's Lower East Side in particular, but it was more about ruined buildings, crumbling walls and earthen lots that were semi-abandoned and fenced off. In this scenario, Jarmusch set his first full-length feature, *Permanent Vacation* (1980), shot as his graduation thesis film for NYU Graduate Film School, which, however, was turned down by the commission at the time. To produce the film Jarmusch used his scholarship money – the Louis B. Mayer fellowship – that had been sent directly to him instead of to the School.[3] This already alludes to a trait of Jarmusch's method of working that would continue in the decades to come: all the phases of film finance are handled directly by him and not delegated to intermediaries, because ownership of the work – in other words the negative – must be the director's, as both the work's creative and financial point of reference. Thus the role of the producer is comparable to that of a collaborator who renders the actual shooting of the film materially possible but does not dictate conditions or influence the creative process. This method of working – often associated with the nebulous and versatile notion of 'indie', or independent, a label that Jarmusch, willingly or not, carries with him everywhere – naturally involves risks. The main risk is of taking for ever to complete a project or, in the worst case, not even finishing it. Having made eleven feature films since 1980,[4] and following a four-year absence from cinemas, Jarmusch still manages to look at this with irony, as demonstrated by his opening response at the 2013 Cannes Film Festival press conference for the world premiere

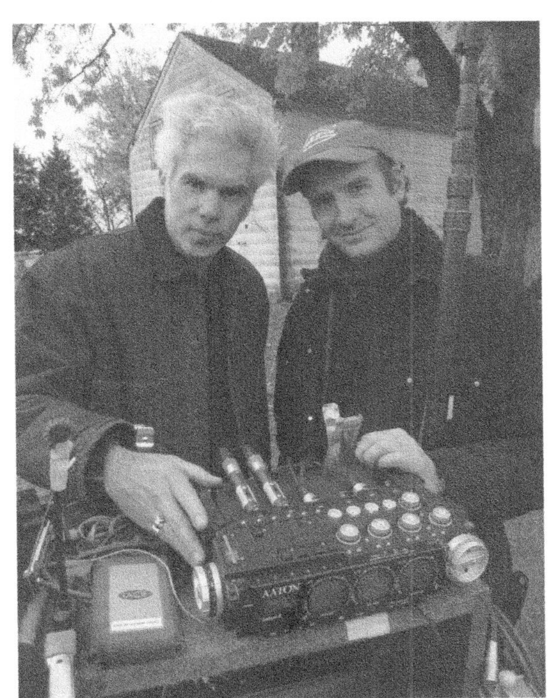

Jim Jarmusch and Drew Kunin on location of *Broken Flowers* with Aaton Cantar recorder.

Robby Müller on location, *Dead Man*.

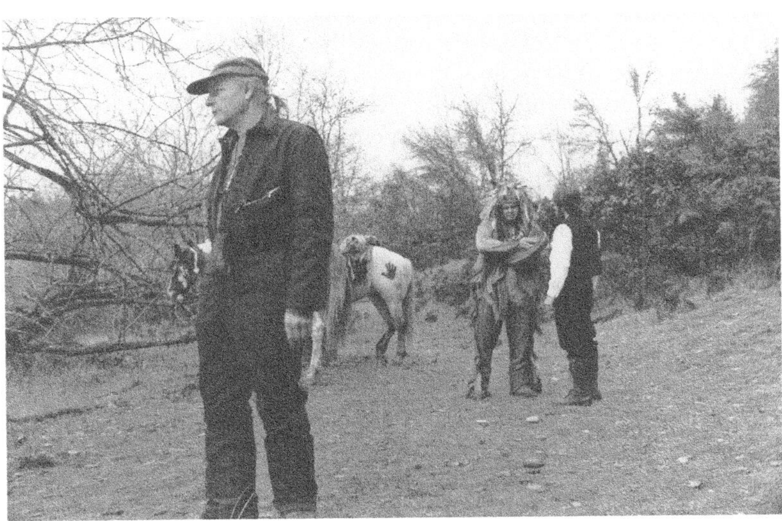

Jarmusch explained in his own words just how much genres are a fluid and personal concept for him, as is evident in *Mystery Train* (1989), his film tribute to Memphis and its musical traditions. In the liner notes for *Mystery Train's* soundtrack CD Jarmusch defined the film as a triptych including 'three separate but connecting stories, like those Japanese films made up of several ghost stories, or the Italian ones consisting of romantic comedies'.[6] However, the genres were dealt with very freely and the episodic structure, Jarmusch added, was only a 'disguise'. The Cannes Film Festival liked the 'disguise' and once again acknowledged Jarmusch's work by awarding *Mystery Train* with the prize, albeit minor, for Best Artistic Achievement. That year the Palme d'Or went instead to *Sex, Lies and Videotape* by Steven Soderbergh, director-symbol of the indie 'fashion' that was about to overwhelm the 1990s.[7] Jarmusch's next project should have been a western provisionally entitled *Ghost Dog*, written in collaboration with author and screenwriter Rudy Wurlitzer, writer of New-Hollywood classics such as Monte Hellman's *Two-Lane Blacktop* (1971) and Sam Pekinpah's *Pat Garrett and Billy the Kid* (1973), but the project never took off. The real causes of this failure, like all projects that never see the light of day, are difficult to ascertain. In certain accounts regarding the project, the blame is placed on the high cost of Cinemascope, while according to others it is placed on Jarmusch's and Wurlitzer's personality clashes and differing creative interpretations.[8] What cannot be argued, however, is that Jarmusch wrote his next screenplay very quickly, and alone: *Night On Earth* (1991) was to be filmed in five different cities, its cast made up mostly of Jarmusch's actor-friends. The moment of suspension of a taxi ride is the narrative nucleus of a film that, at least on paper, must have appeared to Jarmusch like a walk in the park when compared to the tortuous western project he had just shelved. In reality, it was not exactly like that. As remembered by a very diplomatic Frederick Elmes, the film's director of photography:

Night On Earth was really fun, because I'd been a big fan of Jim's films. I'd never met him before he contacted me . . . He had never shot in cars before, so it was a new experience for him to direct a film with a lot of dialogue in moving cars. But I enjoyed visiting the different cities and figuring out how to make these stories work.[9]

Jarmusch instead was more ironically direct in recalling this common experience:

> That was ridiculous. I wrote the film really fast and I was saying to myself 'This will be something real easy to do and I can do it fast.' Then I stepped back in pre-production, realising 'Oh man, this is in four different countries, in five different cities all inside of cars.' Shooting in a car is really difficult and anyone who has made a film in a car interior will tell you, 'Don't ever do that again.' . . . Fred Elmes was the director of photography. In some of the shots when we were towing the car, we had taken away the engine out of the engine cavity and mounted the camera in there. He was riding on the car, operating, sometimes holding a diopter – which allows you to have two different focus areas in the frame – and it was 14 degrees below zero. It was really cold and we were out all night. It was really not an easy film to make. I was deluded when I said, 'This'll be easy, little stories, a few characters.' It was hell.[10]

Night On Earth was liked by audiences but not by critics, who gave the film a lukewarm reception.[11] Four years passed before the making of his next feature film, *Dead Man*. However, Jarmusch enjoyed an intermediate success and, once again, it came from the Cannes Film Festival. In 1993 *Coffee and Cigarettes (Somewhere in California)* won the Palme d'Or for Best Short Film. Starring his close friends Tom Waits and Iggy Pop, the short is the third of the series of 'conversations' with coffee and cigarettes that Jarmusch began to shoot in 1986 (*Strange To Meet You* with Stephen Wright and Roberto Benigni) and continued in 1989 (*Memphis Version* with Joie Lee, Cinqué Lee and Steve Buscemi). Ten years later, in 2003, Jarmusch would fulfil his project to release the complete series of eleven shorts, collected over an arc of eighteen years, as a feature in the cinemas. It is also thanks to the perseverance that distinguishes him that in 1995 Jarmusch finally succeeded in realizing the idea cultivated over the years to shoot a western in black and white, *Dead Man*. Contrary to *Night On Earth*, the film bombed at the box office, but enjoyed critical success, giving birth to ad hoc definitions like 'acid western', lauding the visionary atmosphere, Neil Young's music and the hypnotic pace of this atypical road movie, its protagonist the young bookkeeper William Blake (Johnny Depp) and the cultured Native American Nobody (Gary Farmer).[12] Produced mainly with European and Japanese backing, *Dead Man* was presented in competition at the 1995 Cannes Film Festival and distributed by Miramax, run by the Weinstein brothers, who did not release the film in the United States until 10 May 1996, almost a year after its Cannes premiere.[13]

Jarmusch's next feature film was *Ghost Dog: The Way of the Samurai* (1999), and again, the project's gestation period was a lengthy one: four years separated *Dead Man* from the release of the gangster-samurai movie starring Forest Whitaker as the taciturn killer Ghost Dog. The wait for the new feature film was interrupted by the 'rockumentary' *Year of the Horse* (1997) that Jarmusch was commissioned to make by Neil Young after the Canadian rocker's fundamental musical contribution to *Dead Man*. Together with director/producer Larry Johnson, Young's longtime collaborator, Jarmusch had shot a music video for one of the tracks on his *Broken Arrow* album.[14] 'Let's shoot some more stuff that looks like that video', Young suggested after seeing it.[15] Despite not being accustomed to working on commission, Jarmusch took to the task and, together with Johnson, filmed Neil Young and Crazy Horse's tour, combining it with stock footage from 1976 and 1986 and interviews with the band and Young's father. The method of sampling – or collage – used here also characterized *Ghost Dog*, in which the reference to hip hop is substantial and not merely stylistic. With the feature films of the 2000s Jarmusch instead adopted a narrative technique closer to 'variations on a theme' – as becomes clear in the already mentioned episodic *Coffee and Cigarettes* (2003), the laconic, romantic road movie *Broken Flowers* (2005) and the stylized gangster road movie *The Limits of Control* (2009). Whereas the feature version of *Coffee and Cigarettes*, presented at the Venice Film Festival, was largely snubbed by the critics who considered it stylistically too self-referential and too schematic in its treatment of miscommunication, *Broken Flowers* – the story of Don Johnston, a middle-aged Casanova travelling from ex-lover to ex-lover in search of a hypothetical son – was an unexpected and stunning success. After winning the Jury Prize at the 2005 Cannes Film Festival, *Broken Flowers* became the biggest box office hit of Jarmusch's career.[16] Born from an idea by Sara Driver, his partner and collaborator since university days, and friend Bill Raden, the film stands out for its procession of female roles, an unusual element in Jarmusch's works. Julie Delpy, Sharon Stone, Frances Conroy, Jessica Lange, Tilda Swinton and, in a minor but incisive role, Chloë Sevigny are the leading ladies that Jarmusch chose to surround the apathetic Don, played by Bill Murray.

Chloë Sevigny also plays the lead in the short *Int. Trailer. Night*, Jarmusch's contribution to the collective film *Ten Minutes Older: The Trumpet* (2002). Filmed in black and white by Frederick Elmes, the short tells of an actress during a break in filming of exactly ten minutes.[17] Following the success of *Broken Flowers*, Jarmusch began to concentrate on his idea for a love story through the ages, defined by him as a 'crypto-vampire love story', which, as mentioned, took seven years to make: *Only Lovers Left Alive* was presented in competition at Cannes only in 2013.[18] Before achieving this goal, Jarmusch once again got busy with a variation on the road movie theme with his 'action film without action', *The Limits of Control* (2009).[19] The quasi-mute killer, Lone Man, played by a cold and elegant Isaach de Bankolé, travels from Madrid to the south of Spain, its scenery photographed with equally cold elegance by Christopher Doyle, multi-award-winning director of photography and Wong Kar-wai's regular collaborator.[20] Despite its undeniable aesthetic refinement, the film divided both critics and audiences, and was an unmitigated commercial flop.[21] It is probably for this reason that finding the funds for *Only Lovers Left Alive* was such an unusually long and complicated affair, seriously testing Jarmusch's

Jim Jarmusch and Frederick Elmes on location, *Broken Flowers*.

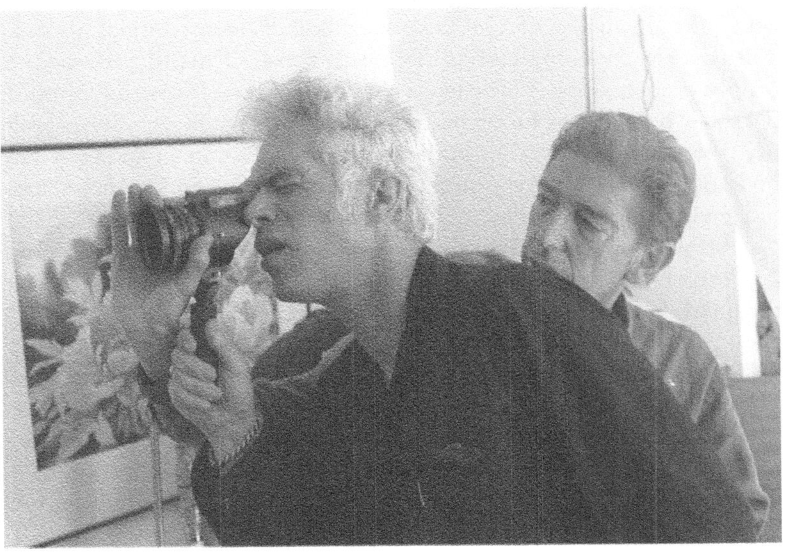

tenacity. Two important allies and enduring collaborators accompanied him on this journey, Tilda Swinton and John Hurt. As Jarmusch pointed out in Cannes:

> Tilda and I were talking about this film and I had a script seven years ago. Shortly after that there was a character for John Hurt and somehow they stayed with this project the whole time. It was very difficult to do but Tilda would never give up. When things would fall apart she would say: 'That means it's not the right time for us to make the film. That's a good thing!' I wasn't sure if that was a good thing but I think in the end it was because . . . here we are! And John Hurt said: 'You just tell me when we are gonna do it and I'll be there.' And he was.[22]

In Jarmusch's 'independent' cinema – the adjective intended as a synonym of 'artisanal' or 'homemade' – the trait of surrounding himself with trusted people, with whom over the years he has built a relationship that goes beyond work and is not restricted to the weeks it takes to shoot a film, thus becomes a true necessity. The example of the production course taken by *Only Lovers Left Alive* is the umpteenth demonstration of this. In a manner comparable in some ways to 'director-gang leaders' like John Cassavetes and Rainer Werner Fassbinder, Jarmusch's work is founded on an idea of 'collective' or 'familial' cinema, even if his style and rhythm are completely different to those of his illustrious and prolific predecessors. A little like a conductor whose leadership is indispensable, but without his orchestra perfectly useless, Jarmusch has built over the years with his slow but constant pace a compact and coherent body of work in which the analogy between cinema and music as 'arts of time' assumes a load-bearing role. In 1984, fresh from his success at Cannes with *Stranger Than Paradise*, when interviewed by critic Yann Lardeau of *Cahiers du Cinéma*, Jarmusch's response to a question about the link between music and cinema was clear:

> I believe in the existence of two likenesses: on one side, playing in concert is similar to acting onstage. To record music in a studio is relatively comparable to working on a film, be it editing or acting . . . I also think there is a similarity between the elaboration of a piece of music, with its tracks and its mixing, and the editing of a film. A link really exists.[23]

In Jarmusch's films sound is never reduced to mere background comment, but becomes an 'open, multiple, dispersed' area of linguistic production in its own right: an area in which a word may 'reduce itself' to noise without annulling communication; an area in which a sound effect may become the bearer of the narrative structure; an area in which the music may assume the role of interlocutor with whom to converse.[24]

For this reason I have chosen to structure my journey (one of the many possible) around the three invisible mainstays that support the acoustic scaffolding of a film. Music, words and noise are thus the three sections of the book around which I have developed my exploration, neither chronologically nor biographically, of the cinema of Jarmusch. Starting from the presupposition that in observing the work of a film director I consider it essential to pay the same attention both to what one sees and to what one hears, in Jarmusch's case I willingly forced the presupposition by favouring the acoustic sphere.

Music is the common denominator of the first four chapters: the formative environment of 'Jarmusch, the musician' from the New York of the late 1970s with the Del-Byzanteens and Dark Day, to his most recent musical collaborations both on stage and in the recording studio with Squrl, the recurring topos of musician/actor, the crucial role played by key personalities such as Nicholas Ray, Wim Wenders, Amos Poe and naturally John Lurie (to whom the third chapter is entirely dedicated), and finally the profound effect on Jarmusch's filmography of so-called black music and the role of two exceptional 'mestizos', Tom Waits and Neil Young. The music section ends with the acknowledgement of Jarmusch as a *musicien manqué*.

In the three chapters of the section *Words* I elaborate on the idea of relativism: intended initially as a 'battle against *verbocentrism*', or rather criticism of the paramount and unquestionable centrality of the verbal language that Jarmusch puts in motion thanks to instruments like polyglotism, the 'proliferation' or 'rarefaction' of the word, the violation of the cinematographic taboo of dialogue comprehension; and then as a more general 'cultural relativism' that finds its natural habitat and roots in the American melting pot.[25] Jarmusch expresses this, among other things, through irony, word games, his obsession with proper names along with, for example, his passion for Dante and hip hop. The *Words* section ends with a chapter on Jarmusch as poet in which I define certain 'poetic characters' in his cinema – Rammellzee, Nobody and William Blake, Ghost Dog, Bob and finally Christopher Marlowe – and observe the broader literary structure that Jarmusch has chosen for many of his films, favouring in particular the episodic form of the short story.

The third section of the book contains two chapters based on the leitmotif of *Noise*. In the first I investigate the narrative and expressive characteristics of noise that, thanks to its semantic flexibility, is capable of 'infiltrating' the other two sound materials, music and word. The last chapter, 'Silence', is based on the double premise that silence helps define sound and vice versa, and that there is no such thing as the total absence of sound. With a final hypothesis, according to which elements of pre-sound cinema converge in Jarmusch's work, I develop the idea of a *Silent-Sound Film*.

In light of this synthesis of the book's structure, a significant clarification must be made: speaking of the 'battle against verbocentrism', silence, relativism, the importance given to noise and *Silent-Sound Film*, one must not think that Jarmusch, in his cinematographic universe, preaches a refusal of communication, *tout court*. If his films abound with apparent vacuums, moments of suspension and pregnant silences, this is due in my opinion not so much to a rejection of communication but more, and this may sound paradoxical, to a reaffirmation of its inestimable value. Terms such as 'incommunicability' and 'alienation' are readily used by critics and film students, and yet Jarmusch's characters, no matter how taciturn they may be and despite frequently venturing across landscapes that turn out to be desolate and silent ruins of 'civilization', never give up *trying* to communicate.[26] Though this does not mean they necessarily succeed. And so the communication channels prosper and grow: from the customary ones of a word that has value only by virtue of its meaning, to those of a word capable of communicating even if its meaning remains obscure, becoming plain sound as in the case of a foreign language (purposely not subtitled); or a word that communicates thanks also to its shape and usage, like the poetic word; or one based on the ironic register founded on wordplay. Jarmusch's way of treating the word – and the other two sound matters – is certainly not hierarchic because not only is sound in no way subordinate to the image, but sound matters are also considered 'equal' to each other, establishing what I have called *sound democracy*. The ideal place to put this into practice is Jarmusch's melting pot. An invisible location, made up of all possible locations, inhabited by singular characters and events: here, William Blake, in an ambiguous game of identities with one of the more visionary of English-speaking poets, may be a young and naive bookkeeper who becomes a merciless killer without really being aware of it; here, thanks to an entertaining linguistic game, metaphorical names of Native Americans and allusively funky ones of rappers are taken to the same level as those of now ageing Italian American mafiosi; here, the lifestyle of a taciturn African American killer, active in the ghettos of Jersey City, may draw inspiration from an antique Japanese code of the samurai; here, the Elizabethan playwright Christopher Marlowe may become a Bohemian vampire living undercover in a café in contemporary Tangiers run by his faithful Moroccan companion, who calls Marlowe 'my teacher' and aspires to become a writer himself.

music

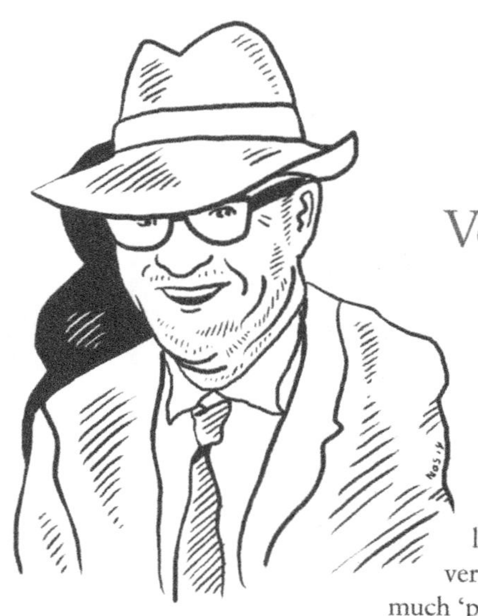

Voices: Amos Poe

1

In the downtown scene of the late 1970s, music and film were very connected to each other. Pretty much 'physically': a lot of the people who made music were also making films or at least acting or doing all sorts of other things in their friends' films. Have you ever played in a band?

Not really, I think if I had ever been a musician I probably would have never been a filmmaker, 'cause it's far more direct, in many ways a more interesting artistic form.

So you made your choice from the very beginning.

I didn't make my choice, I just didn't have an ear for playing music. I wasn't really talented in that. I enjoyed it, and I was certainly turned on by music before film when I was growing up, by the Beatles, Bob Dylan and The Rolling Stones and Jimi Hendrix, all that stuff, that was my influence. Bob Dylan was probably the most important influence in my life, more so than probably any filmmaker, and connected me to my generation growing up certainly. By the time I got to film, which was when I was nineteen, when I started making films, all my films were about music. I mean not about music, but what we would call today music videos.

Something like *The Blank Generation*?

Yeah, but way before *The Blank Generation*, which was six or seven years after.

What was the first film you made?

The first films I ever made with my Super 8 camera were little films of all the songs of The Beatles' White Album, and it was called *The White Film*.

Do you still have them?

I don't, unfortunately. When I was living in some apartment, somebody who was living in there threw all my films out, all my early films, my Super 8 films.

So they are lost?

Yeah, they are lost. Like four years' worth of films. Well, so basically when I started making films, because I didn't go to film school and I didn't know anything about filmmaking, I simply got a Super 8 camera and Super 8 film and I started to read a lot of books and go to a lot of movies. I made these little quasi-experimental narratives based on songs and whatever form of narrative the song would elicit in my brain, I would try to transpose that onto film, almost always working with my friends.

So, even if you weren't a musician, for you film and music were very connected.

Oh, they were completely connected, I mean in the beginning there was absolutely no difference, I had no sophistication, I had no knowledge, I had no education of anything about cinema, anything about music, I was completely naive and primitive and uninformed. It was the most rudimentary thing you could imagine, it was just shooting stuff.

Was it something like an urge?

Yeah, well I knew it was the only thing that mattered to me.

So *that* you knew, and the technical knowledge could come later . . .

Well, *that* I didn't know, maybe, but I sure *felt* it and, yes, I thought you can learn the rest. As soon as I picked up the Super 8 camera and started to make my first film I knew that was what I wanted to do and what I was meant to do, maybe what God had wanted me to do!

And what you're still doing.

Yeah, what I'm still doing, what I'm still passionate about. I couldn't articulate it very well, and that didn't matter. You know, I was living in a very inexpensive apartment, I could get by without necessarily working a job and I could just spend my time making films. That was very satisfying on some level, but I was also screening it only for my friends.

So what were the venues? The famous Mudd Club . . . ?

Well, this is all way before that. I was living in Buffalo, NY, and just screened my films in this little bar on the corner, a little bar called Maxell's on Main Street in Buffalo. They would give me one night every month and I would invite everybody I knew, and everybody would come and have a few drinks, I would screen it and I would have a record player . . .

You used the record player for sound?

Yeah, because there was no sound on my films, so what I would do is I would edit to the songs, to the record, and I would have a quarter inch tape of it. I would put the film to the first frame of the picture and then I would drop the needle on the record and turn on the projector at the same time and then it would go.

So you could say that the record was actually leading your visual ideas, it started from the music, in a way.

Right, and the sync was never exactly perfect, which six years later leads to *The Blank Generation* which was at the time I had graduated to a 16mm camera, and shooting these bands silently!

So you didn't record sound at all.

No, I didn't record sound at all, I had no sound recording equipment, so I just was making silent films of punk bands like Blondie or the Ramones, Patti Smith or Richard Hell. The first person I met in that whole scene was Ivan Kral, he was probably one of the most important persons for me at that time.

He was playing with Patti Smith, wasn't he?

No, we met before he was with Patti Smith. I met him in 1974. I was working in a film company at the time, I needed an assistant and I put an ad in the paper. It was a little company with just maybe ten employees, I was one of them, it was a company called New Line Cinema! Which is now a very big company, it's a billion dollar company, *Lord of the Rings* . . .

Could you say that you helped start it?!

Well, I was there, let's put it that way. Bob Shaye was the one who started it. But anyway, I hired Ivan to work with me at the company. He was a musician, from Czechoslovakia, he was an immigrant, and he was very much into film as well and when I met him he was what you would call a glam rocker, a sort of David Bowie kind of rocker. And we would look at films, hang out, we would go to see bands and stuff and I would bring my 16mm camera and we would start shooting the bands. We made a little film, a half-hour film called *Night Lunch*, which was these bands that we shot silently and we added the music later. It started with a lot of the glam rock bands like Roxy Music, David Bowie and the last act in that half-hour film was Patti Smith. Ivan joined Blondie first and then left Blondie to go work with Patti. And I kept shooting stuff. We shot at CBGB, all the bands in *The Blank Generation* and then after about five or six months of shooting these bands we decided: hey maybe there's a film here! But we had no music, so we had to go to the bands, find the music, record the stuff, mostly on a cassette like this one you are using. Nobody had a record really. Television had one 45 single out, 'Little Johnny Jewel', and we took all these tapes and we transferred them to 16mm mag stock and we went into the editing room. In one 24-hour period we edited the whole film.

It was music of all these bands . . . out of sync.

Yeah. By this point I was a little more knowledgeable, a little more sophisticated and had basically gone through the whole avant-garde experimental film place that I used to go show my films at. I used to go to the Millennium Film Workshop, which was very odd because I was doing these experimental films but they all had this idea of a narrative, and in that time the prevailing taste in avant-garde film was no narrative.

Like Michael Snow, for example?

Yeah, or Stan Brakhage.

There is even this label 'New Narratives', about taking back some narrative elements.

Yeah, but in that time, when I was showing the films, that was very much ostracized, or not ostracized really maybe but marginalized.

Was it because you were telling a story?

Yes, because I was interested in telling stories, and they were not, 'cause they thought that telling stories was very conservative and that the true avant-gardist was more abstract.

Don't you think that that can get quite boring sometimes? I mean, if it becomes almost a formula to follow blindly?

Well, that was what I thought. I thought that as interesting as some of those films were, and some of them were visually very interesting, that ultimately they served no purpose, because the purpose of art was to engage the viewer in an emotional sense or an intellectual sense, as well as a visual sense. Anyway, that's what happened with *The Blank Generation*. And then that film was very ostracized or marginalized because it was non-sync and a lot of people at the time thought it was very amateurish, which it was. But it was inspired too and there were people who saw the inspiration and understood that it was of the time and it had the form that was right for the time.

One could say that it is 'punk' in this respect, because it is sincere and direct, it's like saying: even though we don't have the means, we just do it with what we have.

Yeah. And it was perfect because also the bands at the time were not very professional either and they weren't very good musicians!

Well, it wasn't about virtuosity, but rather about having something to say, wasn't it?

Exactly. And it was about . . . you know, it was . . . true. So anyway, people who did get it got it, and people who didn't get it didn't get it, that was fine, you know, it didn't matter. But it did make me want to make a more narrative film. But I got sidetracked, because the next phase was really Godard and Nouvelle Vague. Having worked in film distribution at this point and understanding a little bit about how that worked I thought well, I could never make a film that anybody would pay money to go to see. Well, *The Blank Generation* only cost us maybe $2,500 to make and we made that money back very quickly, so we already felt that we were professional, in the sense that we had made a film that made more money than it cost. Now it didn't cost very much, so it didn't have to make very much. In literally a couple of weeks we had

paid the film, so that fuelled the fire a little more. It fuelled the fire so
much actually, the grandiosity of it was that I jumped, I literally skipped
a whole step and decided that I wasn't gonna make a film, I wanted to
make a film movement!

You were thinking big.

Yes, I was thinking big and stupid! I wasn't trained to make a film, but
I was grandiose enough to think I could start a movement.

Maybe you were optimistic.

No, I was a visionary and my vision exceeded my filmmaking talents in a
certain sense. But I thought that my filmmaking talents would grow into
my vision, or I trusted that whatever was going to happen was going to
work. I had no idea what was going happen, but I did know that I didn't
want to make anything like 90 per cent of the movies that were out
there. The three filmmakers that were most inspiring to me at that time
were Andy Warhol, who worked with his superstars or his friends and
basically was very economic, used every take, used every frame . . .

In a self-sufficient structure that was producing art.

Right, great art. And John Cassavetes who was working with his friends,
with 16mm black and white, very handmade films that I thought were
very eloquent. *Shadows* and *Husbands* and his whole body of work was
really inspiring to me. I can't even put my finger on why, but I know that
when you're not an academic, or you are not a cineaste per se, you are not
sure how to articulate it, but you do know what you feel. And if you feel it
do it, and if you don't feel it don't do it. I was listening to my gut. And the
third inspiration were Godard and Truffaut and Chabrol and Rohmer, that
all made a lot of sense to me and all those films were very, very inspiring to
me. The whole bohemian downtown, the neighbourhood where I lived,
was all very real. It was Montparnasse. It was the whole thing. Right away
what I wanted to do was a film like *Breathless*: a film that would just
change the perception and if I could do a film like that for almost no
money, then maybe there were other people like me in my neighbourhood
who would also do that. So that if there were, let's say, three of us, or five
of us, or ten of us, or twenty of us making these films, all from one neighbourhood at one time, then perhaps one film could not reach the 'culture',
let's say, but ten films or twenty films or five films could really reach out.
So the idea was to make not a film but to make a movement!

Like a Nouvelle Vague of the Lower East Side?

Exactly! And that was the whole idea that I had. So working from that idea I instantaneously decided that was exactly what I needed to do. And then I met Duncan Hannah, who is still an artist, Eric Mitchell, Patti Astor and Ivan [Kral], who could do the music. I put an ad in the paper, I got a crew and we shot the film [*Unmade Beds*] in seven days and put it together and there it was. And it didn't quite work. But other people saw it and started to say, hey we could maybe do this . . . but then my life went into a really darker area, some personal tragedies or difficulties in my life happened. I wanted to do another film with Eric Mitchell, and then Eric and I came up with this idea of *The Foreigner* reading a book called *The Outsider* by Colin Wilson, which Duncan Hannah had given me. I started to decide that I could make a much tighter narrative, because *Unmade Beds* is really like an essay in a way, it's really about making a nouvelle vague, whereas *The Foreigner* is almost my first attempt to make a real narrative film.

2

Jim Jarmusch often said that *The Foreigner* really inspired him to become a filmmaker when he was still figuring out, back in the late 1970s, whether he wanted to be a musician, a writer, a filmmaker. After he saw your film he decided: I want to be a filmmaker. In 1980 Jarmusch made *Permanent Vacation* and you made *Subway Riders*. Have you ever really worked together?

No, Jim and I have worked parallel but never worked on the same thing. We're like brothers in a way, coming from the same place, same 'parents' let's say. I think Jim is a brilliant artist and filmmaker and always marches to his own drums and he's taught me a lot. You know, *The Foreigner* might have inspired *Permanent Vacation* in a way, but he's taught me more about . . . being who you are.

Do you mean focusing?

Jim is perfectly focused, he's built to be a filmmaker. He knows exactly what he's doing. And he is very, very conscientious, he's built a tremendous career and a body of work that is very, very austere and he is about as artful an American filmmaker as there is. There is no other that basically owns all his own negatives.

That's really an extremely revolutionary thing, isn't it?

Oh yeah, in this industry, in this business. He is probably the best – and this shouldn't be taken the wrong way – but he's probably the best businessman of any filmmaker. He has a lot of respect for his films but he is not greedy. He's whimsical in some sense but he's also very serious, very grounded and he's grown tremendously from when I met him, when he was a very young film student, to where he is today. Jim and I have been friends for a very long time and I have a tremendous admiration and respect for him.

Jarmusch said in several occasions that he loves poetry and what he likes about writers and poets is that they're never in it for the money.

Well, you do need money to make films. It's not like poetry.

Of course, that it is inevitable. Let's say that money doesn't have to be your god.

It's definitely not Jim's god.

And what about *Subway Riders*?

Subway Riders. You know, I had made all these black and white films and I thought well, I should try to make a colour film. But the colours would be very minimalist and very abstract, so I came up with this idea of doing an ensemble film about six characters who go through each others lives. Each one has a different colour and so they are lit with different colours and they clash or they go . . . and it was very noiresque, very druggy.

Would a colour also correspond to a personality feature, like a leitmotif, but in colour and not in music?

Right. The emotions and the colours would go together. There was a blue character, which was John Lurie. That was a very difficult production, because we started shooting in the summer I believe of 1979 and then ran out of money and then finished in January 1980 and then didn't finish editing it until August of '30 and then it came out in '81. It took a lot of time and it was a very, very 'heroin' type of film. A very, very strange film.

How did you manage to keep this crew together for such a long time?

Well, I didn't. That was the problem. John Lurie played the main character in the summer and then, when we went to finish shooting in the winter, he was not available, but he didn't tell us he wasn't available until the night before we were going to start shooting again. John said 'Look Amos, I can't do this. I just can't do it. I have this band now . . .'.

Was it The Lounge Lizards?

Yeah. So that obviously shocked me, I didn't know what to do, I thought that's it.

How did you solve it? Changing the story?

Right, changing the story. I realized what the main character was about. I went home and I sat there and I thought why am I doing this? This is crazy! And then I realized that the character that I was writing about was crazy, and that it was all crazy!

So it made sense again!

So in a way it made sense. What I had to do was rewrite it, so I stayed up all night and I rewrote the film in a sense. A movie starts somewhere and ends somewhere, but there is always a story that happens before the first frame and there's a story that maybe goes on after the last frame. So I realized I had to make another story before we get to John. It was a story about a screenwriter, a filmmaker – *moi* – who is writing about this serial killer saxophone player.

Played by John Lurie?

Yes. He's a serial killer saxophone player who is so obsessed with his saxophone that he plays it in his apartment, but there's a prostitute who lives upstairs from him, who is played by Cookie Mueller, whose colour is red. His saxophone playing keeps her up all the time and she can't stand it. She keeps knocking on the floor so he can't play in his house. He has to go on the street and he plays saxophone at night in these very strange places in New York. His saxophone sounds so eerie and strange that people come to listen to him. When they're listening to him he pulls a gun out of his saxophone case and shoots them. So it's about a musician who kills his audience. The movie begins with a screenwriter, a filmmaker who goes to a producer, played by Bill Rice, to ask him to give him some money to make this film. Throughout the film the character of the saxophone player is played both by the screenwriter and the saxophone player.

So you added yourself as an actor?

Right. The film stars myself and John playing the same character – which is schizophrenic to begin with, and which helps his psychosis. Then there are other characters who come into it: there's the policeman who's looking for the killer and his wife, who is a drug addict; there is this angelic woman, who realizes that the saxophone player is in trouble and is a killer, she has her own dementia which is about being a saint and she wants to save him from himself and tries to enter into his life; then there's of course the prostitute who lives upstairs. So there are these five or six characters who interplay throughout. It's a very poetic New York story, an epic poem . . . a New York street poem.

3

There is a long scene in *The Foreigner* in which Eric Mitchell is sitting on the bed in the hotel room watching television. There is a reportage about the British punk rock scene. Actually this scene made me think a lot of *Stranger Than Paradise*. What do you think the word 'punk' means today, and what did it mean then, back in 1977?

Well, specifically, when you talk about it in terms of *The Foreigner* and that scene in 1977, June '77 I guess, it's a confluence, a meeting and maybe that's what makes the scene interesting at some level. That scene was filmed in the Chelsea Hotel, which immediately brings to mind Andy Warhol and *Chelsea Girls* and that whole thing. So while it's 1977 it brings us back on one hand to the 1960s, to the cinema that inspired me to make films: the last underground New York art film, which was Andy's work, which was very important for me. The struggle between art and film. Especially for someone like me, who was a self-taught filmmaker. I didn't even know there was such a thing as a film school actually, I just thought there was a movie camera and you made films.

How old were you in '77, if I may ask?

At the time we made that film I was 27 years old. And so the idea right away was to put the camera in one place, there was no idea really of montage. There was a very static camera, which relates to *Stranger Than Paradise*. There was a lot of up-framing. Once you decide where the camera should be and what the lens should be used, the actor who's in the frame, Eric Mitchell in this case, goes in and out of frame and creates the language of the scene, so the camera doesn't have to follow.

And then there actually *is* something happening because there's the TV.

Yes, the TV. The TV represents the now. We didn't put a tape on the TV. It just happened to be the show that was on.

So that was a coincidence?

Yeah! It was live.

So it really was a 'chance thing' like Andy Warhol or John Cage.

Yeah, we didn't choose that programme. I said, okay let's put the TV on, because I think the TV is boring and it'd be interesting to have something boring.

And then it was not so boring! Surprisingly there was something quite interesting on TV.

Well, what happened was that actually, if I remember correctly because this is some time ago, there was something boring on another channel and I thought that would be good and then, while we were setting up, somebody turned to another channel and then to another channel and this programme was on. And then I thought, well jee! They're talking about English punk, Britain and the UK, which was semi new at the time. We had been through that punk thing a year before, New York moves very fast . . .

You had already made *Blank Generation* then, right?

Yeah. But *The Foreigner* was also in that genre, or whatever you want to call it. So it seemed appropriate, the character of Max Menace worked well, I thought, with that programme. Here was this European terrorist in NYC, in the Chelsea Hotel in fact, being very alienated, very estranged from reality with the TV referring to something going on in Europe. So the whole mix seemed to make sense: we very, very, very quickly just flipped the camera on and basically let it run.

How long for?

It's got to be eight minutes or something. So the other people behind the camera were going: 'Well, shouldn't we cut?' I said: 'No! Why would we want to cut?'

Because you were actually 'watching' that TV programme.

Well, some people were watching it, there was no video tap so I could see what was going on, but I was looking through the camera.

And of course you could hear it. You could hear the guy speaking British English.

I could see the show through the camera, whereas nobody else could see what was going on in the camera. They saw Eric sitting, standing, doing the whole thing and I just let it run for as long as I thought it worked for. And then finally I think there was a commercial or something that came up.

So you were interrupted.

Yeah, that's when we cut it off. Also because we didn't have that much film, we didn't have any money, we couldn't waste, which was also about the economy of Warhol: everything that you shoot is used in the film.

When I did the interview with Taylor Mead he told me: 'Well, when we shot with Andy everything we shot was it, it was one take . . . and when I shot with Jim Jarmusch it was three takes, which is not very many!'

What did he shoot with Jim?

He is in *Coffee and Cigarettes*, in the last episode with Bill Rice.

Oh right! And Bill Rice is in *Subway Riders* and Taylor Mead is in *Frogs*.

And about this word 'punk', do you think it has any meaning today? Do you think it is important to relate to this word at all?

I don't know. It may be important to some people I guess, but it doesn't have that much relevance to me.

New York, December 2003

1 Flashback: New York Stories

'Between Fourteenth Street and Houston and Avenue B and Bowery, that was the whole world to us.'
John Lurie, transcript from Céline Danhier's documentary *Blank City* (2010)

'Yep, I know that song well. Cale banging the keys, Lou rapping about the only good thing about a small town: getting out of there. You just replace the "small" with "down". That was us.'[1]
Amos Poe, interviewed by the author, Berlin and New York (January 2015)

Coordinates

Distance on the island is measured in blocks, each block a small island unto itself with precise references on the compass. Block down, block up, North, South, East, West. Islands on North America's most famous island of all: Manhattan. The islands/blocks are not made of just stone, bricks and asphalt, but of people too, and groups, scenes: little tribes who gather together according to common interests, necessities or otherwise, curiosities or addictions.

As a foreigner, the sensation one gets wandering around the island is of crossing myriad worlds, separate and yet united. Numerous little planets. One of these planets is the Lower East Side, which measures about 10 square km. Not that big. It is here that, at least since the 1950s all the way through to the '70s and '80s, ideal conditions have allowed the continuity of an artistic scene made up of heterogeneous people, nearly all from outside New York, foreigners to the island. Just like Jim Jarmusch. Or Sara Driver, who recalls: 'You'd walk down the street and there'd be William Burroughs in a three-piece suit . . . The loft I was living in Yoko Ono had made the "Fly" movie.' As artist and designer Maripol put it, 'People like Burroughs and Kerouac and all the Beat Generation, they laid the stones on the road for us.'[2] Jarmusch, himself a long-time resident of the Lower East Side, has witnessed the changes in the neighbourhood over the last decades and remembers key figures who connected those different generations of artists, such as the Palestinian Rafic Azzouni, owner of Rafik Film and Video supply and editing store:

> Rafic was really generous. He had the O-P screening room which you could rent depending on how much money you had. He'd say: 'I need $50' – 'Oh, I only have $10 . . .' – 'Okay, I'll rent it to you for $7!' Every year at Thanksgiving Rafic would invite whoever wanted to come and I remember having my cranberries served by Jack Smith! There was a precedent for underground filmmaking in New York, people like Jonas Mekas and Shirley Clarke, Robert Frank and Jack Smith for sure.[3]

All, or nearly, foreigners to the island, just like Jim Jarmusch.[4]

Akron, Ohio, is a small town once famous for its now extinct tyre industries, from where a young man with literary aspirations and a strong desire to discover a new slice of this world could be forgiven for thinking he had to get out.[5] After a couple of years spent in Chicago, where in 1972 he enrolled in Northwestern University's journalism course, the magnetic pull of the island got to him too. Jarmusch rethought his plans, left Chicago and entered Columbia, where his friends Phil Kline and Luc Sante were already enrolled. It was 1973 and only three years earlier The Velvet Underground, the distorted voice of Andy Warhol's Factory, had played at Max's Kansas City for the last time with Lou Reed.[6] Nico and John Cale had already left the group. Was it the end of an era? Or perhaps simply the natural passage from one decade to another? Following the Factory's golden moment, the 'arty' environment was losing much of its popularity, allowing a return to a more lean and direct approach that would be the fertile terrain for No Wave bands from the second half of the 1970s.

The Ramones set the stage. During a 22-year career, from 1974 to 1996, the New York iconic punk rock band performed 2,263 concerts – an average of 102 per year, nearly nine a month – for two decades. One understands that their influence was huge. But it is not simply a question of numbers. Jarmusch has often said that without the Ramones he would probably never have made a single movie. What inspired him and most of the public was the absolute refusal of virtuosity, their no-frills, fast and direct approach to music and life, the will to identify essence and form. It did not matter what artistic form transmitted the message – if there was one at all. On the contrary, the forms often ended up coexisting.

Generalized tags such as 'Punk' and 'No Wave' are extremely versatile and can define, with all the inherent limitations in their label, both musical and filmic tendencies. Jarmusch was surrounded by many overlapping art forms – from poetry to performance, from literature to music, from music to cinema, from cinema to painting, installation and graffiti – but the passage from one form to the other was not traumatic, in a place and a period in which the supposed 'confines' between the arts were increasingly rare and elusive. The diverse artistic scenes and the myriad ethnicities that populated the city tended to amalgamate. As Italian critic Rosma Scuteri said:

Doing art, practising art, consuming art were all immediate expressions of life's exuberance that glided by without complexes, nor excessive 'aesthetic' or 'linguistic' limits. They were nearly all artists in Manhattan's Downtown. It became an existential category of people and situations . . . During the 1980s in New York, there was an anomaly, immediately absorbed, that rendered that block of contemporary art unrepeatable. For a moment – and only a moment – African Americans were leaders of the art world. The graffiti artists were the first . . . kicking off with an excess of 'physical' energy that found an immediate means of communication. A mobile instrument: the train.[7]

The need to experiment took on new forms and appropriated untraditional spaces: the street and its sidewalks, walls, Subway trains. The youths who flooded the serpentine Subway with colour, often from tough neighbourhoods like the South Bronx or Harlem, did not consider themselves only 'graffiti artists', they were 'writers'. Theirs was more than an art form: it was a rebel urgency, a necessity to exist and appear, so close to life as to identify with it. The 'writing' allowed these subterranean street poets and painters to communicate a name, a style, an idea from the Bronx to Brooklyn, from downtown Manhattan all the way to Harlem, in such a way as to connect those islands that otherwise seemed so far apart.

And the same applied to young Jarmusch: the step from writing to music and finally to cinema was short and homogeneous, just as it was for the 'writers' who, apart from the written word, spread the sounds and rhythms of hip hop that reached New York directly from the sound systems of Jamaica. Music and colour moulded together in a lifestyle, the traces of which have nearly disappeared today.

A film boasting a great documentary value about the hip hop and graffiti scene of the period is *Wild Style* (1983) by Charlie Ahearn.[8] Its cast included icons such as Grandmaster Flash, the DJ considered by many to be the father of hip hop; graffiti artist and 'hip hop historian' Fab 5 Freddy; far-seeing Fun Gallery manager Patti Astor, who at the time enjoyed a successful career as an actress in numerous No Wave films;[9] and perhaps the most influential graffiti artist – Dondi. His tag, a highly recognizable icon, covering all points of the compass on the city's Subway trains,[10] was one of the first to be exhibited in the Fun Gallery. As Fab 5 Freddy recalls: 'People from the Bronx and Harlem and Brooklyn, black and Latino people hanging out with punk and new wave, all these different people were mixing together for the very first time.'[11]

It is right in this scene that Jarmusch made his first moves, at a time in which the merging of the different artistic and musical tribes was a reality shared by one and all. With respect to just how mutually close and physical this contact was, it is worth quoting what Jarmusch recalled about the filming of *Permanent Vacation*:

> We were shooting at John Lurie's apartment at the time. Jean-Michel Basquiat was a friend of ours, and back then he used to stay up all night roaming the streets painting on walls as SAMO, and he'd end up crashing at our places. The funny thing is that while we were filming he was fast asleep under the camera in a sleeping bag. And when we had to shoot the reverse angle we just pulled him out of the way, so that he was never in the shot – but he's actually there, asleep![12]

The celebrated Basquiat, especially thanks to his collaboration with Andy Warhol, was another important link, opening up the Big Apple's more 'white' and elitist environments to the raw jargon of the street. The desire of the arts to contaminate each other was an experience that Jarmusch lived at first hand and one crucial to his formation, both artistic and personal. In New York from the mid-1970s to the mid-'80s

Allie in John Lurie's apartment, *Permanent Vacation*.

the passage between sound and image was in no way traumatic and paid no attention to colour and ethnic origin. It was often about a truly physical coexistence in the same places, the same people. As evoked in 1979 by Italian film critic Renato de Maria,

> The actors and directors, in a continuous exchange of roles – creators of videotapes and Super 8 narratives that constitute the current reality of New York's underground scene – are at the same time the drummers, guitarists and singers of the most important New Wave/No Wave rock bands of the metropolis.[13]

Asynchronism and Super 8: Poe, Nares and Mitchell

The step from music to cinema was thus a short one: films were frequently shown in the clubs where the bands played, the musicians often being the lead actors. Legend has it that the 'movement' took off sometime in 1977, thanks to a load of Super 8 cameras coming into the possession of a local resident, Freddy the Fence, making it suddenly affordable for anyone to make a film.[14] The result was a five-year boom for the Lower East Side's underground film scene. A lot of people started to shoot with a Super 8 just as a lot of people played in a band, and in a large number of cases, as noted, the two things coincided.

A character considered by many to be an initiator of the rush of low-budget films seen all over New York from the mid-1970s to the start of the '80s was an Israeli, American by adoption, Amos Poe. His influence on the 'scene' was far-reaching. British New York-based artist and musician James Nares praised Poe's hands-on approach: 'Amos showed us that you could do films for nothing.'[15] Patti Astor put things into a wider historical perspective: 'You really have to give Amos Poe the credit for starting the next independent film movement after Andy Warhol.'[16] Poe's influence on Jarmusch was perhaps even more significant:

> One of my favourite films, that actually encouraged me to make films, was Amos Poe's *The Foreigner*. When I saw that, in 1978 or so, I got really inspired because he had made a feature film with five thousand dollars. It was so loose and raw, so close to the idea of the music of the late 1970s – so-called punk rock music – where musicianship wasn't important, virtuosity wasn't the main criterion, it was: 'I have something I want to express.'[17]

Before shooting *The Foreigner*, Poe marked the time with a small milestone of the so-called No Wave or Punk cinema: *The Blank Generation*. The title was taken directly from the song/manifesto by Richard Hell and the Voidoids, who like other stars of the downtown scene – Patti Smith, Blondie, the Ramones, Talking Heads, Television, just to mention a few – perform in the film on the small stage at CBGB. As Poe told me, he did nothing more than film the bands on 16mm, going from concert to concert together with his friend Ivan Kral, shooting a sort of diary of that era's underground music scene.[18] But it was a *silent* diary. Poe filmed the concerts without sound, something that began to make his work more interesting and more liable to a certain visionary madness. Later, armed with a portable cassette recorder, he returned to those same bands and recorded the pieces one by one, or retrieved them off the demos, because at the time most of them had not yet made a record. Needless to say, the 'reassembly' of sound on images was asynchronous, reserving surprises and a sense of alienation for the spectator.

If on the one hand this deliberately unorthodox choice expresses the ideas of conscious detachment – especially between performer and audience – and chaos as theorized in punk aesthetics, on the other hand the argument needs simplifying: basically, Poe did not have the necessary equipment to record the bands live. As Italian director Guido Chiesa pointed out, 'The famous asynchrony was no more than the result of Poe's and Kral's lack of technical (and financial) means before becoming the much theorized example of punk aesthetics.'[19] Nonetheless, it is somewhat strange that the asynchrony of *sounds* immediately stands out with respect to the images. Why is there no talk of the asynchrony of *images* with respect to the sounds? Or of a general asynchrony of both? Probably because traditionally speaking the audience of an audiovisual work tends to take the image as the first parameter of its worth, concentrating more on what is seen than on what is heard. As the French composer and theorist Michel Chion pointed out in his classic work on sound in film, *Audio-Vision*:

> At best, some people are content with an additive model, according to which witnessing an audiovisual spectacle basically consists of seeing images plus hearing sounds. Each perception remains nicely in its own compartment . . . the reality of audiovisual combination is that one perception influences the other and transforms it. We never see the same thing when we also hear; we don't hear the same thing when we see as well.[20]

The work of the downtown filmmakers often provided a 'visual track' to be projected at concerts as a backdrop. In *The Blank Generation* we hear an 'audio track' knowingly detached from the images. This practice of separation, in which figure and background alternate, represents a step towards the reaffirmation of the equal importance of sound and vision, as materials put at the director's and at the audience's disposal. The viewer-listener may choose to follow either one or the other, or take an active role in the perceptive act of 'audio-vision', as Chion calls it, editing the two things together in one's own mind. Rejecting a hierarchical model, the image may be the sound's background or vice versa, neither enjoying supremacy over the other. Finally, if the absence of a hierarchy may be defined as *anarchy*, then once again we find ourselves before one of the wider cornerstones of the punk aesthetic. Thus in the case of *The Blank Generation*, instead of the somewhat restricted definitions 'Punk' or 'No Wave' cinema, I would rather opt for the broader idea of *anarchic cinema*.

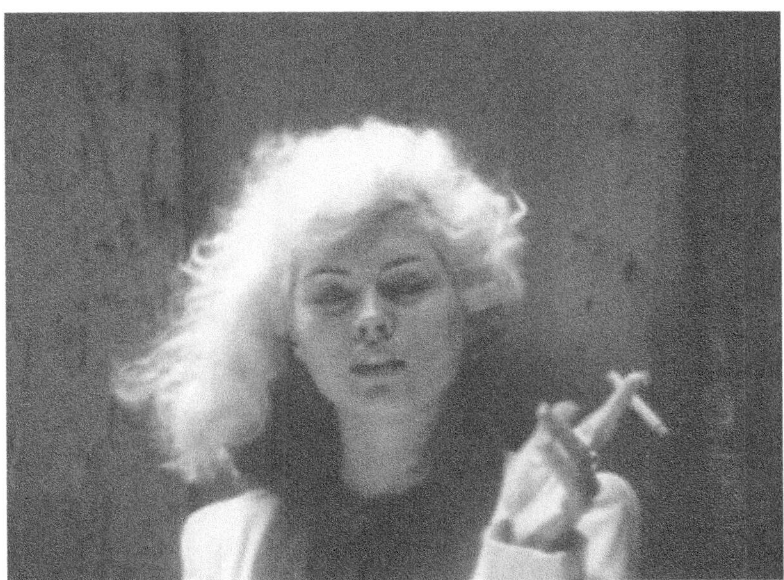

Returning to *The Foreigner*, Poe's film that contributed to Jarmusch's decision to become a director, there is something that strikes whoever watches it or, rather, listens to it: the film was not mixed; there is just one audio track. One hears either the dialogue, the music or the effects, none of which overlaps the other two, as is usually the case. The effect that may bother some spectators is an immediate awareness of the sound as an element in itself, certainly not completely separated from the images but not 'annulled' in the perfect and camouflaged traditional audio-visual illusion. This must also have influenced the young Jarmusch when he saw – and listened to – *The Foreigner* for the first time.

From the thematic point of view, the story of Max Menace – a European terrorist and spy landed in New York City to search for un-defined 'help' from various strange characters, with whom he struggles to communicate – can be interpreted as an anti-American Dream. The foreigner does not find a land of a thousand opportunities. On the contrary, in New York he will come to a nasty end, and will be hounded to the southern reaches of the island in a long final chase sequence. Actor Eric Mitchell, as remembered by Poe, did not stop running for at least twenty blocks, having filmed for seven consecutive days and nights without rest.

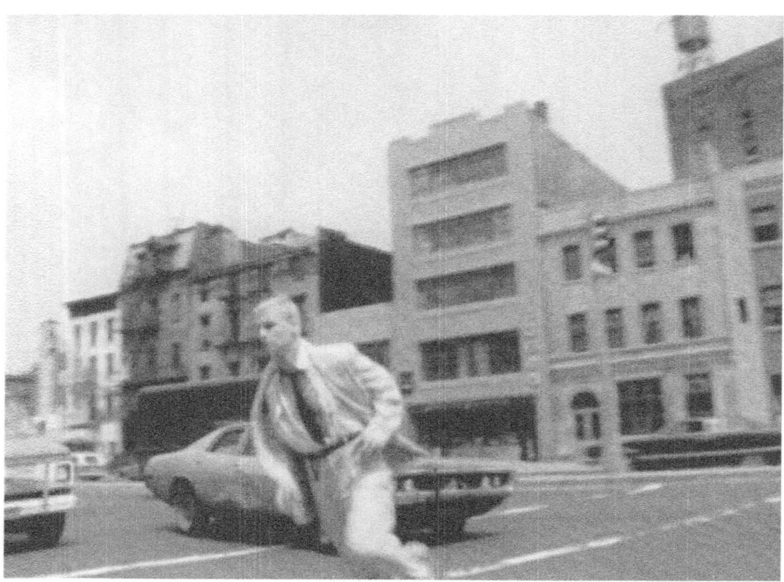

Besides being an actor, Mitchell was also a hyper-energetic director of the downtown scene. A stranger to the island and of French origin, he had already worked with Poe on *Unmade Beds*, the Israeli's more explicit attempt to reproduce the Nouvelle Vague and shoot a film Godard-style, its cast almost identical to *The Foreigner*.[21] True to his real-life persona, Mitchell burst with undiluted adrenaline when playing Max Menace. Apart from the endless running mentioned above, in the fight scene inside the washrooms at CBGB, members of The Cramps attack him with a real knife and cut him up a little. Poe himself admitted that he lost control of the situation and that his futile attempts to interrupt the scene by shouting 'Cut!' were followed literally by the musicians/actors – the knife just kept on cutting.

In 1978, having survived *The Foreigner*, Mitchell, together with artist and musician James Nares and filmmaker Becky Johnston, founded the New Cinema – a small space at 12 St Mark's Place that would at last give visibility to a growing number of directors, and not just its founders. Similarly to many No Wave bands, the New Cinema lasted less than a year. The space, once part of a Polish social club, became the place that allowed people, even if for only a few months and with no more than 50 spectators per show, to see the results of what the Super 8 boom was

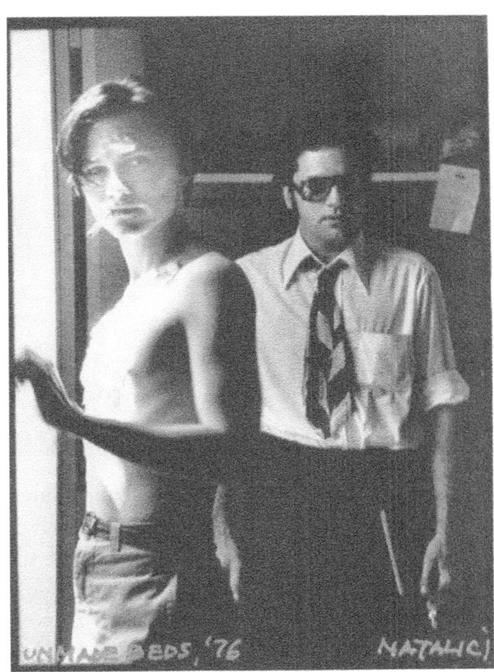

Duncan Hannah
and Amos Poe,
Unmade Beds.

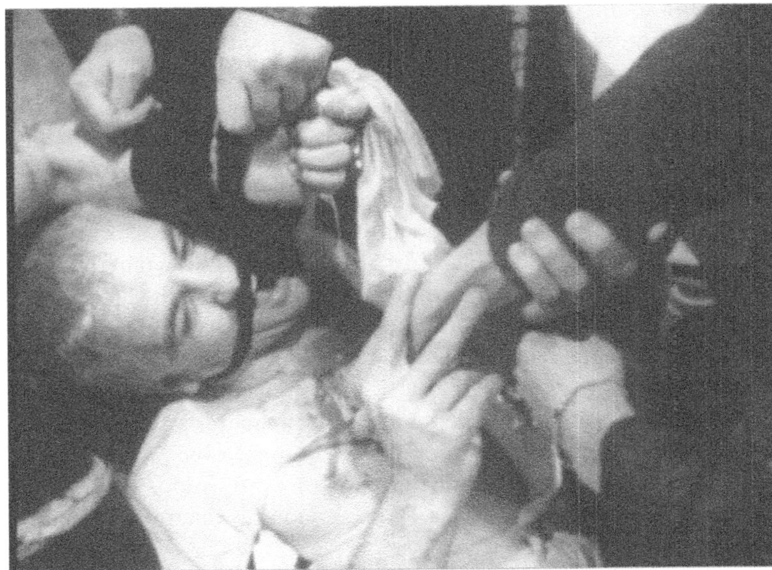

Cut! Eric Mitchell,
The Foreigner.

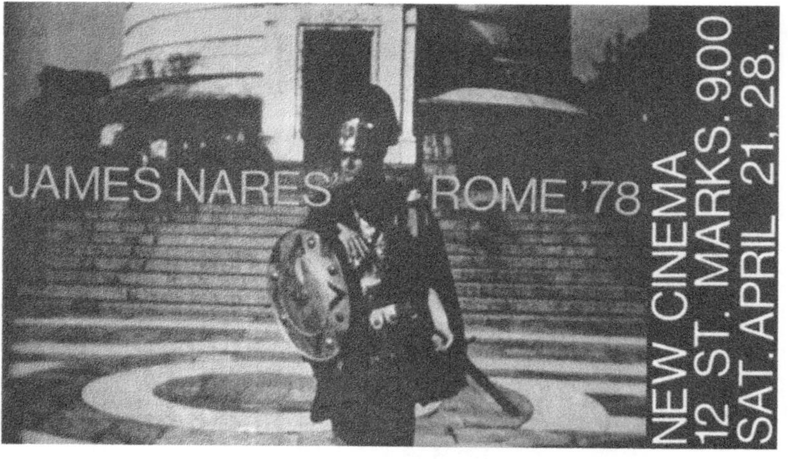

Rome '78 at the New Cinema.

producing in the city, or rather in the neighbourhood. Mitchell and Nares at the time were among the members of the Colab artists' collective, short for the programmatic name Collaborative Projects, one of its objectives being to free artists from the slavery of traditional art venues. The New Cinema fitted the bill perfectly.

The films, as Nares explained to me, were all transferred onto video mainly for economic reasons considering that, in order to be projected, the Super 8 sound had to be duplicated either directly on positive, which usually meant the images were slightly out of focus, or by first creating an intermediary negative and then reprinting the film, which was very expensive.[22] Transferring the film onto video, apart from being clearly more economical, proved to be an aesthetic choice that evidently illustrated the artisanal tendency of the works in question and which freed video from its eternal status of being inferior to celluloid. Before its premature end the New Cinema enjoyed intense success.

Rome '78 (1978) is one of Nares's films that was shown in the small space in St Mark's Place. Nares told me how he had searched for a series of 'Romanesque' locations in the middle of the city, and that all the actors, including the musician James Chance and his girlfriend/manager Anya Phillips, as the Queen of Sheba, were dressed as ancient Romans, despite the wristwatches, cigarettes and other anachronistic devices. The film, which also starred a very young Lydia Lunch – the pale vedette of Teenage Jesus and the Jerks, the porn poetess who would be the star of numerous legendary Cinema of Transgression productions, including

Richard Kern's *Fingered* (1986) – is an irony-ridden take on epics about ancient Rome, inspired in particular by *I, Claudius* (1976), the BBC series depicting the vicissitudes of Emperor Claudius and his infamous nephew Caligula.[23] The children of the 1950s were the first generation to be raised on television, a fact not to be ignored when coming into contact with the work of these filmmakers. In fact, Colab sponsored a series called *All Color News* (1978) for a local cable station. Scott and Beth B., creators of many films of violence, nihilism and sexual slavery with the omnipresent Lydia Lunch, were among the directors who contributed to the station.[24] 'We felt that we weren't getting the real news and this infuriated us', Beth B. said in 2011.[25] At the time, however, practically none of the filmmakers had private access to cable television and thus had to go to bars and clubs to see their own work and that of their friends – just as they used to do at the New Cinema.

Co-founder Mitchell's first experiences with Super 8 were *Kidnapped* (1978) and *Red Italy* (1979). The first, in which bored, young kidnappers – all regulars of the downtown music/film scene – torture a businessman to crackly music from a record player, highlights the idea of No Wave ennui and is noticeably influenced by *Vinyl* (1965), Andy Warhol's personalized interpretation of Anthony Burgess's shock novel *A Clockwork Orange* (1960).[26]

With James Nares on camera and Becky Johnston on sound, *Red Italy* was technically more elaborate than *Kidnapped*, in which the only form of 'editing' was the length of each reel. The film was set in Rome but shot in the Lower East Side, at Coney Island and the Chelsea Hotel.[27] *Red Italy* attempted to recreate a punk and European environment and was defined by Mitchell as 'a portrait of a bored, disenchanted woman in post-war Italy'.[28] As well as Mitchell, the cast included John Lurie and guitarist Arto Lindsay playing a somewhat distorted version of Gene Vincent's classic 'Be-Bop-A-Lula'.

The same trio, Mitchell, Lurie and Lindsay, got together again in a bizarre 'lowest-budget-science-fiction movie', *Men in Orbit* (1978), a 45-minute film in which Lurie doubled as actor and director. He and Mitchell play two odd astronauts travelling through space in a very rudimentary craft: the sofa in the living room. They communicate with Arto Lindsay and Becky Johnston back on 'Earth' through microphones that alter the timbre of their voices, making the improbable dialogue virtually incomprehensible. Between laughs, Lurie and Mitchell eat a hamburger, pretend to sleep and try to shave. *Men in Orbit* is a good example of do-it-yourself aesthetics because the film is literally homemade. Three decades later John Lurie described the approach of that period in a nutshell: 'Nobody was doing what they were good at. The painters were in bands. The musicians were making films.'[29]

In the meantime, the Colab collective continued to make waves. In 1980 it organized two exhibitions that created quite a stir in both the media and the 'scene': the *Real Estate Show* held in a building occupied for the occasion on Delancey Street in the Lower East Side, in which Joseph Beuys was also present, and the *Times Square Show* held in an abandoned massage club in the Times Square neighbourhood, at the time still the haven of peep shows and sex for sale, a far cry from the child-friendly shopping-mall atmosphere that exists today. At this groundbreaking exhibition, photographer Nan Goldin presented a first version of the work in progress that made her famous, her intimately raw slide show *The Ballad of Sexual Dependency*, with Phil Kline's collaboration on the music selection, which included some of the Del-Byzanteens' tunes.[30] Jarmusch participated directly in the show as well, presenting one of his student films, *Cinesthesia*, the name he gave to his first production company. In various interviews, when talking of this film and of a short shown just once at the MOMA – the editing based on a 1934 percussion piece by contemporary composer Henry Cowell (1897–1965) – Jarmusch explicitly expressed the desire that they never again be shown in public.[31] The *Times Square Show* included painting, installation, video and otherwise uncategorized work, giving a good example of the 'lack of borders' ethos between the various artistic scenes that characterized New York at the time.

That same year, in the context of the Super 8 and musical scenes in particular, the paths of Jarmusch and Mitchell also crossed on the set of the film that would reward the French director with fame as instant as it was ephemeral: *Underground USA* (1980). Jarmusch was in fact the film's sound recordist. The film is a remake of Billy Wilder's classic *Sunset Boulevard* (1950) that had already inspired Andy Warhol and Paul Morrissey in *Heat* (1972). Making *Underground USA*, Mitchell thus decided to refer to one of the top products of the studio system, while at the same time hinting at the Factory, which, though still transgressive at the time, had lost its momentum and was moving downhill. As observed by historian Vera Dika, 'The notion of the "remake", especially the remaking of narrative art films, became a kind of Downtown genre in itself.'[32] In Mitchell's work an invisible thread seemed thus to

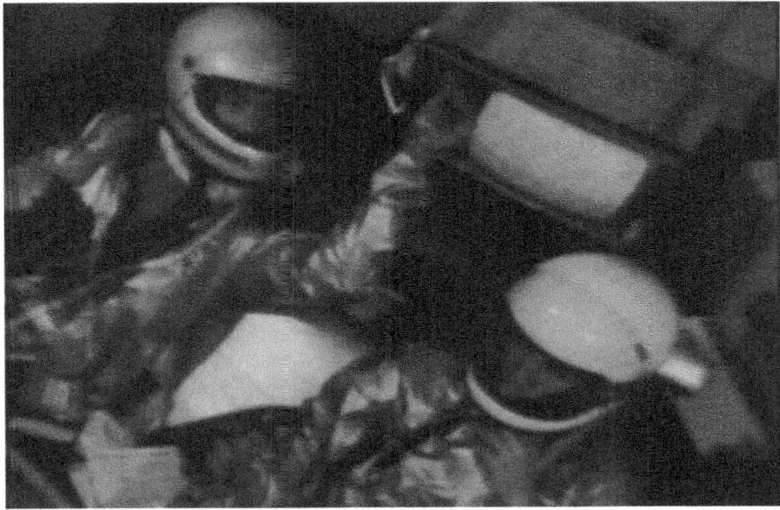

unite the 1950s, '60s and '8os, evoking that idea of continuity among the various generations of artistic scenes that Jarmusch and his friends and colleagues – willingly or not – embodied too.

As in music and in numerous No Wave and Super 8 films of the time, the link with the past was by no means abolished. On the contrary, it was reaffirmed and transformed. What has been often defined as 'No Wave nihilism' was a rather particular one. With her typical 'taste for shock', Lydia Lunch expressed one contradiction about this tag:

> I don't think nihilism is a strong enough word. I hated every-thing. At the same time, I probably laughed more than anyone else. As horrible as it is, you have to fucking laugh, or you are going to kill yourself or somebody else.[33]

Whether speaking of 'hate' or 'nihilism', there exists a basic 'ecology' in the distorted re-reading of the past by many films and a lot of No Wave music. The past must not be thrown away: it must be reset to zero and reconstructed from the rubble, but on a common ground already fertil-ized by others before us. Neither violence, nor nihilism, nor primitivism, nor noise, nor dissonance was invented by No Wave.

No-fashion

To conclude this opening chapter about audio/visual 'coordinates', I would like to refer one more time to Amos Poe, director of *The Blank Generation* and *The Foreigner* and Jarmusch's 'inspirer'. The reason is not only to observe that one of the most emblematic musician-actors of Jarmusch's first films, John Lurie, was cast at the same time by Amos Poe in *Subway Riders*, but also to focus on an important fact that clearly distinguishes Jarmusch's work from that of other directors active in New York during the same period. The distinctive fact has to do with music.

Though amply involved in both the music scene and the Super 8 and film scene of the time, Jarmusch decided not to succumb to the temptation of 'fashion': in neither *Permanent Vacation* nor *Stranger Than Paradise* is 'brandable' No Wave music used.

With *The Blank Generation*, Amos Poe had a great intuitive idea when choosing to document the music scene of the period, but perhaps one should wonder what would have become of his film if, during the following years, the bands in question – the Ramones, Talking Heads, Blondie, the Patti Smith Group, just to mention the most famous – had not hit the big time both inside and outside the United States. Even a film like Charlie Ahearn's *Wild Style* about hip hop and graffiti artists took the road to 'historical documentary'. Its undeniable documentary value, starring some of the leading exponents of the hip hop scene at the time, such as Grandmaster Flash and Fab 5 Freddy, compensates the spectator for some perceivable traces of 'old age'.

As he has stated since the beginning, Jarmusch deliberately set out to avoid using recognizable ingredients easily identified with New Wave or No Wave cinema – particularly with regard to the music but also to the *mise en scène* – as demonstrated by Allie's 1950s look à la Gene Vincent in *Permanent Vacation*, and Eddie and Willie in *Stranger Than Paradise*. In 1980, responding to a question on the absence of period music in his first feature film, *Permanent Vacation*, Jarmusch said:

I kept it out intentionally. I didn't want the film to be seen as belonging to this or that New York or London scene . . . It can be brought into contact with the ideas of the New Wave, but still there is no direct link . . . I didn't want to make a rock 'n' roll film.[34]

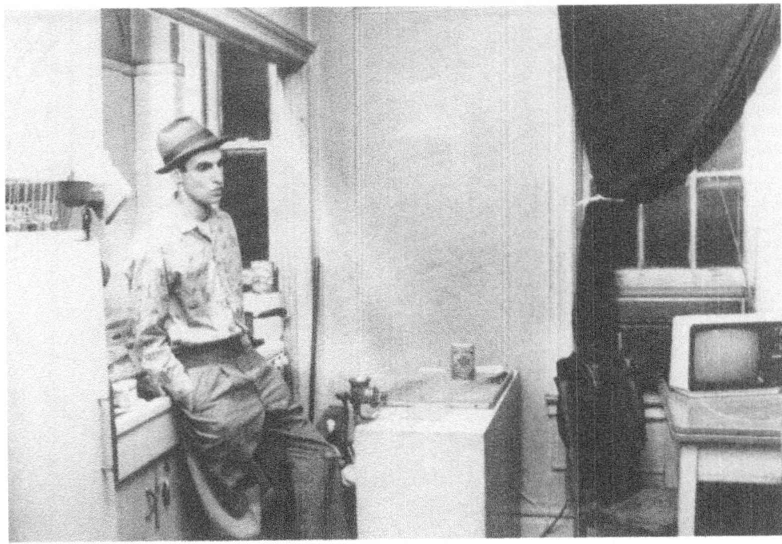

John Lurie, *Stranger Than Paradise*.

A few years later, talking about *Stranger Than Paradise*, Jarmusch again confirmed that 'the reason John [Lurie] and I even got the idea for this film, was because we wanted a story no one would say is New Wave'.[35] If this statement sounds slightly snobbish, it shows Jarmusch's reluctance to identify himself with a given cultural model, no matter how off stream yet predictable. Behind these words the central theme of cultural relativism is already disclosed, confirming Jarmusch as a profoundly *independent* figure even within the 'independent New Wave scene'.

It is also because of this that his first two films in particular, born of a close contact with the downtown music scene, do not run the risk of being labelled as dated, immersed as they are in a characteristic 'timeless' atmosphere, to whose creation the choice of music contributed in a determining way. Imbued with New (and No) Wave music and vision, the young Jarmusch succeeded in not getting stuck with a tag that would have become irremovable.

Voices: Phil Kline

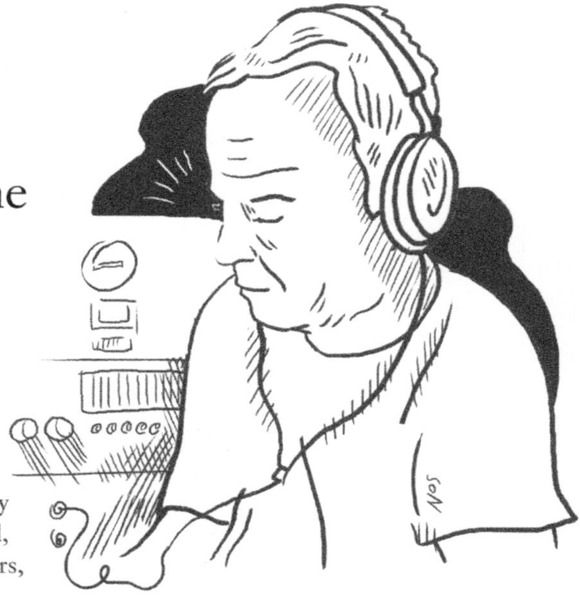

1

Let's go a little bit back in time,
to the Del-Byzanteens days. If
I am not wrong you were the only
professional musician in the band,
which included writers, filmmakers,
painters . . .

I was at a distinct disadvantage! (Laughs)

This was a natural thing in the so-called 'scene' of the Lower East Side.

Right, most bands usually had at least one musician . . . well, it wasn't unheard of to actually be a musician.

It was a scene in which artists helped each other a lot, joining their friends' projects, films and bands most of all. Everybody's eyes and ears, so to say, were open and available for collaboration. Can you tell me something about how the creative process went along in the Del-Byzanteens? And why it didn't really matter to have musical training to play in a band?

For one thing, that particular wave of music that was happening right at that time, was very much a reaction to the perceived artificiality of what had come before. So simplification, paring down, looking for not so much the simplest elements but the purest: rather than a lot of stuff, let's try to find the truth in its simplest way. So, like I just said, being a musician almost put you at a disadvantage, because a musician picks up an instrument and starts playing lots of notes, whereas a non-musician

picks up an instrument and does something more elemental with it. In the case of that particular kind of music, on one hand it was a futurist movement but we had a way of looking at the past too. A lot of the inspiration came out of rockabilly and early forms of rock 'n' roll. In the case of our band we had a bass player who listened to lots of '50s rockabilly. I was more into avant-garde classical and world music, and early minimalism.

Like Steve Reich?

Sure. I was a Steve Reich fanatic. Well, he's one of my idols and was one of my inspirations of the time. I was also really into Egyptian popular music, and Jim was very much into Indonesian gamelan, we listened to that kind of stuff.

Gamelan is also very present in *Permanent Vacation*.

That's right. I remember when that came about. Jim was trying to think of a sound and he actually took one of those *Explorer Series* gamelan records and slowed it down.

So what about the creative process in the band? Did you feel a big responsibility for being the only musician?

Well, truth be told, we weren't the best band and we didn't always have the best flow. What we could do was find a good, mysterious groove. We could really rock. But we weren't so good at turning corners. Once we got in a groove we would just . . . stay there! But the stuff that Jim and I did together, that we did with James Nares and with Philippe [Hagen] was actually very much based on a blend of rock, minimalism, on Indonesian gamelan, which is a kind of minimalist modular process, and that's sort of the way we played too.

I read about gamelan that these concerts can go on for days and nights and it is not considered strange, insulting or embarrassing for the musicians that the audience, at a certain point, sleeps.

Right. Jim and I, I'm not sure if Luc [Sante] was with us or not, but we attended the Brooklyn performance of Robert Wilson's fourteen-hour-long *Life and Times of Joseph Stalin*, we all nodded off in the middle of that. How could you not? The thing ended at 9 o'clock the next morning!

There's one more thing that I wanted to ask you about the Del-Byzanteens: why did you cover The Supremes?

Oh, 'My World is Empty without You'. Oh my god! I'm not quite sure how it all happened, although I do remember something. We were a brand new band, I'm not even sure if we had had our first gig yet. I was waiting for Philippe, our bass player, outside this club downtown, I think it was Tier 3. Philippe, who was our contact guy, was in there talking to the manager, who was a woman – very good in the case of Philippe, 'cause he was a real charmer – and we had this material that we were working on. I do remember something about that arrangement clicking in my head while I was waiting for one hour on the corner for Philippe, but . . . so you wonder why we did it?

Yes.

I don't remember why . . . I think what happened is we had this jam, with a slow, clunky beat and while I was standing outside the club I thought of combining it with the chorus from 'My World is Empty'.

Well, the way things worked in the band a lot and the place where my being a musician would come in, would be when we had raw material I would often be the one who would frame it, so to speak. We have eight measures of this and eight measures of that, so I would organize it and edit it.

So you were really being a composer.

Yeah, but a lot of our stuff was worked on so much together. There are few songs where I maybe composed something. Sometimes we had a jam and I'd write the whole melody or on one or two songs I wrote the whole lyric, but most of our stuff came out of improvisations. We generally used mixed composition.

I think that our greatest failing as a band is that we didn't stay together! I mean, how much can a band do in a year or two . . . That Michael Spano photograph of us in the kitchen, taken when we had the twins [Dan and Josh Braun] playing with us, is beautiful. Michael went on to become a famous, big gallery photographer. The funny thing is that we had already done a photo session with Nan Goldin, but it didn't work out, the situation wasn't right. Actually it wasn't Nan being very much Nan. We were coming up with these goofy ideas and she was trying to photograph them . . . But on the other hand, it's hard to imagine a true Nan Goldin photograph of our band, unless we were all doing something really *bad* together! Nan didn't take your picture unless you were doing a drug, having sex or going to the bathroom! (Laughs)

You worked with Nan Goldin, right?

Yes, quite a lot, in the years in which she was doing her slide show work in progress which was called *The Ballad of Sexual Dependency*, that was pretty much all of her work from the late 1970s. Until she became famous that was her watershed piece. It was a brilliant idea: a slide show with music, but then she just kept culling it, taking out all the bad cookies and just keeping the good ones, keeping the best stuff and rotating it, she was always changing and changing the music a little bit.

What kind of music was it?

That's where I came in. She would come over to my place and bring a lot of records, we mainly used her records, we'd use some of my records too, we also used Del-Byzanteens songs and we would put together something like a DJ show, but it was timed to go exactly with the photographs. So when she was showing her drag queens we'd have Charles Aznavour singing 'What makes a man a man!', for example.

Where did this happen?

She was showing at funky downtown art performance spaces like ABC No Rio or Dixon Place, which was another downtown basementy weird little scene.

And now, are you still working with her?

Oh, she's long gone. I think she spends most of her time in New England and in Europe. When I was in Paris I noticed the ads for the Metro, the suburban train the RER, it said 'photos by Nan Goldin'. A couple. Lovers exchanging kisses before one of them gets on the train. They even look like old Nan photos, because the guy looks Puerto Rican, the girl is half black. I was lucky Nan didn't take too many pictures of me.

You mean you weren't bad enough for her?

Except for one time, I was so bad that somebody made her destroy the pictures! It wasn't me. I won't say any more! (Laughs)

2

You come from Akron, Ohio, right?

Thereabouts, the area. Jim and I grew up in a little town called Silver Lake.

An area that became famous for the big tyre industry.

Yeah, Akron was where Goodyear and Firestone and all the big tyre companies used to be. But don't forget Devo, and Chrissie Hynde! Devo are from a little town called North Hampton, that's one mile from Akron. And Chrissie Hynde is from Akron proper, she's the only one that is really from Akron, she's from south Akron, Garfield High School. Jim and I are from the lilywhite suburbs. There are no black people in Silver Lake! We are as white as the water lilies in Silver Lake. Well it's just as hard to find a Jew in Silver Lake, jeez it's bad, so bad.

What was it that attracted you about New York? And have you ever actually worked with Jarmusch?

Well, if you grow up in Akron and you've got anything on the ball at all it seems to me that your life's goal from a very early age would be to get out of Akron!

Maybe you could use a tyre . . .

Yeah, maybe that's it, your mind is rolling from the beginning . . . the look of the place, the smell of the place.

You've known Jarmusch for a very long time, right?

Yeah, I guess we first met when we were in the sixth grade, which means we would have been about twelve. Well, my family moved to Silver Lake the summer between the fifth grade and the sixth grade and at first we lived on one end of the village and he lived on the other end of the village. But then a couple of years later we moved to a street that's one block away from where he was. We went to the same high school and then I went on to New York to Columbia. Jim went off to Chicago and went to Northwestern. But I guess he didn't like it so much. In the second year of college he came to visit in New York and that same year he decided to transfer to Columbia. Luc Sante started there too, so all of a sudden – boom! – we were all there and we were all very much sort of the poetry crowd. Jim had not yet decided he wanted to become a filmmaker, and I think Luc already knew he wanted to be a writer. I was having problems because at the time I didn't know that I could make the transition from being a writer, which is what I was doing, to being a composer. I knew I really wanted to be a composer but at the time I thought it had to be way too technical and too difficult. I was hesitating over doing it. So first I went into rock 'n' roll!

As a guitarist.

Yeah, as a guitarist. I've been doing that since I was a kid. But it was a while before I had the courage to make the transition, all along I wanted to be a regular art music composer, it just took me a while to get the courage to just say, 'Okay, here it goes.' Actually the music scene of the 1970s and '80s helped a lot because between the minimalism and the electronics it was a lot easier to just come in and be a primitive, a beginner and get away with it. Whereas the complex music that was going on when I was a boy . . . I could have never faked my way through it!

The second part of the question was if you ever actually worked with Jarmusch.

Other than the Del-Byzanteens, no, we never really worked together. I did soundtracks for two of Sara's [Sara Driver, Jim Jarmusch's long-time partner and collaborator] films – *You Are Not I,* for example.

Can you tell me more about that?

You Are Not I is a nice little film. People talk about how unusual Neil Young's soundtrack for *Dead Man* is, 'cause he just sat down and watched the movie and played along with it. Well, that's how I did the soundtrack for *You Are Not I.* I don't know if there was that kind of synchronizing that you can do nowadays and if it existed it certainly didn't exist on my level. I was just sitting there watching it on a TV, with a VHS player and a synthesizer, just playing along with it, running it back and forth. I think Sara gave me $50, bought me a Chinese meal and gave me a hit of speed! A day later I gave her the soundtrack. It was a good way to work!

Can you tell me something about this movie?

Well, it's about a woman in a psychiatric hospital, it's a weird, mind-bending little film because it has a weird twist of reality in it, suddenly what seems to be is turned around on you and so it's a challenge for the filmmaker. To tell you the truth I never read the story, well it wasn't really part of the job for me to read the story.

Is Sara Driver still making films?

I know she's been writing scripts, and I know for some time she's been wanting to make a silent film, but I can't remember if it's completely silent or if there's a gimmick in there. I know the protagonist is a deaf mute. I think the working title was *Deaf, Dumb and Blonde*!

I also read about another project that never saw the light, called *The Garden of Divorce*.
The Garden of Divorce . . .

Weren't you involved in some way?

Yeah. Okay, that's the hidden answer to the other question, if Jim and I ever worked together. He had the idea for a film called *The Garden of Divorce*. He and Luc and I talked about it a little bit. Luc was a script adviser. This is really long ago. Jim had a whole idea there, Richard Boes, who is in some of Jim's films, was supposed to be the actor. I think there was a samurai theme of some sort, I don't remember exactly what it was any more . . . I think this was before Jim had made any features.

Even before Permanent Vacation? I thought it was right after . . .

That's what I'm trying to remember. Maybe it wasn't before *Permanent Vacation*, but certainly it was a long time ago. But I actually started to work on it. After we had that first talk, I went home and wrote three or four musical cues.

So you actually were writing the music . . .

. . . ahead of the film. I just took off with it and started going with it, and actually the film never got made, the music never got used, but then, years later, when Sara made her second film, *Sleepwalk*, she used those cues in it.

So it's a very ecological project!

Yeah, recycled! It seems to me that what I thought of as the opening title sequence she used as her closing title sequence! (Laughs)

And you also told me that even though you have not actually really worked together, you contributed with two very important things: one is a joke and one is a title.

Yeah, well when Jim and I were in college in Columbia he did a jazz show and I had an overnight free-format show where I mixed together all sorts of music. My show was called *Stranger Than Paradise*. And Jim did ask me if he could use that name later on. And there was the crazy joke that Jim put into *Permanent Vacation*, well, I told him that joke.

The Doppler effect joke.

Yeah, the famous Doppler effect joke, but that joke had in turn been told to me by a friend of ours named Matt Kennedy, who heard the joke on the old *Tonight* show with Johnny Carson. The joke was actually the invention of a great old Las Vegas comic named Pete Barbutti. He was like an old beatnik. With the funny flat top fade haircut and the little pointed goatee beard. He was a jazz musician and he often did jokes that involved playing while he told them.

Well, the whole joke is actually about Charlie Parker.

Yeah, it's about jazz musicians, so it was a perfect Pete Barbutti joke. That's a very long explanation for where that joke comes from! Well, it's just interesting how somebody first told it, then say five people went through the chain of this joke and Jim changed it a bunch more.

In *Permanent Vacation* when Chris Parker is going to the cinema and I think he has just heard the joke, in the background you can hear the famous Ennio Morricone theme of *The Good, the Bad and the Ugly*. I always thought it couldn't be accidental.

Well, I do know that as far back as the late 1970s at least we were collecting Morricone LPs. So Jim probably placed that in the movie.

The funny thing is that Morricone, who has a great respect for Sergio Leone, actually does not like to be remembered only for the westerns.

Well, it's maybe not his best music, but it's kind of the best films that his music got in. Actually my favourite music of his is all those mafia films, or suspense and terror films. There are so many amazing films that to Americans are very obscure films we hardly ever see.

Well, Morricone is also a contemporary musician.

That's the stuff I don't like. The concert music of his that I have heard does not equal his cinema music. There was some piece of his I heard last year that is a long cue from one of these gangster movies that was a ten-minute-long track that had a heartbeat going on through it. I don't know what it was, but it was just great.

3

What do you think about Jarmusch's musical choices in general?

Actually directors can sometimes have an interesting effect on musical taste, by what they use. Jim has had a remarkable effect. Well, would people have remembered Screamin' Jay Hawkins so well without that movie [*Stranger Than Paradise*]? He was remembered at a tiny edge of cult appreciation, and all of a sudden everybody knows him!

I wrote that in my opinion Jarmusch's films are really 50 per cent vision and 50 per cent sound, and that there is what I call a sound democracy. That means that to him all sounds are equally important.

Well, you do notice that – there are little exceptions but they're only little bits – for the most part Jim's films do not have conventional composed soundtracks at all. There's no narrative music, even when there's some extra composed music.

Of course there are some masters at that, I think of the Hitchcock–Herrmann connection, for example.

Yeah, true. Morricone did a few good ones too.

Exactly. But not everybody is Morricone or Bernard Herrmann.

I know. The lot of the film composers is dismaying. It's hard to put your finger on what went wrong or what is going wrong and what's been lost there. It was one of those cases where maybe the old studio system worked in their favour, because certain people somehow, if the right person had the power, could protect that composer and let him do what he'd want to do. Obviously Bernard Herrmann was allowed to do six or seven films with Hitchcock in a row, not to mention Welles. It's the movie *Torn Curtain* where Hitchcock said 'I don't like your soundtrack' and the relationship with Bernard

Herrmann ended. The film was a flop, by the way. There is that terrible story. He died just after he finished the score for *Taxi Driver*. The movie hadn't come out yet and Scorsese's office was getting frantic calls from Bernard Herrmann's widow, wondering how she could get the payment . . . he was that broke! It was terrible. But nowadays the film composer is treated just as if he's doing a jingle for a commercial. The people I know who do it, they get kicked around. Of course they are not Bernard Herrmann, they are not Ennio Morricone, nonetheless it seems to be typical that you are just considered zero. When you watch a current film, look at where the composer's name is. The costume designer comes over the composer now. It's amazing how many people are over the composer. They don't get any respect.

This is especially true for Hollywood.

Yeah. I don't know on what level those composers in the old days worked with their directors, but from what I do know about them, it doesn't sound like the relationship was that much more profound than today. Prokofiev or Herrmann just came in last-minute, took a look at it, Hitchcock or Welles would say, 'This is what we want Benny', and Herrmann would go do it. And there's no reason that can't be the case now and I don't know why it isn't. Is it the films?

I don't know. Well, what you just said is exactly what Morricone told me. He has a very humble attitude. He said he is like an *'artigiano'*, a craftsman, who has this ability, but in the end the film is the work of the director, because he is actually composing on the bigger level.

That's the way it should be, I know that you're at the service of the picture but what I heard from the people I know who do it professionally . . . I couldn't stand to be treated like that! Unfortunately, being totally subservient is the nature of commercial work. When I do my concert or theatre music I do exactly what I want to.

And now, as you just told me, you are also starting to make your own films and videos.

What is interesting is that sometimes I do the music first. I've done two of these so far and the first one works beautifully, the music and the pictures go so well.

How long are they?

The first one is about twenty minutes, it's three movements each of which is six or seven minutes long. Although actually it wasn't meant to be a single video, it was meant to be projected on three screens with the boom-boxes surrounding it. It's a piece called *Meditations in an Emergency*, [speaking softly] after a poem by Frank O'Hara . . . I like to steal titles!

Quoting is not necessarily something bad.

Oh, there's no way I can hide that one, anybody who knows anything about poetry in twentieth-century America must know that that's the title of his best book of poems. And about quoting, finally I have come up with a beautiful closing quote: 'Do not fear mistakes, there are none' (Miles Davis).

New York, December 2003

2 Jarmusch, the Musician

'If the Ramones had not existed, I probably would not have made any films.'
Jim Jarmusch at the Buenos Aires Festival Internacional de Cine Independiente, 25 April 2001

'If he had not become such an extraordinary director, Jim would now be a rockstar.'
Wim Wenders, in *Rolf Aurich and Stefan Reinecke*, ed. Jim Jarmusch (Berlin, 2001), p. 8

The Del-Byzanteens: 1

With thickly drawn white Egyptian hieroglyphics on a black background and the group's name in angular, electric purple characters, the Del-Byzanteens hit the scene with their first EP, released on the Don't Fall Off the Mountain label. The year was 1981 and you could breathe music on every street corner on New York's Lower East Side. The EP was followed a year later by *Lies to Live By*, this time with a full seven tracks, three more than on their debut. There is one eye-catching detail on the sleeves of both records: voice and keyboards – Jim Jarmusch.

There is nothing odd about this, though, since playing in a band in New York at the time was almost a compulsory step along a path that did not necessarily lead to a fully fledged musical career. Actually being able to play an instrument was of minor importance compared to owning one or being able to find a loft to rehearse in or a stage to perform on.

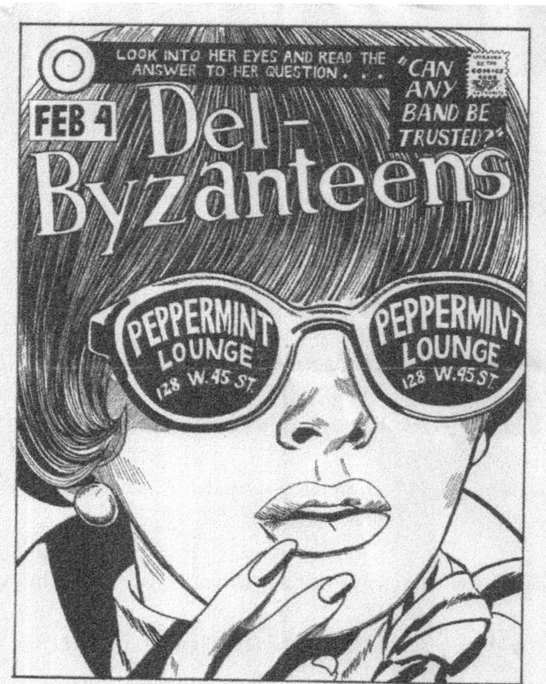

The Del-Byzanteens live at Peppermint Lounge.

Back in the pre-Internet era people got together in intensely physical places that were anything but virtual: Tier 3, CBGB, Max's Kansas City, Rock Lounge, Hurrah, Mudd Club. Not to mention the myriad nameless places and spaces: squats in abandoned buildings, lofts managed by artists, improvised galleries. Many flocked to the Big Apple with its acceptance of new forms of stimulus and insecurities, and its willingness to take in anyone seeking artistic – or any other – form of self-realization, or those just seeking a cheaper place to live. Indeed, public policies of planned shrinkage resulting in affordable rents and numerous empty buildings were among the main reasons behind the birth of the bohemian community on Manhattan's Lower East Side.

The Del-Byzanteens broke up just over a year later. This too was nothing unusual, since most groups on the scene at the time were unlikely to be remembered for their endurance – 'Live fast and die young', as Allie (Chris Parker) says in *Permanent Vacation*.[1] However, velocity is not a quality that particularly interested the young director in his cinema, and especially not in his musical quest. Jarmusch seemed to be more drawn towards rarefaction, repetition and progressive modification.

In *The Trouser Press Record Guide*, David Fricke described the Del-Byzanteens as a band from the 'art-punk' scene, stylistically close to Television and The Velvet Underground.[2] The term *punk*, a typical all-encompassing label that has been stuck on the most disparate of bands and musicians, is generally to be taken with a pinch of salt. Punk's initially self-destructive streak, shouted nihilism and scorched earth approach have little to do with the Del-Byzanteens' music, not even in its supposed 'art-punk' variation. With a few exceptions, the songs have a rather traditional structure of verse and chorus, although they give the impression of circular compositions as they unfold, unresolved to the point of becoming vaguely hypnotic.

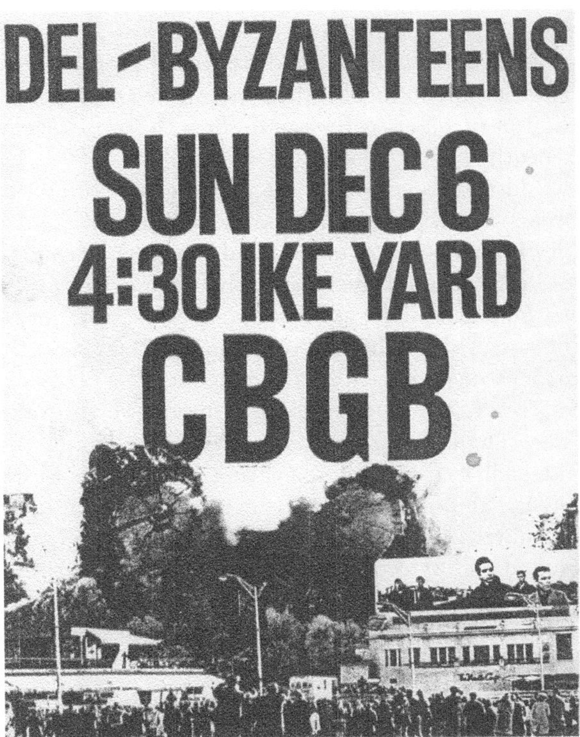

The Del-Byzanteens
live at CBGB.

In the record version of their hit, 'Girl's Imagination', the ostinato bass riff is virtually unchanged for the full six minutes, providing a solid platform for the dream-like vocals.[3] In their cover of the Jaynetts' 'Sally Go Round the Roses' it is the song itself that is already hypnotically repetitive, particularly through the echoing structure of the lyrics that seem to chase and mirror each other. The metallic screech in the background of 'Welcome Machines' is a drawn-out lament over the track's constant percussive rhythm. The instrumental 'Apartment 13' is structured with different movements, alternating diverse rhythms and timbres, creating an overall minimalist, alienated feeling. On the whole the arrangements are sober and without frills, while percussion plays a central role.

Jim Jarmusch and Phil Kline (vocals and guitar, the Del-Byzanteens' only real musician and possibly the 'mind' behind them), apart from going to gigs at the venues mentioned above, were at the time also into minimal music, gamelan and Egyptian pop. The contamination between scant ethnic and percussive elements lost against an electronic background, and the more obscure sound typical to so-called No Wave, make it difficult to label the work of the Del-Byzanteens – but then half the fun of labels is removing them, leaving a clean, smooth surface beneath.

Just like on the Super 8 scene, the link with the past is by no means broken. Of the nine songs on the two records, two are covers of 1960s hits, both by successful girl bands: the Jaynetts and the Supremes. With 'Sally Go Round the Roses', the Bronx trio took the pop charts by storm, reaching the number two spot in 1963, but more to the point is the song's decidedly hypnotic and circular mood, traits particularly present in Jarmusch's early cinema. The other cover version is the Supremes' 'My World is Empty without You', featuring diva-to-be Diana Ross. The Del-Byzanteens gave the song their own twist, creating an indefinable, troubling, alienating atmosphere with an insistent, high-pitched and off-beat note from the synthesizer, the listener taunted by this unrelenting, slightly annoying background pulse. The past is thus evoked and placed in a different context, but is in no way abolished.

As Phil Kline and Luc Sante, who wrote the lyrics to some of the songs on *Lies to Live By*, told me, the band's bass player Philippe Hagen listened exclusively to 1950s rockabilly music while working as a graphic designer and trying to teach himself to play the bass.[4] Becoming a virtuoso definitely was not the main preoccupation for many musicians of the 'scene'. As Jarmusch recalls, 'We often would switch instruments, because back then the idea was not to be professional necessarily but to just express something. So a lot of bands would play instruments they didn't know how to play, or switch around.'[5] All in all, the Del-Byzanteens were not entirely unsuccessful and two of the album's songs, the title track 'Lies to Live By' and 'Girl's Imagination', were used by Wim Wenders in *The State of Things* (*Der Stand der Dinge*, 1982). By 1982 Wenders and Jarmusch had known each other for some time and had even worked together on one of the German director's lesser known but more extreme and ambitious projects, *Lightning Over Water* (1980).

Before going into more depth on this crucial film, it is now time for a flashback, temporarily diverting from the strictly musical path followed so far and focusing instead on broader cinematic connections that help to clear up the context in which Jarmusch took his first steps as a director.

Bridge over the Ocean

In an interview for the Sundance Channel in 1996, while talking about the over-inflated, ambiguous concept of independent filmmaking, in light of the 'indie' fashion of which the Sundance Film Festival is itself to a large extent a clone, Jarmusch mentioned some of the artists that most influenced him.[6]

> To me, people that have been really inspirational – in all forms – are people who stay outside of the mainstream because that's not their expertise or that's not their interest. So people like Robert Frank or John Cassavetes and in the same way, people like Thelonius Monk, or Ornette Coleman. They're not trying to hit a certain niche in the market; they're trying to use their form to express themselves.

I'd like to take a closer look at John Cassavetes. Many agree that the director of *Shadows* (1959) was a crucial link in the development of independent cinema in the 1960s and again in the 1980s. 'Independent spirits' have always existed, yet Cassavetes managed to combine that spirit with a new working method, which in time became exemplary for many who came after him. Dealing with the burning issue of race, and shot in quasi-documentary style on a shoestring budget with its use

Bridge over the ocean, *Shadows*, John Cassavetes (1959).

of Charles Mingus's jazz and street talk, *Shadows* was born of the intense training provided by the actor-director in his workshop, based on improvisation. The film ends with its problems unsolved, just as in real life, de facto violating Hollywood storytelling traditions, which require clear-cut endings. In 1960 Cassavetes triumphed at the Venice film festival by winning the Special Jury Prize, earning himself the reputation as 'America's answer to the French Nouvelle Vague'.[7] By rejecting Hollywood, where nonetheless he continued to work as an actor to fund his own productions, Cassavetes's work built a solid 'bridge over the ocean', which many will choose to cross in both directions for years to come.

In 1975, during his last term at Columbia University, Jim Jarmusch travelled to Paris where he ended up staying a whole year. At the Cinémathèque Française he got to know the works of Japanese directors Ozu and Mizoguchi, of European *auteurs* Bresson and Dreyer, and, possibly more surprisingly, of American directors Sam Fuller and Nicholas Ray. Indeed the director-critics of the Nouvelle Vague had long since started the process of rehabilitating many U.S. directors, previously relegated to the cage of rigidly defined genres – Hitchcock being the most famous case in point. While breathing new life into those same genres,

Godard famously stated: 'Had cinema not existed, Nick Ray would have invented it.'

The 22-year-old Jarmusch went to the Paris Cinémathèque almost every day, thus discovering America anew – from a distance, through the eyes of a foreigner, of a European. 'I was particularly struck by Nicholas Ray . . . In America I had already seen *Rebel Without a Cause* (1955)' he explained in 1984.[8] This first filmic encounter with Ray was to be followed by a second, much closer to home, with far-reaching consequences. On returning to New York, Jarmusch decided 'for the fun of it' to enrol in the New York University Graduate Film School, and was incredulous when admitted on the basis of some writings, an essay on cinema and a few photographs. László Benedek, at the time director of the graduate film programme at NYU's School of the Arts, and who twenty years earlier directed Marlon Brando in *The Wild One* (1953), was responsible for the first meeting between Nicholas Ray and Jarmusch. Due to his lack of tuition money, Jarmusch was about to quit his last year, when Benedek introduced him to Ray who had just been given a teaching position. The two immediately liked each other: Jarmusch became Ray's assistant, and Ray his mentor. Benedek was able to help Jarmusch get a fellowship – as Jarmusch wryly recalled, 'a Louis B. Mayer fellowship, the guy who destroyed Erich von Stroheim's film *Greed*!' – which enabled him to work mostly with Ray during that last year at NYU.[9] The old 'Hollywood rebel' trusted the young student and gave him advice which proved crucial to his future choices, regarding two points in particular. First, he should never set foot in Hollywood, otherwise his future as a director would be completely and irreversibly ruined.

> Nicholas Ray told me something, he repeated it many times and at the beginning I thought he was joking, but then I realized he was serious. He told me: 'Never go to Hollywood, not even for a simple visit, never go there at all! You will be destroyed!'[10]

The second point was brought up by Jarmusch fifteen years later in an interview with the *Cahiers du Cinéma* on *Dead Man*:

> The most important thing he taught me is to think about each scene in itself. He always repeated to work on one scene abstracting it from the one that comes before and the one that comes after. 'A series of good scenes make a good story', he told me.[11]

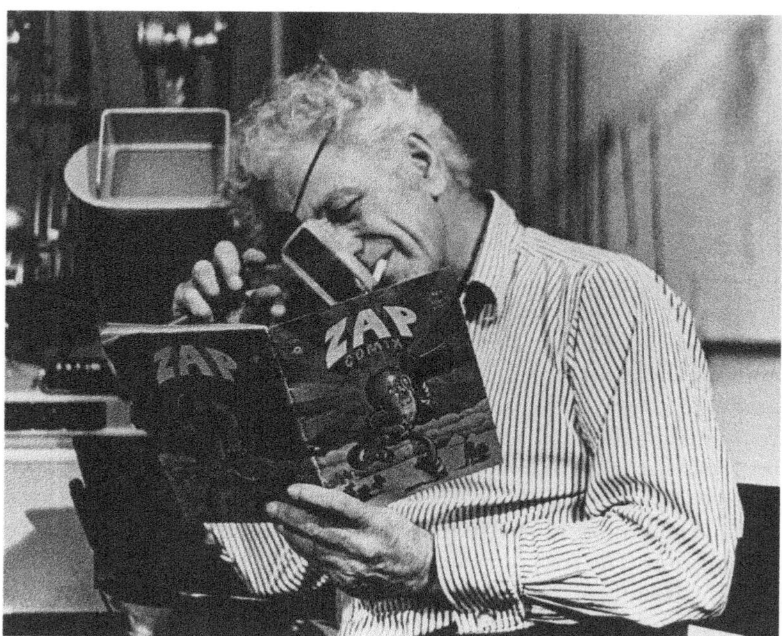

The pupil appeared to follow his teacher's 'metaphorical' advice almost overly to the letter, particularly in *Stranger Than Paradise* and *Dead Man*, in which every individual scene stands materially alone, physically separated from the next one by a length of black leader, sometimes even for a few seconds. In *Stranger Than Paradise*, working on a tight budget required that every scene be shot in one sequence to make the most economic use of the film stock, whereas in *Dead Man*, the black leader intervals are a clear aesthetic choice to give the story an increasingly dream-like quality as the character wanders lost in an alien landscape. Despite these differences, one could be forgiven for thinking that in both cases Jarmusch, without being overly loud about it, is taking a swipe at traditional Hollywood storytelling where scenes blend into one another, building towards a definite climax that Jarmusch's films apparently never wish to reach.

Meeting Ray was fundamental to the young Jarmusch, in more ways than one: it was through him that the budding director became involved in the previously mentioned project *Lightning Over Water*, during which he met Wim Wenders. Whereas Jarmusch's first serious encounter with cinema occurred in France at the Paris Cinémathèque, it was now Europe, ideally personified by Wenders, one of the most 'American' of its directors, who crossed the Atlantic to New York to shoot his personal tribute to the maestro of *Johnny Guitar* and *Rebel Without a Cause*. As mentioned earlier, when referring to Cassavetes, the 'bridge over the ocean' between Europe and the U.S. can, of course, be crossed in both directions.

Nick's Movie

Lightning Over Water was a radical project. The superimposition of life and cinema, of reality and its depiction, was complete, even though Wenders's visual 'expedient' of alternating video and 35mm attempted to highlight their separation. Nicholas Ray played both himself and a character treading a thin line between documentary and fiction. As if wanting to stress that cinema cannot bestow immortality, whether to its creator or its spectator, Wenders and his team filmed Ray as he moved closer to death, terminally ill with lung cancer. 'I knew he wanted to work. To die working', Wenders says in the film. Nicholas Ray's end is

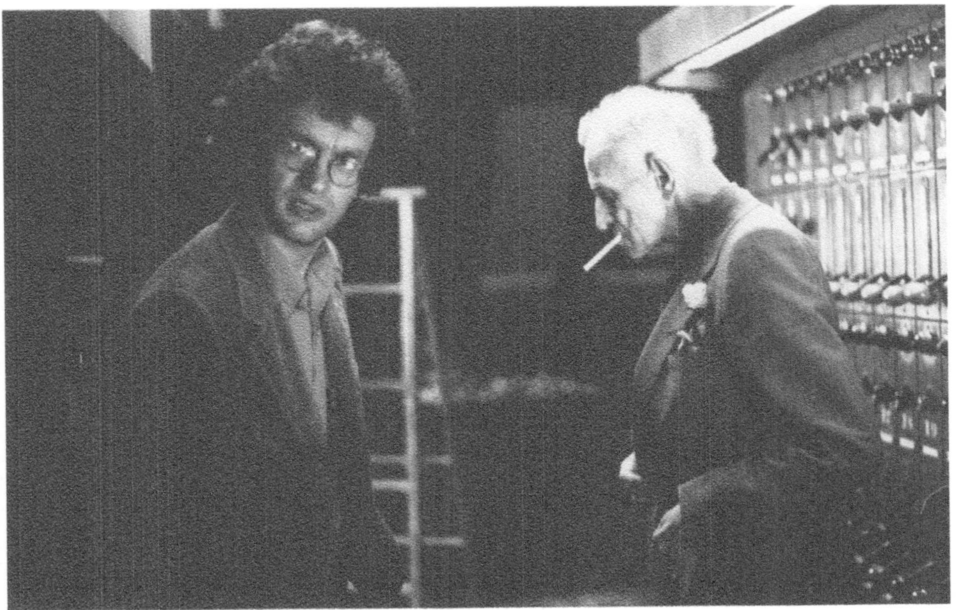

extraordinary. His final gesture is to look into the camera and, eliminating any cinematic fiction, utter his last word: 'CUT!'

In June 1979, two days after Ray's death, Jarmusch started shooting *Permanent Vacation*.[12] It is unthinkable to imagine that Ray's young assistant would not be deeply moved by this entire event, and his relationship with Wenders would not be strengthened. The German director's favourite themes – travelling, wanderings, the lack of or search for an identity, being a perpetual foreigner, and the importance of music ('My life was saved by rock 'n' roll' is still one of his most famous statements[13]) – are a clear indication that the two are at least partly on the same wavelength.

When speaking of waves, the closing shots of both Wenders's *Lightning Over Water* and Jarmusch's *Permanent Vacation* come to mind. Notwithstanding the fact that both stories and settings are quite different, these shots actually seem very similar. The clear, blue skies, the water, the Manhattan skyline and a boat sailing into the distance – a Chinese junk[14] in *Lightning Over Water*, a steamer in *Permanent Vacation* – are the elements common to both. At first one might think that this is due to the older director's influence on Jarmusch, who had not yet turned 30 and was shooting his first feature film. But that would be a mistake. Why? Some clues can be found listening carefully to the acoustic layers of the two sequences.

In *Lightning Over Water*, the film crew meets on the Chinese junk carrying Nicholas Ray's ashes. On board words overlap; it is difficult to

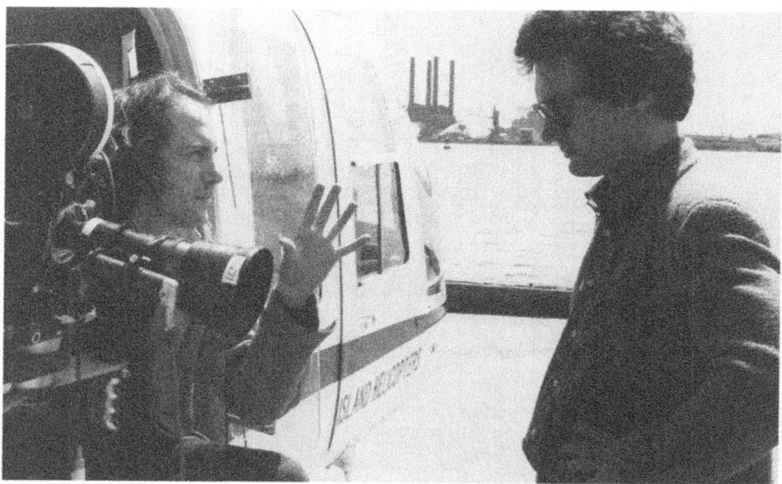

Aerial shot, *Lightning Over Water*.

focus on one single conversation and a cinematic taboo is broken as dialogue becomes incomprehensible. The emotional confusion is compounded by the tangle of sound and language. The final image, the one I am focusing on, unfolds as follows: a swaying aerial wide shot, the junk shrinking in size, the island of Manhattan in the distant background. During the first seconds we can still hear fragments of the crew's voices, then a saxophone and a piano strike up a melancholy tune. Words fade as the camera starts its reverse flight, the frame freezes and shakily handwritten words appear superimposed on the screen: an excerpt from Ray's diary that Wenders's voice helps us decipher. The sound of his off-screen voice is the last dynamic element, which continues to flow over the frozen image, now resembling a silent-movie caption. In fact, the last sequence is introduced by a title card – 'Epilogue' – making Wenders's ending linear and clear-cut.

Let us now look at the final sequence of *Permanent Vacation*. Young Allie Parker cannot live without drifting; *elsewhere* is the only place possible for him. At the end of the film, in what he still believes to be the beginning of a new life, he arrives in port prior to boarding the steamer – it is no coincidence that Paris will be his final destination – where he meets his double: a young Parisian who has just arrived in New York, and who is also searching for his new 'Babylon'. After exchanging a few words, they are interrupted by the steamer's horn calling passengers on board. Here again we hear an off-screen voice: that of Allie talking about his goodbye note. As we will never know exactly what was written on it, the message is left open. In the final subjective shot, seen from Allie's point of view, we stare down from the steamer's deserted deck at the fast-moving waters below, while in real time the Manhattan skyline slowly shrinks into the distance.

If in Wim Wenders's final shot, which includes the Chinese junk in the field of vision, the spectators are mere bystanders, in *Permanent Vacation* we are actually *on* the boat, and therefore part of a departure that feels more like a beginning than an end. John Lurie's saxophone blends in with the slow, constant and, at times, slightly dissonant Indonesian gamelan, which follows Allie's wanderings throughout the film. Lurie improvises variations on the theme of 'Over the Rainbow', an important and recurrent element of the film, which according to film critic Joyce Roodnat 'is *the* melody expressing desire and trust in an ideal *elsewhere*'.[15] The saxophone chases the chorus with an irregular rhythm, jumping from one octave to another, becoming increasingly higher in pitch, and giving the impression of a goal that remains unattainable in spite of the incessant movement.

Unlike the clear-cut ending in Wenders's 'Epilogue', here we are projected forward or, rather, in a circle. It is the same story, about to start again, only somewhere else. Jarmusch's subjective shot, together with the layer of sounds and the length of the real-time sequence, all contribute to creating a hypnotic atmosphere, which is circular rather than linear, open rather than conclusive. Behind two apparently very similar sequences two visions and two messages appear, totally independent of each other and crucially defined by the deliberate use of sound.

Celluloid

The above should not detract from the importance that the encounter with Wenders had on the young Jarmusch who, like any budding filmmaker, was dogged by a constant and costly problem: film stock.

In 1982 Wenders was in Portugal shooting *The State of Things* (*Der Stand der Dinge*) in black and white, a story involving a film crew forced to stop work because it runs out of money and film stock. Ironically enough, just under an hour's worth of raw stock remained unused by Wenders's production. The German director decided to give it to Nicholas Ray's ex-assistant who, in the meantime, had founded his own production company, Cinesthesia, with Sara Driver, his girlfriend and collaborator. As John Lurie told me, he suggested Jarmusch use this precious raw stock to shoot a short.[16] Wenders's production company, Grey City Film, and producer Chris Sievernich agreed, but demanded to keep the negative and the rights to the finished film. French cineastes Jean Marie Straub and Danielle Huillet also decided to help the young filmmaker, by giving him one roll of negative film, which Jarmusch used as the black leader to create that feeling of suspension between each scene of what would become his second feature film, *Stranger Than Paradise*.

Shot over a single weekend in 1982, the 30-minute short that later turned into the first episode of *Stranger Than Paradise – The New World* – was supposed to be shown before the screenings of Wenders's movie. But, as is often the case, things turned out differently. Jarmusch was set on making a feature film, but he lacked the funds to finish shooting. Once again he crossed the 'bridge over the ocean' to try his luck at the European film festivals. When in 1983 the film was awarded the Jury's Prize at the Rotterdam Festival, new opportunities opened up for Jarmusch.

A meeting with the young German producer Otto Grockenberger, who decided to sponsor the project, turned things around. Finally, *Eating Raoul* director, Paul Bertel, helped Jarmusch buy back the rights from Grey City, and the German public TV network ZDF co-produced the entire endeavour. After a long period of careful preparation, and not without some initial adventurous twists, Cinesthesia was ready to resume shooting. As Sara Driver recalled, the first half hour of *Stranger Than Paradise* was shot very fast, in one weekend, but was in danger of never seeing the light of day due to a run-in with one of the first backers of the project. Driver literally had to steal a 35mm print of the film from his office, something she is rather proud of to this day.[17] In January 1984, after almost three years, *Stranger Than Paradise* was about to take definite shape. From about $7,000 spent on the initial 30-minute film, the final cost had climbed to about $120,000, which was still very little. In March, almost by miracle, Jarmusch managed to send his film to the Cannes Film Festival just in time. He did not win the Palme d'Or, which, as fate would have it, went to Wenders's *Paris, Texas*, but he was only too happy to accept the prestigious Caméra d'Or, the award given to the best debut film. As Wenders stated in 2001, '1984 was a good year for both of us.'[18]

But there is another twist to this tale, with celluloid once again taking centre stage. One of Jarmusch's production assistants on *Stranger Than Paradise* was Guido Chiesa, a young Italian from Turin with a passion for music and cinema. Following his experience in the U.S., Chiesa decided that cinema was his future and, like many a young novice director before him, stumbled upon the inevitable lack of film stock. One of his first films, *Black Harvest* (1986), had in his own words 'a rather unique production process, with all the hallmarks to become a small "legend" of independent cinema'.[19] Chiesa shot it using film left over from *Stranger Than Paradise*.

Chiesa remembered that when Wenders was about to shoot *The State of Things* in 1982, his director of photography, Henri Alekan, wanted to use 500 ASA Kodak, a highly sensitive film no longer sold, so the producer had to search for it in storerooms all over the world, since Kodak would not have been able to produce it in time. In the end so much film was shipped to the set that some was left unused and Wenders decided to give it to Jarmusch, who with the film made the first part of *Stranger Than Paradise*. Since three years had passed before the funding was secured to complete it, the producer was able to order the film needed directly from

Kodak, requesting more than was necessary. Jarmusch, well aware of the constant 'stock problem' young directors were confronted with, decided to give Chiesa, his friend and production assistant, the remaining film.[20]

It seems fair to say that history repeats itself.

The Del-Byzanteens: 2

In any art form based on collaboration it is often the group dynamics that determine what course creativity will take. If any. The Del-Byzanteens were short-lived, precisely because the group struggled to find the necessary cohesion. Apart from Jim Jarmusch, the line-up included Phil Kline on vocals and guitar, Philippe Hagen on bass and twins Josh and Dan Braun alternating between drums and percussion. Part-time members of the group included Luc Sante who contributed by writing some of the lyrics, and James Nares on percussion.

Of these seven people only Phil Kline continued to work with music, mainly as a composer, his distinctive style born of a childhood obsession: recorded loops. His 'boombox symphonies', composed for an orchestra of dozens of portable tape recorders, are built on the layering of mostly electronic sounds, on repetition and overlapping loops. Following the same principle – separate music tracks played simultaneously at slightly differing speeds – Kline's 'Unsilent Night' has been a Christmas classic since 1992, quickly becoming a cult performance-procession that takes place every year in the streets of Lower Manhattan and beyond.[21] Besides being the only 'real' musician of the Del-Byzanteens, Kline is also one of Jarmusch's oldest friends. Together with Luc Sante, they went to Columbia University and, during the first half of the 1970s, studied with David Shapiro and Kenneth Koch, prominent representatives of the New York School of Poets.

For Luc Sante poetry and literature remained focal points and helped him forge an American identity in a way that only a non-American could do. His home town is Verviers, a Belgian town close to Liège, but New York welcomed him with open arms. As is often the case, it takes an outsider to really see the adopted city he lives in, a successful result being *Low Life*, a heartfelt though unsentimental account of New York's slums, chronicling in great detail the years 1840 to 1919.[22] It was thanks to this book that, ten years later, Martin Scorsese hired him as a historical adviser for *Gangs of New York* (2002). With the Del-Byzanteens, apart from being one of three inseparable friends and participating behind

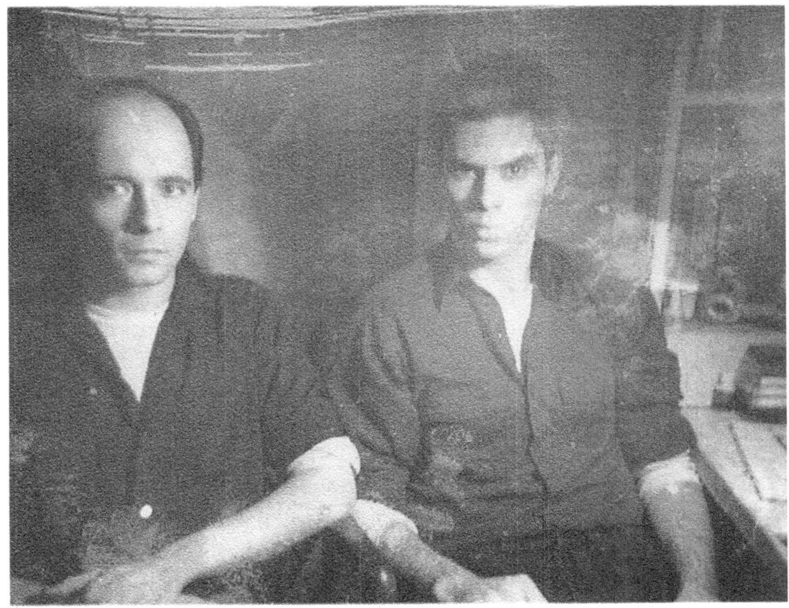

the scenes as mentioned above, Sante wrote the lyrics for 'Lies to Live By' and 'Girl's Imagination'. The chorus of the first song – 'If I only have one life, let me live it as a lie' – has an amusing story to go with it.[23] Is it a remnant of existentialism? Intellecto-punk cynicism? Disillusioned spleen of youth? Not at all. As Sante told me, he got the idea from a 1960s shampoo commercial, or rather its slogan: 'If I only have one life, let me live it as a blonde.'[24] Irony, a trademark of Jarmusch's cinema, is behind this somewhat breezy though poetic ode to mendacity. Lies sometimes help us to survive. Lies without malice help gauge one's self-confidence, gauge how much to believe in one's potential – enough to go on stage with little musical skill to display. Having something to say and saying it with the means at one's disposal is what matters. And that is something one cannot lie about.

As mentioned, bass player Philippe Hagen was more graphic designer than musician, and the Egyptian hieroglyphics against a black background was his idea. He also recalls where the band's name came from:

The name Del-Byzanteens refers not to the Byzantine Empire in Constantinople, but to the adjective. You can have a 'byzantine argument', the most famous example is 'How many angels can dance on a hatpin?' and it was in the sense of the adjective that we used that name: as something being obscure, convoluted, not immediately clear.[25]

When playing bass Hagen could do little more than 'follow instructions', but it hardly mattered since the minimalist atmosphere and tribal sounding loops of the Del-Byzanteens' music concealed any eventual 'technical shortcomings'.[26] Hagen was an expert at networking, so thanks to him the group got signed up for gigs. Most of the time advertising was by word of mouth, and whether or not a group got the chance to perform somewhere often dictated its line-up and choice of songs.

The Braun twins, Dan and Josh, played drums and percussion with the Del-Byzanteens, contributing to the group's somewhat tribal sound. However, this was not their first venture into the field of music: in 1979 they had formed the No Wave group Circus Mort together with poly-instrumentalist Michael Gira, who later went on to develop a cathartically brutal sound with his band, Swans. Like so many groups at the time, Circus Mort soon broke up, following the release of only one album.[27] More recently, the Braun twins successfully broke into the film business, creating a parallel with Jarmusch's move from music to cinema. It is certainly not by coincidence that their company Submarine, formed in 1998, co-produced the documentary *Blank City* (2010) by French New York-based director Céline Danhier. The film is a kaleidoscopic procession of interviews and archive material immortalizing the leading players of the New York scene at the end of the 1970s and early '80s, including Jim Jarmusch, Eric Mitchell, James Nares, John Lurie, Amos Poe, Debbie Harry, Lydia Lunch, Nick Zedd, Fab 5 Freddy, Patti Astor, James Chance . . . the list is endless![28] Danhier explained to me the reason behind her stylistic choice that, due to the rapidity of the editing and the monumental quantity of information, leaves the spectator feeling dizzy at times: 'I see them as hints: if you really want to see the whole film, you have to do some research and find it or go into a retrospective.'[29]

One of the prominent members of the *Blank City* cast is James Nares. Besides being an active filmmaker in the Super 8 scene, he played percussion on both the Del-Byzanteens' records. In more recent times he reduced his commitment to the music scene to concentrate on his career as an artist. However, looking at his single-brushstroke paintings that recall Japanese calligraphy, it is evident that rhythm and experimentation with time still are among his main artistic preoccupations. Before contributing to the rhythm backbone of the Del-Byzanteens, Nares played guitar with James Chance's band the Contortions. As Chance recalls, at the Contortions' first gig Nares did not actually have a real guitar and 'was playing this plastic kid's guitar',[30] confirming that owning an instrument of any kind often got the job done. Just as in any self-respecting movement, it was standard practice for No Wave bands to swap members and cooperate with each other: infatuations, break-ups, falling in love or falling apart was what shaped the line-ups of the downtown bands.

Jarmusch also collaborated briefly with another group, Dark Day, founded by Robin Crutchfield in 1979 after leaving DNA.[31] As Crutchfield recalls:

> Our first concert as Dark Day was played at The Mudd Club . . . Phil Kline was the guitarist, friend of writer/co-worker Luc Sante at the bookstore where I worked. He was also best friends with Jim Jarmusch and was pursuing an interest in film music.[32]

It is a small world, especially in New York. Jarmusch was a guest keyboard player with Dark Day for a gig at Tracks N.Y.C., with Phil Kline on guitar. Gradually though, Kline drifted away from the band to concentrate more on the Del-Byzanteens, which he felt was more his own project. Déjà vu: the break-up of yet another band.[33]

What springs to mind, while trying to find the common thread in the intricate variabilities of these figures, is a basic concept that comes back time and time again: curiosity and willingness to experiment with all and any art forms. Jarmusch seemed to have a fairly clear project in mind, or at least he displayed the determination to define it, and his experimentation deftly moved from literature to music to cinema. The downtown scene was a fertile ground, in which music, images and words actually inhabited the same places and often, sometimes even simultaneously, the same people.

'If he had not become such an extraordinary director, Jim would now be a rockstar.' Saying this, Wenders might have overstated things somewhat. Jarmusch is certainly an extrovert, but he tends to shun the limelight. He might be closer to a 'hipster-artisan' at the service of cinema, an 'underground' Ennio Morricone (even though far less prolific than the Italian maestro), with perhaps just a touch of Buster Keaton's silent poetry.

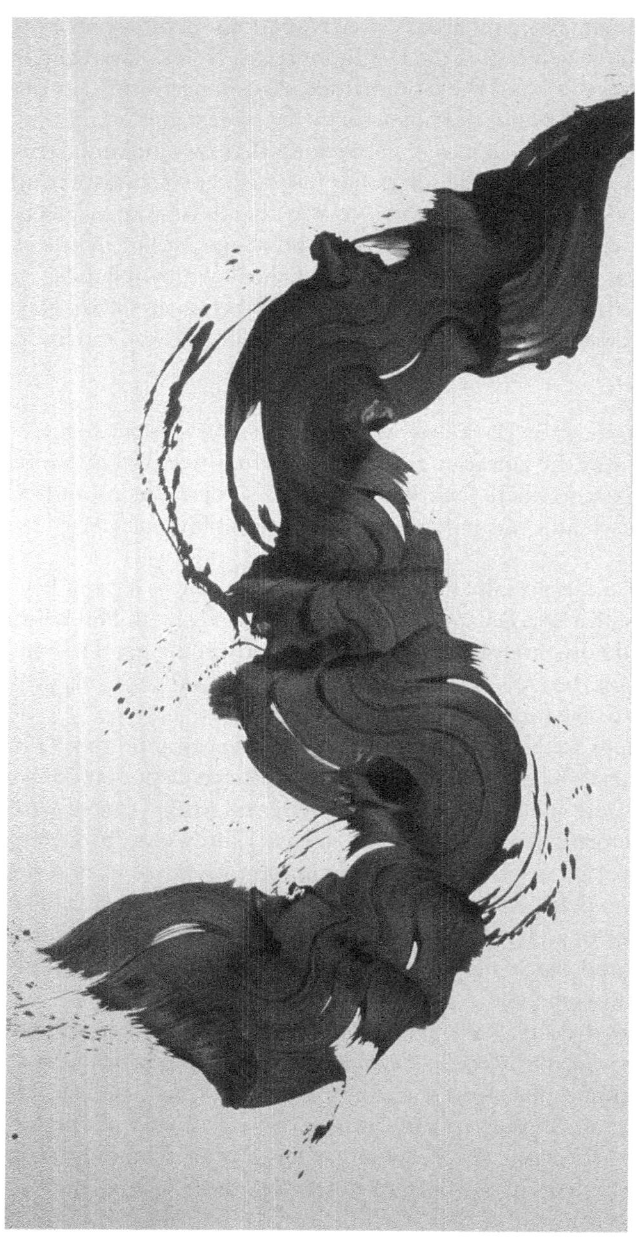

James Nares, *Half the Time*, 2003, oil on linen.

Sqürl Coda

Mentioning Morricone is by no means accidental, seeing as how over the years Jarmusch has been gripped by a progressive return to making music. As he told DJ and pop star Moby in 2010,[34] after a hiatus of more than twenty years, the Del-Byzanteens' ex-keyboard player finally returned to composing, recording and performing live. What seemed a foregone conclusion finally took form in his most recent films – *The Limits of Control* and *Only Lovers Left Alive* – for which Jarmusch composed part of the score. The reference to Morricone is thus motivated by this new role of composer (and instrumentalist) that Jarmusch, not without a certain prudence, has now taken upon himself. In 2001 and 2006 I had long conversations with the Italian maestro from which I drew that when Jarmusch, together with his collaborator-and-musician friends, embarks on the creation of the acoustic landscapes in which he chooses to immerse his films, he has the same *artisan-at-the-service-of-film* attitude embodied by Morricone.[35] There is a sort of defiant humility, an individualistic deference, but without an ulterior motive, in the way in which both Jarmusch and Morricone talk of the almost magic power, difficult to explain rationally, that music stirs in those who listen to it.

Until these more recent developments, one of the 'strategies' chosen by Jarmusch to stay connected with music had been to work

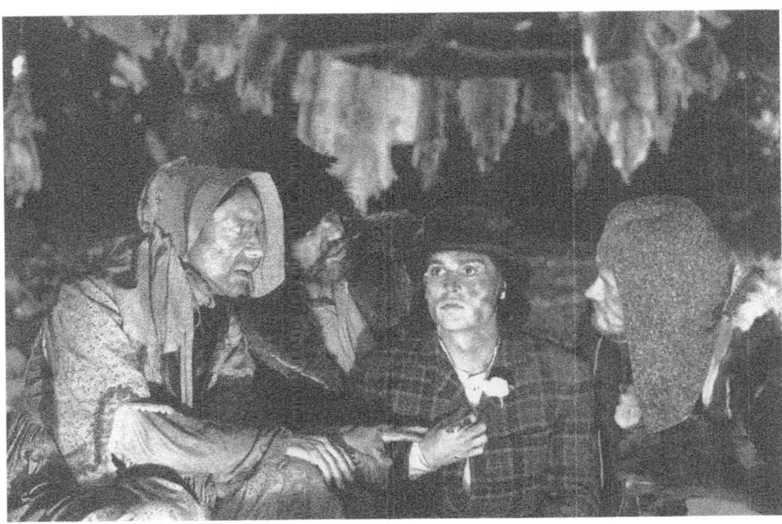

Musician-actors:
Iggy Pop (left),
Dead Man.

frequently with musician-actors, a category that seems almost ubiquitous in his casts. Countless musical faces have populated his films, making this into a typical 'Jarmusch touch'. John Lurie, Richard Edson and Eszter Balint in *Stranger Than Paradise*.[36] Lurie again and Waits in *Down By Law*. Screamin' Jay Hawkins, Joe Strummer and a little cameo by Rufus Thomas in *Mystery Train*. Iggy Pop in *Dead Man*.[37] A long list of musicians including rappers RZA and GZA, percussionist E. J. Rodriguez and rockstars Jack and Meg White of The White Stripes in *Coffee and Cigarettes*.[38] Jarmusch wishes to capture on screen the spontaneity and the immediacy of playing onstage that musicians are accustomed to. The strong bond with musician-actors, chosen for their abilities as performers, signals that intuition often draws him to them.

Jarmusch's more recent feature films – *Broken Flowers*, *The Limits of Control* and *Only Lovers Left Alive* – show a radical change of direction, musician-actors being practically absent from the casts. What at first may seem very surprising, almost a betrayal of that specific 'touch', could perhaps be explained by the mentioned progressive return to Jarmusch's own music-making. To tackle now the composing of music for his films, years and years after his sketchy, youthful music career, Jarmusch has in some way completed a cycle. He has taken a crucial step towards reawakening that same spirit of collaboration and contamination, lifeblood of the New York scene in which he started his journey

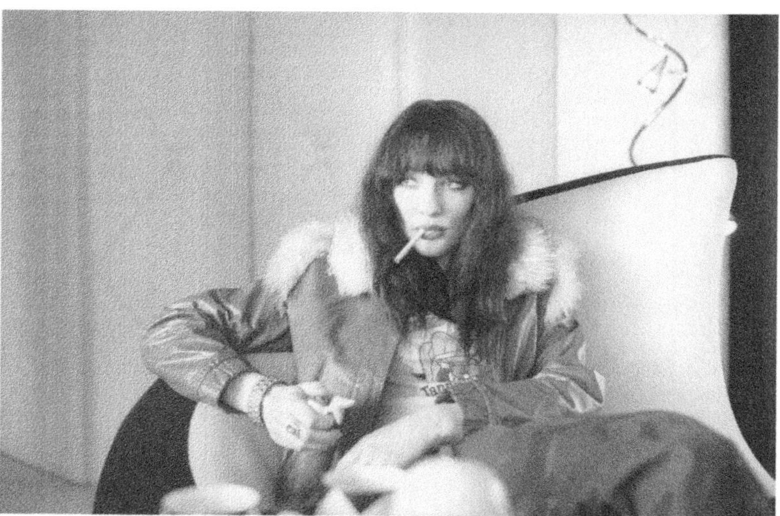

Cate Blanchett as Shelly in *Coffee And Cigarettes*.

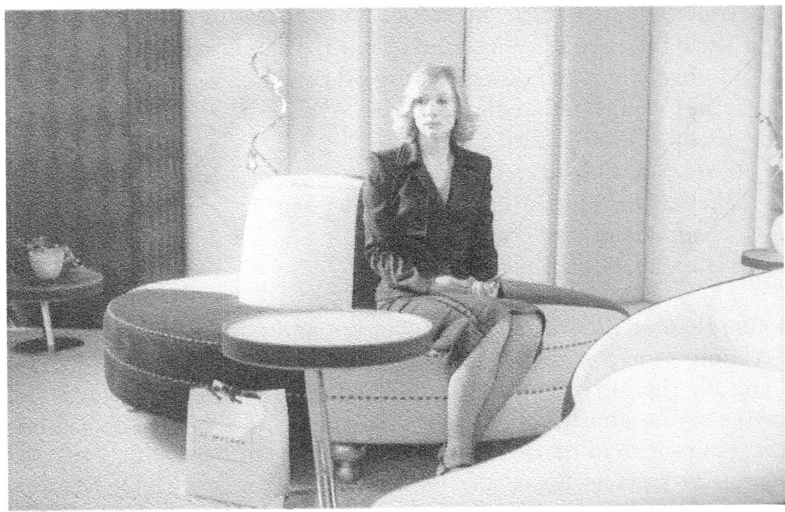

– a 'fluid scene' in which the step from performing on stage in a club to performing in front of the camera was not as long, or as hazardous, as one might have thought.

Naturally, there are new collaborations to enrich this 'reawakening'. The band initially named Bad Rabbit before being renamed Sqürl consists of Jarmusch (guitar), Carter Logan (drums and percussion) and Shane Stoneback (organ, carillon and audio engineer). As explained by Jarmusch:

> We made some music under the name Bad Rabbit for *The Limits of Control* and put an EP out.[39] After that we have been continuing to make music . . . But then we found out that there was a band named Bad Rabbits and another guy Bad Rabbit, there were a lot of rabbit names at one point, like there are a lot of wolf names, so we went for Sqürl![40]

This name had been in the pipeline for some time, as revealed by an extract from *Coffee and Cigarettes*, particularly the episode *Cousins*, with Cate Blanchett in the dual roles of Cate and Shelly, two apparently identical, but quite different cousins. When Cate asks Shelly to describe her new boyfriend's band, Jarmusch uses the moment to show off one of his typical linguistic quid pro quos based on names:

Cate: I'd love to hear the music. What does it sound like?
Shelly: It's really . . . it's kind of hard, it's industrial, kind of
    throbbing . . . I don't think you'd get it.
Cate: Well, what are they called?
Shelly: They're called Sqürl.
Cate: Squirrel?
Shelly: No, Sqürl. You know like they say here: S–q–ü–r–l, with
    an umlaut over the U. Sqürl.
Cate: Oh, Sqürl. I get it. Right.

Regardless of the correct pronunciation and punctuation, Sqürl are certainly in step with Jarmusch's idea of *music-cum-landscape*. The hypnotic rhythm of the songs, which seem intent on expanding time, merge harmoniously with the dilated images of *The Limits of Control*, the gangster road movie set in Spain. Lone Man (Isaach de Bankolé) repeatedly visits the Reina Sofia museum of contemporary art in Madrid. On each visit he stops to contemplate a single painting, and then moves on. The fourth and last painting of the series is *Gran Sàbana* (1968) by Antoni Tàpies, an artist described by Jarmusch as 'a Spanish painter who was one of the first to start incorporating found textures of things: dirt, brass, objects'.[41] The painting that Lone Man gazes at is in fact a simple white sheet with its four corners slightly rolled up to create four points, glued to a white canvas. It is over this image that the beat-less and fluid mordant notes of Bad Rabbit are heard. Jarmusch's distorted guitar projects an allusion to a film screen onto the white surface, hinting at the potentiality and depth of cinema itself, almost as if wanting to annul the static bi-dimensionality of the pictorial image, transformed here into moving images thanks to the motion picture camera. There are also various internal references to some of the film's specific scenes, as pointed out by Jarmusch:

> Tàpies' painting just looks like a sheet, which echoed to the girl in the sheets and that picture frame Lone Man looks at in the house: a painting just covered by a sheet.[42] I was just trying to find variations again and echo things throughout the film.[43]

And yet in my opinion the image of the white surface, the folds and wrinkles of which Jarmusch surveys as though a landscape, blended with his music, opens up vistas far broader than a couple of quotes

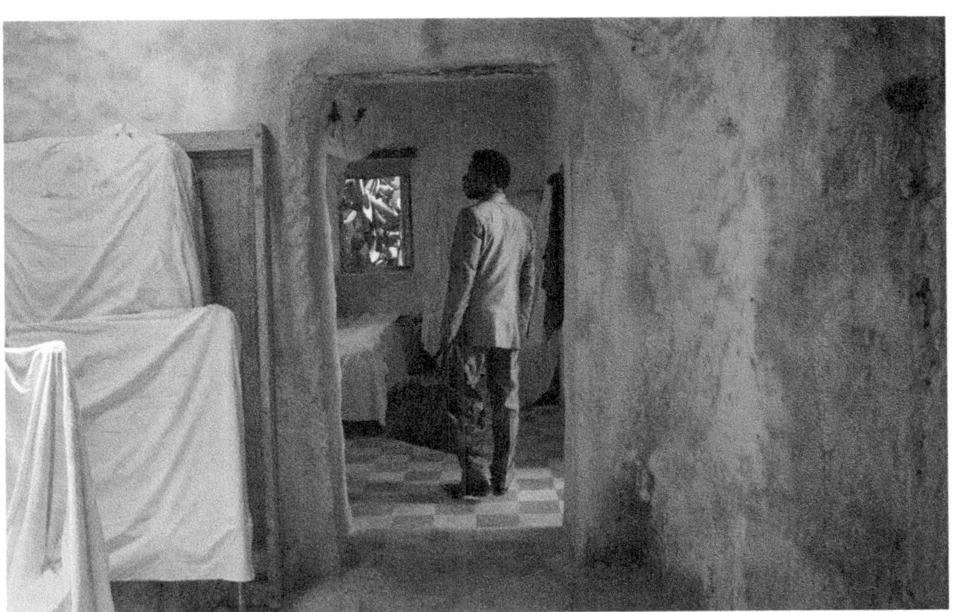

that are self-referential and perhaps even a little didactic. In the white monochrome image that hypnotizes Lone Man, who cannot take his eyes off it, the power of the music's projection and appeal assumes – as far as the spectator is concerned – the crucial role of rendering the passage of time perceivable and, in some way, visible. Lone Man probably does not feel it, but that is of little importance. The spectator may live the experience of 'watching the passage of time' as the music takes him into the apparently static images of the white canvas, the potential starting point for all possible images.

Along with Squrl, Jarmusch is taking the experiment on *music-cum-landscape* even further thanks to his collaboration with Dutch lute-player Jozef van Wissem. As Jarmusch told John Schafer on Radio WNYC:

What's so beautiful about Jozef's music is he uses very minimal structures like palindromes . . . I see it like he is painting the foreground and the details and I'm putting a kind of wash of the background in of clouds and trees . . . I really think of it as Jozef's music and I am like . . . on film sets you have a guy called

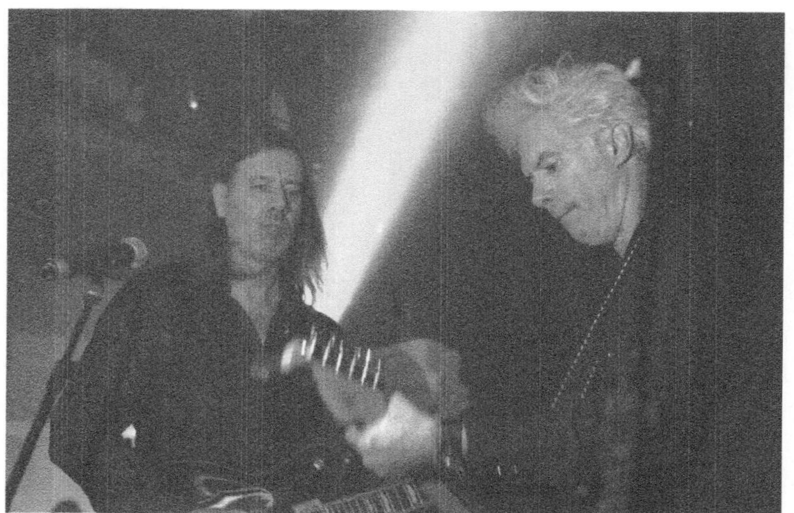

a 'scenic' who paints all the backgrounds, you know, if you need
a wall touched up or to make it look older, and I'm kind of the
scenic guy in this duo. I really like that position a lot because I
love music that has spaces in it that make it cinematic.[44]

For Jarmusch, the connection between cinema and music is thus wholly
natural, one might even say congenital. His approach to the instrument
is completely physical, particularly in creating the backdrops to van
Wissem's melodies. Jarmusch's body position in relation to the ampli-
fiers, the movement of the guitar and the volume knob all become
crucial elements of his playing. The specific chords are thus enriched by
this physical quality that makes each performance distinctive. The collaboration between Jarmusch and van Wissem has proved to be highly
prolific, as testified by their numerous releases: two albums came out in
2012 alone – *Concerning the Entrance into Eternity* and *The Mystery
of Heaven*.[45] The previous year Jarmusch played guitar on a track of van
Wissem's album *The Joy that Never Ends*.[46] And on van Wissem's most
recent work, *It is Time for You to Return*, Jarmusch collaborated again
on guitar, on the track 'Invocation of the Spirit Spell'.[47] As one can
deduce from the rather high-sounding titles, the lute-player's inspiration
comes from Catholic mystics, a fact that is echoed in the hypnotic quality of the pieces that feed on the *trance* tradition of so much sacred

and ritual music. On *Concerning the Entrance*, on the track 'He is Hanging by His Shiny Arms, His Heart an Open Wound with Love', instead of playing, Jarmusch recites brief verses from St John of the Cross (1542–1591) over the final notes of van Wissem's lute.

Regardless of this more or less mystic and Catholic vein, their most important collaboration, not only from a musical point of view, but also a cinematographic one, is without doubt the work on the score for *Only Lovers Left Alive*. To mark their concert at PS1, at New York's MOMA, Jarmusch described how they work together:[48]

None of the score for *Lovers* is really written for specific scenes. Jozef wrote quite a few lute pieces for the film, so there will be solo lute pieces as score. Myself, Carter Logan and Shane Stoneback have a band together called Squrl and we've started adding stuff to what Jozef already gave us. What we'll have is a kind of modular score. Sometimes we'll add to them or even take his lute away to make it a more rock 'n' roll thing. Other times it will be only his lute, or it may be his lute with drums and feedback or just another guitar . . . One of the main characters in the film is a musician, so we'll create his music too . . . He is a virtuoso violinist, but in the present day he's making experimental, avant-rock, drone music. So the two things kind of go together in the film as well.[49]

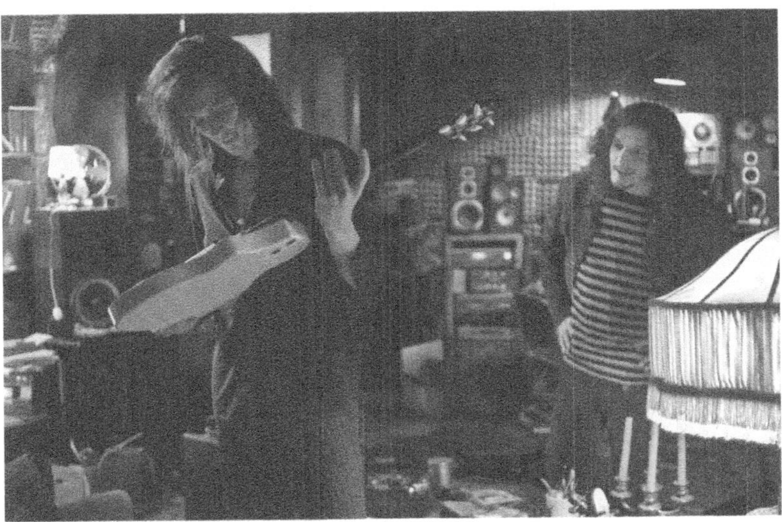

Ode to the vintage guitar, *Only Lovers Left Alive*.

The duplicate nature of the antique 24-stringed lute, and contemporaneous landscapes painted by the electric guitars, thus inspired Jarmusch in the creation of the musician character, who is also split between past and future. His Detroit hideout looks more like a recording studio, in which Jarmusch concentrated an exhibition of vintage/nerdy equipment with unmistakable evocations for a music lover: analogue Telefunken gear, Revox tape machines, Neumann microphones.[50] The entire opening sequence in Detroit could be defined as an 'ode to the vintage guitar': the young 'pusher' Ian brings Adam some new jewels, such as a 1959 Supro that the vampire wants to name William Lawes in homage to the seventeenth-century British composer, whose funeral music Adam is especially fond of. As the guitar 'history tour' continues we are introduced to a 1960 Swedish Hagström, an early 1960s Silvertone and a Gretsch Chet Atkins that almost causes Adam accidentally to reveal his most important secret.

Adam: I once saw Eddie Cochran play one of these . . .
Ian: Wait, you actually saw Eddie Cochran play?
Adam: Yeah, on YouTube.

Later in the film Adam will ask Eve to use her power to date anything she touches on another rare instrument in his collection – an acoustic 1905 Gibson. Jarmusch's selection is certainly that of a collector, stylistically ranging from 'surf guitars' to blues and rock ones, the Chet Atkins being '*the* classic country music guitar' along, of course, with the early Gibson.[51] The idea of an almost mythical past embodied by these instruments adapts well to Jarmusch's own musical passions and obsessions, and it is no accident that he chose the city of Detroit as a setting. After the u.s. premiere at the New York Film Festival in October 2013, Jarmusch explained:

> Detroit is a city I really deeply love . . . As a child it was almost mythological, Detroit, as this Paris of the Midwest and very different to Cleveland, which always felt culturally secondary. And now, what's happened with Detroit is very tragic and sad and unusual, maybe not so unusual, I don't know . . . So I was drawn to it visually and historically, for its musical culture and industrial culture, its kind of post-industrial visual feeling.[52]

The ruins of Detroit's glorious past are immortalized by Jarmusch during Adam and Eve's nocturnal car rides: the Packard Plant, 'where they once built the most beautiful car in the world', and the Michigan Theater, built in the 1920s, once a glorious venue for concerts and theatre, where 'mirrors used to reflect the light of the chandeliers', now turned into a car park. Jarmusch's sparkle of hope in the future of Detroit materializes in a short dialogue exchange between the two pale lovers:

> Eve: But this place will rise again.
> Adam: Will it?
> Eve: Yeah. They have water here. When the cities in the south
> are burning this place will bloom.

Referring to this mythical place from Jarmusch's youth, it is quite natural to think back to the small-town boy from Akron, Ohio, whose career moved on from the 'Paris of the Midwest' to a path on which the link between music and cinema has proved to be fluid and devoid of obstacles. Now as in the past. The first steps with the 'not-quite-teenager-band' the Del-Byzanteens were essential, and for this reason I will close this visual and acoustic journey about 'Jarmusch, the musician' with the

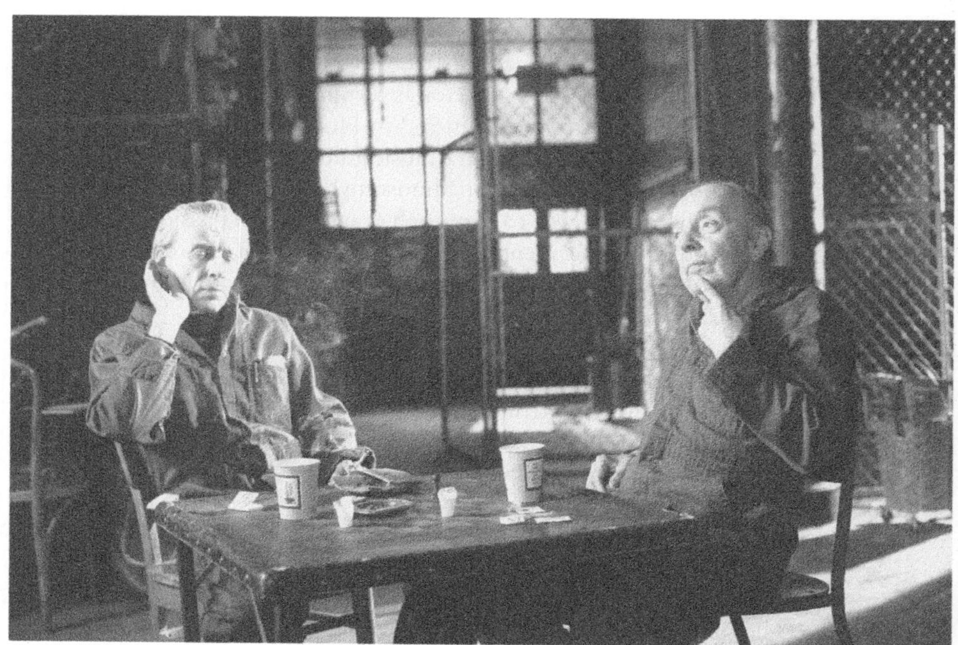

mention of a projected partnership, with one of his band mates of the early days, composer Phil Kline.

What brought these two ex-university companions together again after more than 30 years, professionally speaking, is the shared passion for a celebrated figure whose life bridged the nineteenth and twentieth centuries: the Serbian, naturalized American inventor Nikola Tesla (1856–1943).[53] Jarmusch summed up the greatness of Tesla in one of the eleven episodes that make up *Coffee and Cigarettes* entitled *Jack Shows Meg His Tesla Coil*, starring musicians Meg White and Jack White of The White Stripes. The Tesla Coil is capable of producing high tension – essentially homemade lightning – that emits a penetrating sound like a popping metallic buzz. Nikola Tesla's theory on the nature of the Earth, as Jack explains to Meg, is quite fascinating: Planet Earth is considered a 'conductor of acoustic energy'. A definition of this sort could not escape Jarmusch, who inserted it as the central force of the episode with Jack and Meg, and again in the film's concluding one – *Champagne* – starring two of the Lower East Side's oldest mythical figures: Bill Rice and Taylor Mead.

Downtown legends: Bill Rice and Taylor Mead, *Coffee and Cigarettes*.

It is Meg who puts Tesla's theory into practice, using the spoon as a drumstick on the coffee cup. Hit, the cup produces a clear, penetrating sound. The acoustic energy that the physicist talked about radiates in every direction, as if to say: everything is sound. An exchange of dialogue between Jack and Meg clarifies even better Tesla's importance. After asking Meg whether she remembers the little fluorescent light on the Barbie make-up mirror she used to play with as a child, Jack goes on to list all the technological innovations that would not have been thinkable without Tesla's inventions and experiments: fluorescent light, alternating current, radio, television, X-ray technology, induction motors, particle beams, lasers . . . Jack is convinced that paying more attention to Tesla's ideas would have made the world a better place: a world in which mass communication, transportation and energy would all be free for everyone. 'That's why they discredited him in the end: for free energy.' This economic-political element is a rare example in Jarmusch's filmography; he does not generally take such an explicit position on arguments of this type. And yet he made an exception with respect to Tesla. The tag of 'mad scientist' pinned to the revolutionary inventor has obviously never gone down well with Jarmusch who, via the dialogue of Jack White, expresses other motivations that, in his opinion, led to the powers

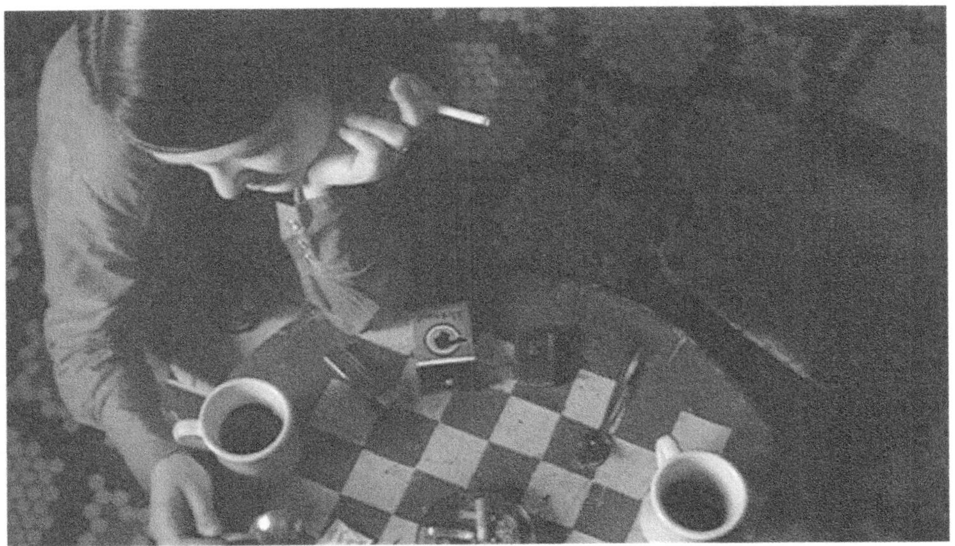

Conductor of acoustic energy. Meg White, *Coffee and Cigarettes*.

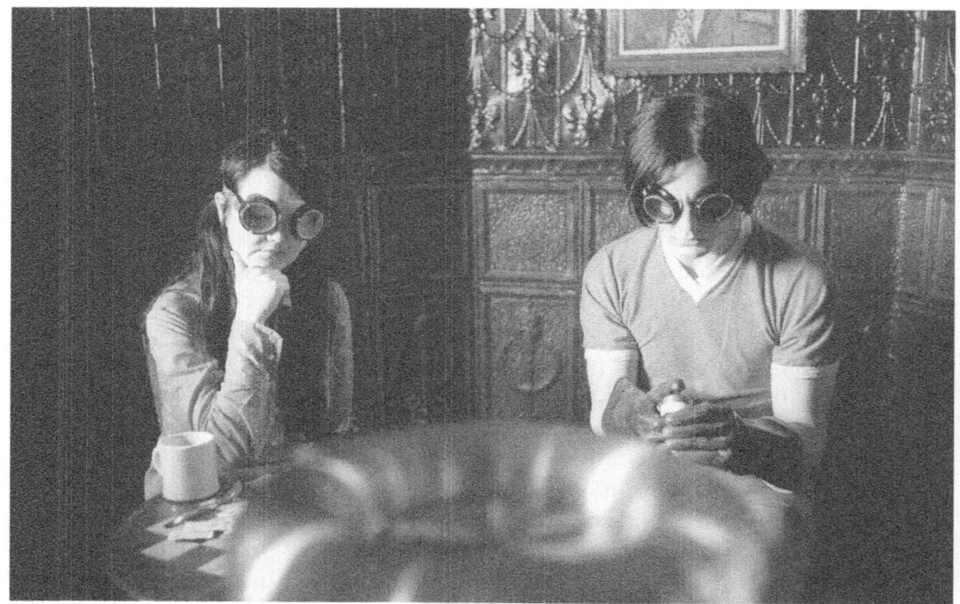

that be labelling the visionary inventor a 'half-forgotten' figure in the history of scientific revolutions.

A decade after *Coffee and Cigarettes*, Jarmusch mentioned Tesla again in a dialogue between Adam and Eve in *Only Lovers Left Alive*. Adam, depressed to the point of getting suicidal, is complaining to his centuries-old wife Eve about the wrongdoings of the 'zombies', as Jarmusch's vampires call us humans.

> Adam: I don't have heroes.
> Eve: What? What about your blessed scientists?
> Adam: The scientists? Look at what they've done to them.
> Pythagoras slaughtered. Galileo imprisoned. Copernicus
> ridiculed. Poor old Newton pushed into secrecy and alchemy.
> Tesla destroyed. And his beautiful possibilities completely
> ignored.

Jarmusch's future project with Phil Kline, announced as *Untitled Tesla Project*, is not planned as a biographical documentary or a film of fiction or an album, but rather an opera.[54] It will take the form of a theatrical show with music and a powerful visual component, orchestrated in collaboration with Robert Wilson.[55] The political component echoed in Adam's 'anti-zombie' dialogue is likely to become part of it. Wilson's striking, minimalist aesthetic will probably also play an important role. But despite the nebulous atmosphere necessarily surrounding any project that has been in the making for some time and not yet reached its final stage, there is one thing that Jarmusch seems to be very sure about and that has a lot to do with his specific musical obsessions. As Jarmusch remarked in 2009 about his personal involvement in the project, his input would be mainly visual while all the music would be by Phil Kline. Only on one – strictly musical – point would he guarantee to insist: the presence of some electric guitars.[56]

Voices: John Lurie

1

I am very interested in the way
you break the supposed borders
between different art forms:
directing, acting, composing,
playing, painting, writing. A painter
can 'fix' one moment in time and
freeze it, so to say – in a duration that whoever watches the picture
determines – whereas a musician, just like a filmmaker, creates a duration,
as he or she is literally working with time. You are presently very active as
a painter. What is the relation between painting and making music – if
there is one for you?

I find, first of all, with acting and with music that that moment, when it
really happens, when it really works, it seems to stop time. Or it slows
time down so much that you perceive reality differently. There is something different with painting and with music, particularly with music.
We would do concerts and I would record it every night. I would listen
to it that same night or the next morning, so I would go over the notes
with the band, what they called the 'dreaded notes' and I would say
things like: 'Ah, that's a B flat there after this section. That's going too
fast, when you come out of this, it's got to be slower. Don't play that
high note there, wait two bars.' You know, I'd do that all the time. So
I'd listen to the tapes and make notes, but I would often think that we
had done a bad concert, because, at the time it happened, I would
remember the mistake: the time something was a little bit too fast, the
time we were just too loud coming out of the soft section, and so on.

So I'd think: 'Damn! That wasn't good tonight.' Then I'd listen to the
tape again and it would be remarkable how much great music was in
there that I had not remembered. And a similar thing happens with
painting. You start to paint, you think you've been painting for twenty
minutes and you're into it, and you look at the clock and it's six or
seven hours later. And when I had the show here at Roebling Hall, one
of my first shows, when the paintings came out of the box, when they'd
all been framed, I thought: 'Oh my god, how did I do this, when did this
happen?' You almost blank out, John disappears and something else is
happening. So when the best music and the best painting for me happens
is when you blank out . . . well, with acting it's a little different. Is that
answering your question?
Absolutely.

2

In my opinion the music you composed – especially the music for films
– allows the listener to travel to many different places and cultures. I
think of Bartók, Africa, gamelan, the Mississippi: a sort of sonic melting
pot in which there is no distinction between so-called 'high' versus 'folk'
or 'popular' culture. I especially like how you deal with repetition, to
me it works in a very visual way, and it gives a true signature to your
music. What do you like – if you like it – about repetition and about the
'cultural melting pot'?

Well, that's hard to answer all in one thing . . . I've always been interested
in repetitive music where it becomes hypnotic, trance music. So certain
kinds of African music, certain Indian music, even when I heard Philip
Glass for the first time back 25, 30 years ago I thought it was great.
Well, it allows the mind to go to a different space rather than going
A – B – C – D . . .

Like another level.

Yeah, another level. And the listener then is affected in a different way,
than if you're playing a concerto or something. But, you know, my
musical influences are so broad, from Tibetan to Balinese to Edgar
Varèse to Charlie Parker to Mingus to Fela to . . . I mean, you just take
the different things out of there that hit you and then it all goes into one
thing. Then of course your musicians also have to be able to do that. So
the musicians really have to understand *music*, rather than just styles of

music. Because that seems to be a real problem with culture and society, that everything has to get compartmentalized. The reason why we had trouble with the business of The Lounge Lizards, for example, is they could never figure out where we should go in the store. There were record companies telling us they knew that we were immensely popular but did not know where to put us: in the jazz department, in the rock section, in the African department, in the classical. So marketing has always been an enormous problem for us.

Wasn't there also this definition 'fake jazz'?
Yeah.

What was that about?
We had played our first concert in 1979, and it was even an accident. Jim Fourrat asked me who was a good band to open for Peter Gordon and I said: 'My band.' But I didn't have a band . . . My brother Evan had just moved to New York and Steve Piccolo, who I had a band with in high school, worked on Wall Street and we just threw this thing together.[1] Arto Lindsay and Anton Fier were in it too. We played and it just happened to be that everybody was there that night. The dressing room door flew open and all these people came in asking 'what do you call this music? It's unbelievable. What is it?' And, not even thinking, I said 'oh it's fake jazz'. I didn't even think. So then some journalist wrote it down.

Well that's crazy – from there it even reached me, decades later.
Yeah, I know, but that's just lazy journalism to me, because it hasn't been what I would call 'fake jazz' since about 1979, so anybody who writes that now is just a lazy idiot.

The common obsession of putting labels on things all the time.
Yeah, they have to have a label. It would be good if they got it right.

Sometimes it is difficult, though, when you're trying to describe something. The effort is in trying to use your imagination and avoid labels.
Yeah, but if something is indescribable it's more likely infinitely more beautiful. Something that can be described – if it's an art – is in trouble, if you can *really* describe it. Especially with music and painting.

About all these influences that you just mentioned, I think you did find
a common line in them.

Do you know a photography book from the 1950s called *The Family
of Man*?² It's a book my parents used to have, with a lot of really nice
photographs, but it would be some poor farmers and then some African
people and then some . . . you know. Music should be the same. I don't
see why limit yourself to just one thing.

What music do you listen to right now?

Well, when I got sick I couldn't listen at all, because it was hurting me,
I couldn't. And I also have a sort of bitterness about what happened
with me and the music business. I'm just starting to listen a little bit,
what did I listen to, I can't tell you . . . I listened to something the other
day . . . I listened to Sly and the Family Stone.

For a long time, for almost two years, I didn't listen to anything, because
I have these neurological problems and to me the sound of music was like
fingernails on a blackboard. It was just going through me, it was painful. But
it's getting better and better. I'm halfway better now. I wouldn't even be
sitting here doing this with you. I was really sick. Not just a little sick.

Oh, well, if you don't want to.

Oh it's okay, I don't mind talking about it. That's one of the reasons I'm
so pissed about the guy you're writing the book about . . . Because he
abandoned me when I got sick.

Okay, so let's go to him then.

Okay.

Right. Just a very short one about Jarmusch.

Yeah, all right.

3

How much freedom does Jarmusch leave to the composer? And how
much to the actor?

As far as being a composer he is wonderful, because he would sometimes take a whole piece out, but he won't mess with it. Whereas with
Hollywood you have to give each instrument on a different track and

they can decide, for example, to take the bass out, and it is usually some dope doing it. It's unbelievable, they can ruin it. They can change the complete nature of what you've done. You write a piece for fourteen strings, bass, banjo, percussion. They take everything out except for the banjo and percussion, you know, just like that.

But they are raping the music.

For real! But they pay you so much money that you try not to think about it. Well, what I was doing for a long time was that I had my own record company, I was completely independent, I would do a Hollywood film score for half a million dollars and then take the money and put it into my own record company and my band.

Strange and Beautiful Records?

Yeah. But it was so much work that I finally just collapsed . . . but Jim was really excellent at allowing you freedom and was very respectful, even though I remember we had an unbelievable fight. On *Stranger Than Paradise*, he wanted a string quartet. It came out because the characters were Hungarian. Me and Eszter [Balint] used to listen to Bartók, we used to have almost like a little class: we would listen to Bartók and follow the scores and we were teaching ourselves how to write a string quartet. So then we decided to do a string quartet for that, but Jim did not want me to see the film, the scenes. It was now a big secret.

So you had to write the music without seeing the film?

Well, I refused. He asked me to just give him some pieces of music and I said that it was insane to ask somebody to write the music and not be able to see what they were writing the music for, because you have to feel the tempo of the scene. I thought it was disrespectful to the music in a way, it's like saying 'oh, any music will do'. There's a real knack, and I think I'm quite good at it, putting music under a scene without getting in the way of the scene and yet not being this new-agey kind of music and finding the right tempo. The motion of the car, of the person walking, the rhythm of something. Finally Torton went up and videotaped the scenes off the Steinbeck while he was editing. Not a secret, it was all allowed to happen, so in the end I did it from those little videos. But he is very good, Jim is very hands-off, he didn't even come to the studio on later projects. It's almost the best thing about him. Really. Because he lets you alone and he left all the music completely intact.

And what about the acting? How much freedom does he leave in that?

See there's a whole thing that becomes very bizarre. You know how *Stranger Than Paradise* came about, he was working on this movie *Garden of Divorce* . . .

Which never happened.

Right, it never happened. Then Wim Wenders had given him fifteen minutes of film and he didn't really know what to do with it. He was agonizing over the *Garden of Divorce* film. I just pushed him really hard that we should just make a little movie with the film that he had. I asked him who he'd want to use. He said he wanted me and Eszter [Balint]. I was in a break from rehearsal with the band, at Squat Theatre, upstairs on the phone – I remember this moment – and I said, why don't you make me a Hungarian, a gambler, I don't want anybody to know, I've been here for some years, and Eszter is my cousin. She comes to stay with me. I can't stand her being here and I eventually warm to her. Jim agreed to it. Then we shoot the movie, there's no script and, you know, I'm fairly aggressive and creative and so I'm coming up with ideas. My feeling is I wrote about 50 per cent of the dialogue. Jim claims there's a script that I've never seen. But then, when it all comes out and is done, Jim is the genius and I'm an interesting character that he's discovered and I'm playing myself, you know? That's how I was portrayed to the press. And that really bothered me greatly. Because then people thought I was the person in that movie: I wasn't acting.

And what about *Down By Law*?

That was different. There was a script.

There was Roberto Benigni.

Well, it was all Benigni. To me it was all Benigni and Robby Müller that made that movie great. Me and Tom [Waits] were there as colouring, but it was all Benigni.

Well . . .

I thought our characters weren't well developed and you couldn't really sink your teeth into anything. It was all Benigni.

But without this triangle it wouldn't have worked.

Well, yeah. He set it off nicely, that is a really good combination of people and you have to give Jim credit for that.

It couldn't have been just a Benigni monologue.

No, it couldn't be. But that's my same problem with *Coffee and Cigarettes*. He's got these fascinating people and it's just because they're so fascinating that the movie is any good at all. And there is a certain talent, a sort of Andy Warhol talent behind getting interesting people together and he's done a lot with that, but honestly I find it very weak. I got a lot of problems with the guy. So I don't know how far to go and also with getting sick, how I was left alone . . . I'll tell you the whole thing: you can put it right in there.

When did you get sick?

Well, I had something wrong for ever. For a long time I was just aching and getting dizzy. I would have brain fog, I couldn't think right, and it would come and go. I could always do what I had to do, but then, I would go on tour and I would collapse afterwards; I would do a film score and I would collapse afterwards, but I thought, well, maybe this is what happens to people when they work really hard, but it just got worse and worse. Finally I closed the office down, and then I started getting really sick. I had all these bizarre neurological problems, and I was having these attacks where electricity would be going through my body, and my heart was exploding and my pulse and my blood pressure were sky-rocketing and then plummeting and they couldn't figure it out. That's when I started getting all these tests and was basically locked in my apartment, seeing nothing but doctors.

So you couldn't play.

Oh, I couldn't play at all. That much exertion would just start the whole thing again. I was really scared.

Of course. So what were you going to tell me?

This is later, in May 2003. *Coffee and Cigarettes* is coming out the same week as I'm having my first opening in New York. The opening is just terrifying, because I haven't been anywhere near a room full of people in two years, so just the social anxiety alone was unbearable.

Renée [French] is in *Coffee and Cigarettes* from 1992 when she was
my girlfriend. It is the episode where she's sitting in the restaurant with
the coffee . . .

And where E. J. Rodriguez who plays the waiter annoys her by pouring
a refill and she says: 'Why did you do that? I just had the right
combination.'

Yeah, that's it. So I remember that morning. She'd never acted before
and acted in Jim's film, you know, so it's a big thing for Renée. Jim's
name is coming up a lot that week, because he's having his premiere and
I'm having my opening and I really wanted this to be something special
for Renée. A lot of people I know were in *Coffee and Cigarettes* and
Renée particularly. Jim basically is out of my life, but because of the
Renée connection and *Coffee and Cigarettes* I start to think about him,
and I'm on my way to the psychiatrist. I had started to see a shrink
because I was so furious with doctors that I needed someone to complain
to. I am in the cab on the way uptown and I am thinking, this time if
I see him I'm not letting him off the hook any more. Because when Jim
stands in front of you, there's something really beautiful, genuine and
real about him, and you kind of love him like he's your little brother.
And I said to myself, next time I see him, I'm going to really have to let
him know what a phony I think he is. Because he really abandoned me
when I got ill and then was rude about it. I would call him and he
wouldn't return my calls. And this is on my mind the whole way up to
the psychiatrist. I get out of the cab at this crazy corner. I have vestibular
problems, so any kind of motion causes me to really get dizzy, but it also
goes right into me. My whole neurological system starts to shake, that
corner is just crazy and I'm leaning into a tobacco stand to keep from
collapsing and I see this guy's elbow.

Okay . . .

And I know it's Jim. With thousands of people around I'm seeing halfway
up a block and I see an elbow, and I know it's Jim. For real. I see he leans
back, I see the white hair and it really is Jim. It was just one of those
bizarre things. So I walk up and I think: 'Ah, I can't deal with him right
now.' I look, and now he's smoking a cigarette further up the block . . .

He has not noticed you.

He hasn't seen me. So I go to walk on the street to avoid him, and then

I look again and he's gone. I think, fine. I get back on the sidewalk, start to walk and then suddenly he's right in front of me. And his walk is so vulnerable and unassuming that my heart just went out to him. Jim had this strange form of facial paralysis, Bell's palsy. It's one of the symptoms of Lyme disease and now I've done so much research on medicine . . .

Because that is what you have?

It's 99 per cent sure, I can't be positive but yes, it seems like it because I'm getting better. I'm taking the antibiotics and after a year I'm 50 per cent better. So either my body would have gotten better on its own or the antibiotics are killing something. Well, so I see Jim and he's had Bell's palsy, which is one of the symptoms of Lyme disease. I had seen 60 doctors before I discovered myself on the Internet the possibility of the Lyme disease and I thought he might have it and nobody's told him. And so I felt that even if he was Hitler I would have to tell him he might have this disease. And I go: 'Hey Jim.' He stops and I tell him the whole thing. It was kind of nice to see him. He says he's going to go to my art opening. I say: 'Good, I want to know what you think, call me after you go.' And – this is such a weird story – then I go into the psychiatrist office, I'm waiting at the elevator, and Jim comes running into the building. I say: 'Where are you going?' He says: 'Ah, I've an appointment on the top floor' – and I know he doesn't want me to know he's seeing a psychiatrist, because I know that that is what all the offices on the top floor are. 'Do you see a shrink?' He says, 'Yeah, this is my regular appointment.'

Believe it or not, for two years we've had the same time, same day of the week, and I've been going to the same office, the exact same place. For two years. And I haven't seen him once. Until this time I'm thinking about him and I see his elbow. So isn't this crazy?

It is absolutely crazy. You weren't seeing the same doctor, were you?

No. But we were in the same office, and it must have been weird for the shrink because I complained about Jim from time to time . . . And he couldn't say anything like he knew. So then, then Jim calls me the next day and he tells me there's a doctor he wants me to see. I am very interested and he says he is going to call me with her number and he is going to see my show . . . and I never hear from him again. But it was good because, you know, I'm writing this book and I'm way past the Jim Jarmusch chapters. I thought, God if I decide that this guy is a nice guy

I'm gonna have to go and change my whole fucking book. It's gonna be too much work to make up with Jim. I have to stay away from him. It's just too much trouble. (Laughs)

The book – is that the autobiography? I heard a radio interview in which you were talking about it, saying, 'This is the slowest thing I've ever done.'

Oh my god, writing . . . And you have to go back and back and fix it. Try to remember, what was I thinking there? It's really a painful fucking thing. But let me just add . . . with Jim it's so weird, because I really feel like a fellow traveller with him. I think he's got heart. And I think he's really smart and I feel connected to him in some way and yet I'm so disappointed and so hurt.

That's a very strong connection though – being so hurt, being so deeply disappointed. You wouldn't be that to someone who . . .

Right, if it were just some sleazeball, I wouldn't care, but every time with him it's just like with some girl you like you make the same mistake all over and over. Even though he's not that seductive, he just seems genuine and his presence seems genuine, and his actions are completely contradictory. I'm sure a lot of people feel the same way about me: John Lurie's music is so beautiful and he's such an asshole. But I think in the end he's just kind of weak and that's what disappoints me. I really found with being sick the reason why the people stayed away is 'cause they were cowards.

Do you think he might be a shy person?

He's way shy. He's really shy.

Maybe that's part of it, don't you think?

Yeah, but I just demand a certain amount of at least honesty. He's got to be able to say: I'm shy. Because he's not a bad guy. I worked in the music business and in Hollywood, I know *bad guys*, I'm not sitting here complaining about any bad guys, I knew going in these were bad people and I watched my ass, but with Jim it's kind of like . . . Damn! I have a deep love for him and at the same time I don't know if we'll ever work it out. I would even go so far as to hire an arbitrator or a psychiatrist to sit there and not let him get away.

Really?

Yeah, like couples counselling, I would do it, absolutely.

You are very passionate about it.

Passionate, I don't know, I am passionate about people being account-
able. But I wouldn't be thinking about it if you weren't here. You didn't
ask me about Ennio Morricone, who's also in your book.

No, I didn't.

You want to?

Sure.

Yeah, let's talk about Ennio Morricone. Well, I think music of the last
half of the last century, the best of it, is film score, because there is no
other place for serious music by orchestra with colour. Nobody ever
hears it, you could be a classical composer and just forget about it. So
the really great composers like him and Bernard Herrmann, even John
Barry, I think they are brilliant. It's like combining popular music and
classical music, but Morricone gets so many colours. This weird
harmonica thing and this great fuzz guitar, especially with the Leone
things, but he did a lot of great, great soundtracks.

I would like to have him listen to the Neil Young score of *Dead Man*,
and ask him what he thinks about it, because of the western, you
know?

Oh, I see. Yeah, you should try that. I heard he's very serious, Benigni
talks about him being very proper.

The thing that I found very interesting is that when you talk to him
about the soundtracks he really wants to be thought of as a composer,
also for his contemporary music.

I've never even heard of it.

He sees himself as an '*artigiano*', a craftsman, when he's composing the
film scores.

I understand that.

The director is the main man and I am here to serve the film: that's his
approach.

Yeah, I understand that.

He has some kind of humbleness about it, and then he wrote these incredible scores. In my opinion the amazing thing about him is the timbre.

Yeah, I don't even know how he did it. He gets some stuff out of there, weird things out of weird instruments or weird things out of normal instruments. And combinations of voices with instruments, really smart, different, so much colour. I auditioned for *Once Upon a Time in America* and I was very close. I went back several times and met with De Niro, and I really wanted it. I hadn't been in a movie yet.

Did you audition as an actor?

Yeah. And when they hired James Woods they thought we were too much the same type, and I also made Robert De Niro look like a midget so . . . I didn't get the part. But I still knew that Morricone was gonna be doing the score and I thought I really want to hear what Morricone does for an American gangster movie. But then I wasn't so impressed. It was more of a romance.

It was very romantic music.

Yeah, it was nice, but I really thought he was going to blow the whole thing out of the water. There are very few people I think of as somebody who could do something better than me, in almost any field, I'm just like that. With Morricone I really thought this guy will nail you, he's gonna blow you away, what he does with a gangster movie . . . He probably wouldn't have even survived Hollywood now, they don't even let you do a good score, there's no way to do a good score.

Well, this thing you told me earlier is just terrifying.

It's not even somebody who knows anything about music. It's somebody whose uncle works at MGM so now they're in the position of deciding. Nine o'clock in the morning, he hasn't had his coffee and he says, 'I don't like violins.' And so some poor guy who doesn't want to lose his job, some music editor, takes all the violins out of your score. Just like that. Or they do this other thing: you hired good musicians, who have rhythm, you got a good bass player and it's grooving and you got it. The movie has to be locked, it has to be edited for you to do the music so it really works. They can't go editing the movie after the music. So then they start to cut a few frames out, and they say, well let's just take a few frames out of the music. I mean, you can't do that.

You just ruined the whole groove. You have to have no sex in your bodies to know that the groove has just been ruined? They just wreck what you do. And so then I finally thought, okay just do it for the money, don't care about it, just write shitty music, get it done, they won't even know. But I couldn't. I could never do it.

Well, I can see . . .

But the movie is gonna suck, nobody's gonna see it. And anyone who does see it is an idiot anyway, so I thought, okay, write some shitty music just take the money and put it towards your own music, there's no harm in that, but something in me would never . . .

Did you think it would be a violence to yourself?

No, I thought I could do it. It was only because I'm so compulsive that I couldn't. I thought there was no blame in this, but I just couldn't. You know, when you do the music for a bad movie and you have to watch the scene over and over again, it's just like torture. Oh, oh no please. I can't see them again!
    Sorry, I gotta lie down now.

Sure.

This was too much energy for me.

New York, March 2005

3 John Lurie, Gamelan and Minimal Music

'What you realize when you've done it for a while is that all music works with any image, but all music changes every image.'
John Lurie, quoted by Marc Ribot[1]

'One of the great lessons I learned from being in the band with John is that he was never afraid to say something like: "This should be really precious, or this should be really naive or really vulnerable", 'cause those are words you don't hear musicians use too much, especially when playing kind of muscular instrumental music. So the idea was basically to do whatever we wanted to do, which is a philosophy I still follow. And that makes its own style, it becomes its own style.'
Erik Sanko[2]

All four of Jarmusch's films made in the 1980s bear the enduring mark, visual or acoustic, of John Lurie, who wrote the music and also acted in the first three of them: *Permanent Vacation* (1980), *Stranger Than Paradise* (1984), *Down By Law* (1986) and *Mystery Train* (1989). The sounds and images of these four films defined the 'Jarmusch style' in an incisive way and the contribution from The Lounge Lizards' saxophonist leader was crucial to asserting it. What does this particular style consist of? How can it be defined or described? As John Lurie said in the interview opening this chapter: 'If something is indescribable it's infinitely more beautiful. Something that can be described – if it's an art – is in trouble.' Jarmusch's four films of the 1980s with particular regard to the rapport with John Lurie's music are rendered homogeneous by the *rhythm*, both visual and acoustic; a *rhythm* that escapes the logic of

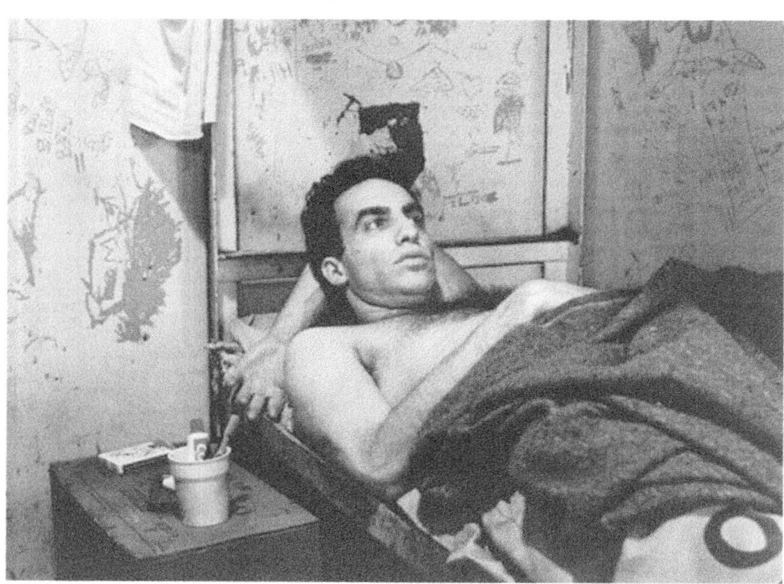

an extenuating search for a Hollywood-style climax, and that, on the contrary, slides by us, our eyes and especially our ears with a hypnotic pace, certainly not hurried, though certainly not static either. We know that both cinema and music are arts that unfold in time, their duration determined by the writer, director or composer, with maximum precision. The basic material with which he works is mostly made up of 'time', as clearly exemplified in the very fitting definition by the great Russian director and poet Andrei Tarkovsky, who considered the film director 'a sculptor of time': someone who removes the superfluous from an imaginary block of time, leaving only the essential to define the film's *rhythm*.

At this point, it is useful briefly to define certain notions from musical terminology to avoid creating confusion between *tempo*, *metre* and *rhythm*. The musical *tempo* is determined by the velocity of the isochron impulse – such as the beat of the metronome – and it is only in rapport with it that the rhythm, the metre's internal division, may be defined, for example, as tight, loose, regular, irregular, ostinato or syncopated. Often mistakenly called tempo, another term that needs defining properly is *metre*. The metre is nothing more than a cluster of impulses determined by a strong accentuation – for example, in the case of duple metre every two impulses, like marching music, and in the case of triple metre every three impulses, like the waltz – which better explains the definition of rhythm as internal articulation to the metre. The *rhythm* in music is always evaluated with respect to the tempo, never isolated. It is not strictly correct to speak of a slow or fast rhythm per se, as is often the case in everyday conversation, because the 'slowness' or 'rapidity' of the rhythm in question depends exclusively on the unit of the chosen temporal measure: a tempo of 120, 60 and so on, always considering the impulses of the metronome, or the tempo traditionally codified as *moderato*, *allegro*, *andante* and so on.

Having made these considerations, one may better evaluate the precision and the beauty of the declarations made by Tarkovsky with regard to time and rhythm:

> The dominant, all-powerful factor of the film image is *rhythm*, expressing the course of time within the frame . . . One cannot conceive of a cinematic work with no sense of time passing through the shot, but one can easily imagine a film with no actors, music, décor or even editing.
>
> . . . Although the assembly of the shots is responsible for the structure of a film, it does not, as is generally assumed, create its rhythm. The distinctive time running through the shots makes the rhythm of the picture; and rhythm is determined not by the length of the edited pieces, but by the pressure of time that runs through them.[3]

The pressure of time . . . And what better element is there to articulate this 'pressure' than music? In this specific case, John Lurie's music. A characteristic of Lurie's sound is, without a doubt, to proceed with an expanded, rarefied and repetitive rhythm that is strongly linked to the traditions of American minimal music,[4] or rather the type of music developed in the United States, starting from the 1960s, based upon the principle of micro-varied repetition or:

> Static variations (intended here as gradual and almost imperceptible differentiations of elements around a stationary nucleus), that aims to reconnect to the Oriental concept of music as a hypnotic factor of contemplation.[5]

Alberto Basso's definition is spot on, because in quoting the oriental concept of music, one connects to that 'ethnic' element that can in no way be separated from the immense wealth of inspiration from which Lurie draws his artistry. His passion for the most disparate types of music is too vast to be confined to American minimalist traditions. Africa, Pigmy, Asia, Indonesia, gamelan, blues, Bartók and Albert Ayler are just some of the reference points that come to mind when thinking of Lurie's scores.

Urban Gamelan

Until the more recent *The Limits of Control*, in which Jarmusch gets a credit as 'additional musician', and *Only Lovers Left Alive*, in which his band Sqürl is credited, his first feature-length film, *Permanent Vacation*, is the only one in which his name appears, alongside John Lurie's, as composer of the music.

There are three principal ingredients in the film's musical mix: a piece of American music and film history like *Over the Rainbow*, free jazz improvisation and Indonesian gamelans. *Over the Rainbow* is an important and in no way casual reference in *Permanent Vacation*, which is shown by the recurrence and frequency of real and proper musical quotations: like John Lurie's nervous saxophone improvisations on the theme, to be found in both the final long shot on the steamer and towards the middle of the film, when the street musician, John Lurie himself, encounters Allie, his one and only metropolitan spectator. But the references to the song are not only musical: very explicit ones exist also in the film's dialogue.

Consider the clever joke on the Doppler effect, surely inspired by the figure of Charlie Parker. The funny story is told to Allie by a strange, amusing and seemingly stoned African American (Frankie Faison) at the entrance to the cinema where, as chance would have it, Nicholas Ray's *The Savage Innocents* (1960) is being shown. Until this moment the atmosphere of the film has become steadily heavier and heavier. The scene follows the sequences of Allie's visit to his mother, who is shut up in a psychiatric institute, and the outdoors encounter with a Hispanic girl (Maria Duval), in the grips of a sudden 'sung crisis' in which she bungles the lyrics of 'Cielito Lindo'. The girl is crouched on an iron staircase in a desolate environment, as if to show that mental illness can bypass even the locks of an institute, and that bars can be created outdoors or quite simply in one's own mind. The joke is extremely cynical, if not macabre. Allie's face shows not the slightest emotion when it finally comes to the punchline of what can be defined as a 'sound joke'. The comic nucleus of the story is based on the – difficult to describe in words, but easily singable – Doppler effect: that physical propriety of sound for which, moving its source in space, the same sound undergoes a variation of pitch.[6] The ambulance siren, mentioned in the joke's punchline, at last reminds its dying protagonist – the depressed saxophone player who just jumped off a building – of the melody of 'Over the Rainbow', which he was trying in vain to remember.

The movement of the sound source produces a transformation of our acoustic perception. If one thinks of Allie's state of constant wandering, thanks to this brief and effective story, Jarmusch succeeds in transmitting two types of movement: the physical one in the shape of sound 'in motion' and the psychological one contained in the sense of the funny story, or the dream, the desire to find that ideal somewhere else. In this case it is Paris, where the musician had hoped to be if not understood, at least listened to. Is this simply a reference to Charlie Parker, the 1950s saxophonist who was ahead of his time? Or does it also refer to the protagonist Aloysius Christopher Parker who, when introducing himself at the beginning of the film, says: 'If I ever have a son he'll be Charles Christopher Parker, just like Charlie Parker'? While we hear

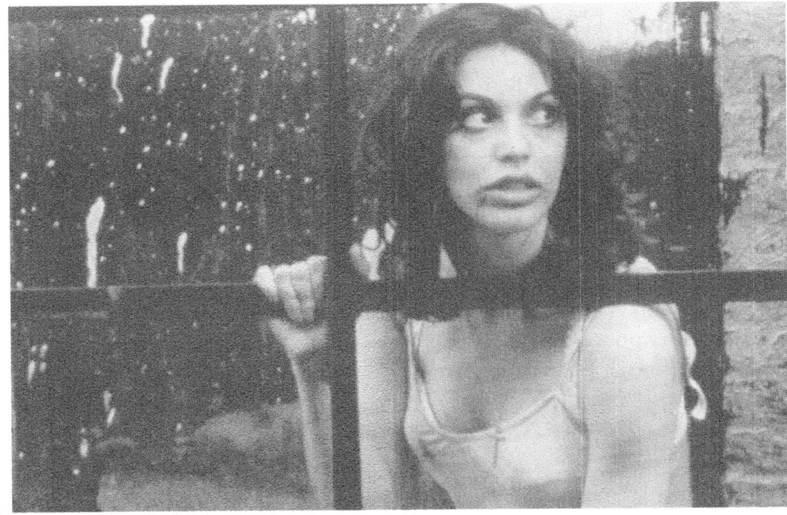

'Cielito Lindo',
Maria Duval,
Permanent Vacation.

Allie's voice, 'postcards' run across the screen, freeze-frames of typical Jarmusch environments, never the face of Allie, who, as we will discover at the end, is already in Paris, and who adds:

> So here I am now, in a place where I don't even understand the language, but, you know, strangers are still always just strangers. And the story? This part of the story, well, it's how I got from there to here, or maybe I should say from here to here.

Movement is thus 'immobile' and accompanied by the perception of always finding oneself in the same place, in spite of the moving, be it mental or physical.

John Lurie's improvisations on the alto sax are mostly variations on the *Over the Rainbow* theme. The tradition of the American musical, on one side, and the dream of a better, unreachable somewhere, on the other, are both celebrated. Thinking about it, they might be one and the same thing, filtered and brought up to date by the free jazz experimentation. When Allie meets the street saxophonist one night, Lurie asks him what he wants to hear. The answer is immediate and clear: 'I don't care, as long as it's vibrating.' Through music, Allie – 'the kid with the replaceable head'[7] – searches for a somewhere far from the Lower East Side's post atomic scene of 1979, the year the film was shot.

Lurie's visionary sax often superimposes the third musical ingredient I mentioned, Indonesian gamelan. As Jarmusch declared in an interview in 1980, he used original gamelan recordings and then slowed them down.[8] Specifically, he chose Javanese gamelan, which is traditionally slower than Balinese gamelan, electronically adding a little reverb and eliminating some frequencies. One of the principal points of gamelan music is that the various instruments that make up the ensemble – xylophones, gongs, bells, metal sheets, bamboo – play the same melody with rhythmic variations, and this explains the hypnotic and circular modulation. The rhythmic structure varies within an entirely homogeneous melodic framework. Such an approach adapts perfectly to the atmosphere of a film like *Permanent Vacation*. The passage of time, the duration of the piece seems to become palpable, while 'the things that happen', the actions, which in musical terms could be likened to the melody, are far more volatile and less significant.

Gamelan's musical system confronts us not so much with 'songs' as it does with a 'state'.[9] Just like Jim Jarmusch's film. The constellation

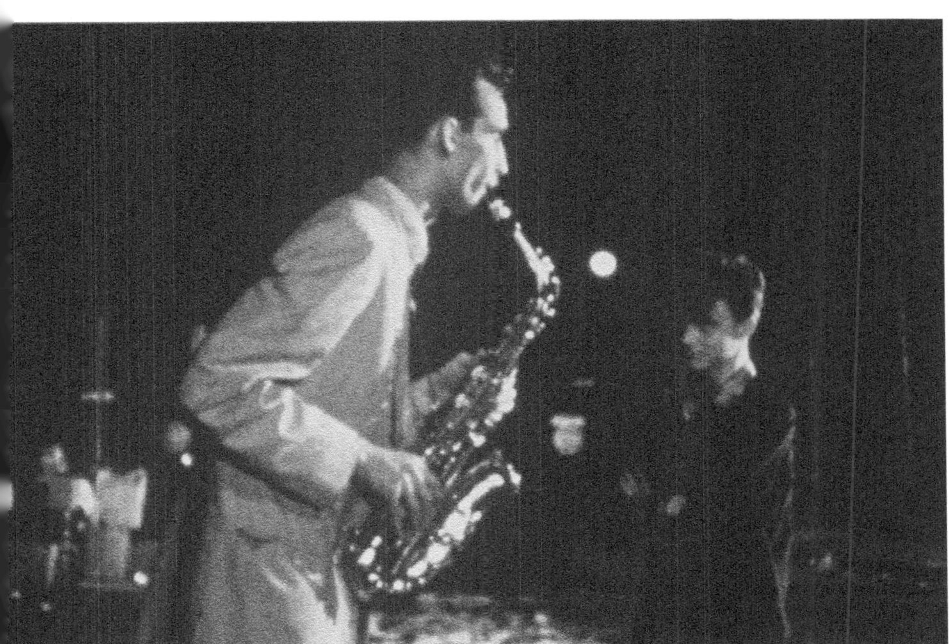

of events that makes up Allie's vagabonding has an almost casual nature about it. His decisions are made without a pre-established plan, without a motive dictated by ambition or precise desires. Thanks to the gamelan music, the New York scene is likened to those moonlit fields where Javanese orchestras play for days and nights, to an audience that nods off to sleep and then wakes up again, participants in an event that adapts to the organic and unexpected rhythms of life. Not that the young music lover Jarmusch had any fanciful ethnomusicological ambitions, let that be clear. What interests him is the circular and unsolved atmosphere offered by gamelan. To make it sound more urban, more New Yorkese, he often superimposes Lurie's equally hypnotic but at times restless saxophone over it. The mixture of these two seemingly distant worlds produces an effect of alienation and at the same time familiarity on those who listen. If on one hand we wonder what Indonesian gamelan might have to do with the Lower East Side, on the other the saxophone takes us on an urban ride.

Paradise Quartet

East and West, minimalism and ethnic music: limitless sound suggestions from which Jarmusch draws without reserve, keeping his own originality integral. However, with *Stranger Than Paradise* the sound journey took him not to Asia but to Eastern Europe and back to the United States. The two musical mainstays on which the film relies are in fact original compositions by John Lurie for string quartet, inspired by the Hungarian composer Béla Bartók (1881–1945), and Screamin' Jay Hawkins's classic 'I Put a Spell on You'.[10] As in *Permanent Vacation*, Jarmusch and Lurie renounced any temptation to use musical elements identifiable with the No and New Wave scene to which both belonged and that rocked New York during the film's long period of gestation: as mentioned, it took almost three years to go from the 30-minute first 'draft' – *The New World* – to the completed feature-length version.

References to Bartók come up during the film, and beyond it as well. Two of the leading characters of *Stranger Than Paradise* – Willie/Bela (John Lurie) and Eva (Eszter Balint) – are of Hungarian origin. Balint actually is Hungarian, having come to New York from Budapest as an eleven-year-old. The Squat Theatre, founded by her father, the playwright and actor Stephen Balint, was her teenage island, inhabited by countless artists and musicians. It was on this island that she was noticed by both Jarmusch and Lurie, devoted regulars and animators of the Squat's musical programme. The Hungarian origins of the film's two cousins, Eva and Willie/Bela, are confirmed by the musical tone of the Paradise Quartet's performance.[11] Lurie told me how together with violinist Balint he would listen eagerly to the Bartók quartets and then compose music for string instruments together with her.

Though the credits on the original record mention Evan Lurie, John's brother, as the arranger, guitarist Marc Ribot, who at the time still wandered the Lounge Lizards universe, maintains that in the final stages of the record's arrangement a major contribution was made by the quartet's Jill B. Jaffe, noted for also being a member of the Philip Glass Ensemble and for having been involved in the soundtrack of *Koyaanisqatsi* (1982) by Godfrey Reggio. According to what Ribot told me, it was she who, in the shortest time imaginable, seeing that the recording studio and the musicians were not available for long, arranged the beautiful and hypnotic melodies composed by Lurie.

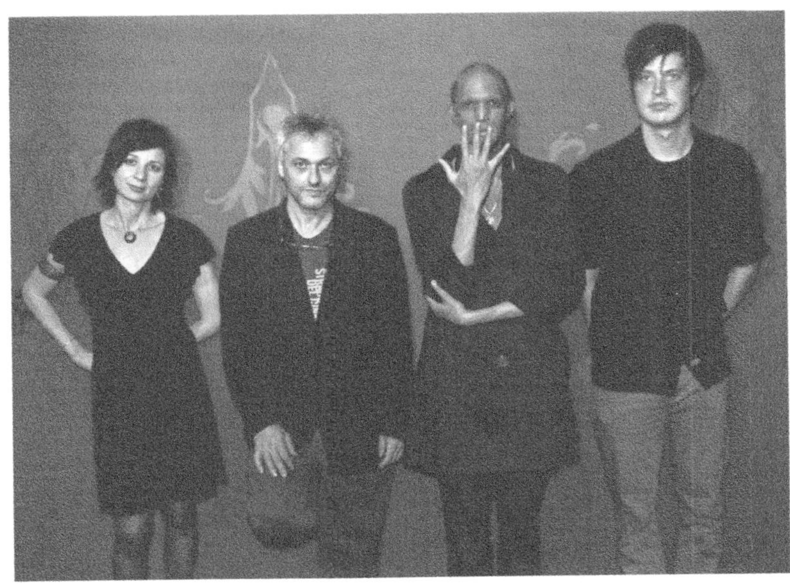

Apart from influences and collaborations, the fact remains that the spirit of Bartók is strongly felt in the film, determining much of the atmosphere, and that John Lurie was the main catalyst of that presence. Bartók had studied ethnic music in depth, and his interest in popular Hungarian and Balkan music and songs was responsible for his collaboration with composer and ethnomusicologist Zoltán Kodály, in the collection and study of the documents of this very rich folkloric tradition.[12] In *Stranger Than Paradise*, as in *Permanent Vacation*, principles linked to ethnic music and to forms of contemporary minimalism are interwoven. In some ways, thanks to his interest in ethnic music, John Lurie has moved closer to the Bartók sound in its repeated and cyclical reprises for strings, especially in relation to biting timbres, to percussive modulations and to an atmosphere that is partially folkloric, despite being taken from contemporary experience.

Another leading exponent of the downtown scene, David Byrne of Talking Heads, for whom Jarmusch in 1985 filmed the video for 'The Lady Don't Mind', made the link between ethnic and contemporary music even clearer. Talking of his experience with Bernardo Bertolucci for *The Last Emperor* (1987),[13] he said:

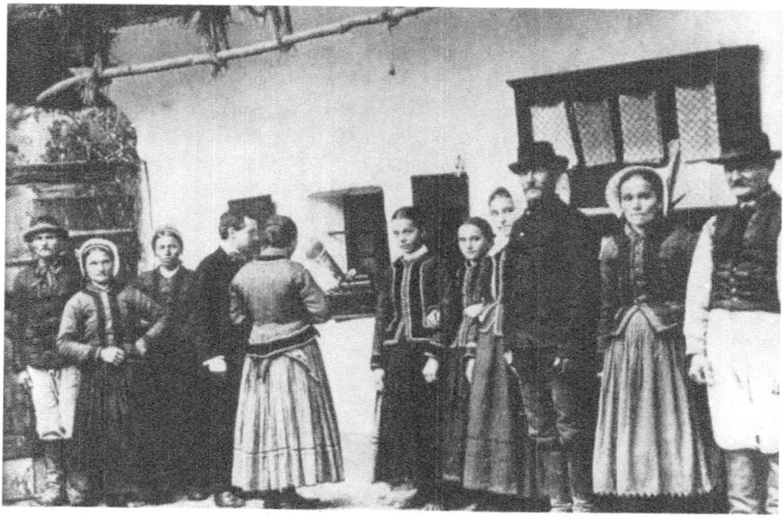

Béla Bartók recording folk music in Hungary (1908).

I listened to a lot of Chinese music that they brought back, that was different from what was commercially available here, and it seemed to run this complete spectrum from Western rock to real percussive things to music that sounded like *Bartók meets John Cage*.[14]

In *Stranger Than Paradise* something immediately strikes one as odd: Jarmusch is extremely parsimonious with Lurie's compositions. The moments during which the strings of the Paradise Quartet are heard can be summed up in three categories: the first, when the characters are alone with themselves, like, for example, in the last of the three episodes – *Paradise* – filmed in Florida, when a slow panoramic shot reveals Eva sitting alone at a concrete table by the beach, having been abandoned for the umpteenth time by the two male characters; the second, during the lengths of black leader separating one scene from the next, when the absence of the picture allows the music to assume even greater powers of suggestion, as well as the function of instrumental link between the shots; the third, in certain travel sequences in which Jarmusch decided to use more rhythmic and percussive musical passages, as if almost wanting to simulate a sense of movement. In particular, the fastest staccato is used in the scene of the three characters' much-anticipated arrival in Florida, perhaps to highlight a climax, a goal only theoretically reached: as witnessed by both Eva and Willie in different moments of the film, every place ends up looking alike and a real 'goal' appears not to exist at all. One just has to think of *Down By Law*, for example, in which the New Orleans prison cell is more or less identical to the shack where the three fugitives Jack, Zack and Bob manage to spend the night. This recurring theme in Jarmusch's films is reaffirmed by the principle of repetition that is established by the music. Far from furnishing a mere comment to the images, the music structures, enriches and gives a supplementary sense to what we see before us. However, it is surprising how 'little' music – in terms of length – there is in *Stranger Than Paradise*, especially with regard to how much it contributes to determining the film's overall atmosphere.

To confirm how 'less' can still be substantial with respect to 'too much' that generally ends up cancelling itself, I would like once again to invoke David Byrne:

> After I'd done music for a little bit of film here and there, I started to notice, say in Spielberg films, that some of those were wall-to-wall music. In *Indiana Jones*, for example, music started at the opening credit and didn't stop till the last credit, maybe one little bit of silence for a reel change or whatever but that was about it.

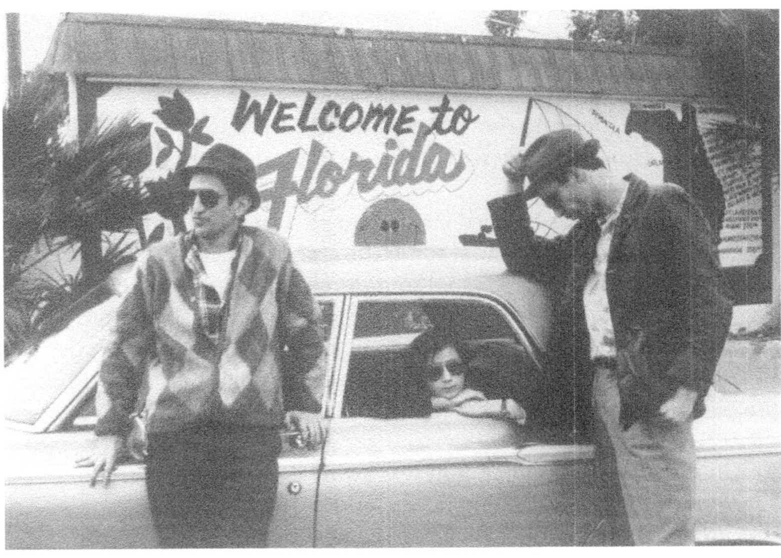

'Paradise', *Stranger Than Paradise*.

And it was almost all cued for hits in the action, punches and explosions.[15]

Jarmusch's approach on the contrary is gradual and 'parsimonious': the moments with music are apparently casual, but it is because they are so rarefied that they have such an impact, even though there is no precise sync with the images. Jarmusch does not create climaxes in the traditional sense, and events must not be underlined; they simply happen, as in the real world. The music behaves in the same way. With its measured presence it transforms an apparently banal moment – in which, action-wise, perhaps little or nothing happens – into a unique moment, rich in atmosphere and, in its own way, made to appear magnetic, as in the memorable sequence in which the three characters contemplate Lake Erie, frozen, practically invisible and as snow-white as the windswept sky.

In the same way as in *Permanent Vacation* and Indonesian gamelan, here the string quartet seems vaguely out of place with respect to the film's locations, but it is this character of the music's 'uniqueness within the ordinary', united with its sporadic use, that justifies the apparent inconsistency. Amos Poe got it right when he said: 'The worst sin you can commit in movies and music is have the music describe exactly what is happening on-screen.'[16]

Liquid South

After Asia, Europe and the United States, Lurie's sound exploration is enriched in *Down By Law* with a new territory that is both geographical and musical.

Apart from the southern United States, where the film takes place, it is South America that burst upon the scene this time. The musicians who played on the film's original soundtrack composed by Lurie include percussionist and berimbau virtuoso Naná Vasconcelos, from Recife, and eclectic guitarist Arto Lindsay, born in the United States but raised in Brazil before coming to New York as a teenager and powerfully joining the No Wave scene. Lindsay remarked:

In the Sixties, Brazilian pop was aware of many other styles. Brazil was to the side, not in the middle, of everything. People loved all kinds of music – from the Beatles and the Rolling Stones

THE LOUNGE LIZARDS

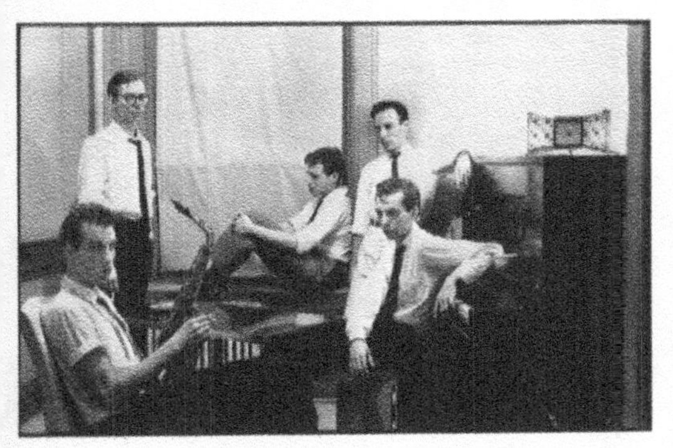

Album cover,
*The Lounge
Lizards* (1981).

to Brazilian folk, to avant-garde music like John Cage, to serialism, to 20th century classical music.[17]

Lindsay's Brazilian education and consequent musical sensibility are on the same wavelength as the geographically open and by no means hierarchical approach that is fundamental for a composer like Lurie. It is no accident that the start of their collaboration coincided with the dawning of The Lounge Lizards at the beginning of the 1980s. Lindsay was the group's first guitarist who, following the New York pattern, would leave the band shortly after the release of their first record entitled *The Lounge Lizards*.[18]

Vasconcelos enriches Lurie's compositions thanks to the strongly 'ethnic' timbre of his percussions, played together with long-time member of the Lizards, Puerto Rican E. J. Rodriguez, one of the musician/actors in *Coffee and Cigarettes*.[19] It is the fifth track on the *Down By Law* album – 'Please Come To My House' – that reveals in a particularly evident way the mix between the scratchy style of Lindsay's neurotic guitar and the warmth of enveloping wood, the roundness of Vasconcelos's percussion instruments. In actual fact, the two confirm that No Wave and 'ethnic' or 'black' musical traditions cannot be separated easily.

This is highlighted in the prison escape sequence: the three fugitives, as if by magic, find themselves running through an underground drain, until finally re-emerging in daylight. The prison's penetrating alarm manages almost to drown out Lindsay's guitar splashes, but if you really listen you can just about hear them. Continuing their escape, Bob, Jack and Zack are forced to cross the bayous of Louisiana that are as desolate as they are spellbinding. The magnetic wide shot on the water, in which the ratty old rowboat is followed from a distance, is marked by the 'piercing' sound of Lurie's distraught harmonica.[20] A single note, as annoying as the buzz of a mosquito, echoes until finally disappearing across the

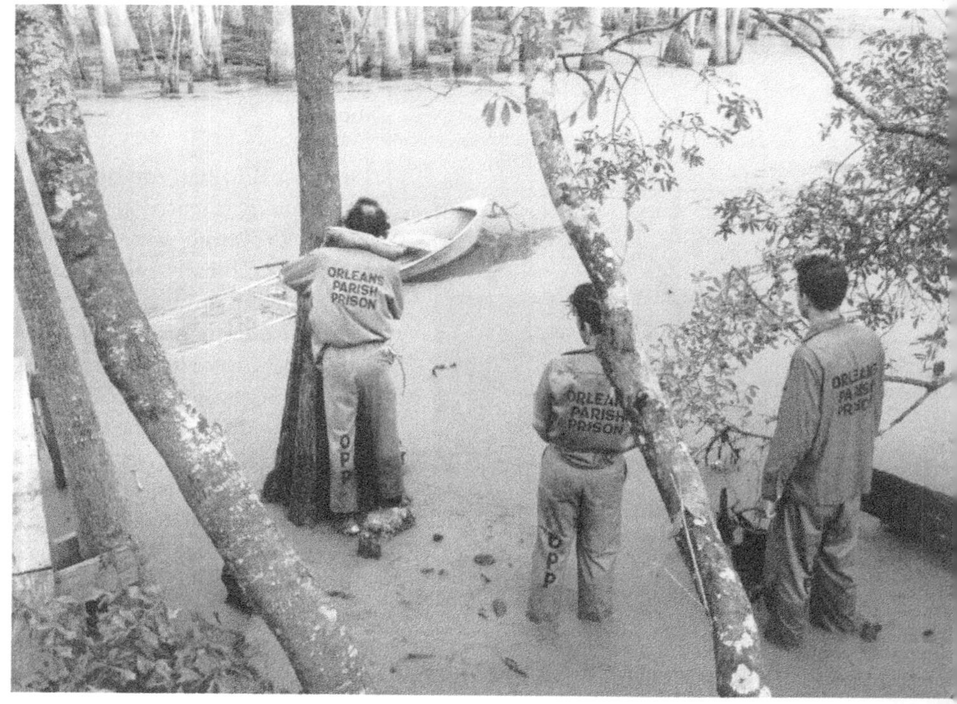

monotonous, glassy surface of the water. It is obvious right from the first moment that the leaking rowboat will come a cropper.

After surviving its sinking, the escape, that gets slower and slower due to the lack of a real pursuer, switches to a muddy terrain through the trees of the swamp. This time we hear Vasconcelos's percussions duetting with Lurie's saxophone to create liquid and solitary sound environments, organic but not mimetic with respect to the images. The dilated and fluid rhythms of the wooden instruments take the three fugitives by the hand and accompany them on their aimless drifting. The saxophone's melodic lines move as slowly as the three soaked demoralized heroes, dragging their wet feet behind them.

Bob will save the situation, as he already did in a totally unexplained and inexplicable way when breaking out of prison. Just as in a fairy tale, in the midst of nowhere, a small house/tavern run by a young Italian woman (Nicoletta Braschi[21]) appears out of the blue. No one knows it yet, but Bob has reached his final destination. Jack and Zack,

Bob, Zack and Jack in the bayous, *Down By Law*.

brave talkers, but cowards deep down, had sent him on ahead alone towards the mysterious house in the woods. Bob, who in the meantime has fallen in love at first sight with his fellow Italian, has forgotten about the other two fugitives, who are out in the cold waiting for news. 'She has asked me to stay here forever and ever like in a book for children,' Bob announces to his two stunned companions, who have finally made it into the house and are digging into the pasta like two starving boys. The following morning Jack and Zack go their separate, but interchangeable ways. Neither knows where it will take them. They are so interchangeable that, before taking off, the two exchange coats and thus part of their individual identities.

With the two walking away in opposite directions, Jarmusch once again gives us the liquid sound of Lurie's saxophone that works its way into Vasconcelos's enveloping percussions. It is the same theme already heard during the aimless trek through the swamps, as if to say that their traipse will continue and that their goal remains distant or illusive. Or perhaps it does not exist at all.

Ambulatory Music

Blues, soul and minimalism: one could thus summarize the musical palette of the film following *Down By Law* that Jarmusch again decided to shoot in the South. This time the destination was a city with a totally 'musical' reputation – Memphis, Tennessee, the home of *Memphis soul*, of legendary studios like the Stax and the Sun Studios, and naturally one of the most famous mansions in the history of rock 'n' roll, Graceland.

Lurie's original compositions are particularly helpful in exemplifying another characteristic use that Jarmusch makes of music, a veritable musical feature, or rather what I would like to call here *ambulatory music*.

In 'Far From Yokohama', the first of the three episodes of *Mystery Train*, this sound 'trademark', in which music and motion are inseparable, is clearly established. The episode's lead players are two teenage Japanese rockabillies, Jun and Mitsuko, on a pilgrimage to Memphis. The stages of this initial sequence, which lasts about twelve and a half minutes, are: the end of the rockabillies' train ride and their arrival in Memphis station, where the brief encounter with one of the undisputed fathers of Memphis soul, Rufus Thomas, takes place; the couple's visit to the legendary Sun Studios; their various daytime and nocturnal ambulatory sequences in search of Mitsuko's idol, Elvis Presley; and finally the arrival at the hotel, where the other two episodes of the film will come together. The *ambulatory music* is distinctly audible in four moments, the start of the characters' walkabout corresponding to the first musical note, the end of the walk corresponding to the last.[22] The first two walks, immortalized by the fluid and unfailing lateral tracking shot, a real Jarmusch touch,[23] are accompanied by the more bluesy of the two John Lurie *ambulatory music* themes used: 'Mystery Train' (parts B, 'Banjo Blues', and C, 'Chaucer Street'). Jarmusch's musical choices demonstrate his coherent drive to underline the 'mobility' of the music, as articulation in space-time, in relation to the characters' physical movements. When I talk of movement, I am not referring to anything sudden or unexpected, but something rather more distended that allows one to feel the passage of time, by virtue of its slowness. Or perhaps, rather than slowness it is more appropriate to talk of strategies of dilation, much used in road movies, a genre to which without a doubt *Mystery Train* leans towards. In order to reaffirm this principle of dilation, Jarmusch uses Lurie's two variations on the mentioned blues theme better to highlight his position. The blues is characterized by a codified and structured rhythmic and melodic progression, in which the listener's expectations are rarely disappointed. Usually three musical phrases of four bars are structured around three main chords, the metre being a solid 4/4. What the blues manages to create, also thanks to this definite structure, is a veritable sound route, a road, one with precise stages made of chord progressions that are repeated right up to the conclusive release. Speaking of roads, routes and stages, it becomes clear how Lurie's blues creates an essentially 'mobile' sound structure, *ambulatory* to be exact, in which the movement is often circular, reaffirming the principals of dilation and repetition so dear to Jarmusch. Furthermore, historically the blues was born as an itinerant musical genre, starting from the last decades of the nineteenth century, which is deeply reflected in its same rhythmic substance. The blues singers, the songsters, often moved around because of diverse environmental and economic circumstances, and their history is difficult to separate from the bigger picture of the African Americans' socio-economic situation. It is not only a type of music that induces or provokes the movement, but more a veritable 'music *in* motion'.

The second *ambulatory music* theme, 'Tuesday Night in Memphis', is based on a more repetitive, minimalist criterion and has a frequentative structure, based on repetition, on which various tonal swings are inserted. These swings help Jarmusch to accentuate the dynamic sense of the music even more, once again confirmed by the characters' wandering. In perfect sync with each tonal change ulterior visual 'swings' happen on the screen: Jun and Mitsuko take turns to carry their cumbersome red suitcase, the minute girl now leading the way; the two teenagers enter the frame from the opposite side to the previous tracking shot, thus changing the direction of their walk and disorienting the spectator; one of the rare words of dialogue of the 'ambulatory moments' is uttered: 'Cadillac!' Each one of these 'events' is underlined with precision by a slight tonal shift in the music.

Lurie's *ambulatory music* and the characters' pilgrimage, both physical and psychological, confirm, consent and detail the spatial and temporal dilation process especially essential in *Mystery Train*, but also in Jarmusch's films of the 1980s mentioned thus far.

And because I have talked about walking and routes, I would like to conclude with an observation on the respective artistic routes taken by Jarmusch and Lurie.

One may agree on the fact that, in a few words, Jarmusch's route took him from music and literature to film, naturally not forgetting that these three forms of expression all remain solidly at the centre of his artistic universe. Film – images and sounds in motion – has, however, clearly gained the upper hand.

Lurie, on the other hand, after an explosive but not particularly long career in music and cinema, turned his talent to painting.[24] From a purely 'temporal' form like music, his current research focuses on painting, freezing the image in time. If Jarmusch's research is mostly dedicated to *rhythm*, as defined by Tarkovsky, namely the 'pressure of time that runs inside the shot', Lurie on the contrary no longer seeks to react against the said 'pressure', but chooses rather to throw the baton directly at the spectator, who receives an impression of the work within a few seconds and then determines for exactly how long he will stand in front of a painting. The 'time of life' prevails over 'cinematographic or musical time' strictly dictated by the director or the composer and the images – along with the words and phrases of inimitable cynical and at times tragicomic irony that constellate Lurie's paintings – immediately produce infinite associations in the mind of the viewer that endure for an unspecified amount of time.

James Nares, the painter and musician amply mentioned as percussionist of the Del-Byzanteens, wrote words that are spot on in his

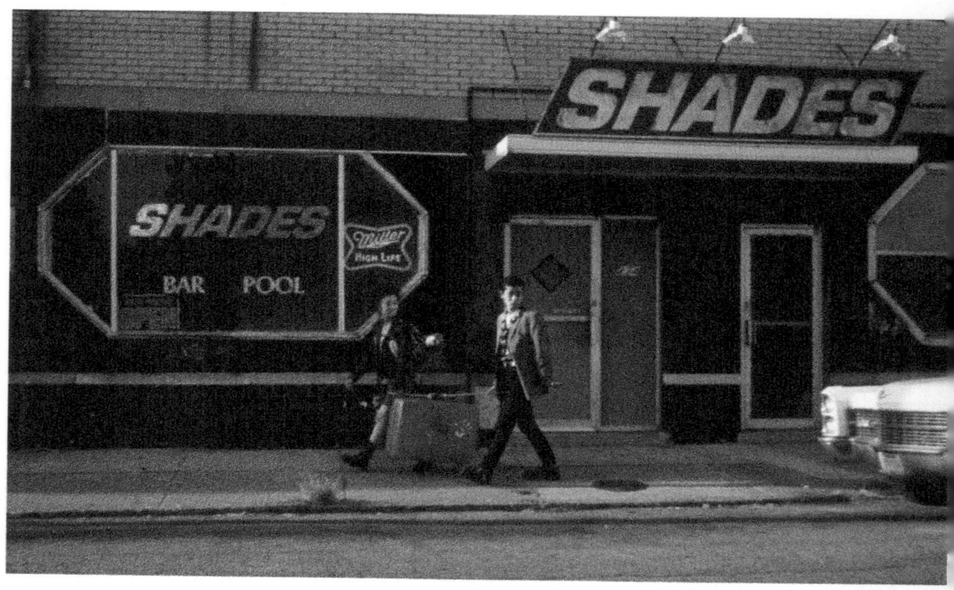

afterword to the inspiring collection of paintings published in the volume *John Lurie: A Fine Example of Art*:

Ambulatory music, *Mystery Train*.

> Perhaps the best thing Lurie's work does is something that art seldom achieves: it makes you laugh (even if you're not quite sure why). It's funny. Funny here is no joke, though: it's a funny that skews the mind, leaving a sense of elevated perplexity in its wake. Not exactly dark. Certainly not light. It's baffling, rude, sweet, and crude – but never nasty, mean-spirited, or dumb. Rather it is an honest irreverence . . . They make perfect sense and none at all: I am a Bear. You are an Asshole. God is God.[25]

John Lurie, *I am a Bear. You are an Asshole. God is God.*, 2005, watercolour, oil pastel and ink on paper.

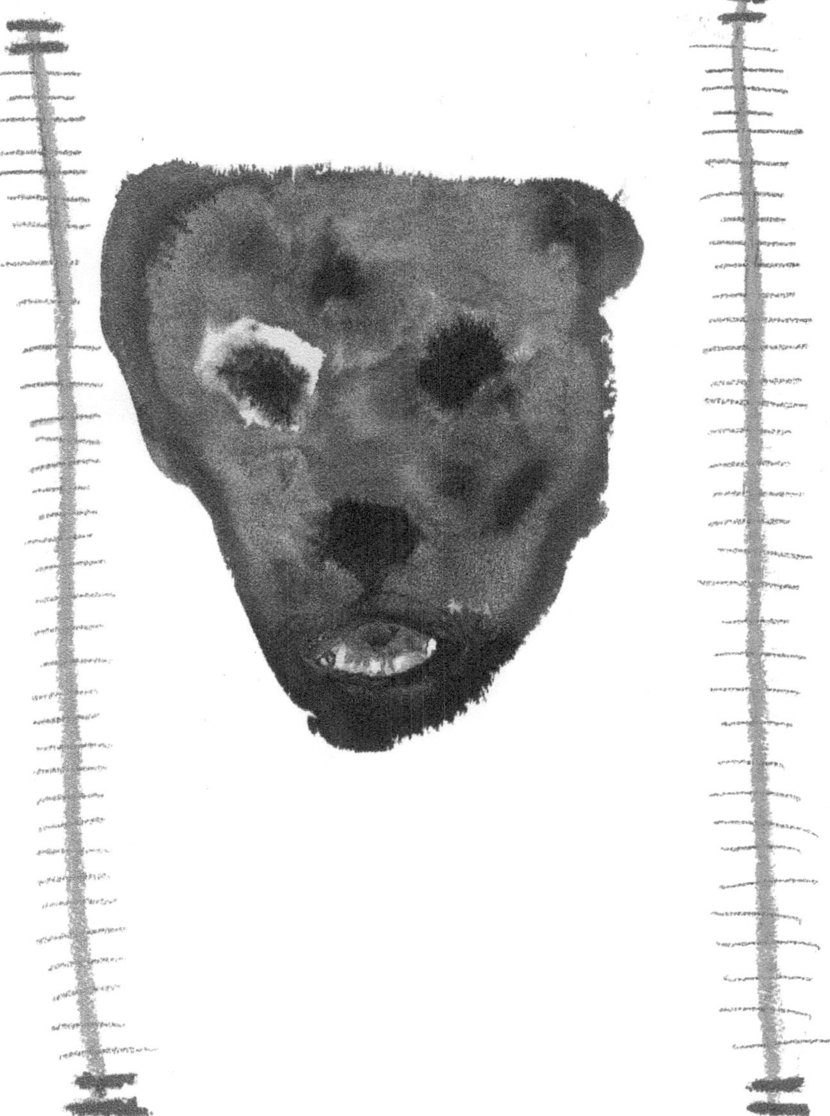

What does 'Indie' Really Mean?: Prologue to a Conversation with Marc Ribot

One of the questions in my book is: what does independence or rather 'indie' mean in film, if it has a meaning? And in my opinion, it has pretty much lost its meaning.

To me its original meaning is questionable as well. In records what it means is this: a long time ago, there was always the marginal, there was always stuff not many people wanted to buy so capital was not interested in producing it. The larger record companies weren't interested in, for example, 'race records', black music or country music but when they saw it was developing a market . . .

What do you mean by 'race records'?

I'm talking about black music from the 1920s. At the beginning of the '20s it was seen as a marginal market but eventually record companies realized it could sell, so they took over some of the labels and artists they could sell best. The only difference between then and now is that for complicated reasons instead of taking over marginal record com-panies that are becoming popular, larger companies find it more profitable to keep them as separate entities, maybe buy a percentage of the label, and just sign the label to a distribution deal. Okay, there is still a tiny marginal independent distribution network, but most of what has been called 'indie' music is simply another way of structuring a business relation, and, in spite of infinite hype, not necessarily a beneficial one for most artists.

There is a difference in my opinion when you talk about auto-production: I distribute it, I produce it myself and then I can say that I am independent, because I am economically independent from a system.

Right. But then how many people can say that they produced and paid for a movie themselves? Okay, the budget on *Stranger Than Paradise* was very low. But still, it took at least a year, I'm sure, of their time – how many people can afford not to work for a week!? Let alone a year. And even if it had a super-low budget of, let's say, $100,000, how many people 'independently' have that kind of money sitting around?

Absolutely. Film is really one of the most . . .

It's a very cruel medium.

Yes, really cruel. What Jarmusch often does, is to get the money abroad: Japan, Europe, the broadcast companies in Europe that have co-produced many of his films. One thing that is really extraordinary is that he actually owns his negatives.

Right, that is extraordinary. Well, it mirrors some of the issues for indie music. Artists who develop themselves whether musically or in film as 'indie' are not outside capital. They are in a stage in their career in which they are choosing to represent themselves as outside capital. And nothing is outside capital. 'Hipness' is capital and can be cashed in at the bank at a later stage, and is.

So, anyway on with the Jim Jarmusch interview. All this is to say: I really like Jim's films but – and it seems Jim feels the same way – about the whole myth of independence I couldn't care less!

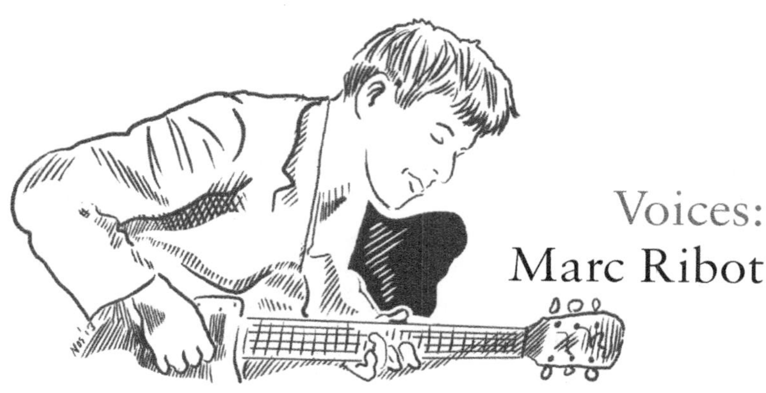

Voices: Marc Ribot

1

You played with John Lurie and The Lounge Lizards. And of course with Tom Waits. So, in a way you have a 'double musical link' to Jim Jarmusch. Have you ever actually worked together and can you tell me something about these experiences?

You mean worked in the studio with Jim Jarmusch?

Yes.

Well, Jim was in the studio definitely for *Mystery Train*, I don't remember whether he was there for *Down By Law*, he may have been. I had very limited participation in that score. Both of the film scores that I was involved with for Jim were composed by John Lurie.

Also *Stranger Than Paradise*?

No, I wasn't on the score of *Stranger Than Paradise*. But I did like it. The music for that film was also composed by Lurie and contains a kind of joke: it's a film about Hungarian immigrants who are doing everything in their power to assimilate to what they believe is America, and the score references the style of Hungarian composer Béla Bartók. It's a case of the film score as a return of the repressed. Lurie composed some really strong themes. By the way, I think the entire score according to what I heard from Jill Jaffe, whose string quartet recorded the score, was done in one [three-hour] session, because it was low budget and so they couldn't afford the musicians for a long time. Although it was John's concept to do it as Bartók, I suspect it was Jill and her quartet who helped translate John's ideas into the language of Bartók.

Wasn't it quite common at the time for artists to share a lot?
Not only at the time, it is now as well.

Yes. That is a crucial and beautiful aspect of both music and filmmaking.
They're collective.

Exactly. And it's different than the work of a painter or a writer, not wanting to compare anything, but just looking at the differences.
Yeah, by the way, I'm not protesting the way things are legally structured, it's all fine with me, I'm just saying that's the way it is. Anyway, there was definitely some kind of collaboration with Jill Jaffe and her string . . . now was it trio or quartet? I forgot.

It was a quartet.
Right. Anyway, so I didn't participate in that film score but I did the next two. I had a fairly minimal participation in *Down By Law*. I did mostly banjo and trumpet, I play a very small amount of trumpet . . . I think John is a very gifted film composer. I've worked with him on a number of projects, he's really got something.

He has a very visual way of making music. When I listen to his records, and also to other things like the Marvin Pontiac record, or other scores he made, or the work with The Lounge Lizards as well, it always brings me some images. And he really likes minimalist atmospheres and repetition.
That's right, he comes partly from a minimalist tradition. I think it's true that his music is very visual, although it probably does not produce the same images for me that it does for you. But that's another story . . . (Laughs)

2

In Jarmusch's films there is a very strong 'presence' of black music. I think especially of *Mystery Train* – with all the Memphis soul/Stax references, there is also Rufus Thomas in the film; he has a short cameo where he says '*arigato*', when he is talking to the two Japanese kids.
Yeah, he appears as a kind of god of Memphis . . . I once visited Rufus Thomas at his house in Memphis.

Okay, and what about it?

He has a nice house. And, by the way, he really *is* the god of Memphis.

So that's one side, that Memphis thing, there's also Screamin' Jay Hawkins, there's a lot of black music. And then of course *Ghost Dog – RZA* and the Wu-Tang Clan. On the other hand, his own musical experience with the Del-Byzanteens and with Dark Day fits more in the so-called 'No Wave' scene of the Lower East Side that you were also part of. One could say that in Jarmusch's 'melting pot of sounds' there is a lot of space for different things. What do you think about this?

Well, first let me just say that you can't separate No Wave music from black music. The people who were involved in No Wave had a common edge with the punk scene. But first of all what was the punk scene? I'm not gonna get into it but there's a very well-known book by this English guy . . . youth cultures and . . .

Do you mean Dick Hebdige?

Yeah, Dick Hebdige. Anyway, it's about the connection of punk to black music and culture. I mean okay, Malcolm McLaren put together the Sex Pistols after having heard Richard Hell's band the Voidoids, which included Robert Quine, not black, but a real scholar of black music. Quine's playing was strongly influenced by Ike Turner.

I read an interview with Lydia Lunch in which they asked her what's punk, who's punk, why punk, this whole obsession about punk, and she said well, that's actually a label that they put on me because I was wearing black and I was dyeing my hair and . . .

Maybe she was just wearing black because it's easier that way, you don't have to wash it as often and it's practical, you know, and in the winter it's a little warmer.

Exactly. And she said that punk was like rock 'n' roll, it was just fast rock 'n' roll.

Yeah, that's right. It was a retro movement in some ways with a rock root, so in that sense it was a type of black music. The other element of New York No Wave music that English punk didn't have was a certain amount of jazz influence. But it wasn't jazz à la Charlie Parker. If there was one common denominator to the whole thing, it was Thelonious

Monk. In a way, the whole thing was a reading of Thelonious Monk not as progress but as . . . I don't know, something else, as stripping down. Thelonious Monk started playing medium tempo solos and slow ballads, playing slowly, playing like a composer, stressing ideas over chops, allowing disjunctions and rough edges to appear in the music, at the time when all the beboppers were busy showing how fast and seamlessly they could play. At the height of modernist 'progress' he brought back elements of early stride piano style. So one way you can see it is 'he expanded the vocabulary, he was moving forward' but other people might say 'no, he was trying to move backwards'. The Lounge Lizards' first gig, I wasn't playing in the band yet, but their entire first gig they only knew one song and I think it was 'Well You Needn't', a Monk tune. You know, James Chance, I've worked with him and he's somebody who doesn't have a whole lot of tunes memorized but he can play entire chunks of Monk tunes.

James Chance of the Contortions?

Yeah, the saxophone player. Monk was also key for Zorn and a lot of other 'downtown' players. So I would say Thelonious Monk was a common denominator, a key to that scene. There was also contemporary classical influence, minimalists, John Cage et cetera. I guess it was a lot of white *people*, but the music was closely linked, through rock and a particular part of jazz, to black music.

I am always curious about one person: Rammellzee.

Rammellzee! Yes, I have one of his records. I have it on vinyl.

He also acted in *Stranger Than Paradise*, a short cameo, and he has a lot to do with what hip hop became after, don't you think?

Right. He was very early influence on a lot of people.

Do you know where he is now?[1]

No, I don't have a clue. I had his records and I probably met him a couple of times. Rammellzee. Let me see if I can find it . . .

What music are you listening to now?

I listen to Albert Ayler a lot. He was another important figure, a sax player. Oh here's the Rammellzee. It's a great record by the way. It won't do us much good because the record player is broken. I have to get it fixed. But the cover is kind of cool.

I think that Jarmusch's films have what you could call a musical and poetical structure. It is possible – in my opinion – to recognize refrains, strophes, rhymes, if you think about the episodic structure. For example in *Coffee and Cigarettes* there are some shots that come back, or in *Mystery Train* there are some literal quotations – so they really can work like rhymes, in a way.

You mean quotations from within the same film?

Exactly.

As well as quotations from outside . . .

Yes, quoting is very important in his aesthetic vision. So, both film and music are arts of time. They have a duration that the musician, composer or filmmaker determines. What do you think about this?

I think it's a good observation on your part, I would agree with it. Maybe Jim's having played in bands had some influence on this – recurring shots that structure the film like the repeating chorus in a song. I think what you are saying is true in general for film. Film editing is all about rhythm. What's also interesting for me in Jim's films is the *type* of rhythm. I sense there is a correspondence between a certain kind of flatness, a lack of an arc, or a very subtle arc, and what we were also doing at a certain point in the music scene. I was trained as a blues player basically or a rock player, so I was trained to construct solos that would start at a certain place and build and build to a climax, to a climactic moment and then fall off a little bit to a coda and then end. But when I started playing in The Lounge Lizards, and started to listen to No Wave and free jazz, this idea of climax was being questioned. Let's put it this way, there was another idea at work: the idea of doing a solo that was just a bunch of events, or a solo in which the dramatic arc was flat. Things would happen but the point was pointlessness.

That gives a really great opportunity to the viewer/listener to participate, because there is more space to fill in your own ideas. The rhythmic structure of course partly determines the atmosphere, but at the same time as a viewer/listener I don't feel that the director is taking my hand and telling me how to feel and – like in Hollywood films – shouting: Now, laugh! Now, cry!

Yeah, that's right. Maybe he's not telling you what to feel because he doesn't care if you feel anything.

Speaking of rhythm, Jarmusch has a very big interest in poetry. Luc Sante, whom I spoke to, confirmed that Jim is actually writing a lot of poetry.

Oh, I had no idea.

But he is very private about it. He doesn't show it to many people. It's a very personal thing.

Yeah, I know. I have enough respect for poetry that I don't show mine either! (Laughs)

The last one is just an open question. Is there anything you want to say about Jarmusch, or about something else?

Well, you know I'm not really a film critic, I like Jim's movies . . . Well, actually another thing that I remember from the early 1980s was that everybody was putting a 'postmodern' tag on Jarmusch's stuff. I suspect Jarmusch saw a lot of the downtown Super 8 film stuff that Eric Mitchell, John Lurie, James Nares and others were involved in. And the thing about those movies is the pacing: when you watch *Men In Orbit* by Lurie or *Red Italy* by Mitchell, for example, there are funny moments, but they take so long to happen, there's so much hanging around that the narrative breaks down and you just think 'Oh, there's some guy standing in front of a camera.' So I suspect Jarmusch was influenced by that, and got some of that same tag. Bands I was in at the time also did a lot of quotation, focusing on the surface, using movie music, noise, bad jazz and so on. Quotation and irony, so-called postmodernism, blah, blah, blah . . .

Didn't they also call the Lizards a 'fake jazz' band?

Yeah, 'fake jazz' and all that. But everybody I knew was basically over that and looking for a way out by around 1985. I mean, at a certain point it became clear that there had been some kind of change and all the sincere, heroic modernist-type sensibility looked stupid or dated. And there was a moment when people thought 'oh, this new sensibility is something that should be announced and celebrated' but for me it was a very short moment. I mean, maybe we're all subject to some kind of postmodern condition, but it seems more to me now like a disease than like something really fabulous. So quite a while ago people who invented that artistic response were already looking for another thing.

Not that it's necessarily possible to find one, but the celebratory attitude towards irony, distance, et cetera, is now what seems dated to me. And when I look at the projects I was involved in during the 1980s and early '90s, projects that had that kind of po-mo tag, I find myself liking them in spite of, not because of, those elements. I think Jarmusch's stuff transcends the moment it came out of, and that 30 years from now, when nobody knows or cares who was hip in 1985, *Stranger Than Paradise* for example, will be seen as a beautifully made film, a movie with a lot of soul, about immigrants.

And really funny.

New York, December 2003

4 Memphis Hip Hop, Mestizos and Samurai

'If Elvis Presley Is
    King
Who is James Brown . . .
    GOD?'
Amiri Baraka, 'In the Funk World' (1969), in Amiri Baraka, *Digging: The Afro-American Soul of American Classical Music* (Berkeley and Los Angeles, CA, 2009), p. 116

'So there was a new breed of adventurers, urban adventurers, who drifted out at night looking for action with a black man's code to fit their facts. The hipster had absorbed the existentialist synapses of the Negro, and for practical purposes could be considered a white negro.'
Norman Mailer, 'The White Negro: Superficial Reflections on the Hipster', *Dissent* (Fall 1957)

Among the multiple ingredients, be they music, words or images, that make up Jarmusch's melting pot, there exists no cultural hierarchy, no imposed tradition that is worth more or less than another. When approaching these wide-ranging facets, the routes that can be taken are thus countless.

I would like to extract and explore – somewhat liberally – a route that, as universal as it may be, is homogeneous from a 'chromatic' point of view: it is the deep track dug in the fertile terrain of Jarmusch's cinema by *black music*, merely defined for now as the music composed and performed by black or simply non-white musicians and artists. Two important exceptions close the chapter.

Since *Permanent Vacation*, the *black* or *non-white* sound universe has populated Jarmusch's films in an assiduous and natural way with a parade of names, from Earl Bostic and an imaginary Charlie Parker (*Permanent Vacation*) to Screamin' Jay Hawkins (*Stranger Than Paradise*); from Irma Thomas (*Down By Law*) to Junior Parker, Otis Redding and Rufus Thomas (*Mystery Train*); from RZA and the Wu-Tang Clan (*Ghost Dog*) to Mulatu Astatke (*Broken Flowers*); from – and here we have the two exceptions – Tom Waits (*Down By Law, Night On Earth*) to Neil Young (*Dead Man, Year of the Horse*). If you wanted to guess a route, the journey would no doubt start in the United States, with all the historical and cultural infiltrations linked to the cradle of the melting pot; infiltrations that would naturally lead back to the black continent and traditional African American music.

Bebop Meets Voodoo Jive

If, on the one hand, Jarmusch has often insisted that he has no particular interest in virtuosity, preferring the more genuine and unsophisticated artistic forms, on the other it must be said that, in musical terms, his passions include one of the most virtuosic traditions in the history of African American jazz starting since the 1940s: bebop. The virtuosity of the musicians who planted the seeds of this genre, like Miles Davis, Dizzy Gillespie, Max Roach, Art Blakey and, naturally, Charlie Parker, is based in particular on the exorbitant speed of solo performances, on the use of complex harmonies, on the importance given to improvisation and individual interpretation, and on the refusal to fall back on the sort of regular and reassuring rhythmic structures favoured by the popular big bands of the period, such as Duke Ellington and his Orchestra, just to mention one of the most famous.

In *Permanent Vacation* the presence of Charlie Parker is felt from start to finish, even though Jarmusch chose not to use his original pieces. Instead, he opted for Earl Bostic, a saxophonist admittedly not as well known as 'Bird', but who certainly did not lack extraordinary technical talent. In support of this claim it is worth quoting an excerpt from a rare interview with jazz icon Pharoah Sanders, the acute and unmistakable tenor saxophonist on John Coltrane's *Meditations*:

> I remember one time, he [John Coltrane] asked me if I could get
> a low A on my saxophone. I told him, no, I didn't know how to

do it. I would have to put my knee in my bell to get a whole step down from the B flat. He mentioned that Earl Bostic could do that without putting his knee into the bell.[1]

In *Permanent Vacation*, we hear what Earl Bostic is capable of in the magnificent dance scene in which an almost trance-like Allie spins around and around, pirouetting and snapping his fingers, as though on an imaginary stage. Bostic's rigorously diegetic solo performance booms from the record player sitting on the floor of the almost bare apartment. Moments before its start we hear a police siren fading into the distance. It is one of the rare almost carefree moments of the film, even if the hypothetical dance partner Leila, Allie's girlfriend, instead of joining in the dance, stares out of the window. During Allie's wild performance she turns her head a couple of times with the hint of a smile, but otherwise remains motionless on her chair, her gaze vacant. The exhausted dancer's dialogue at the end of the scene explains the imaginary line that, for Jarmusch, links Bostic to bebop: 'Sometimes I think I should just live fast and die young . . . and go in a three piece white suit like Charlie Parker! Not bad, uh?' We hear Bostic, but the presence that hovers over the scene is that of Parker from whom Allie, among other things, takes his name: Aloysius Christopher Parker. One can thus identify analogies also in the microcosm of the variegated post-war North American jazz scene, especially with regard to virtuosity and the particular importance given to the individual performance. Charlie Parker, Earl Bostic and Allie – performer or rather primo ballerino in an imaginary domestic setting, the stage being his bare room – are three expressions of the same individualistic and solitary spirit. Jarmusch condenses these different and yet homogeneous 'notes' onto one track, 'Up There in Orbit', a tongue-twister for alto sax, as fast as it is prominent for its audio impact on the rest of the film.

In fact, until Allie's dance sequence, the soundtrack has relied mainly upon the slowed down Indonesian gamelan, confirming once again Jarmusch's boundless approach that roams and alternates between jazz and traditional ethnic music. Bostic's single is heard just this once, until an exhausted Allie finally lifts the needle off the record. Jarmusch's use of the piece is respectful, because he does not interrupt it, and measured, seeing that, despite the importance of jazz to the film in general, and to the character of Allie in particular, this is the only time we hear it.

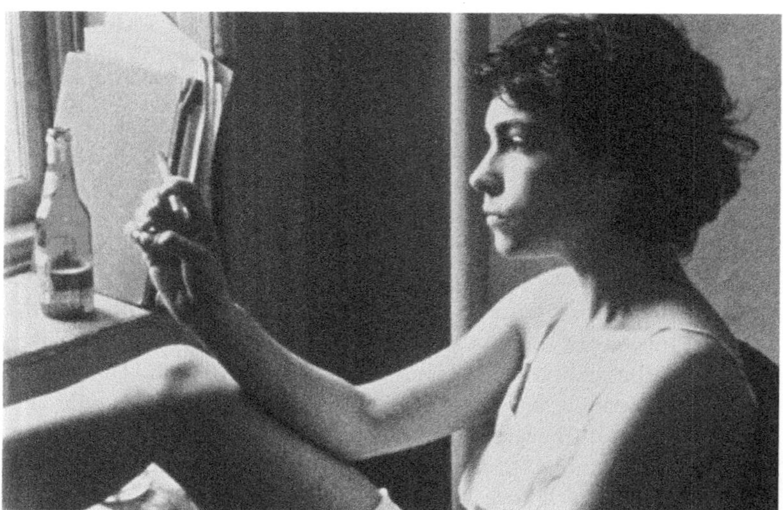

Leila's vacant gaze, *Permanent Vacation*.

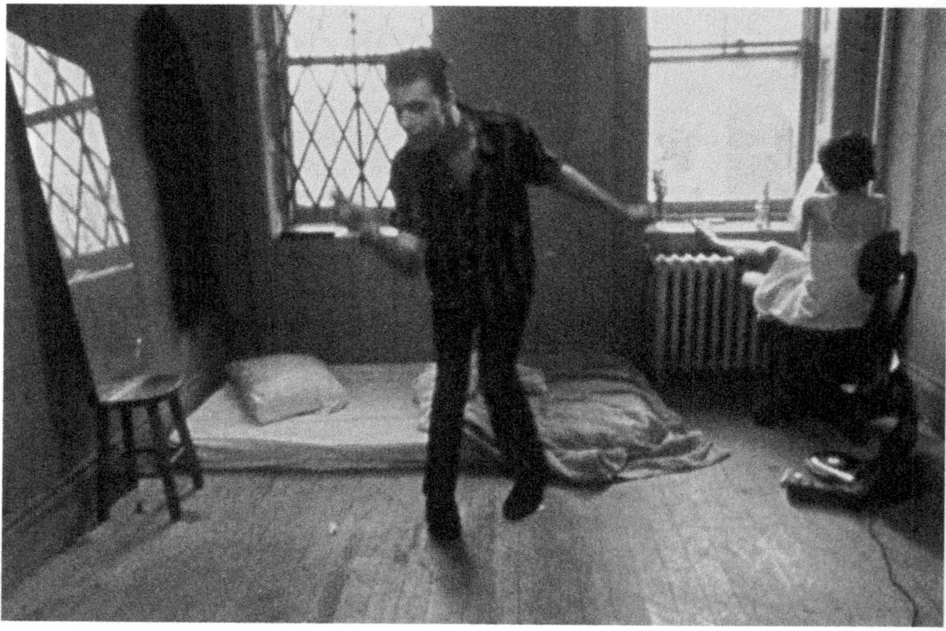

'Up There in Orbit' Allie's dance, *Permanent Vacation*

John Lurie's original saxophone improvisations are, on the contrary, more frequent and perhaps less 'sober' in their free jazz dimension. They feed a more hypnotic sound texture, which is assimilable to the gamelan, once again demonstrating that an analogy is possible even amid seemingly very distant musical hemispheres. Instead, Bostic recalls the jazz universe, even if with great virtuosity, almost sotto voce, within the film's general musical economy. In this sense, what comes to mind are the Bartók-like instrumentations for string quartet in *Stranger Than Paradise*, which are extremely incisive regardless of being parsimoniously used.

In fact, in *Stranger Than Paradise*, it is not just the strings that Jarmusch uses sparingly. The other musical mainstay, which comes under the non-white category dealt with here, is a single song, though repeated four times: the classic by Screamin' Jay Hawkins, 'I Put a Spell on You'. On one side, there are obvious economic reasons to explain the use of a single song – the rights cost the production $10,000 on a budget of just over $100,000 – while on the other the concept of repetition is a stylistic, almost existential mode very dear to Jarmusch. In 'I Put a Spell on You' repetition is expressed on a number of levels: an 'external' one regarding the song's textual repetition during the film, and an 'internal' one concerning the level of the very structure of the ballad, which is built on verse and refrain, in triple metre. In other words, a waltz. The use of this typically European music form makes ulterior observations possible.

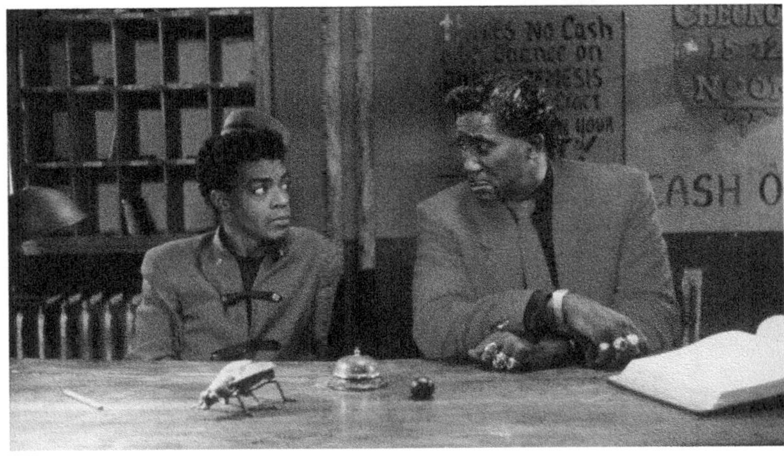

Cinqué Lee
and Screamin'
Jay Hawkins,
Mystery Train.

During the film's long opening lateral tracking shot, young Eva's first gesture on arriving in New York from Budapest is literally to 'switch on the soundtrack' by pressing the play button on the cassette recorder held firmly in the same hand that is gripping a large paper bag. The ensuing sounds coming from the recorder are naturally those of 'I Put a Spell on You'. Willingly, Jarmusch crosses the 'bridge over the ocean' with Bartók and the waltz, giving him totally European musical cues, while the images that flash across the screen could not be more American – as is also confirmed by J. Hoberman's comparison of the urban land-scapes in *Stranger Than Paradise*, and the extraordinary, celebrated photographs of Robert Frank's *The Americans*.[2]

If, from the musical metre's point of view the 'oompah-pah, oom-pah-pah' of Screamin' Jay's piece can trigger a European waltz-like feeling, then from the point of view of the song's function in the film one could turn this idea around and come up with a hypothesis that has more to do with the identity of a European girl just landed in the United States. 'It's Screamin' Jay Hawkins and he's a wild man, so bug off!' says an irritated Eva to cousin Willie/Bela in 'The New World', the film's first episode, in which they still barely know each other.[3] Gruffly, Willie turns off the cassette recorder that Eva has just switched on to dance to, her steps circular and rhythmic, in the bare one-room apart-ment where Willie has reluctantly put her up – a scene reminiscent of

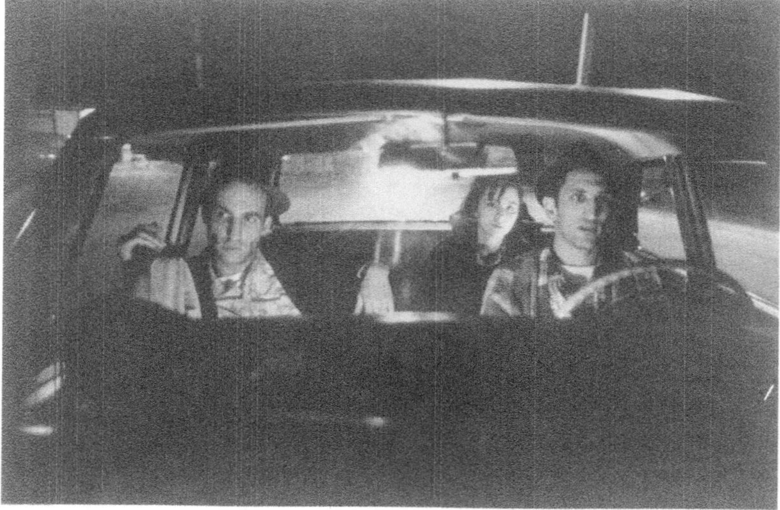

Driving music, *Stranger Than Paradise*.

Allie's dance in *Permanent Vacation*. The young Hungarian immigrant does everything she can to be accepted by the male characters, particularly by her cousin who is initially offhand, and uses the song – literally *screamed* by the great black performer, himself originally from Cleveland where the film is partly set – as an instrument, a cultural foothold, this time all American, to assert her identity as a new citizen of the New World. Her 'main man', Screamin' Jay, is her first ally in this endeavour and becomes the quintessence of 'Americanness' for Eva. When, in the third and final episode, 'Paradise', the three lead characters drive through the night to Florida, Eva turns on the cassette recorder again. Willie/Bela's reaction remains the same. On hearing the first note he protests by lowering the brim of his 1950s hat over his face. Eddie, on the other hand, greets Eva's music with a sly smile and declares: 'I like it . . . It's driving music!' Two against one. Screamin' Jay wins. And Eva, too, in the throes of her exhausting battle for a new American identity.

The image of the three characters on the road brings to mind another trio of cinematographic outsiders who are also engaged in hand-to-hand combat with American identity or, rather, with the American Dream: namesake Eva (Eva Mattes), Herr Scheitz (Clemens Scheitz) and Bruno S., protagonists of *Stroszek* (1977) by Werner Herzog. The pessimistic vision of the Bavarian director, however, imbues an epilogue that is way more tragic – and surreal – than the closing of *Stranger*

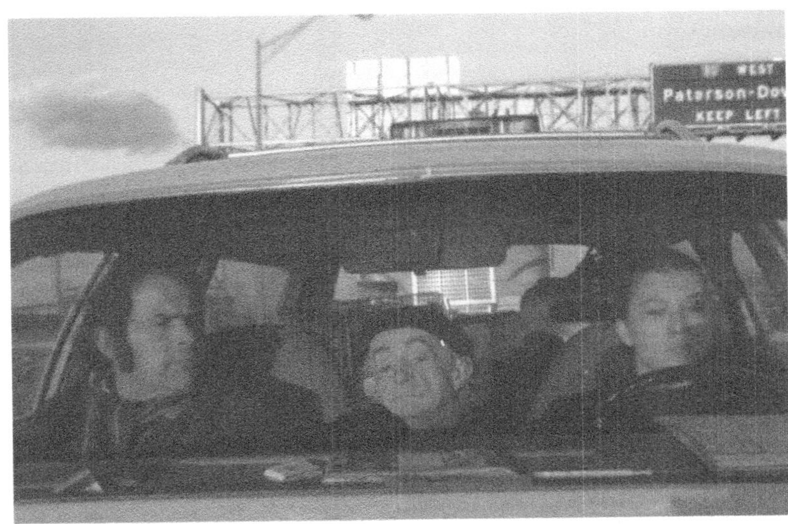

Land of opportunities, *Stroszek*, Werner Herzog (1977).

Than Paradise. For the three German characters, who have crossed the 'bridge over the ocean' on the run from Berlin and had an illusory taste of a new life in the land of opportunities – wonderfully symbolized by the prefab mobile home which just as it has arrived will depart again, leaving them literally homeless – the clash with reality will be unbearable.

There is a crucial difference between the two films. In *Stroszek*'s epilogue, man has completely disappeared and animals have gained the upper hand. This should not be mistaken for a glimmer of hope founded on a last redemption of 'nature versus civilization': on the contrary. Herzog's prolonged closing shots of animals locked up in small display cases are both absolutely bizarre and disturbing: the dancing chicken constantly operating a miniature fake piano, the drum-playing duck and the rabbit switching on the siren of a small fire engine are the shreds of nature, irreversibly contaminated by 'civilization' but at the same time exhilarating and ridiculous. Jarmusch's three outsiders, Eva, Willie and Eddie, will separate at the end of *Stranger Than Paradise*, but the viewer can sense that there will be a life 'after' the film. Though it is true that their attempt at communicating did not quite work, perhaps there will be another attempt in the future. Screamin' Jay's waltz is a far cry from the piercing piano loop, annoying and repetitive, which the chicken dances to, as well as from the wild siren played by the rabbit and the senseless hits the duck mechanically makes on the drum. In contrast to Jarmusch, Herzog annuls any hope or suggestion of dialogue, whether present or future.

Sixteen Coaches Long

It might seem incredible, but before shooting *Mystery Train*, Jarmusch claims never to have set foot in Memphis.[4] Thus his first encounter with one of the undisputed music capitals of the United States, one of its vital centres or, if preferred, one of the umbilical cords that joins African American music culture to the African continent, came about exclusively through music: acoustic encounters that fuelled a desire to shoot in Memphis the film that had the major task of following the two hits *Stranger Than Paradise* and *Down By Law*.

The year 1989 also saw the release of the *Coffee and Cigarettes (Memphis Version)* episode, again set in Memphis, that in 2003 went on to join the parade of eleven shorts, its 'protagonists' being coffee and tobacco. Apart from these two basic materials, the short stars Steve

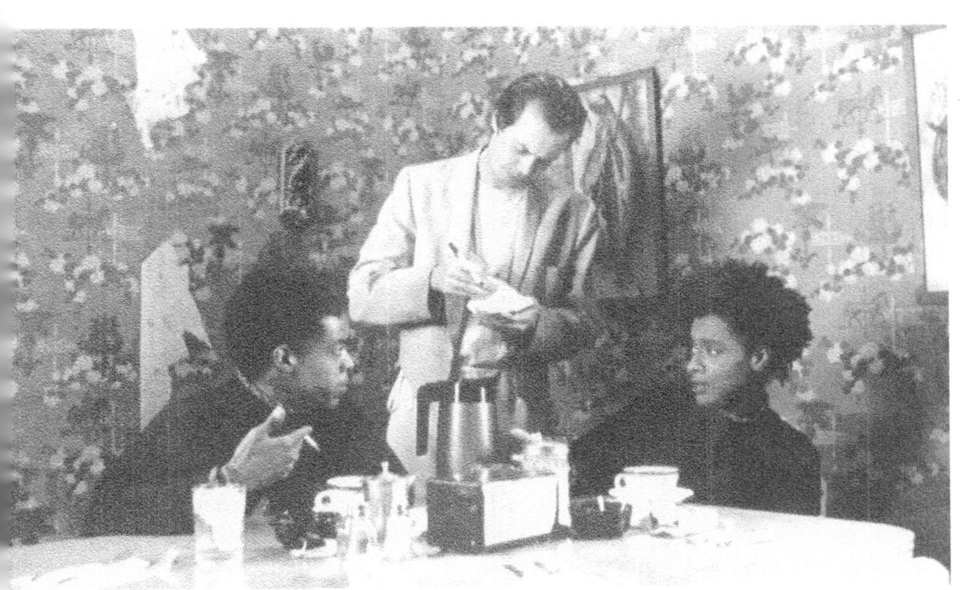

Buscemi, Joie Lee and Cinqué Lee. The latter two are respectively sister and brother of an illustrious friend from Jarmusch's university days, Spike Lee. Joie and Cinqué, seated at a table in an anonymous Memphis diner, tease and annoy each other like ill-behaved kids before getting into a heated argument with Steve Buscemi, the greasy and deathly pale waiter. Initially, the argument seems to question the quality of the diner's coffee, but it is not long before we understand that Jarmusch wants to go somewhere else. Thanks to a musical dispute, we come to one of those rare moments that his work hints as being 'political'. Without being too subtle about it, brother and sister question Elvis's integrity when recording songs written by African American composers like Otis Blackwell and Junior Parker. The siblings believe that denying them access to the celebrity these two composers so richly deserved was a pre-meditated act by Elvis and that the so-called King was no more than a heartless fraudster. 'Elvis robbed their music!' a fighting Joie shouts, an opinion that stuns the waiter/Buscemi, a loyal subject of The King. The accusation is echoed by Cinqué who, without batting an eyelid, adds: 'My favourite Elvis quote is: "The only thing coloureds can do for me is shine my shoes."' However, the scene closes in a pretty upbeat mood, thanks mainly to Buscemi's comic and surreal tale about 'Elvis's evil twin'. In fact, it was he and not the real Elvis who did and said all those bad things, who wrecked his brother's health and career in Las Vegas. A bizarre theory, yes, but one responsible for the peaceful solution of the racial clash among the three.

Going back to *Mystery Train*, almost in defence of the siblings' theory, Jarmusch included both the successful version of the title song by Elvis and the lesser-known version by Junior Parker on the soundtrack CD. The piece was written in 1953 by Parker together with Sam Phillips, the founding father of Sun Records, and was Elvis's final recording with that legendary label before he signed with RCA and achieved planetary success. Right from the first note, two vastly different approaches are clearly evident.

Junior Parker is driving a comfortable, old, coal-driven locomotive, its rhythmic cadence wrapped in a thick cloud of steam. The piano, guitar, drums and saxophone arrangements mimic the tone of this mysterious old train, and Parker's soft and nocturnal voice seems to tell us that this ride will never end. Who knows when the song's leading characters, the two lovers separated by the train, will be reunited?

Elvis, on the other hand, is at the controls of a high-speed train, his almost metallic voice driving home the fact that the train that took away his beloved will not get a second chance. His 'It never will again!' rebels against the fatalism of the blues, its tone decidedly more accentuated than the same phrase by Parker.[5] Both Scotty Moore's guitar solo and Elvis's voice have something lucid and fast about them, an almost aggressive touch if compared to the awkward, shambling pace of Parker's train that the purist Jarmusch let run along with the end credits.

While in *Permanent Vacation* the presence of Charlie Parker, though highly important, is purely hinted at, in *Mystery Train* the figure of Elvis is a fundamental, almost ubiquitous presence/absence that breezes through the entire film, and makes up part of the narrative structure. His voice, heard constantly on the radio singing 'Blue Moon', marks the timeline of the film's three episodes, and helps us understand that the on-screen actions take place contemporarily. The voice of radio DJ Tom Waits — or should we perhaps call him Lee Baby Simms?[6] — announces 'The King' at the end of 'Domino' by Roy Orbison, another hero of the Sun Records stable. Pictures of Elvis are on the walls of every room in the Arcade Hotel where a large part of the action takes place. Johnny, played by Joe Strummer of The Clash, is nicknamed Elvis, thanks mainly to his greased-back hair and 1950s rock 'n' roll look. It is interesting to note how the two Japanese 'pilgrims' from the first episode never agree on Elvis's mythical role. Mitsuko is the victim of a true personality cult: she compares the image of Elvis not only to Buddha and the Statue of Liberty, but to pop 'queen' Madonna too, and in fact it is surprising to discover that a strong likeness really does exist. In sharp contrast, Jun stubbornly insists that Carl Perkins, often hailed as the father of rockabilly, was the greatest of all. Perkins, the white guitarist who worked in the cotton fields, and one of rock 'n' roll's greatest unsung heroes, started his career in the above-mentioned Sun Studios in 1954, a year after 'Mystery Train' was recorded. Nonetheless, Mitsuko remains implacable; nothing will threaten the love she feels for her hero. In order to be free to admire the statue of Elvis, at whose feet they are seated, the girl has no alternative but to gag her stubborn companion who, with his bizarre Japanese accent, continues unperturbed to repeat the name of Carl Perkins. Furthermore, Elvis is the protagonist of a very rare 'supernatural' moment in the cinema of Jarmusch: the apparition of Memphis's most famous ghost in the hotel room of the stunned Italian tourist Luisa, in the second episode suitably entitled 'A Ghost'. Referring to the double of the illustrious phantom, cultural critic Greil Marcus did not miss the chance to cut to the quick by branding the actor Stephen Jones as 'perhaps the least convincing Elvis . . . in the history of Western civilization.'[7]

Notwithstanding these particulars, The King's function in the framework of the film, which is based upon the variations of a theme principle, is not merely decorative, but structural. Elvis helps to give the spectators a temporal, spatial and even thematic orientation, regardless of the more or less political or qualitative interpretation they wish to give his character. For Johnny, who hates his nickname and would rather be called Carl Perkins Jr, Elvis was an exploiter of black musicians. For Mitsuko, Elvis is a legendary figure, a dogma not to be disputed. For Luisa, he is a mysterious and incomprehensible apparition, a ghost who, in answer to the question from the bemused woman on what he is doing in her room, calmly responds: 'I don't rightly know, ma'am' and then vanishes. If the opinions can thus diverge, what remains undeniable is the central role played by Elvis as a mythical character, and by Graceland as a mythical setting that, in fact, will never be reached by the two pilgrims, Jun and Mitsuko.

A methodical and passionate lover of music, Jarmusch could not, however, heap praise solely on the 'boy who stole the blues'. In fact, he draws inspiration on the musical universe not only of Sun Records, but

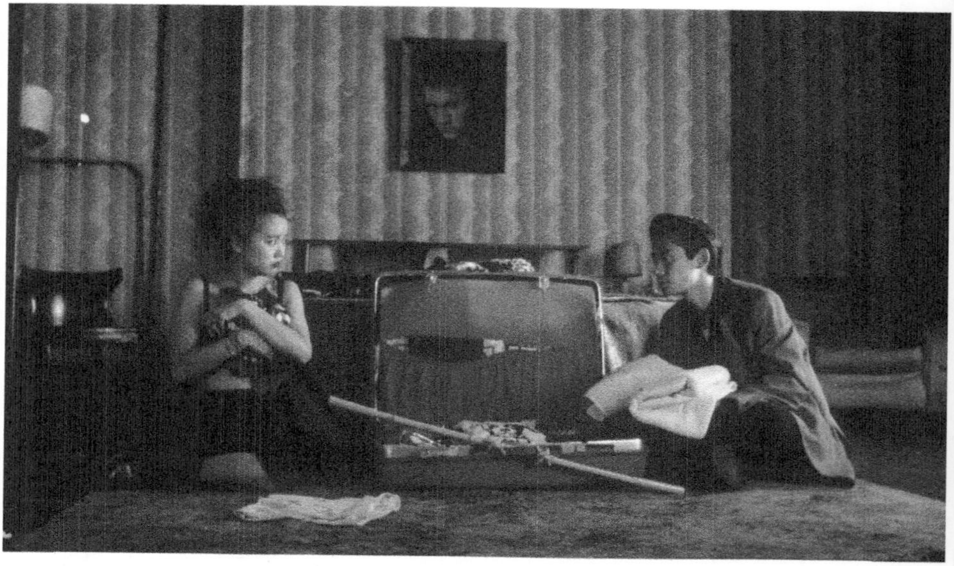

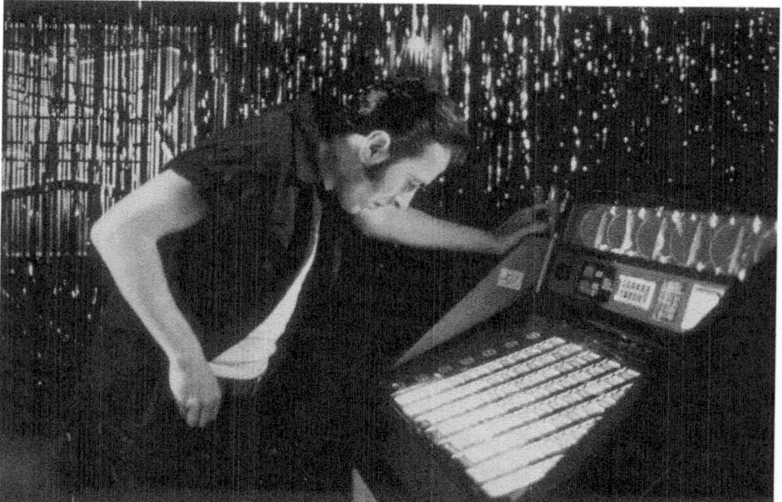

Ubiquitous Elvis,
Mystery Train.

Johnny/Elvis,
Mystery Train.

also of Stax: the record labels that made the Memphis sound a household name, the former with rock 'n' roll and R&B, and the latter with Memphis soul. In 'Lost in Space', the third episode of the film, the music on the jukebox in the Shades – the bar/pool hall where the only white, Johnny/Elvis, who has just lost his girl and his job, drowns his sorrows – is a serious tribute to the traditions of Memphis soul: Rufus Thomas, Bobby 'Blue' Bland, Otis Redding, The Bar-Kays, all artists linked to Stax Records. Jarmusch does not just refer to this label in a purely acoustic way. When a totally wrecked Johnny, having been carried out of the Shades, goes in search of an all-night liquor store, we see the abandoned building that once housed Stax Records. Today, not even the graffiti on the wall filmed by Jarmusch remains to pay homage to one of Memphis soul's historic sites. The building was torn down in 1989 and those images immortalized in *Mystery Train* are among the last to appear publicly, acquiring a relevant documentary value.[8] Stax Records had already risked extinction in 1967 when Otis Redding, just 26 at the time, and four members of his band, The Bar-Kays, died in a plane crash in Lake Manona one month before the release of the record that would have guaranteed him enduring fame '(Sittin' On) The Dock of the Bay'. Thanks to his unique voice, to his natural ability to move audiences worldwide, Redding had rightfully earned himself the title King of Soul, not without some allusion to the other oft-mentioned King of Rock 'n' Roll. The record 'Pain in My Heart', played on the Shades jukebox, is a perfect example of Redding's vocal talent, and comes close to the fatalistic blues incarnated by Junior Parker. 'Someone please stop this pain in my heart' is the desperate plea that ends the piece.

With a pinch of nostalgia, Jarmusch refers to a glorious and apparently faded past, while at the same time managing to bring it back to life through his story and characters: the first among many being Johnny/Joe Strummer. In both his roles, on-screen and in real life, the 'modern Elvis' reaffirmed the link between past and present on one side, and between the black and white musical universes on the other. Johnny quotes Malcolm X and listens to Stax records; Joe Strummer and The Clash have always fed off black music, managing to unite worlds only apparently distant from each other like British punk rock on one side and ska, reggae, zydeco, Jamaican dub and Memphis soul on the other.

The link to the past is, again, not even remotely contested by Jarmusch. Music, particularly in a blatantly musical film like *Mystery Train*, becomes an especially valuable accomplice in reawakening the past to fuel the present. Jarmusch's network of references and quotes, pedantic to some, structural or just amusing to others, is not intended as a pretentious, elitist show-off but rather as his personal celebration of that past. A phrase credited to Jean-Luc Godard on the question of originality in art seems to hit the nail on the head, and is willingly quoted by Jarmusch: 'It's not where you take things from. It's where you take them to.'[9]

Hip Hop and Pigeons

Staying on the black music trail in Jarmusch's filmography, one inevitably arrives at two particularly emblematic films from this point of view: the gangster movie *Ghost Dog: The Way of the Samurai* – the story of the taciturn killer with a passion for literature and pigeons, up against a shabby and elderly gang of Italian American mafiosi – and *Broken Flowers*, the road movie about ex-Latin lover Don Johnston on a pilgrimage to find a hypothetical son. In the first, the score is entrusted to RZA, born Robert Diggs, the brains behind the New York hip hop collective Wu-Tang Clan, while in the second Jarmusch uses original music by the Ethiopian maestro Mulatu Astatke, creator of the sound he named Ethio-jazz.

Continuing the above discussion on *Mystery Train*, it is not an exaggeration to say that *Ghost Dog* is a film that literally feeds on quotations. The variety of references extends from cinema to music, from literature to cartoons, to Jarmusch's very own filmography. The director, not without his customary irony, defined the film as a 'samurai-gangster-hip-hop-Eastern-Western'.[10] Instead, in *Broken Flowers* the variations- on-a-theme principle that is very dear to Jarmusch structures the film. During his travels, Don Johnston finds himself in similar situations – surprise encounters with lovers from the past, five to be exact, one of whom is no longer alive – but set in different circumstances and locations. Both these storytelling strategies, the *quote* and the *variations-on-a-theme*, have a solid foundation in Jarmusch's musical choices. I would like to observe *Ghost Dog* first.

Hip hop is a genre based upon sampling, in other words upon quotes of existing materials, what in graphic terms could be compared to collage or cut-up in literary terms. For RZA and friends cut-up is the ultimate method of working, with traits that can be described as ecological and minimalist. On one side, thanks to the altered juxtaposition of the elements, the original material is 'recycled' and transformed into

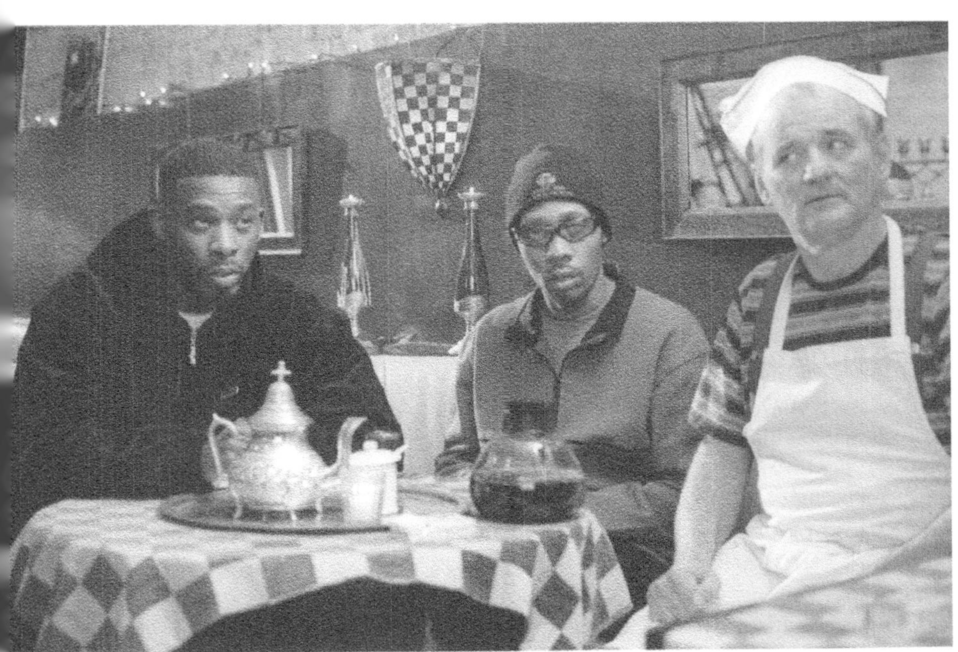

something new while, on the other, a rhythmic and melodic modulation built on a repetitive loop is created, using the minimum of the material available. Not only composers of minimal music à la Terry Riley, but hip hop too puts into practice what film critic Jonathan Rosenbaum happily called 'the minimalist paradox', according to which 'the less your work does, the more these things matter'.[11] Within an apparently monotonous structure each variation, whether on a tonal, rhythmic or textual plane, has an enormous impact on the listener. Each detail becomes meaningful and form and style may even become subject-matter. And this is perhaps why the producer, or rather he who materially and technically gives shape to the sound that will be recorded in the studio, that RZA has covered in almost all the Wu-Tang Clan's works, plays a central and by no means accessory role in any hip hop musical production. RZA personally encouraged Jarmusch to use his music like the pieces of a 'sound mosaic', to compose and undo as he wished. 'Cut it up, edit it, mix it together – I don't care.'[12] This is the hip hop approach embodied by RZA. In *Ghost Dog*, through the use of his music, based mainly on hypnotic loops, dilated rhythms and Asian-sounding bells and gongs with a ritual mood, Jarmusch confirms the practice of sampling and quotes that he has chosen as the mode of interpreting the film in its broader sense.

Without intending to make an infinite list, one can in fact observe how single scenes recall films from the past. The final showdown between the modern samurai, Ghost Dog, and his 'boss', Louie the mafioso, imitates Fred Zinnemann's classic western *High Noon* (1952), in particular with the chiming bells during the gunfight, as pointed out by Juan A. Suárez.[13] The role of Ghost Dog feeds on numerous film characters, from Alain Delon, the lone protagonist of Jean-Pierre Melville's *Le Samouraï* (1967), who kills wearing white gloves and lives in perfect isolation with his canary, to Clint Eastwood in Sergio Leone's *A Fistful of Dollars* (1964), who shares his mannerisms and meditative, taciturn attitude with Ghost Dog. And finally let us not forget Elia Kazan's classic *On the Waterfront* (1954), in which Marlon Brando, just like Ghost Dog, keeps pigeons on a roof.[14]

As told by photographer Martha Cooper, who has documented New York's street art since the end of the 1970s, 'It's a very classic New York thing, keeping pigeons on the roof and trying to capture other kids' pigeons. It's a sort of game.'[15] This game often becomes a full-blown contest, and it is not unusual for someone to capture a pigeon and then demand a small ransom to return the bird to its rightful owner. The

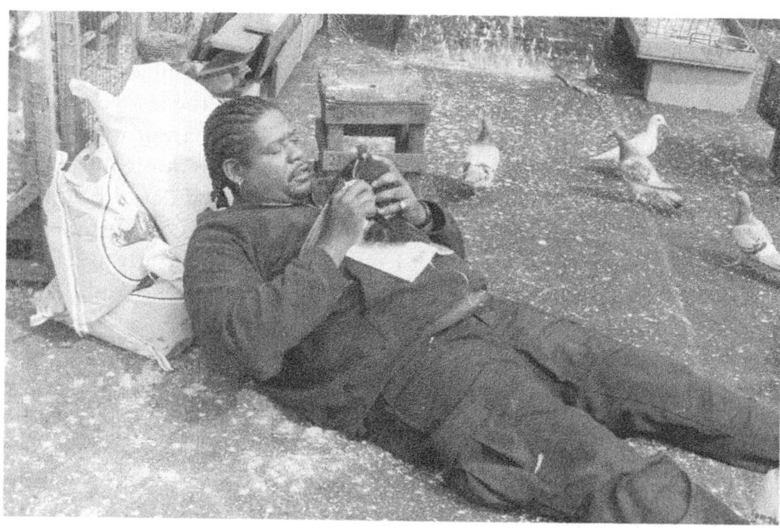

Message bearers, *Ghost Dog: The Way of the Samurai*.

personal touch that Jarmusch wanted to add to this particular urban sport is killer Ghost Dog using pigeons not as racing birds but as rapid, precise and unsuspected message bearers, in order to communicate with his mafioso 'boss', Louie.

Putting aside movie quotes and this small carousel of references to classics of the 1950s and '60s, it can be surmised that for the pigeons theme Jarmusch found an ulterior source of inspiration, one closer to home, in a New York artist very dear to him and who was very active in the heyday of New York's hip hop and street art: graffitist or, better, writer Dondi, real name Donald J. White, who died on 2 October 1998, less than a year before the presentation of *Ghost Dog* at the Cannes Film Festival in May 1999. As told by colleague and fellow graffitist Zephyr, Dondi kept pigeons on the roof and, just like Ghost Dog, spent hours with them separated from the rest of the world.[16] On top of that, Dondi had been a cast member of the classic hip hop film *Wild Style* (1983) by Charlie Ahearn along with many other names of the scene such as Grandmaster Flash, Fab 5 Freddy and Rammellzee.[17]

Sixteen years after the release of Ahearn's film, it is the first shot of *Ghost Dog* that really hits home: an aerial POV shot, in which the spectator sees the city through the eyes of a pigeon, flapping its wings in time with RZA's hypnotic beat and loops while flying above its neighbourhoods oblivious to man-made confines like streets and buildings.[18] On Ghost Dog's roof, where the pigeon finally lands, Jarmusch evokes a piece of history in which he also took part. Granted, the gentle giant Forest Whitaker seems to have little to do with the early 1980s hip hop scene by playing a lone killer, brooding and precise, a modern samurai who lives according to the dictates of the *Hagakure*, the Japanese samurai's ancient code of conduct. Moreover, the film is set in Jersey City and not in New York, the idea having been to find the most anonymous of urban environments.

However, the citation in this case is neither literal nor didactic, and nor does it mean to be. What interests Jarmusch is a lighter affinity, not necessarily faithful from a strictly nominal or topographic point of view, one that is possibly even subliminal, but born from the deep roots of a shared past. Ghost Dog could not have existed without Dondi, nor without the artistic and music scene around him, regardless of the citation structure used by Jarmusch; just as Dondi probably could not have existed without the Brando of *On the Waterfront*.

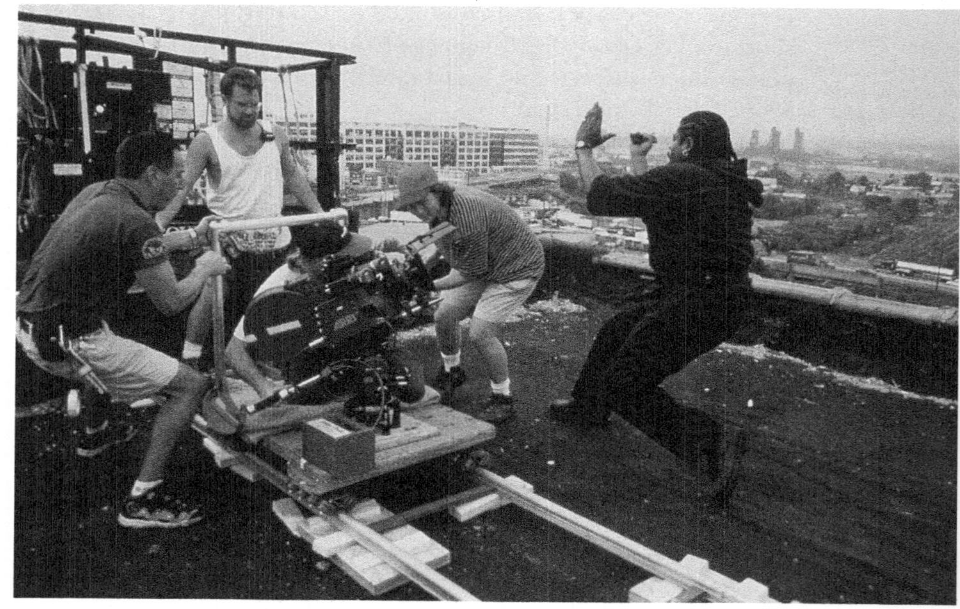

In this sense, Ghost Dog brings to mind another principal player of Jarmusch's filmography, whom I will only touch upon for now: William Blake, the naive bookkeeper from Cleveland played by Johnny Depp in the anti-western *Dead Man* (1995). From beginning to end, Depp's character is totally unaware of being the personification, at least nominally, of the great British poet. On the contrary, his Native American travel companion, Nobody (Gary Farmer), is very familiar with the work of the visionary poet and thinks that the young bookkeeper, the unwitting killer, fatally wounded and constantly on the run, is the reincarnation of the dead William Blake. A ghost. Ghost Dog, in spite of having a name that does not immediately bring to mind any famous figure, is inspired by numerous other killers from the annals of cinema. And yet, as in Blake's case, Ghost Dog lives the 'citation' ploy unwittingly. He bears it upon his broad shoulders with great levity. The 'samples' of the numerous players – Brando, Delon, Eastwood, just to mention the more obvious, and perhaps also Lee Marvin and Toshiro Mifune – that make up the character of Ghost Dog are used by Jarmusch according to the already mentioned advice from RZA: to cut, edit and freely assemble, just like a music track in which the different parts that make up the piece take

on a new originality. The typical techniques of hip hop, the sample and
the quote, the collage and the cut-up, thus determine not only the style
but also the deeper structural elements of the film, like the character's
personality. *Ghost Dog: The Way of the Samurai* is the proof: the form
on some occasions may become the content.

Ethio-jazz Meets Bebop

In *Broken Flowers* there also exists a deep musical analogy at the
heart of the film. The soundtrack is mainly based on original pieces
by Ethiopian composer and vibraphonist Mulatu Astatke, the recognized father of Ethio-jazz, a style he kick-started more than 40 years
ago. Were it necessary to identify a genre for *Broken Flowers*, then
'slow episodic road-movie' or 'sad romantic comedy in stages' could
be two possibilities. As mentioned, Don Johnston is a middle-aged
ex-Casanova searching for his unknown hypothetical son, whose existence is announced in an anonymous letter at the beginning of the
film. Encounters with ex-lovers and potential mothers punctuate his
journey, which can be traced to the variations-on-a-theme mechanism.

Winston and Don,
Broken Flowers.

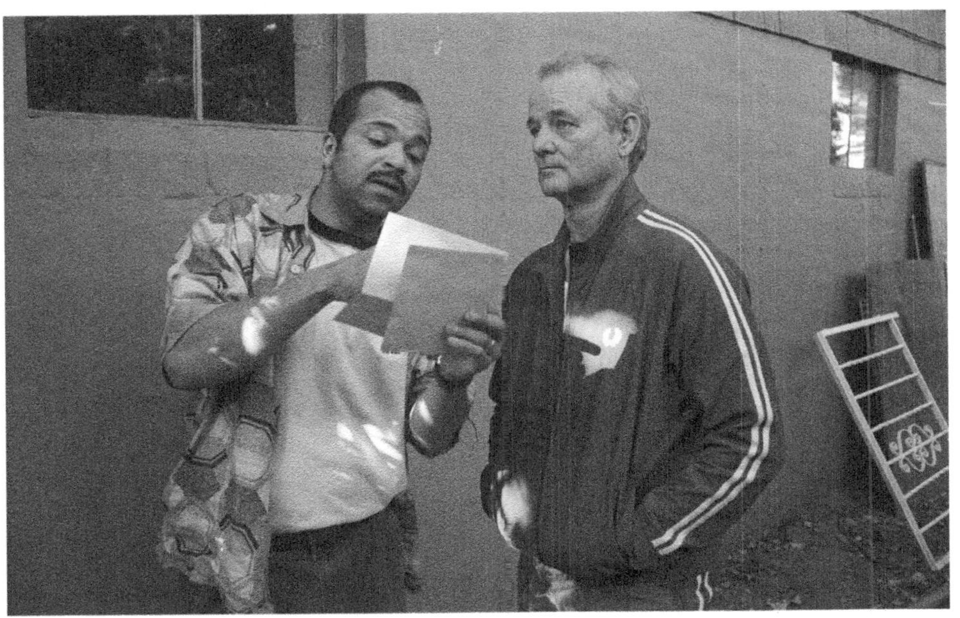

Each woman corresponds to a different environment, with or without a new man, and the presence of each alludes to an equally different past: all variations on the theme of the unexpected and multiple developments of human relationships. But for the first encounter with the still-beautiful Laura, played by a radiant Sharon Stone, the others will have neither a positive nor a particularly reassuring outcome – on the contrary.

The only warmth given the taciturn and listless Don comes from the fluid and all-encompassing Ethiopian music, his faithful travelling companion. Jarmusch fell so much in love with Mulatu Astatke's music that,[19] to justify the massive use of his compositions, he made Winston, the character embodied by Jeffrey Wright who spurs Don into going on his travels, an Ethiopian. Apart from street maps and the addresses of his ex-lovers, Winston also gives Don CDs for his emotionally complicated journey and insists he listen to them, convinced as he is that 'Ethiopian music is good for the heart!'

One of Mulatu Astatke's talents is to have created a seriously happy mix between traditional Ethiopian music and jazz, with particular regard to the timbre and the choice of instruments: vibraphone, brass, organ and guitar. In Mulatu's compositions in *Broken Flowers* – 'Yegelle Tezeta', 'Yekermo Sew', Gubelye'[20] and 'Ethanopium' – a specific type of variation on a theme is used originating from the bebop jazz lingo of the 1940s of which Mulatu found models and analogies in the traditional music of his country. Contrary to what usually happens, rhythms and melodies (variations) change while the harmonies (theme) based upon hypnotic pentatonic scales dictated by Ethiopian tradition remain constant. In short, pentatonic scales are scales without semitones made up of five notes not dissonant from each other. The absence of semitones annuls the hierarchies between the notes because it eliminates the functions of tonal tension that the semitones normally determine, in such a way that no note overwhelms another by playing the role of resolution-note (tonic). The two tonal models, major and minor, are thus indiscriminately contained in these scales that adapt very nicely to create a circular and unsolved general atmosphere: the perfect sound environment of Don Johnston's uncertain journey into his past. The constant theme around which the rhythmic and melodic variations express themselves is thus of a harmonic nature or, to use a more cinematographic comparison, of an environmental nature or rather a genre; as in a film noir or a romantic comedy the overall atmosphere is also determined, for example, by the photography or by the set design.

Just like the principle of quotations and samples in *Ghost Dog*, a mechanism of a musical nature like a particular type of variation on a theme – namely the variations typical of bebop and Ethiopian tradition – was used by Jarmusch to structure the film's general progress. Nothing points to this being a completely intentional or conscious choice, and yet it is noticeable in retrospect.

And perhaps, apart from the effective publicity campaign, the awesome cast – Bill Murray, Sharon Stone, Jessica Lange, Tilda Swinton among others – and even the Jury Prize won at the Cannes Film Festival in 2005, it is possible to find in this indisputable *harmonic analogy* of sounds and images one of the keys to the film's extraordinary success. It grossed almost $47 million, making it the most lucrative of Jarmusch's films. It is rather probable that the producers of Focus Features, a rising star at the time and one of today's acclaimed realities in the production and distribution of art films, who financed *Broken Flowers* with France's BAC Films, would disagree with the *harmonic analogy* theory,[21] but I – and perhaps Mulatu Astatke – would beg to differ.

Mestizos: Waits and Young

'White Negro' and 'White Indian'. These two intentionally risky definitions justify the presence in this chapter, dedicated up to this point to black – or rather non-white – music, of Tom Waits and Neil Young, two musicians fundamental to the Jarmusch universe.

Tom Waits, a Californian of Norwegian, Scottish and Irish origins, has made many of the so-called typical African American traits his own, such as the use of a rich vernacular of word games, of improvisation, of semantic drifts, in other words a fantastic and personal form of *slanguage*.[22] Neil Young, a native of Toronto, Canada, has always supported Native Americans and indigenous peoples in general in their battles for self-determination, and has held nothing back when accusing the white invader of crossing the ocean with 'galleons and guns' to spread death and destruction.[23] One just has to mention the titles of the two classics, 'Pocahontas' and 'Cortez the Killer'.

Clearly, from an epidermal point of view, the two characters in question have very little black about them, an irrefutable fact that demonstrates how foolish it is to commit to schematic categories, let alone 'ethnic' ones. In fact, what is 'black music'? Are there such things as ready recipes, canons to be obeyed, rules that determine the structural qualities of so-called black music and those who play it or compose it? I do not think so. Instead, I would like to quote American musician and music critic Sasha Frere-Jones who, in his noted article 'A Paler Shade of White', explains the difficulty of tracing with scientific certainty the origins of traditional music and cultures in general:

> In the case of many popular genres, the respective contributions of white and black musical traditions are nearly impossible to measure. In the 1920s, folk music was being recorded for the first time, and it was not always clear where the songs – passed from generation to generation and place to place – had come from . . . In 1952, the record collector Harry Smith released *Anthology of American Folk Music*, a highly regarded compilation (and, later, a source for Bob Dylan), which showed that white 'country' performers and black 'blues' artists had recorded similar material in the 1920s and '30s, singing about common legends, such as 'Stackalee', over similar chord progressions. Even the call-and-response singing that is integral to many African-American church services may have been brought to America by illiterate Scottish immigrants who learned Scripture by singing it back to the pastor as he read it to them.[24]

To be recognizable, the multiple styles – and not only musical – must submit to the rules or codes that determine them, such as the metre of a blues or a waltz, but also a haircut or the width of a pair of trousers. One cannot say the same about the people who adopt such styles. In this sense Waits and Young are, as with all artists, immune to schematic categories and may easily slip into a chapter on 'black music'.

Having established this fact and before moving on to take a closer look at Jarmusch's collaboration with these two titanic and now officially recognized mestizo musicians, I would like to add a few observations about the idea of the 'White Negro'.

According to German critic Klaus Walter, a leitmotif of Jarmusch's cinema could be the so-called White Negro, theorized by Norman Mailer in his famous essay of 1957: namely, that the aspiration of white hipsters is to shake off the 'square' tag and to imitate the liberating speech and behavioural patterns of black people.[25] Walter demonstrates persuasively that this 'White Negro' behaviour can be found in many of Jarmusch's characters – from Allie in *Permanent Vacation* to Sonny

Valerio in *Ghost Dog*, and even to the Elvis evoked in *Mystery Train* —
and in much of his film music.[26] One of his objectives is to demonstrate
how these collaborations, which Jarmusch calls upon regularly, are, as
Walter defines, an integral part of a supposed 'master plan of *hipster
casting*', planned by Jarmusch as a calculated promotional objective
for his career.[27] The common denominator of said 'master plan' could
be summed up in the leitmotif of the whites' aspiration to be black: a
'White Negro', be he actor or musician, deliberately hired by Jarmusch
to guarantee him success.

Personally, I would like to overturn the argument. I do not believe
that Jarmusch, purposefully or otherwise, meant to develop an intentional strategy in order to build a body of work through the years in
which the collaboration with particular actors or musicians, commonly
recognized as 'hipsters' (John Lurie, Tom Waits or, more recently, Jack
White and Meg White of The White Stripes, to mention a few of the
more famous) was merely functional to his success. In my opinion,
Jarmusch's regular collaborations with musician-actors/hipsters are
linked to other reasons.

As Jarmusch willingly declares, his greatest source of inspiration is
music itself, his first love, far more so than the cinema: 'When I started

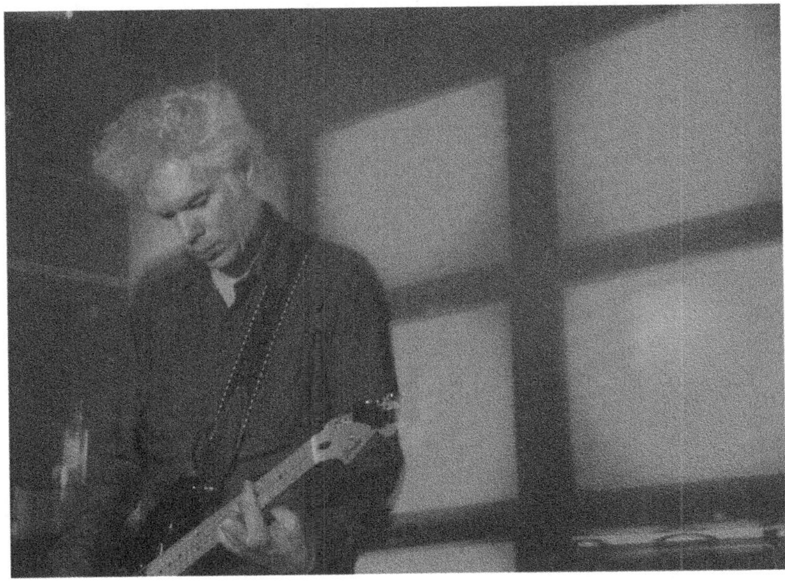

Sqürl live in Berlin,
2013.

out making films, I was a musician', an unequivocal affirmation that confirms his musical affinity.[28]

> I still get the most inspiration from music . . . More of my friends certainly were musicians rather than film people and probably still are. Although, I know a lot of film people now who are close friends, like Aki Kaurismäki, Claire Denis, and Roberto Benigni, but the majority of my friends are still musicians.[29]

At times, there is a palpable, almost reverential aura of respect in Jarmusch's rapport with musicians – often his friends in life – whom he chooses as actors or composers for his films: I am thinking of characters like Neil Young and Tom Waits, along with RZA, Mulatu Astatke, Screamin' Jay Hawkins, among others. Jarmusch's passion for 'black music', rather than be ruled by an artificial 'master plan' divided into complex postmodern calculations based on citations, ellipses and theoretical schemes, is in my opinion based on two fundamental facts: Jarmusch is simply and unequivocally a great lover of music; Jarmusch is slightly less unequivocally, but at least with respect to his principal profession and with a touch of cynicism, a *musicien manqué*.

The habit of always surrounding himself with musicians, in life as in his films, is a point in favour of this last hypothesis. The cinema prevailed over what could quite easily have become a career in music, and not necessarily a successful one. More recently, with a 30-year film career on his shoulders, the *musicien manqué* picked up the guitar again and went back to making music actively. Evidently, notwithstanding his success as a film director, the Del-Byzanteens' ex-keyboard player, born in 1953, realized that for years he had lived minus an instrument fundamental to the expression of his art and creativity. This is a healthy return to a passion that Jarmusch never really turned his back on. On the contrary, he continued to feed it throughout the years, even if not always in an actively hands-on way.

Waits

Jarmusch's personal music contribution to the three films I would like to focus on now, *Down By Law, Night On Earth* and *Dead Man*, is 'limited' to the involvement of two music legends, Tom Waits and Neil Young.

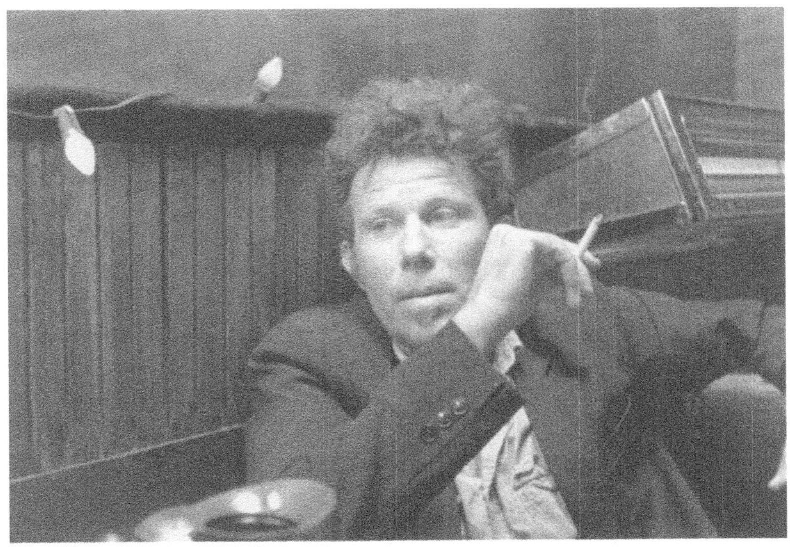

According to Jay S. Jacobs, Jarmusch's collaboration with Tom Waits began in the 1980s with *Down By Law* after they met at a New York party in honour of Jean-Michel Basquiat.[30] In *Down By Law*, the Californian songwriter is present in two roles: as an actor playing the part of taciturn DJ Zack, stage name Lee Baby Simms, and as the composer of the opening and closing songs, 'Jockey Full of Bourbon' and 'Tango Till They're Sore', both released on the album *Rain Dogs* (1985).

The previous record, *Swordfishtrombones* (1983), saw the end of the 'piano-bar arrangements' so typical of Waits's earliest work, and it was also the first to be independently produced together with his wife, Kathleen Brennan, and distributed by Chris Blackwell's Island Records.[31] The arrangements based on percussions and instruments with atypical timbres, somewhere between noise and music, and the surreal atmosphere described in the lyrics, like the magnificent and cynical jazzed spoken word of 'Frank's Wild Years', astounded the critics who unanimously elected *Swordfishtrombones* as a true watershed in Waits's career. Two years later, *Rain Dogs* continued the same experimental and innovative course.

The unmistakable 'Jockey Full of Bourbon' that literally opens *Down By Law* feeds on a very southern, almost Cuban, sound, thanks mainly to the hot and versatile guitar of Marc Ribot, here enjoying his first collaboration with Waits.[32] Jarmusch picks up on this aspect of the song immediately and plays it before the opening credits over the suggestive tracking shots of the streets of New Orleans and Louisiana's flooded bayous, giving precious insights into the environment and general atmosphere of the story. Almost like sharp rhythmic whiplashes, the editing cuts of this sequence rock to the beat of the song and its limpid tones. The music stops the moment the tracking shots reach their destination: the two bedrooms of Jack, the luckless pimp played by John Lurie and of Zack, the withdrawn DJ played by Tom Waits, where their respective bedmates, Bobbie (Billie Neal) and Laurette (Ellen Barkin), lie on their sides apparently asleep. It is the simple action of the two girls opening their eyes that literally switches the song back on again.

This entire sequence is a good example of alternate editing; it moves with symmetric linearity. The images and sounds are linked by a minimized harmony made up of a few gestures, recurring set-ups and tracking shots. Waits's almost whispered voice adds a sweet roughness, and stresses the lyrics at times surreally, as in the chorus in which he tells a little bird to fly home because its house, where its children are, is on fire. At other times he almost echoes the images before they appear on the screen: he sings about himself being out in the street, full of bourbon and unable to stand up, just like the way the character Zack/Waits sits disconsolate and drunk on the street corner, amid his few possessions, after the furious quarrel with his girlfriend Laurette, who has just thrown his things out the window. In the same strophe Waits talks of a probably jammed two-dollar pistol that won't shoot: in perfect sync with the lyrics, Bobbie the young hooker, while lying in Jack's bed, takes the pistol and aims it almost playfully at his back without pulling the trigger.

'Tango Till They're Sore' is the second piece by Waits played in *Down By Law*. Jarmusch uses it during the end credits, in symmetrical balance with the opening of 'Jockey Full of Bourbon'. The piece, a dissonant ballad played on the piano and accompanied by the trombone, has a more folk music quality to it than the first one and adapts well to the all-'Italian' ending of the film, summed up in the catchy morning dance scene played by Roberto Benigni and Nicoletta Braschi. Victims of love at first sight, the two diminutive immigrants dance glued one to the other, exaggeratedly swinging hips and pelvis to the tune of 'It's Raining', the classic song by New Orleans soul queen Irma Thomas. Lurie and Waits, co-stars and composers respectively of the film's music and songs, are sitting at the table amused and slightly incredulous by the performance of the two Italians, who had to come all the way to Louisiana's bayous to meet and

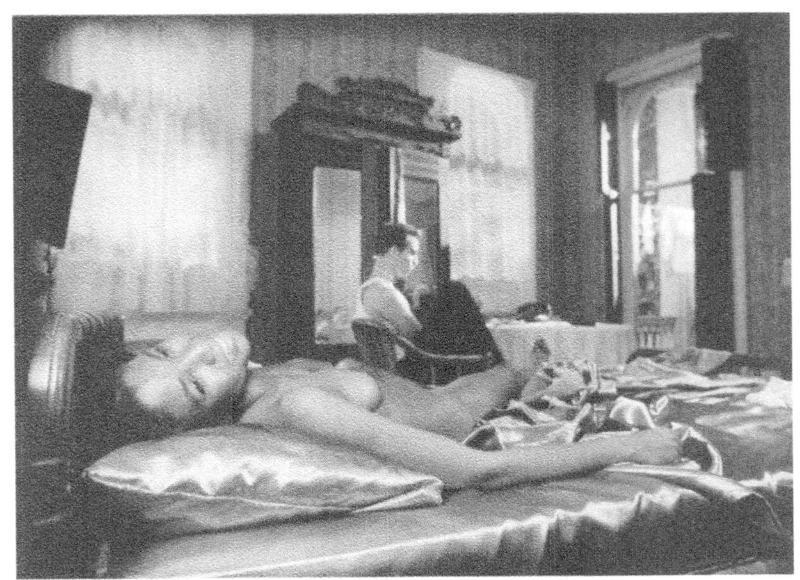

Bobbie,
Down By Law.

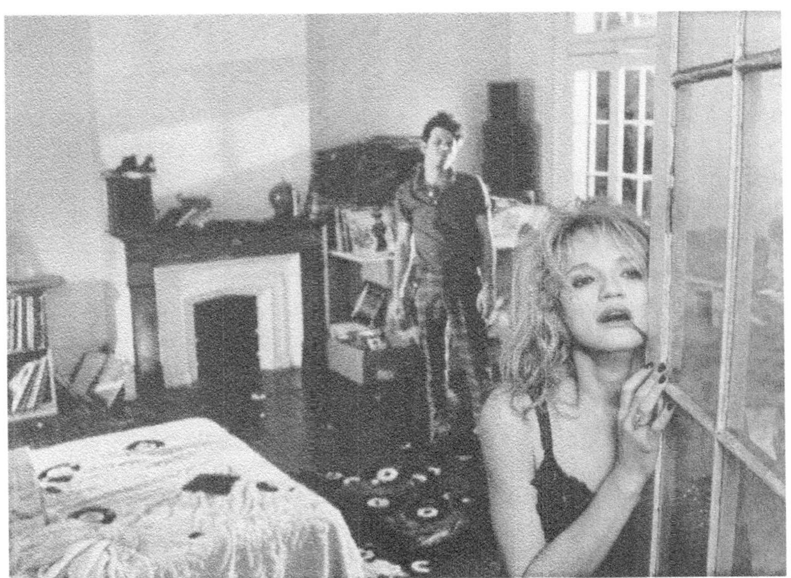

Laurette, *Down
By Law.*

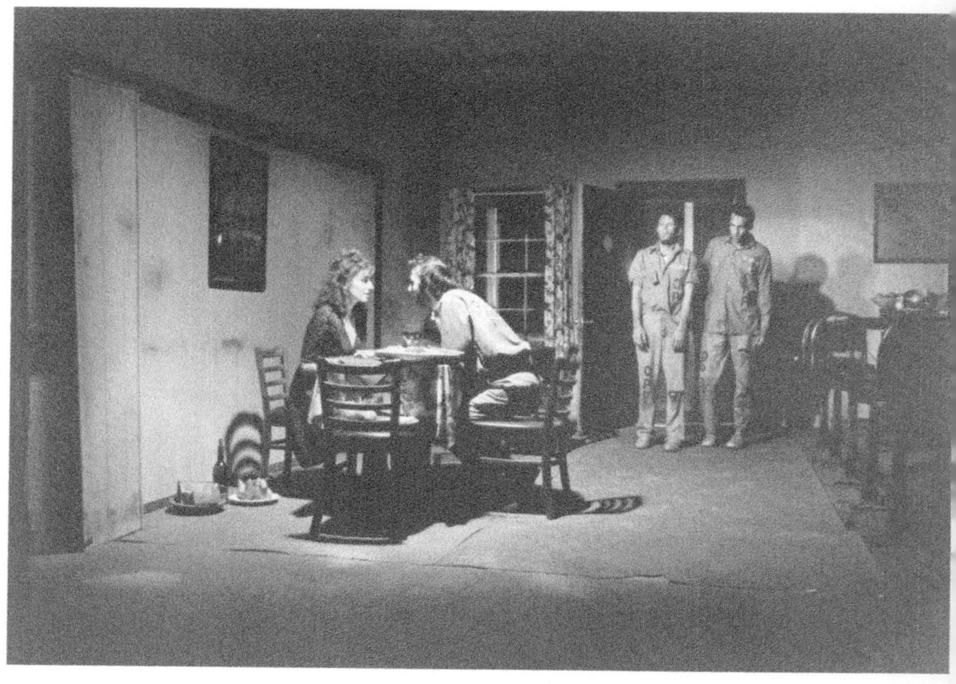

never leave each other again. Set between Waits's opening and closing songs, John Lurie's scintillating instrumental score adds another southern and liquid dimension.

Love at first sight: Bob and Nicoletta, *Down By Law*.

Most of the compositions for Waits's next collaboration with Jarmusch, *Night On Earth*, are instrumental. The five episodes in which space and time play a central role are set in five taxis in five different cities – Los Angeles, New York, Paris, Rome, Helsinki – and run from evening to dawn. The episodes occur simultaneously with Jarmusch inserting an interval, a quasi 'title', between one and the other: a shot of five linear clocks on a wall showing the respective time of each of the five cities. The camera zooming in to a particular clock tells us where the next episode takes place.

Waits's original soundtrack also plays on the idea of time passing and respects the exact beat of each second, while trying to mimic the ticking of the clock's hands. The moment in time is the same, but the location changes. In accordance with this idea, both static and dynamic, Waits's compositions, thanks to the slightly different arrangements, are

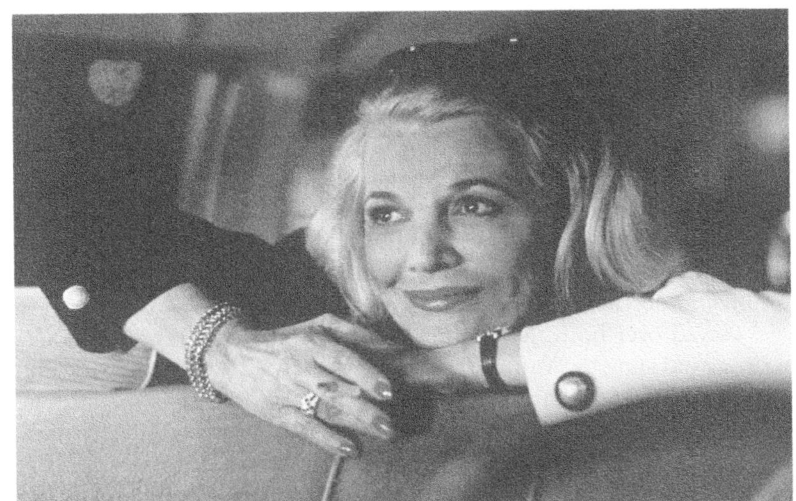

'Los Angeles
Mood': Gena
Rowlands, *Night
On Earth*.

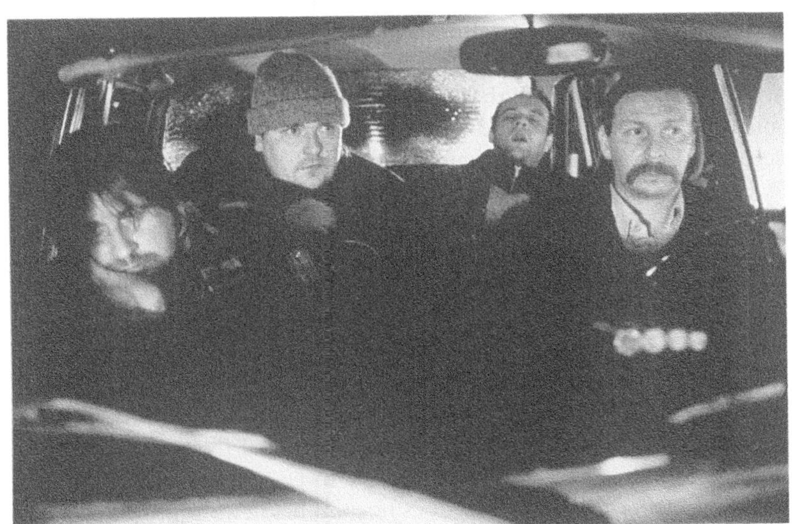

'Helsinki Mood':
Matti Pellonpää
(driver), *Night
On Earth*.

mostly variations on a constant melody and at times harmonize with the starring city. For example, in 'New York Mood' the theme is entrusted to the metallic and urban sound of a trombone, and in 'Los Angeles Mood' to the upfront sound of a biting electric guitar, whereas in 'Helsinki Mood' the theme, played instead on a harmonium, overlaps the sounds produced by the tubular bells, be they drummed or blown as a wind instrument, that bring to mind a cold, slightly desolate Nordic landscape. If on one hand Waits attempts to 'mimic' time thanks to the precise rhythmic beat, on the other he definitely tries to pin down characteristic timbres to describe the locations without relying on easy stereotypes.

Played over both the opening and closing credits, the two songs written and sung by Waits, 'Back in the Good Old World (Gypsy)' and 'Good Old World (Waltz)', are once again variations on a theme. The first version is characterized by an elaborate and energetic rhythmic arrangement, with typically 'Waitsian' timbres and percussions that evoke a weird nocturnal and surreal atmosphere. The second version can already be heard before the start of the end credits, and enriches the last sequence of the bitter Finnish episode: as day breaks, Aki, the taxi's last customer, dazed by alcohol, is left alone sitting on the freezing snowbound sidewalk with his head bowed. The song in this case is much slower and more melancholy: the accordion and the harmonium seem almost to whine with their vaguely off-key accompaniment behind Waits's driving and melodic voice. As a whole the compositions for *Night On Earth* thus try to assonate with the images, while keeping the composer's personality intact, thanks especially to the particular timbres and to his unmistakable voice.

Finally, with regard to voice, I need to mention *Mystery Train* in which Waits is present by his 'absence' in the role of the invisible nocturnal radio DJ, an incorporeal character made up exclusively of 'sound'. DJ/Waits announces Roy Orbison's 'Domino' and Elvis Presley's 'Blue Moon' at exactly 2.17 a.m. at various moments of the film, helping the audience realize the simultaneity of the three episodes. The narrative function of Waits's voice thus goes beyond being a simple 'refrain', or timbric/stylistic trick, but is one of the instruments that allows the spectator to unravel the 'temporal tangle' wound by Jarmusch. Thanks to the radio, Waits's voice is virtually everywhere simultaneously, impossible not to hear, and is one of the invisible keys there to help us understand what is binding the events of the film together.

Young

The last important protagonist of this chapter is the 'mestizo' Neil Young, writer and executor of the soundtrack to the powerful and poetic anti-western *Dead Man*. Jarmusch admits quite adamantly to having always been an admirer of the Canadian rocker, as shown in the booklet of the film's soundtrack CD, described as 'music from and inspired by the motion picture and performed by Neil Young', a clear reference to his way of working. With a method similar to that of pianists during the silent era, Young improvised on the guitar to a first raw cut of two and a half hours that he insisted on watching three times without interruption over the course of two consecutive days. As Jarmusch recalls: 'There was some talk with him having a rhythm section, bass and drums, but he said to me "You know, I don't need that because the rhythm of the film *is* a rhythm section and I will just add a melody to it."'[33] A good part of these improvisations remained in the definitive edit at the exact point Young first played them, creating a perfect example of synthesis and union between sound and vision. Jarmusch described the encounter with Young as almost inevitable:

> I was listening constantly to Neil and Crazy Horse while writing the script for *Dead Man* . . . Crazy Horse even performed in Sedona, Arizona, during our shooting period and a large number of our crew attended the concert. From the very start of the project there were hopes of Neil Young performing music for the film, but I was never very confident that this would actually happen. When Neil finally saw an early cut of *Dead Man* and then agreed to score the film, I was ecstatic . . . Neil eventually played pump organ, detuned piano, and acoustic guitar, but the largest percentage of the music is from electric guitar.

A significant characteristic that unites Young's music and the complex atmosphere of the film is related to the key category of *dilation*, both spatial and temporal. Starting briefly from a more general discourse, it is clear that in cinema the strategies of dilation can differ depending on the director and the historic context: sometimes by privileging *space*, as in the case of landscape expansion – in John Ford westerns, for example – or the expansion of space itself, thanks to movement and travel, as in Wim Wenders's road movies; sometimes by privileging *time*, as in the consistent profound work of Russian director Andrei Tarkovsky, who apropos of the expansion of time in relation to the cinema wrote:

> Just as life, constantly moving and changing, allows everyone to interpret and feel each separate moment in his own way, so too a real picture, faithfully recording on film the time which flows on beyond the edges of the frame, lives within time if time lives within it; this two-way process is a determining factor of cinema.[34]

Time, in all its expansion and dilation, must thus 'live' in film, as it does in life beyond the screen.

Going now from the general to the particular, the long opening sequence in *Dead Man* – William Blake's train trip west – expresses perfectly the idea of spatial dilation that is shown in the character's physical movement, as it should in a road movie. However, the trip of naive, disorientated Blake is without doubt also one of time, seeming to run backwards at great speed: the more he goes west, leaving behind 'civilized' Cleveland, the passengers become increasingly rougher, ending with wild, bearded hunters who have no qualms about shooting buffalo from the moving train.[35]

The length of the sequence that acts as a prologue to the opening credits is about eight minutes, of which only the last two minutes 54 seconds are enriched with words: the dialogue between the scary engineer (Crispin Glover) and Blake. The first five minutes of the film, vital to determining its general atmosphere, are almost silent. Naturally, this does not mean there are no other sounds. The music, the hypnotic timbre of Neil Young's electric guitar, was inserted by Jarmusch over certain images at precise moments: none over the numerous close-ups of Blake sitting on the train, and only sporadically over the engineer's sometimes frightening comments and the bookkeeper's cautious responses during the last part of the sequence. The shots in which the music returns regularly are the 'link' images that show the connecting rods and the wheels of the smoking steam locomotive hurtling along the tracks: shots that *represent movement* and, with it, spatial dilation. Young's guitar improvisations, abandoning a clear melody and instead making use of a more abstract musical language, enrich and highlight the recurring brief rhythmic sequences more directly linked to movement. Jarmusch wants to accentuate the idea of 'departure', both in space and in time, and to do so uses music, that precious ally.

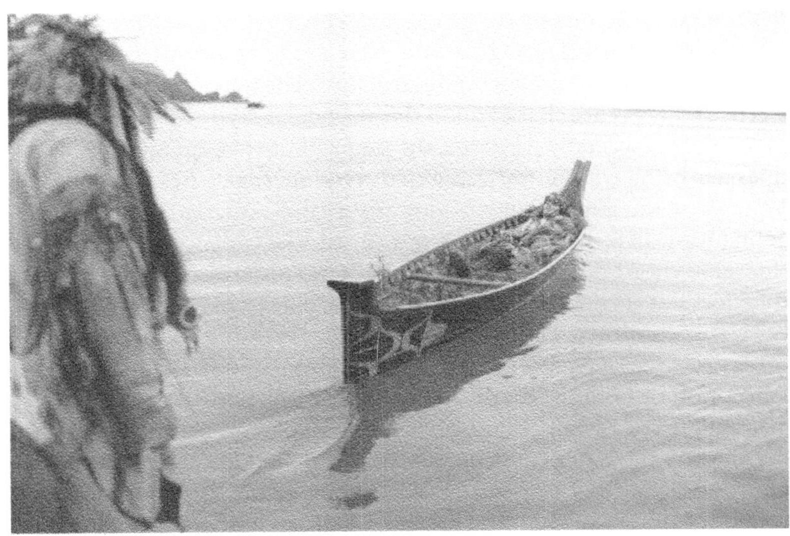

During the course of the film, Young allows himself instead to be transported by numerous melodic variations on a vaguely country theme, irregular from a rhythmic point of view but recurring nonetheless; this too, after all, is a form of dilation.

But it is in the last sequence, solemn in its simplicity, that an ulterior and unmistakable affirmation of this strategy is easily recognizable. A fatally wounded Blake has reached the end of his life's journey. His travel companion Nobody places him in the canoe already prepared with cedar branches for the final challenge with the open sea, the dilated location par excellence where water and air meet, as the train fireman revealed to Blake in his cryptic message at the beginning of the film:

> And doesn't this remind you of when you were in the boat? And then later that night, you were lying, looking up at the ceiling, and the water in your head . . . was not dissimilar from the landscape, and you think to yourself, 'Why is it that the landscape . . . is moving, but . . . the boat is still?'

In the last sequence, where water and air are about to touch, in what way does Young's music help Jarmusch to dilate space further, and with it also time, as with the smoky locomotive in the opening sequence?

The answer comes to us in a very clear way: through the recovery of a rhythm's cadence. During the film, Neil Young's score often renounces a regular and harmonic rhythmic structure. The hypnotic quality of his electric guitar is also based upon this particular stylistic choice. Unlike many films, especially westerns, the moment of the protagonist's death does not bring with it any effect of resolution. Blake dies to a chord of Young's acidic guitar, but it is not an isolated, solemn closing chord. While we watch the canoe drift out to sea, the cadenced repetition of the same chord initiates a regular rhythmic progression: it is a chord that does not close, does not present an end, but opens a new cycle, a new beat, a new journey. This way, thanks to the rhythmic pulse, the spectator is given the opportunity to project in advance and expand their own perception of both the music and the scene.

Symmetrically, the film opens with a departure and closes with a departure – the latter being qualitatively different but by no means less linked to the idea of movement and dilation – that seems thus to reach its highest and most definitive level: it is a dilation beyond the space and the time of life itself. The Native American concept of the circularity of existence, as embodied by Nobody and experimented by the young bookkeeper of Cleveland, who by the end of the film has adopted the look both physically and mentally of a Native American and prepared himself for the journey 'beyond the mirror', is not so far from that of the real William Blake, of the real-life poet. In a 1996 interview, Jarmusch paraphrased the poet when he quoted fitting words to end this reflection: 'Once old William Blake was asked what he thought of death: he said that, for him, it was like getting up and going into another room.'[36]

Year of the Horse

Jarmusch's closeness to Young's music is such that, following *Dead Man*, he shot his one and only 'rockumentary' by express wish of the portrayed musician himself.[37] The Canadian songwriter and his music thus became the storyline of Jarmusch's new work: *Year of the Horse*. The film began without a precise story in mind, the original idea being simply to shoot something and see what came out.[38] It documents Neil Young's *Broken Arrow* European tour performed with his band Crazy Horse in 1996, punctuating the concert images – which were 'proudly' filmed in Super 8, 16mm and video Hi8[39] – with stock footage from 1976 and 1986.

The low-tech quality of the filming tries to capture the rough and passionate spirit of the music, and succeeds in part. However, Jarmusch does not appear to be at ease in much of the film, almost as though Young's personality were too overbearing. Notwithstanding the frequent declarations of mutual respect and esteem, both before and during the shoot, one cannot help sensing a certain discomfort in Jarmusch the director, or rather the documentarian, with respect to the legendary Neil Young, who was clearly on top of things. As Young said:

> The last thing you want to do is ruin what it is that you're filming, and I think that Jim understands that the consciousness of the camera is adverse to the Muse, and is contrary to the goal. So we don't want to be thinking we're making a movie, and they don't want to make a movie of us thinking we are being filmed. Nobody wants that . . . So it's really important that it'd be that way: with the long lenses, sneaking in there, zooming in there, through the atmosphere, with the low grade film, breaking up in front of your eyes, listening to a distorted sound, seeing a

Jim Jarmusch and Neil Young, 1997.

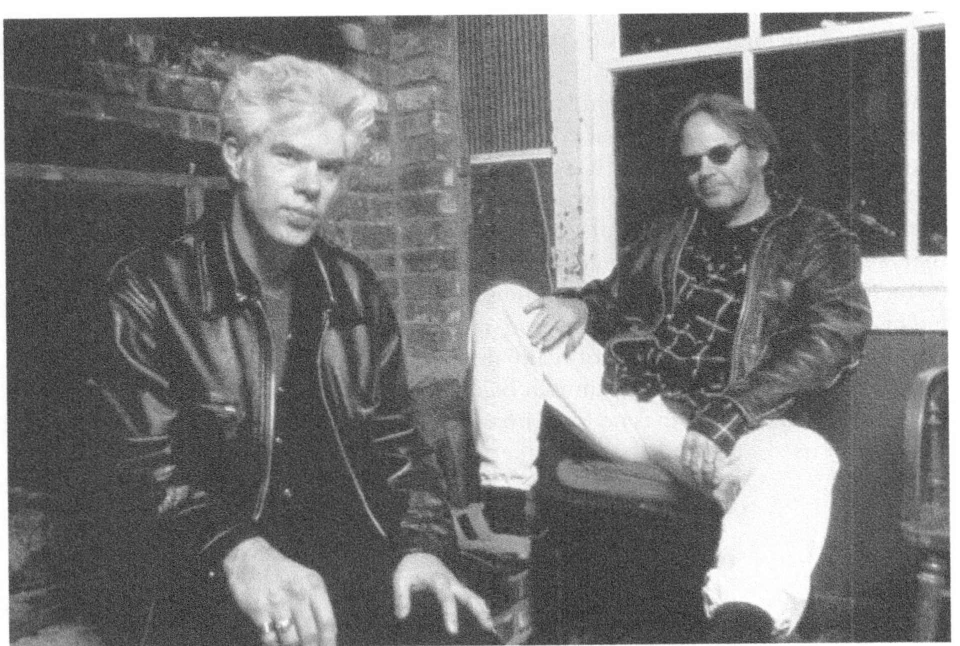

distorted picture . . . So I think he did an excellent job of capturing us without disturbing us. Much like a nature film.[40]

The songs played live – only eight in a film of 106 minutes – on average last from eight to thirteen minutes and, even if alleviated by images both from stock footage and from what was filmed during the tour, can be considered a little exhausting, even for the most dedicated fan. The reason is that Jarmusch allows the music to get the better of him, choosing pieces that have seemingly endless solos. Trying to capture the live event on screen is a difficult undertaking, practically impossible, as defined in a cynical but spot-on way by Frank 'Poncho' Sampedro, the Crazy Horse guitarist who replaced Danny Whitten, who died of a heroin overdose in 1972: 'That's not gonna capture anything. No matter what he asks, he'll never get it all.' Even though the stock footage is well chosen and amusing, and the interviews with the band members and collaborators, including Neil Young's father, are edited in a rapid and charming way, Sampedro turns out to be right.[41] However, the filmmaker must be praised for also having included the not too subtle criticism in the final cut.

One of the high moments of the film is an exhilarating exchange between Jarmusch and Young while travelling on the tour bus. Jarmusch reads some of the more graphically brutal passages from the Old Testament, and explains to Neil Young that God is trying to exterminate the human race because it has turned out to be nothing more than a major 'fuck up'. After listening to a particularly fierce passage from Ezekiel, Young comments: 'I planted a bunch of trees and I thought they were gonna be one way and they turned out not the way I wanted them, so I chopped them all down!' Jarmusch promptly responds, laughing his head off: 'Who do you think you are? God?!'

In this insert, which does not really match the rest of the film, for once you do not pick up on Jarmusch being in awe of Young and the scene works. The musician is no longer on the invisible throne to which Jarmusch raised him, and the filmmaker resumes the role he is good at: directing.

words

Voices:
Masatoshi Nagase

1

Jim Jarmusch has often said in interviews that from his first trips to Japan he would bring back home Japanese movies in the original version.[1] He watched them with no subtitles without making sense of a single word of the dialogue but still understanding perfectly the characters' feelings.

Interviewed by Jonathan Rosenbaum in 1994, Jarmusch said: 'The language of acting is not primarily a spoken language. You can read how people feel or where they're at emotionally, without knowing the language they speak. My first experience was directing Japanese actors for *Mystery Train*.'

I know the script had been translated and obviously there was an interpreter on set, but can you tell me more about how it worked in practice? How did this non-verbal communication function during shooting?

After arriving in Memphis the rehearsal lasted about a week. There was of course a script. However, throughout the entire rehearsal, we were all trying to get the best out of each scene, each cut, developing each situation with our own ideas, elaborating ideas, not sticking to the script itself. It really was some rehearsal. And the film was, after all, focused mainly on music.

Could you say that music literally helped in communication?

In the beginning, when I participated in the audition with Jim Jarmusch,
I had no clue what sort of film *Mystery Train* was. Back then, I was
hanging out a lot with rockabilly friends in private and I often wore
a pair of rubber-sole shoes. I showed up at the audition in those shoes.
Jarmusch was apparently surprised by seeing anyone in Japan wearing
such shoes at the time. I told him that there were tons of guys out there
in Japan wearing them.

Well, shoes definitely play a big role in the whole rock 'n' roll mythology.
'Blue Suede Shoes' is the first example that comes to my mind. So your
shoes walked you right to Memphis.

Well, just shortly before the audition, I lost a very close friend who was
the vocalist of a rockabilly band. Throughout the entire shooting in
Memphis, I never told Jarmusch a word about it. Given the fact that my
friend was a rockabilly musician, Memphis was a sacred place for him.

I'm sorry. So there was a very deep connection being in Memphis.

Yes, absolutely. A day before I left for Japan after shooting was over,
I really didn't feel like going home, in fact, I didn't want to go back
and was just hanging out by the swimming pool in the courtyard of the
hotel all alone. Then, almost all of the crew came down to the courtyard for some personal farewells, wished me good luck, cheering me
up. At the very last, Jarmusch himself came down and we talked alone.
For the first time, I told him about my rockabilly friend. I also told him
that together with my friend we used to talk about his films like *Stranger
Than Paradise* and *Down By Law*. We talked about our dreams and my
wish was that hopefully one day I would act in such films. It was really
a dream back then. I also told him that I believed my friend's sprit
guided me to meet Jarmusch. And he said, 'Your friend must have
been with you here in Memphis.'

I know that Jarmusch flew to Japan to cast Jun's role. What did he ask
you to do in the audition?

At the first call, we talked through an interpreter, but not about
movies at all. We talked for maybe one hour mostly about the music
we liked. And that was all. I really thought that I hadn't got the part.
Surprisingly, there was a second call, which took place in a hotel

room. There, I was given a situation and was asked to do some improvisation. Something like 'just move around'. I don't recall every detail now. One thing I remember is that I was just touching a coffee spoon the whole time, as if trying to bend it with my psychic ability! And then the audition was over. They said 'Okay!' I think the audition ended in laughter and smiles.

So you were really into music before getting involved in the film.

At the time of the film, I had lots of rockabilly friends and liked to listen to rockabilly music. Even though originally, my favourite has always been punk music. Jarmusch introduced me to Iggy Pop in person!

How was it working with Screamin' Jay Hawkins?

I just loved him. Of course I knew the song 'I Put a Spell on You' before I met him. I have released two albums myself. In the first song on the first album, Screamin' Jay recorded a back-up chorus for me. For the second album, Iggy Pop and Joe Strummer, each of them wrote a song for me. I am very thankful to Jim for that.

So Mystery Train really was a turning point for you.

Yes, absolutely. Basically, I have always been a big fan of music rather than a cinema freak. During the shooting, Jarmusch spent a whole day explaining about Memphis as the sacred place for music as well as for music history. The roots of music itself, the Southern music, the south as the centre of music . . .

For his more recent film The Limits of Control Jarmusch has collaborated with the Japanese noise band Boris. Are you into noise music – such as Boris or Keiji Haino – too?

Most of my friends are musicians rather than actors. Basically, I like music in general and I listen to all kinds of genres.

2

Music always plays a crucial role in Jarmusch's films and is as beautifully eclectic as his taste. Do you think music and cinema are related to each other and if yes in which ways?

I like films that have a rhythm just as if you were listening to music. This is a style of directing that is exactly represented by Jarmusch's films. I like films in which I can feel music, even if you can't hear any sound. In some films you can actually feel the music in silence.

In the book I wrote a chapter about silence and, for example, the composer Toru Takemitsu used silence in a very interesting way. What is silence for you, is it an important part of your work as an actor?

Well, I met Mr Takemitsu together with Jim Jarmusch! Generally, as an actor, I am not crazy about films that overflow with explanatory dialogue used only to illustrate a scene. I feel that's rather for radio dramas or TV series. How can I say this? I do believe in films which reflect emotions without a dialogue. For example, conveying emotions just by shooting a tree or an empty field, not necessarily by filming a character as a person with expression. As an actor, I believe in building a character before the shooting and delivering emotions from any angle during the shooting. What I like, for example, is when you can feel the character is sad just by a back shot rather than showing a close-up of his sad face full of tears. I think it is an actor's work to reflect and express the meaning between the lines into a film. This is my philosophy.

3

Jarmusch, it seems to me, criticizes the usual functions of verbal language. He does so by often using silence or an 'overdose' of dialogue. This, I argue, opens up broader ways of communication for the audiences, encouraging them to be more active and to use their own imagination. What do you think about this?

I see your point. It could be possible. Jun was characterized as a very quiet person in the script. I can think of two things. First, Mitsuko is talkative and my character Jun is almost mute. So this contrast is interesting and enjoyable for the audience. Second, presenting such different people as a couple, such an opposite attraction, is a funny side of the film to the audience. I feel that the two of them – Jun and Mitsuko – make one complete person. But I don't want to be misunderstood: it is not because of a negligence in the direction that Jun is such a silent character. There are plenty of clues, hints of Jun's unsaid character everywhere in the movie for the audience to understand. For example, he only takes photos of so-called irrelevant things.

Right, and Mitsuko complains about it. You are also a photographer in real life. What is your approach to photography?

Apart from when I'm shooting portraits, I would rather consider myself as a 'Jun' type of photographer. I hardly take touristic photos. I like to take photos of things which the majority would overlook, or not even notice.

In *Mystery Train* the 'sound of words' plays a huge role for the non-Japanese-speaking audience. Jarmusch preferred to use subtitles as he is very critical of dubbing an actor's voice. What do you think of dubbing in general? Have you had personal experiences in dubbing?

As an actor, I obviously prefer subtitles and to be able to hear an actor's real voice since the voice is part of acting, part of art. I do also understand there are countries where films in the original version with subtitles are not well received by audiences. I have never done any voiceovers for any actors.

Is there anything else you would like to add about Jarmusch, or about something else?

After *Mystery Train*, I have had opportunities to work in international productions, in different countries and languages. And I learned from Jim Jarmusch that creating a film has no boundary of language. Jarmusch is the one who taught me that we have a mutual language called Film. Even after all these years, I adore and respect him from the bottom of my heart. Not only for being an exceptionally great director – he is truly a great person. I would be most grateful if I could be with him on set again. But even without a professional relationship between director and actor, I really respect him as a wonderful human being with whom I would like to stay in touch as a friend for ever.

Tokyo, April 2013
Translated by Yoko Kim Kondo and Miya Yoshida

5 The Battle Against Verbocentrism

'Any sound is music already . . . sometimes I just make up sounds
and don't know what they mean . . . Then, I play the sounds back
and listen to them like a foreign language, and I say: "If this *was*
a foreign language, how would I decipher it?" And pretty soon,
I realize certain words are starting to form. *What* are they saying?'
Tom Waits, interview with George Varga, *San Diego Union Tribune*
(3 October 2004)

The spoken word is generally interpreted based on the meaning it con-
veys. One rarely reflects on the word's indispensable carrier structure,
its simple acoustic 'wrapping' or linguistic 'signifier'. A mix of sounds,
or rather a collection of impalpable, invisible 360-degree vibrations,
bears the weight of every concept, name and definition in all imaginable languages: a highly demanding task. And yet in the cinema, as in real
life, the *sound* of words as a rule is less in evidence compared to their
content. Nevertheless, having said this, one must not think that words
are not given due attention in the cinema: on the contrary, if we imagine a hypothetical hierarchy within the film's layers of sound then the
word, and with it the voice, rules supreme. This idea is clarified by
Michel Chion, a key author on the topic of cinematographic sound:

In stating that sound in the cinema is primarily *vococentric*,
I mean that it almost always privileges the voice, highlighting
and setting the latter off from other sounds . . . And in voice
recording what is sought is not so much acoustical fidelity to
original timbre, as the guarantee of effortless intelligibility of

the words spoken. Thus what we mean by *vococentrism* is almost always *verbocentrism*.[1]

Words are at the centre of communication in cinema because man – also beyond the confines of the screen – has a marked tendency towards verbocentrism.

In his audiovisual analysis, Michel Chion has pinpointed different 'types of words' or rather three 'modes of speech in film': theatrical speech, textual speech and emanation speech.[2] The first two are the more frequent, the third, on which I would like to concentrate, is the more cinematographic, but strangely the rarest.

The theatrical speech is the perfectly intelligible verbal expression spoken by the actor, the line of dialogue in other words, and more often than not in sync with the image. The textual speech, a definition hinting of some form of literary analogy, is that spoken by an off-camera voice. It often functions as a narrator who comments upon or even acts as an external guide describing what is taking place on screen. A classic and paradoxical case of textual speech is Billy Wilder's *Sunset Boulevard* (1950). At the beginning of the film, the body of Joe Gillis, the story's leading character played by William Holden, is shown floating face down in the swimming pool at the luxurious and bizarre mansion of ex-silent movie star Norma Desmond (Gloria Swanson). It is the off-camera voice – or textual speech – of Gillis, or rather the voice of a dead man, who tells us in a long flashback how he came to such an awful end.

The third mode is emanation speech. Chion defines it as a word whose function within the film's general economy is minimized and that 'generally continues to go unnoticed, inasmuch as it is anti-literary and anti-theatrical'.[3] But in what way 'emanation'? This type of word does not necessarily trigger the action, or explain/comment on the events shown to the spectator, just as it might not be perfectly intelligible or audible. It is a word that 'emanates' from the character, that makes up part of his features, in a way similar, for example, to his physical mien, but is not strictly functional to the story's progress or the film's actions. While losing its central role, the word thus finds itself on the same level as the film's other sound layers – music and noise – that at times can even overwhelm it.

In this sense, a fitting example of emanation speech is contained in the epilogue of *Last Tango in Paris* (1972), the Bernardo Bertolucci

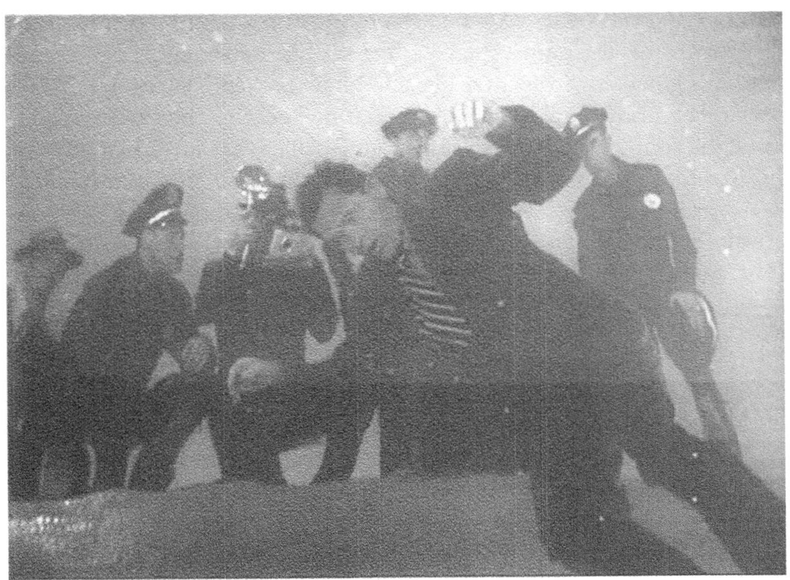

classic. The impetuous and anti-conventional sexual relationship between the two main characters is based on their refusal to reveal *the word* that apparently contains the identity of a person: the name. During the final sequence at the exact moment when the young and fearful Jeanne (Maria Schneider) finally reveals her name to her aggressive anonymous lover, Paul (Marlon Brando), there is a gunshot, its explosive sound drowning out her voice. Paul does not hear the name, which evaporates into thin air. In a state of total confusion and still holding the gun with which she fatally wounded Paul, Jeanne mumbles a few lines until her words are gradually overwhelmed by the music of Gato Barbieri.

The incomprehensibility of dialogue is a rarely violated cinematographic taboo, and yet the young Jarmusch did not hesitate to do it in his first film, *Permanent Vacation*. In the sequence of Allie waking up on the roof of a downtown building, with the New York skyline framed between the Empire State Building and the Chrysler Building behind him, the words the youth mutters to himself are totally indecipherable. The thought that there might have been a banal technical problem behind this apparent 'oversight' is quite plausible, but it is then disproved after about a minute by the first of two perfectly audible lines that Allie 'shoots' in the face of the spectator: 'This gun is my legislative gun.'

After saying this, Allie retreats for a moment back into that mumbled territory of his reasoning, then rectifies the line for the spectator's benefit: 'This gun is my legislative branch! Now that's it.' Therefore, Allie's previous and incomprehensible emanation speech is not an oversight, quite the contrary: it is a conscious sound device that Jarmusch successfully used in an attempt to narrow the gap between film and real life.

Apropos of this, I think it appropriate to quote Tilda Swinton, co-star in *Broken Flowers*, the *Limits of Control* and the 'crypto-vampire love story'[4] *Only Lovers Left Alive* – on the subject of sound, and the sound of words in particular, when we talked in Berlin in 2005:

> I think there is an idea in a kind of theatre related cinema, drama related narrative cinema, which is that people – and this comes very often from the writing and very often from the direction and also from the acting – (the idea that people) know *exactly* what they want to say, they absolutely have the words to express what they want to say – right here and now! – and they say it to each other very clearly and articulately and they don't stop until they have said everything they want to say. And then the other person is absolutely listening in a fully dilated sense and gets it and gives the perfect answer. And mind me, that's just not quite the way the cookie crumbles and that's not what life is like! So much more interesting to me as an audience member is to see a face on a screen that's searching for the words, that's searching for the way to reach articulacy and to see doubt in a face and to see the conflict between thought and some kind of articulation.[5]

The sequence of Allie on the roof is proof of how linguistic rarefaction, and violating the taboo of dialogue intelligibility, paradoxically brings film closer to real life, rather than move away from it, demonstrating the fact that human communication is capable of travelling on ample and varied planes, like that of emanation speech.

Chion quotes various directors – Tati, Fellini, Tarkovsky, Ophüls – who have used techniques of word relativization. I would like to add Jim Jarmusch to the list, who is a particular admirer of the strategies that the French theorist calls 'rarefaction', 'proliferation' and 'multilingualism'. It is worth demonstrating this now through a few examples, but considering that the use of foreign languages in Jarmusch's cinema is so frequent and rich with nuances it deserves to be given its own space in the next section.

The *rarefaction* of the word's presence is a constant in all Jarmusch's films, from the mute wanderings of Allie (Chris Parker) in *Permanent Vacation* to the more recent taciturn nameless Lone Man (Isaach De Bankolé) in *The Limits of Control*. The character of Zack/Lee Baby Simms (Tom Waits) in *Down By Law* is also emblematic: a radio DJ whose words have to be literally dug out of his mouth. Even William Blake (Johnny Depp) in *Dead Man* is not particularly loquacious, due possibly to suffering a fatal wound, while the depression of Adam (Tom Hiddleston) in *Only Lovers Left Alive* leads him to express himself through music rather than words.

Certain exceptions confirm the rule. In the first place and again using Chion's terminology, the construction of the dialogue in *Ghost Dog* approaches the more traditional one, being prevalently based on textual speech. Nevertheless, it is a significant and not merely anecdotal fact that the film's central character, the killer Ghost Dog (Forest Whitaker), lives in isolation on the roof of a building, communicating with the outside world thanks almost exclusively to homing pigeons, and speaking as little as possible. In *Broken Flowers* the dialogue is in a certain sense also more traditional, but the long silences of Don Johnston (Bill Murray), the melancholic lead character in search of a nameless son, contrast sharply with this apparently more canonical approach.

By *proliferation* Chion means the furthest extremity to rarefaction. The excess of words coincides with the annulment of the word itself and, in extreme cases, of communication in general. In this case too, various examples confirm Jarmusch's interest in the relativization of the word.

In *Dead Man*, long-winded killer Conway Twill (Michael Wincott) – one of the three gunmen hired by the gruff Dickinson (Robert Mitchum) to avenge the death of his son – will end up losing the most precious gift of all due to his uncontrollable loquacity: the more frightening of the three killers, the silent Cole Wilson (Lance Henriksen), fed up with his colleague's unstoppable flood of words, shuts him up with a single, sharp gunshot, off camera on top of that.

In *Mystery Train*, there are two very evident examples of linguistic proliferation. The first is embodied in the guide, played by the lively Jodie Markell, who accompanies the two Japanese 'pilgrims' Jun and Mitsuko through Sun Studios. She speaks in such an agitated, speedy and garru-lous way, and without taking breath, that the effort of describing the musical actions in the historical recording studios turns out to be quite futile. At the end of the visit a visibly exhausted Mitsuko just manages to utter: 'She talks so fast, I'm all worn out.' Jun remains silent, but is no less dazed than his companion. Again, in *Mystery Train* the same principle of communication annulment due to verbal overdose is expressed by Dee Dee (Elizabeth Bracco), the ex-lover of Johnny (Joe Strummer), as well as one-night roommate of Italian newly widowed Luisa (Nicoletta Braschi). Dee Dee, freshly separated and on the verge of leaving Memphis, is totally incapable of listening, her one and only concern being to escape the flow of words littering her confused mind and, in doing so, over-whelm everything she comes across. She will inevitably end up alone with her own monologues. The words that the chatty Dee Dee uses to describe her Johnny are emblematic:

> He's really cute. He's from England . . . he's got the cutest accent, you know the way they talk over there? I just love the way they talk. I love the way he talks, when he does talk. I mean, he never says anything. How am I supposed to know what he is thinking if he never fucking says anything!? I mean like, maybe I talk a lot or something but at least that's better than not talking at all! . . . I should look for another type of boyfriend that talks more than I do but I guess that's kind of impossible . . .

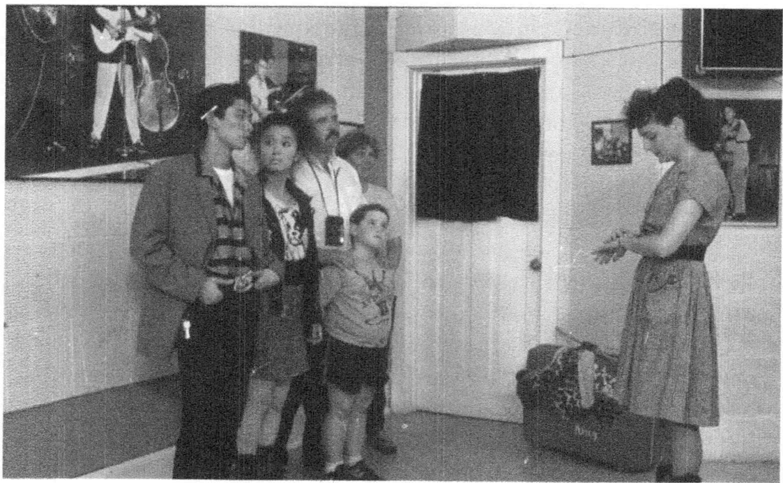

Verbal overdose, Jodie Markell, *Mystery Train*.

Jarmusch's irony is palpable and it is easy to imagine that one of the causes of the collapse of Dee Dee's and Johnny's love story is the girl's verbal exuberance.

One must not think, however, that for Jarmusch the techniques of relativization of the word observed thus far allude to the impossibility *tout court* of communicating or even to negating the importance of the word itself. On the contrary, the point that Jarmusch is trying to make is really quite simple, almost obvious: communication between human beings – actors or not – does not necessarily come about through the spoken word. Once this fundamental fact has been established, paradoxically the 'relativized-word' may assume a greater importance, for the moment it is freed of its habitual and exclusive function as the 'bearer of significance', the spectator's opportunities to explore the communicative areas less associated with its immediate literal content are broadened. For example, I think of the poetic word often used by Jarmusch, the *sound* of which takes on a supplementary and impalpable meaning. Or of foreign languages, understood partially or not at all by the audience, that nonetheless do not renege on their own varied communicative potential.

Travelling Words: Polyglotism and Foreign Languages

Foreign languages are among Jarmusch's favourite territories of enquiry. It helps to quote Chion again when dealing with the theme: 'A few films have relativized speech by using a foreign language that is not understood by most of their viewers. A related strategy is to mix several tongues, resulting in their mutual relativization.'[6] All the variations proposed by Chion – foreign languages not understood by the majority of spectators, with and without subtitles, a mixture and overlapping of idioms – are represented steadfastly in Jarmusch's films, authentic models of linguistic contamination. Ever since *Permanent Vacation*, bilingual characters have crowded his filmography, and it is worth taking a rapid and chronological look to have a clearer idea – even merely quantitative – of this particular phenomenon.

In *Permanent Vacation*, shortly after visiting his mother in the psychiatric hospital, Allie meets a visibly psychotic Hispanic girl crouched on the exterior staircase of a semi-ruined building. Unaware of Allie's presence, she speaks to herself and sings in Spanish. As soon as she notices the intruder, she immediately starts to shout at him in English, telling him to get lost.

In *Stranger Than Paradise*, Hungarian dominates the scene thanks to the characters of Eva and Aunt Lotte, while *Down By Law* introduces Italian, personified by Roberto Benigni and Nicoletta Braschi. The Tuscan rascal improvises in Italian – partly subtitled – at various moments in what has been rightly defined as Jarmusch's film on language par excellence.[7]

In *Mystery Train*, Jarmusch's linguistic interests switch to Japan with Masatoshi Nagase and Youki Kudoh in the episode 'Far From Yokohama', back again to Italy with Nicoletta Braschi in 'A Ghost', and finally to the unmistakable British English of Joe Strummer in 'Lost in Space': Strummer's accent makes a fundamental contribution to establishing a strong linguistic identity that distinguishes him from the other characters.

Jarmusch reaches the apex of his language mix in 1991 with *Night On Earth*, in which five nocturnal taxi rides take place in as many different cities. The first episode of the series, shot entirely in Los Angeles, is the only one in which no other language but English is spoken. However, the determining feature of the two leading characters is their different linguistic accents: the young cab driver, Corky (Winona Ryder), who dreams of becoming a mechanic, uses street slang peppered with swear words; the rich Beverly Hills talent scout (Gena Rowlands) expresses her individuality through an impeccable style and a more refined English, though by the end of the ride she is not averse to a little patois.

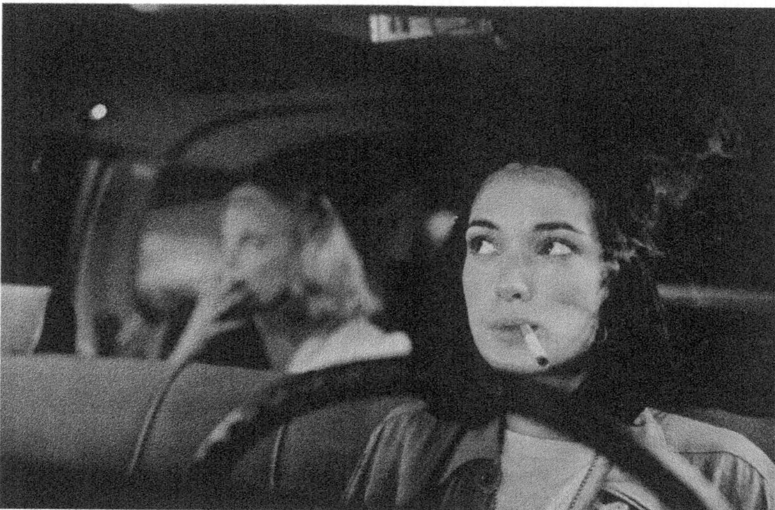

Corky (Winona Ryder), *Night On Earth*.

New York is a real melting pot, a fact confirmed by the linguistic mix that Jarmusch adopts in the relative episode: Yo-Yo (Giancarlo Esposito) gets into the taxi driven by Helmut (Armin Mueller-Stahl), an East German clown from Dresden. His constant remarks about Prague and Czechoslovakia and the occasional word in German, not subtitled, completely bewilder Yo-Yo, who has scant knowledge of European political geography.

The Paris episode is spoken entirely in French. The first clients of the Ivory Coast taxi driver are two Cameroon diplomats. In the second part of the episode their African-French accent is replaced by the Parisian accent of an exuberant blind girl played by Béatrice Dalle.

The fourth and penultimate episode, which takes place in Rome, brings Italian once more to the fore, or better the somewhat Roman-accented Tuscan of taxi driver Roberto Benigni. His rather bawdy vernacular takes on the soft, peaceful Italian of his client, a priest played by Paolo Bonacelli, who will not survive Benigni's verbal onslaught, too devastating and finally lethal for his elderly heart.

Finally, the fifth episode moves to Helsinki where all the characters speak Finnish. It is important to notice that the third, fourth and fifth original episodes are completely subtitled, thus preserving the *sound* of the different languages spoken. However, the Italian version, for example, was completely dubbed, altering a good part of the aesthetic

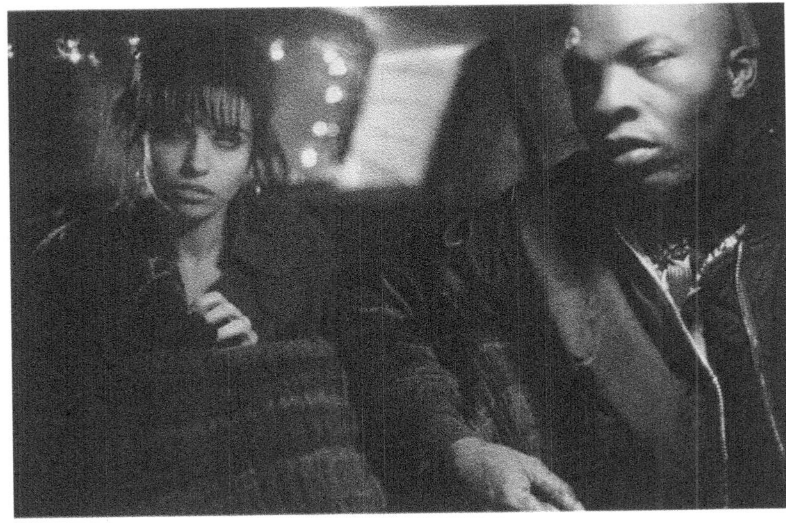

Feeling sound:
Béatrice Dalle,
Night On Earth.

that Jarmusch wanted to give the film thanks particularly to the diverse idioms that inhabit it.

In the films that followed *Night On Earth*, the variety of languages continues relentlessly, almost as though it were a necessary and unfailing condition of the director. In *Dead Man*, as confirmed to me by the Cayuga actor Gary Farmer, who plays the role of Native American Nobody, English is joined by five different Native American languages: Makah, Crow, Cree, Blackfoot and Cayuga.[8] In the next film, *Ghost Dog*, apart from a smattering of Spanish, French returns as the principal foreign language, thanks to the character of Raymond, the ice-cream vendor played by Isaach de Bankolé. Apart from the various slangs and variations of English – British, Australian, New Yorkese/hip hop, Italian American – in *Coffee and Cigarettes* it is French and Italian that return once again.

Broken Flowers seems finally to bring us the first exception to the rule, because one cannot really talk of bona fide foreign languages in the dialogue. And yet, wanting to give the discussion a decidedly paradoxical tone, the character of the determined Dr Carmen Markowski, played by Jessica Lange, is a highly peculiar interpreter or, as she defines herself, an 'animal communicator'. In the doctor's elegant office, where she sees her 'patients' and their owners, what stands out is her book with the eloquent title *Animal Vernacular*. The incredulous Don cannot help but stare in utter amazement when his charming ex admits to him with great seriousness that after the death of her very affectionate dog Winston she discovered a particular gift: the ability to understand the language of animals. 'I don't read animal minds', Carmen reassures him, 'but when they want to communicate I can hear them.'

In *The Limits of Control*, the gangster road movie set in Spain, Jarmusch returns to the more canonical and identifiable human idioms, the languages this time going from Creole to French to Spanish to Japanese and finally to Arabic. Even the password with which during the film different symbolic characters make themselves known to Lone Man, the silent nameless gangster, is one of 'linguistic' colour: '¿Usted no habla español, verdad?' 'No . . .' is the constant response, one that fails to hide a certain irony considering that Lone Man is practically mute from beginning to end, and little does it matter whether he speaks Spanish or not.

Finally, in *Only Lovers Left Alive*, in a brief exchange between Eve (Tilda Swinton) and Marlowe's companion Bilal (Slimane Dazi) at the

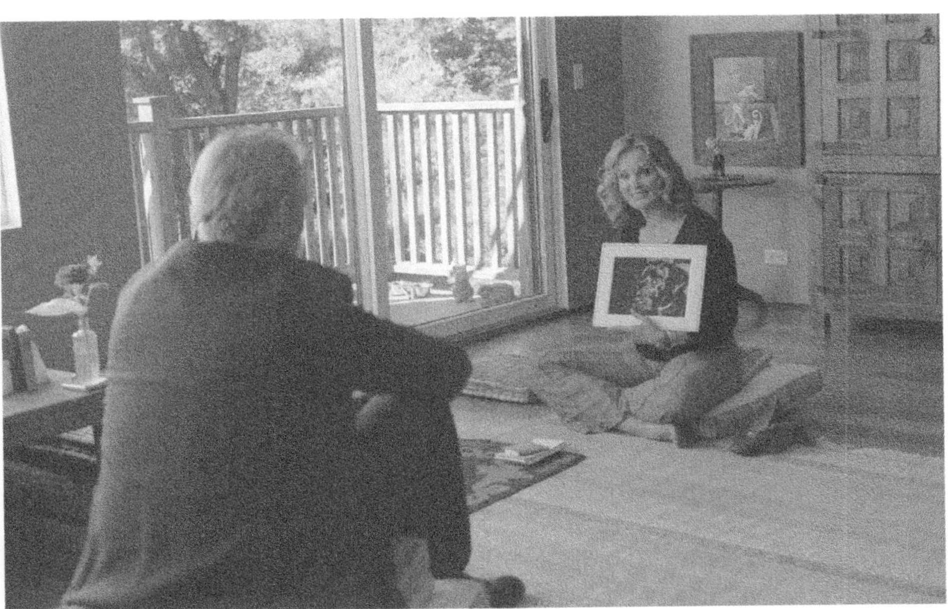

Tangier Café Mille et une Nuits, Jarmusch could not resist the temptation of including a few words in Arabic (not subtitled), before switching back to English.

The Invisible Translation

This survey clears up, also from a purely quantitative point of view, the dominating role played by languages – and the *foreigner's perspective* – in Jarmusch's cinema from his beginnings to the present day. A perspective in which disorientation and linguistic difficulties instead of obstructing communication amplify its possible channels and multiply their devices, sometimes in a totally irrational manner.

There are numerous moments in Jarmusch's cinema when translation is called for: Willie translating Aunt Lotte's Hungarian dialogue for Eddie in *Stranger Than Paradise*; Bob's constant question in *Down By Law*, 'How do you say in English when . . .?'; the bizarre English translation by the two Japanese 'pilgrims' in *Mystery Train*; the consecutive French/English translation in the opening sequence of *The Limits of Control* regarding the task that Lone Man must see through to the end;

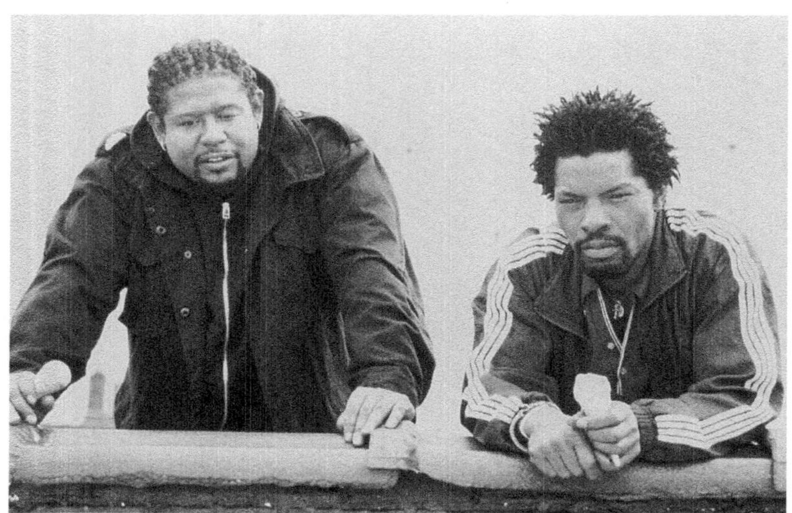

Invisible translation:
Forest Whitaker
and Isaach de
Bankolé, *Ghost
Dog: The Way
of the Samurai*.

I could continue. However, I would rather talk of a single film in which Jarmusch puts into practice a vaguely surreal strategy that I would define here as 'invisible translation': *Ghost Dog: The Way of the Samurai*.

The dialogue between the African American Ghost Dog (Forest Whitaker) and the black francophone Raymond (Isaach De Bankolé) is based upon this particular form of translation. On numerous occasions the ascetic, taciturn killer – the roof-dweller who uses homing pigeons to communicate with the outside world – and the bubbly Haitian ice-cream vendor declare themselves to be 'great friends' even though they do not speak the same language. Despite this 'minor inconvenience', they understand one another perfectly, responding to each other's questions as if they had the help of an invisible interpreter, a situation that has without doubt irrational consequences, but in which communication is guaranteed by simple repetition. Almost regularly, when Raymond speaks French, Ghost Dog, helped by the highly punctual *invisible translation*, intuits and repeats the equivalent in English. Accordingly, when Ghost Dog says certain things in English, Raymond intuits and repeats the same in French, sometimes taking the words out of Ghost Dog's mouth as if he were truly capable of reading his friend's mind. Through this particular method of translation, Jarmusch makes use of *repetition*, a format very dear to him: the same concepts expressed through acoustic wrappings all different from each other.

Jarmusch is not interested in explaining *how* this small 'linguistic magic' works. What matters is that the communication between the two friends is saved. To be certain that audience comprehension is also guaranteed, Jarmusch subtitled the French dialogue even though tempted not to do so. Asked whether he ever considered releasing the film in America without the English subtitles, Jarmusch answered:

> Yeah, I did, but I thought it was really funny and important to know that, even though they don't literally know what the other is saying, somehow they do know, but without knowing it through linguistics. I thought it was an important part of their friendship that they were sort of repeating what the other one said without knowing it themselves, so I decided to keep the subtitles.[9]

An emblematic sequence for this type of multilingual communication used by Jarmusch, and in which subtitles are indeed fundamental, brings a third language into play: Spanish. Raymond invites Ghost Dog onto the roof of a building to show him the impossible endeavour that he considers the work of 'un génie!' Looking down from the terrace, the two friends watch a man busy building a fair-sized boat on the roof of a building below them. Sailing the boat will obviously be a serious problem, but the man does not appear to have considered this, or at least not

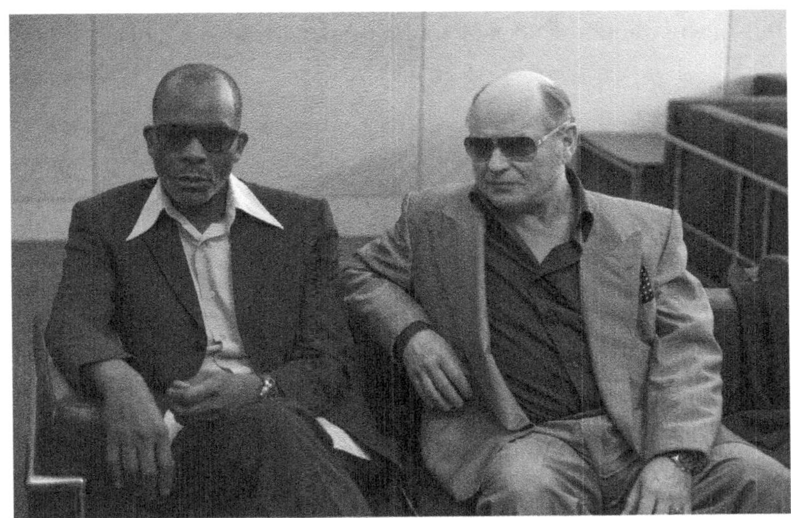

Consecutive translation: Alex Descas and Jean-François Stévenin, *The Limits of Control.*

enough to worry about it, like a lone urban Fitzcarraldo. Following Ghost Dog's comment in English, 'It's amazing. But how the hell is the guy ever gonna get it down from there', Raymond shouts down to the man in French: 'Quelle magnifique bâteau! Mais une fois terminé, vous n'aurez plus qu'à voguer dans les nuages avec?' (What a magnificent boat! But when you've finished, what are you going to do – set sail on a nice cloud?) The man's response, in Spanish, could not be more to the point: 'No entiendo. Sigo trabajando!' (I don't understand! I have to keep working!) In this atmosphere of 'linguistic promiscuity' between the two friends, Spanish pops up to trouble the waters of verbal communication even more, creating a disruptive comic effect.

Speaking of comedy, boats and impossible situations, what comes to mind is a hypothetic reference to one of Jarmusch's most dearly loved directors, Buster Keaton. In the 1921 film *The Boat* the great 'sad-faced comic' builds a vessel not on the roof of a building but, just as crazily, on the ground floor of his house. Needless to say he will have to destroy the entire building to get it out, and this will be just the first in a series of surreal cataclysms. On a more realistic note is the catastrophe that overwhelms Ghost Dog immediately after the amusing sequence of the boat on the roof: returning to the terrace of his hideout home he discovers that his beloved pigeons have been wiped out brutally. In the space of seven breaths – as decreed by the Code of the Samurai – Ghost Dog decides to carry out his very own mute vendetta, a decision made in absolute silence, this time without the need of translation, neither visible nor invisible.

Imperialism

The *foreigner's perspective* plays a central role in Jarmusch's cinema, a fact confirmed by the constant use of languages, with or without translations. It is this perspective that offers the director a particular point of view from which also to confront themes of a social-political character, and the instruments efficient enough to help in this endeavour are often foreign languages. However, it would be a waste of time to look for an explicit judgement or political or ideological viewpoint in Jarmusch's filmography. In 1985, in light of the success of *Stranger Than Paradise*, Jarmusch explained:

> I don't think something that's explicitly ideological serves any
> kind of even subversive purpose anymore in America, because if

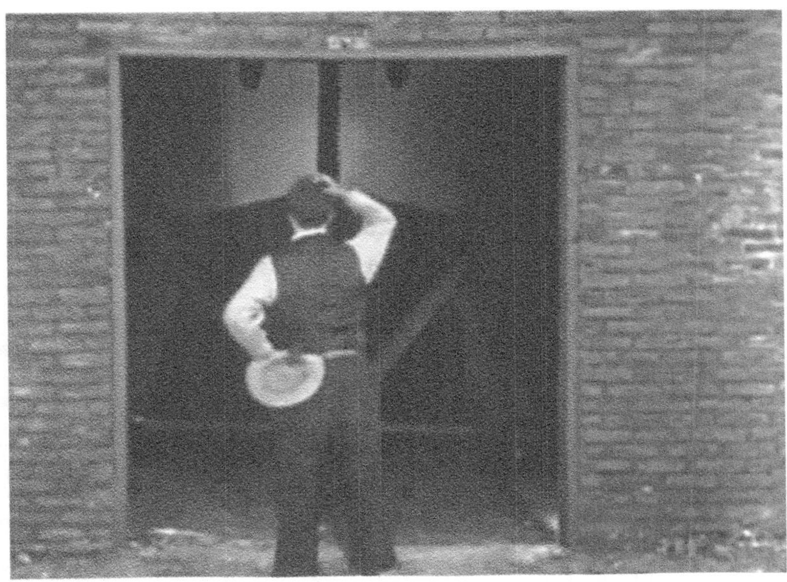

you make a political statement that is completely direct then you're only reinforcing opinions of people who would agree with you anyway, and the people that don't agree with you won't agree with you – you're not changing anybody's way of thinking. So I feel I would never make something that was directly political or ideological.[10]

Irrespective of whether or not one agrees with this statement, one must concur that Jarmusch has kept faith with this vision over the years, with perhaps one exception.

At the end of the more recent *The Limits of Control*, the generically named character 'American' has all the characteristics of an allegory of economical and/or political power or even of American imperialism. The American has the traits of a powerful and unscrupulous business-man/wheeler-dealer, who works in an armoured compound, watched day and night by special units in riot gear, as well trained as they are inefficient, as the film's epilogue will demonstrate. As so rarely happens in the cinema, Jarmusch has succeeded in immortalizing – quite by acci-dent – a surprising and decidedly political *premonitory image*. The shot of this walled-in compound, located in southern Spain and photographed

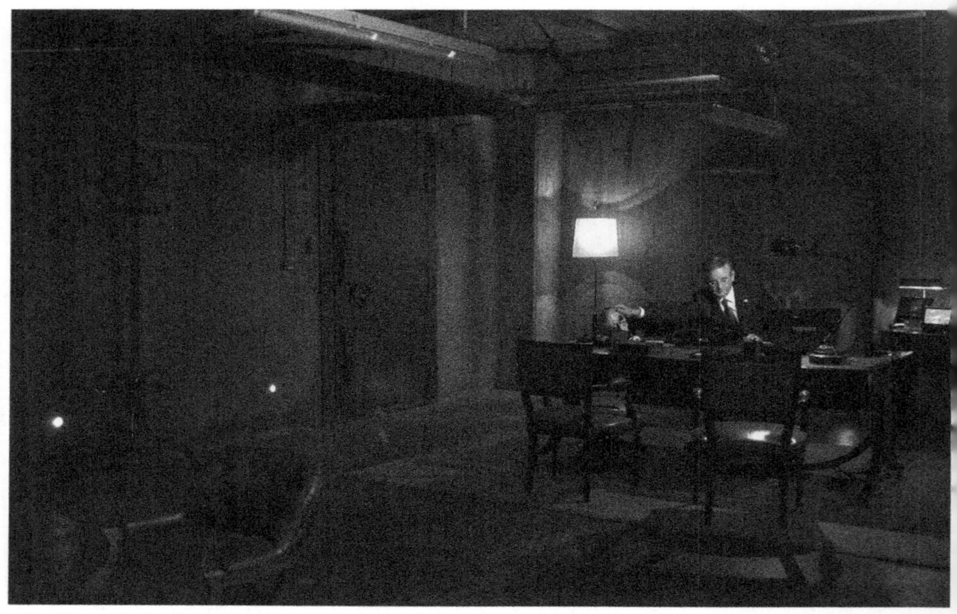

for Jarmusch by Christopher Doyle, has much in common with the image of another hideout: one, however, that has nothing to do with cinema – the now-demolished compound at Abbottabad in Pakistan, where American Navy Seals claimed to have found and eliminated the Al Qaeda leader, Osama Bin Laden, the graphic images of which were sent around the world simultaneously by all the major news agencies on 2 May 2011, only to be quickly forgotten again. However, precisely because it is a *premonitory image* it cannot be considered intentional or explicitly political, not even in this case.[11]

The American, *The Limits of Control.*

So where do foreign languages play a deliberate role in conveying arguments of a social-political nature in Jarmusch's cinema?

If we want to share the opinion of Slovenian philosopher and psycho-analyst Slavoj Žižek, who considers English the language of imperialism, one could attest that even an American director's simple use of a language other than English is in itself a political statement. As he recently confirmed in Berlin, Žižek believes that the privileged use of English – in scientific research, politics, economics and international cultural debate – equates with an attempt to destroy the peripheries of thought: today, at the global level, what can and cannot be done is decided in English.[12]

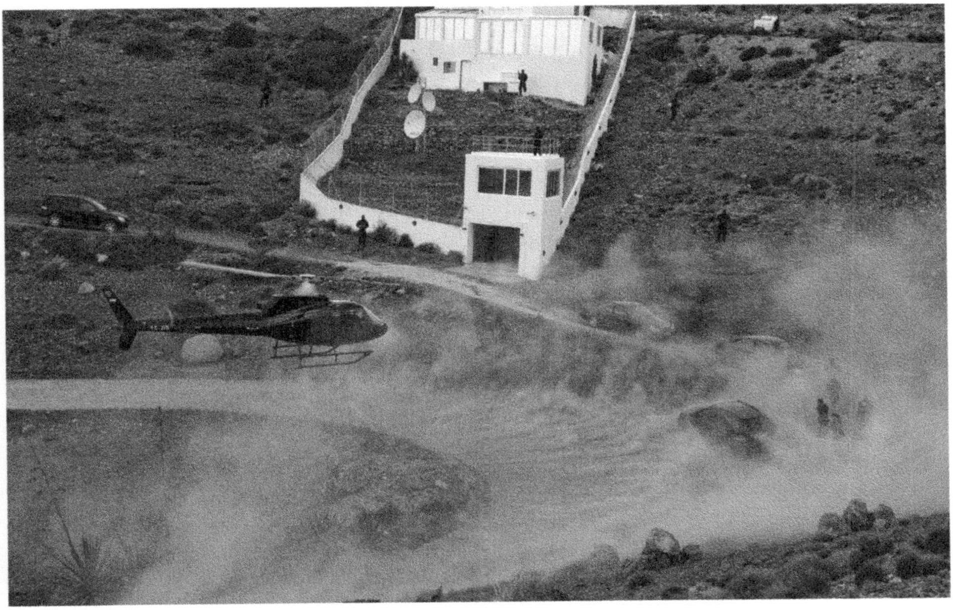

Premonitory image:
the compound, *The
Limits of Control.*

The Abbottabad
compound,
Pakistan, now
demolished.

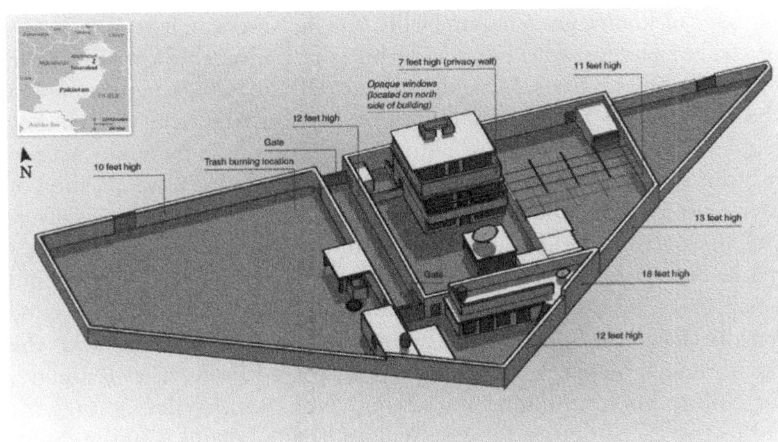

Going from generalities to the specific, I have picked out some sequences in *Stranger Than Paradise*, *Mystery Train* and *Night On Earth* in which Jarmusch alludes to certain recurring themes of a social-political nature through the use of languages and their nuances. The themes are racism/discrimination and the desire to integrate on the part of a minority.

Racial intolerance is lived in close-up, particularly in *Mystery Train* and *Night On Earth*. In 'Lost in Space' – the concluding episode of *Mystery Train* – it is not two different languages that come face to face but American English, characterized by a particular black and southern touch, and British English, spoken exclusively by the most British of all Jarmusch's film characters, The Clash frontman Joe Strummer (Johnny). It is Johnny, a white European, who hears and openly denounces the problem of racial discrimination, particularly virulent in Memphis, a city that represents not only an important slice of America's music history, personified by ivory-white king of rock 'n' roll Elvis Presley, but also the infamous history of slavery and its widespread use. Paradoxically, Johnny appears to be the only one not to tolerate the omnipresent 'King Elvis' icon in a city where numerous other 'idols', not necessarily white, should be remembered and celebrated. What really freaks him out is the sarcastic nickname given to him by his African American friends, habitués of the bar Shades, who because of his very impeccable 1950s rock 'n' roll look call him Elvis. Little does it matter that Johnny never misses a chance to be his friends' champion of African American rights; they regularly discriminate against him, the European with the funny accent. It is this that renders the way Jarmusch handles the delicate question of racial intolerance more articulate and in no way clichéd. Johnny's diversity, apart from the colour of his skin, is mainly characterized by a marked *linguistic diversity*. He does everything possible to get over it and be accepted by his African American friends. He frequents the same bar, listens to black music and even shoots and seriously wounds the openly racist owner of the liquor store, played by Rockets Redglare, for calling his friend and ex-work pal Will (Rick Aviles) a 'nigger'. Following the shooting Johnny, Will and fellow drunk Charlie (Steve Buscemi) seek refuge in a hotel room, where Johnny cannot understand why the umpteenth picture of Elvis dominates the scene. Jarmusch's answer comes at the end, where he does not hesitate to add a final touch of cynicism:

Johnny: Why is *he* fucking everywhere?! It's a black hotel, a black
    neighbourhood, black dudes working on the desk . . . why don't
    they have a portrait of Otis Redding or Martin Luther King?
Will: That's 'cause this is a white *owned* hotel. They just got the
    brothers working here!
Johnny: I see what you mean . . .
Will: Don't worry, next time, Johnny, we're gonna ask for the
    Malcom X Suite!
Johnny: That's right!

After this exchange, once again Will uses a discriminatory name –
'snowflake' – when addressing Johnny, whose response clears up his
position even better: 'Are you gonna start that racist shit again?! It ain't
our fault. We didn't choose to be white! Right, Charlie?' Through
Johnny, Jarmusch reaches a synthesis as simple as it is indisputable,
faced with which Will can do nothing but heave a loud, annoyed sigh.

Moving onto the second film, in the Parisian episode of *Night On
Earth* Jarmusch again tackles the racism theme, not from the traditional western point of view, white against black, but as discrimination
within the same ethnic group, in this case black Africans. Ivory Coast
immigrant taxi driver Isaach de Bankolé, a very visible bandage on his
forehead, drives his vehicle somewhat dangerously through the streets
of Paris, his passengers being two African diplomats (Pascal N'Zonzi
and Emile Abossolo M'bo) on the eve of an important meeting with the
Cameroon ambassador. The language spoken is French and again in
this case, as in *Mystery Train*, there are different accents in conflict
with each other: the strong African accent of the two diplomats and
the standard European accent of the unlucky driver – unlucky because
the diplomats, both drunk and high on their professional success, poke
fun at him and especially at his immigrant status. When their 'joke'
becomes too intolerably offensive the driver suddenly stops the taxi and
throws his rude passengers out, unfortunately forgetting to make them
pay for the ride. Once again the theme of racial discrimination is
expressed through *linguistic diversity*, but in a way contrary to the
generic expectations of a Western audience. It is the characters deemed
the weakest – the two Africans with their strong accents – who end up
discriminating in a very offensive way the naturalized second- or third-
generation citizen, who speaks a decidedly more European French.
Speaking the language of the country that has taken him in is certainly

not enough to render the man immune to the two passengers' intolerant verbal attack – on the contrary. And as if that were not enough, at the end of the episode the taxi driver has to put up with the bigoted racism of a white French driver. Following their nocturnal collision, the unsubtle exchange between the two is highly eloquent:

French driver: Look where you're going! We're not in Africa!
Cab driver: You bloody racist!
French driver: I'm not a racist . . . but you drive like a black!

After English and French, the language that Jarmusch uses to touch on the second political theme – or rather a minority's desire to integrate – is Hungarian.

In *Stranger Than Paradise*, the level and personal concept that each of the three Hungarian characters has of his or her own integration in the grand American social-cultural melting pot is what, among other things, differentiates them. From the oldest to the youngest they are Aunt Lotte (Cecillia Stark), her nephew Bela/Willie (John Lurie) and Eva (Eszter Balint), Bela's cousin. The elderly aunt lives in Cleveland, but behaves as though she had never left Europe. She insists on speaking Hungarian, which is made perfectly clear at the start of the film by her phone conversation with nephew Willie, who pleads with her to speak English. When Willy and his friend Eddie (Richard Edson) turn up at the aunt's small Cleveland home to visit Eva, who had left New York a year earlier, the elderly woman ignores Eddy, who clearly has no idea what she is saying, and insists on speaking to Bela/Willie in Hungarian. At times, Aunt Lotte 'Hungarizes' her English by adding Hungarian suffixes, inventing neologisms like 'pick-olni' (pick up) and 'movie-ba' (go to the movies), the effect highly comical to a mother-tongue spectator. Aunt Lotte's relationship with American culture could be defined as a *voluntarily missed integration*. It is quite evident that America, Cleveland in particular, has never usurped the memory of her European homeland and its traditions. The first thing that the rotund lady of the house offers her two visitors is in fact her native food: goulash, peppers and chicken soup. When her young visitors ask for beer, Aunt Lotte responds in Hungarian: 'No, I have no beer. This is better than beer, much better!'

With Bela/Willie, the situation changes diametrically: he stubbornly refuses to accept his origins, a fact that for the most part coincides with his refusal to speak Hungarian. Willy needs constantly to assert his

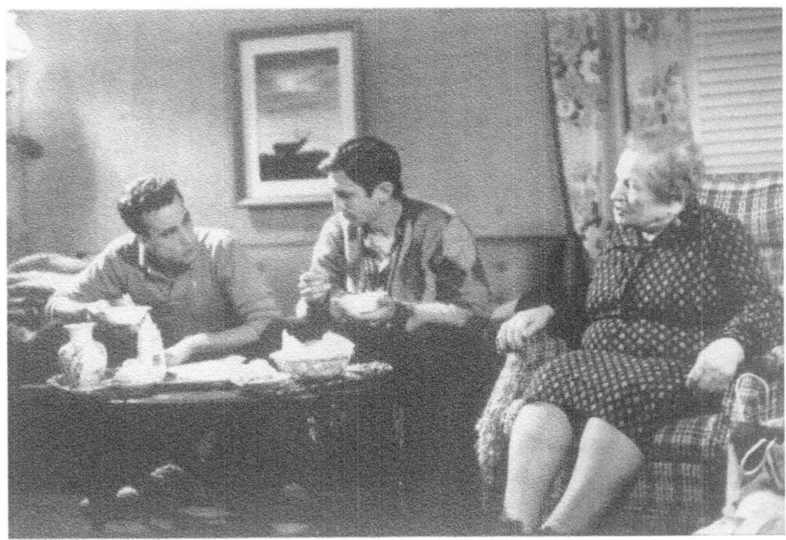

acquired identity, even though there is something undoubtedly ambiguous about the phrase 'I am as American as you are!' that he addresses to Eddie with great determination. Jarmusch does not give us definite elements to show that Eddie is 100 per cent 'American' and so the ambiguity remains, perhaps in order to underline the fact that 'the American identity' is made up of a thousand other identities. Paradoxically, at the end of the film it will be Willie who finds himself – really against his will? – on the day's only flight from Florida to Europe. As luck would have it, the destination turns out to be Budapest. Willie's condition thus reflects a *superficial integration*.

Teenager Eva, who had initially decided to take that very same flight to Budapest, will instead choose the path to integration by remaining in the States. Right from the start she struggles to speak English, using Hungarian only during her very first encounter with testy cousin Willie, who wastes no time in laying down the linguistic rules of his apartment: 'Here only English!' When he and Eddie visit Eva in Cleveland and Willie says, 'I wish Aunt Lotte would just speak English', Eva responds immediately: 'She's so stubborn, just like the rest of the family.' To show how hard she is trying to adapt to Cleveland's local customs, Eva works in a fast-food restaurant and often goes to the cinema, her hero still being Screamin' Jay Hawkins, the 'wild man' who has

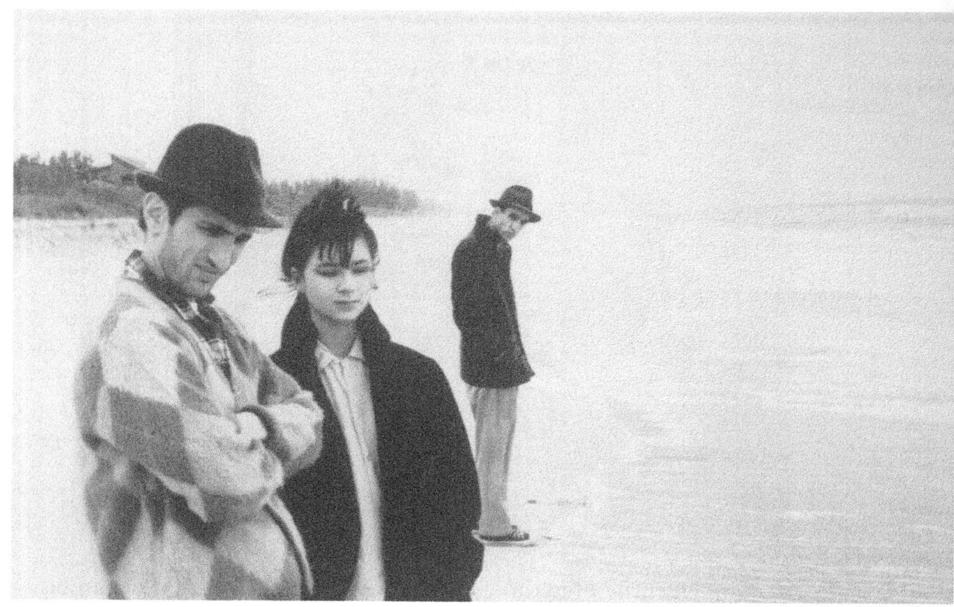

nothing even remotely Hungarian about him.[13] In 'Paradise', the third episode of the film that took almost two years to complete, the linguistic metamorphosis of a now far more self-confident Eva corresponds with the real improvement in Eszter Balint's linguistic skills. In her case, one can quite easily talk of a *resolved and successful integration*.

In the light of these examples, it is now more apparent that language is a privileged instrument with which Jarmusch handles themes of a social and political character, even if not in a too explicit or deliberately ideological way, thus remaining consistent with his declarations quoted at the beginning of this section. The 'filter' of foreign languages helps Jarmusch avoid the risk of becoming didactic, and allows him to touch upon themes like racial discrimination and integration in an articulate and original way. Staying within the same linguistic-political range, a separate section is dedicated to *Dead Man*, the film in which Jarmusch ventured into the realms of languages far more remote than those dealt with thus far, languages seriously threatened by extinction.

Superficial integration: Willie/Bela, *Stranger Than Paradise.*

Genocide

> I think it's in *The Searchers* where John Ford had some Indians
> who were supposedly Comanche, but he cast Navajos who spoke
> Navajo. It's kind of like saying: 'Yes, I know they are supposed to
> be French people, but I could only get Germans, and no one will
> know the difference.' It's really close to apartheid in America.[14]

The Kwakiutl and the Makah tribes are the protagonists of the final
sequences in *Dead Man* at the Native village on the banks of the river.
Granted that Jarmusch's intention certainly was not to shoot an eth-
nological film on the tribes of the northwest, nonetheless, when coming
into contact with them he started out by paying particular attention to
their native languages, a rare phenomenon in the cinema, especially in
westerns.[15] Tag Gallagher, author of *John Ford: The Man and his
Films*, expressed this concept even more directly: 'As Ford observes in
Cheyenne Autumn (1964), it is white words, white language, that have
been our most potent weapon against Indians.'[16] Violent, humourless,
taciturn, barely capable of speaking elementary English, frequently
unable to conjugate verbs, communication made possible thanks only
to drums and smoke signals . . . These are just some of the classic
stereotypes initially suggested and then consolidated by American
cinema, which started during the silent era and lasted well into the
late 1940s.[17] The advent of the Talkies at the end of the 1920s also
meant giving voice to Native Americans, and thus their own language.
In one particular case, which is worth mentioning, this problem was
solved thanks to an absurd technical stratagem. In the mid-1930s series
Scouts to the Rescue, the language of the 'savages' was simply reproduced by replaying their English dialogue backwards, the result being
a bizarre and quite incomprehensible 'Indian'. The Native Americans
were directed to move as little as possible, and their close-ups were
then simply printed backwards, their dialogue in perfect lip-sync with
the 'reverse English'.[18]

That the identity of a people and a culture lives on through their language is a fact well known to Jarmusch, but not necessarily taken for
granted in the cinema. For this reason, going back to *Dead Man* and in
particular to the treatment of the diverse Native American languages
used in the film, it is important to underline that actor Gary Farmer —
born in Ohsweken, Ontario, into the Cayuga nation — who plays Nobody,

wanted more time to rehearse in the Makah language, which has a very complex pronunciation, to be certain he did not mispronounce the words. As Jarmusch pointed out, 'Makah was incredibly difficult: Gary had to learn it phonetically and read it off big cards. Even the Makah people had trouble, because it's a really complicated language.'[19] But Makah is not the only Native American language spoken in the film. As explained to me by Farmer, the Native American languages spoken in *Dead Man* are five: Makah, Crow, Cree, Cayuga and Blackfoot.

> One has to figure that there are a lot of the older people here in my own community who can speak up to three, four, five languages. Maybe twenty years ago it was not uncommon for people to speak many languages. Nobody's family, as I remember it, was Blackfoot and Crow and those two tribes were confrontational to each other for sometime. Being an outcast and also being versed in English, it made much sense to me that if anyone travelled around the Americas at that time they would be knowledgeable of language. So it was important to me as a character trait of Nobody that if he actually came to the Makah, he would speak Makah . . . There was also another language I used, I know for sure that is Cayuga, my own language . . . And we also used Cree. My girlfriend was Cree, she spoke it, and I spoke Cree to her.[20]

Despite the linguistic variety that Jarmusch tried to depict in the film, Farmer pointed out how challenging it is working with non-Native directors and remembered feeling frustrated during the shoot because the Makah extras were not 'allowed' to speak. The reason, as Farmer told me, was that the production was running out of money and could not 'upgrade' the Makah to characters who could have their lines of dialogue in a script. While the silent Makah people, who look almost like 'ghosts' to the hallucinating, dying Blake, in combination with Neil Young's guitar landscapes, add to the 'dreaminess' of the sequence, in Farmer's opinion a conversation might have given the scene a 'more real' feeling. For Farmer the main challenge working with non-native directors lies precisely in the difficulty at maintaining the cultural integrity, something he worked very hard at, but that he found disrupted by the film's editing. 'I guess that's why we try to maintain our own vision in filmmaking. And that was difficult. Although Jim is better than most, way better.'[21] In his effort at trying to maintain the integrity

Farmer talks about, Jarmusch had Nobody's girlfriend in the film help him with the Cree dialogue: 'Michelle Thrush, who's in the film, spoke Cree and is Cree. We wrote some dialogue together and then she translated it with someone else who was even more fluent.'[22] In the nocturnal fight sequence between the young Cree woman and Nobody, sparked by a guiltless William Blake turning up unexpectedly and putting a brusque end to their love making, what strikes the spectator is a detail of major importance: the Cree dialogue is never subtitled.

Nonetheless, the woman's anger is quite comprehensible and palpable, even without grasping the words with which she expresses her uncontrollable rage. The same goes for the other sequences in which a Native American language is spoken: there are no subtitles and this clearly was not an oversight. By not adding subtitles Jarmusch declared that he wanted to pay a small tribute to the people who speak those languages, and who are thus deliberately privileged, contrary to Western audiences: 'I didn't want it subtitled. I wanted it to be a little gift for those people who understand the language.'

So if on one side this choice can be interpreted as Jarmusch's personal contribution to the preservation of languages in constant threat

Native languages: the Makah, *Dead Man.*

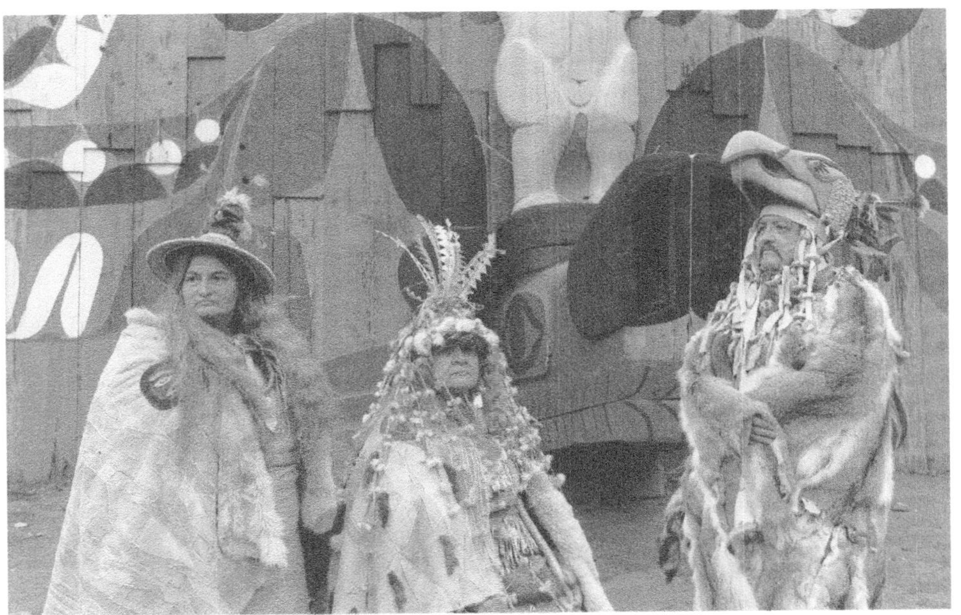

of extinction, on the other it is an aesthetic elaboration involving the film's acoustic landscape: it is thanks to the lack of subtitles that, once the problem of content has been eliminated, the *sounds* of these rare languages become almost music-like to the spectator's ear, a strongly evocative music.

Apropos of this, the sequence in which Blake and Nobody arrive at the Makah village on the banks of the river is emblematic. From the *dead man*'s point of view the line between life and death, between reality and vision, is by now extremely narrow and confused. The sounds of the words, as incomprehensible to him as they are to us, add a strong dose of hallucinatory irrationality to the entire sequence. Blake's walk in a semi-conscious state across the Native American village works musically as a reprise, since it returns to his walk at the beginning of the film, his arrival at the gloomy city of Machine. In both cases, Blake appears as one of the figures most dear to Jarmusch, that of the outsider: someone disoriented by the surrounding environment. Blake does not feel at ease with either the whites who cheat him, fatally wound him and accuse him of a crime he committed in self-defence, or with the Natives who are too distant from a cultural and linguistic point of view.

It is of major importance to Jarmusch that Nobody, the lone and cultured Native American, finds himself in an existential condition much like that of the young bookkeeper from Cleveland: another outsider, another reject. Nobody is of mixed blood, half Blackfoot and half Crow, as he tells Blake when responding to the white man's naive but sincere question: 'Nobody, shouldn't you be with your own tribe or something?' Nobody responds: 'My blood is mixed. My mother was Ohm-gahpi-Piikani. My father is Apsáslooke. This mixture was not respected.' Like Blake, Nobody was also driven away. The two travelling companions, ostensibly so different in appearance, literally find themselves in the same boat.

At the end of the film when Nobody lays Blake in the canoe that will take him on his final journey, Jarmusch conjures up one final 'gift': 'Also the joke about tobacco is for indigenous American people. I hope the last line of the film, "But Nobody, I don't smoke . . ." will be a hilarious joke to them: "Oh man, this white man still doesn't get it!"'[23] In the face of Nobody's continual requests for tobacco, Blake insists on responding in the same way every time: 'Nobody, I don't smoke . . .'. Even at the very end, Blake unfortunately fails to understand that smoking has a fundamental ritual function in Native American culture. Or perhaps, as would seem plausible, Blake understands this only too well and his final line of dialogue is meant as a joyous and ironic separation from life on earth, one last joke for his friend/guide Nobody. Regardless of linguistic or cultural boundaries, Blake, who is now lying motionless in the canoe, has ended up identifying himself with both the native rituals and the visionary English poet himself.

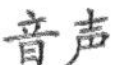

音声

A word or a phrase can be expressed in multiple ways: as a collection of sounds, a series of graphic signs, sometimes even with a single gesture or look. In the cinema some of these forms of expression can coexist simultaneously, as in the frequent case of a film acted in one language while subtitled or dubbed in another, in which layers of words overlap each other. Such layers of superimposition can also increase in number: a film shot in one particular language, then dubbed into another, which usurps the original, and finally subtitled with a third. As observed about the rare Native American languages, non-subtitled foreign dialogue does not frighten Jarmusch, who, in using it systematically, shatters one of the greatest cinematographic taboos: the intelligibility of dialogue at any cost.

In *Down By Law*, Bob (Roberto Benigni) has just broken out of prison, when fellow escapees Jack and Zack abandon him on the banks of the river because he cannot swim. He is left alone with his fear of water and the sound of the baying dogs in the near distance. In the original version of the film Benigni's monologue in Italian/Tuscan is without subtitles: an ulterior confirmation that, as far as Jarmusch is concerned, spoken language is not the only possible form of communication, and, as in the nocturnal fight scene in *Dead Man* between Nobody and his Cree girlfriend, the spectator is left on his own with a foreign language that he does not necessarily understand.

The same happens in the New York episode of *Night On Earth*. When Helmut (Armin Mueller-Stahl), the East German taxi driver, is not expressing himself in his strongly Teutonic-accented English, he often mutters something in German – not subtitled – to passenger Yo-Yo. Again, Jarmusch does not care that a part of the dialogue is 'lost'; the authenticity of Helmut's German is more important than the 'intelligibility at any cost' of every single word spoken.

Obviously, things change when whole scenes are acted in a language other than English, such as in the Paris, Rome and Helsinki episodes of *Night On Earth*, and the 'Far From Yokohama' episode of *Mystery Train*, in which the lead players speak predominantly Japanese. In these cases, Jarmusch prefers subtitles revealing his great reluctance, if not a bona fide aversion, to dub the actors. With *Down By Law*, for example, it is not a banal detail that a condition of the film's foreign sales was that it would not be dubbed, but subtitled where deemed necessary.

> I did allow *Down By Law* to be dubbed into French, but on certain conditions, Roberto would have to dub his own character and the dubbed version could not be shown until half a year after the premiere of the original version, and in Paris the dubbed version could be shown only if the original version was playing in some other theatre. But it was just an experiment, I don't like dubbing, I don't like the fact that the voice is changed. [24]

Unfortunately, this clause was not applied to *Night On Earth*. As already mentioned, in the Italian version all the numerous foreign languages were dubbed without exception, thwarting most of the puns and word games and misrepresenting a fundamental element of the film: the acoustic and rhythmic nuances of the different languages.

The great importance of the *sound of words* is particularly evident in the 'Far From Yokohama' episode in *Mystery Train*, in which Jarmusch measured up to the rhythm and timbre of Japanese. Jun and Mitsuko's love sequence, apart from being a rare sex scene in Jarmusch's filmography, is emblematic. The verbal exchange between the two youths is, to say the least, surreal in its comedy. Shortly after making love, his pomaded rockabilly hairstyle still immaculate, Jun asks Mitsuko: 'Do women always worry about their hairstyle?' It is evident that Jarmusch wants us to reflect on the uselessness of talking at any cost at any time. The above phrase, made even more absurd by its context, cannot help but irritate Mitsuko: 'What are you talking about? In all the times we've made love – and this is number eleven – I've never once thought about my hairstyle! And if that's what you're thinking, try shaving first next time . . . it hurts my face!' The sound of Mitsuko's words, the scene shot in Japanese with subtitles, is something like that of a crazed machine gun, and this sound explosion accentuates unequivocally and onomatopoeically the girl's angry and incredulous reaction. For the big slice of the audience that does not understand Japanese, sound and meaning are here materially separated and not merged into a single word that can be understood without any mediation (in this case guaranteed by the subtitles). The audio-spectator, to use Chion's terminology, thus has more freedom and more room for his own creativity. While interpreting the literal meaning expressed by the subtitles, Mitsuko's 'machine gun vocal blast', made exclusively of sounds, offers the opportunity to add sense to the scene in an intuitive and individual way. Because the spectator is asked to make this creative effort, requiring greater concentration, I maintain that the *onomatopoeic sound* of Mitsuko's anger, together with the subtitles, creates a paradoxically more explosive effect than her words would have had if they had been dubbed into English, or any other language.

The same goes for Jarmusch, who does not necessarily use the spoken word when communicating with his actors:

> Language is very important to me. I love the way language takes on slang, gets mixed up by different influences, different cultures. And I like working in other languages. In *Mystery Train*, I got the chance to direct actors in Japanese, which I don't speak. And I don't speak Finnish, and I don't really speak Italian though I understand it somewhat.[25]

Onomatopoeic sound: Mitsuko, *Mystery Train*.

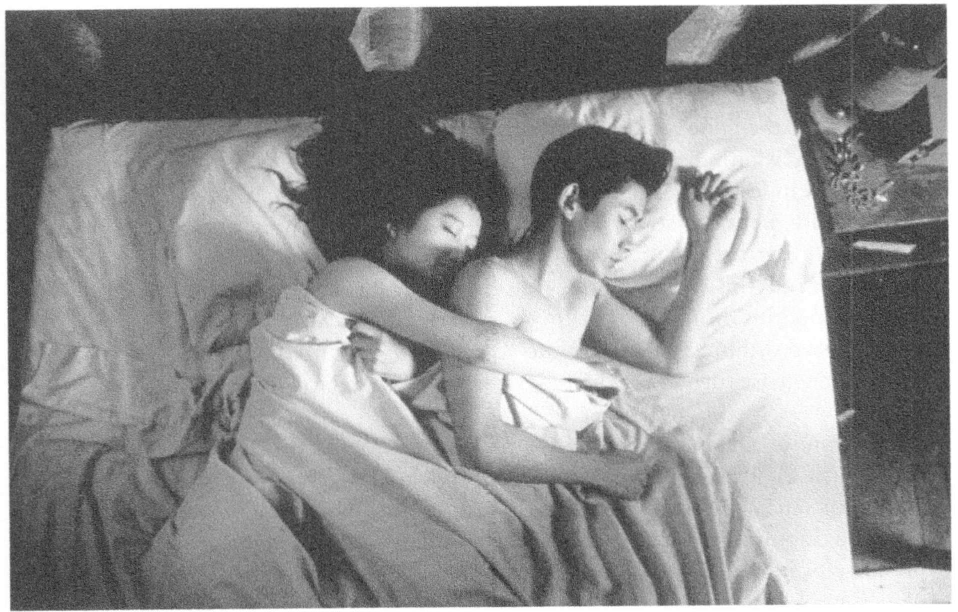

Even if working on the set was simplified by the use of interpreters, a good part of the communication with the actors took place on more intuitive levels. On top of that, and speaking from the *foreigner's point of view* so dear to Jarmusch, a common thread running through both the episode 'Far From Yokohama' and the rest of the film is precisely the attempt to communicate and be understood.

Jun and Mitsuko personify the Japanese language, not without certain differences. While Jun's character played by Masatoshi Nagase is profoundly taciturn, because of both his attitude and his actual difficulty in speaking another language, Mitsuko is undoubtedly the driving force with regard to verbal communication. It is she who regularly attempts to speak English, albeit in a quirky fashion. On entering the hotel where they will spend the night, she opens with: 'Hello! Goodnight!' and, even in situations in which gratitude is quite superfluous, the phrase she uses most is 'Thank you!'

Actually, there is another character in the film who 'speaks' Japanese: Rufus Thomas, the father of Memphis soul. The white-haired man meets the two teenage tourists on their arrival at the Memphis train station, and asks them for a light. After an initial linguistic misunderstanding, the three finally get the drift of things and before going their separate ways Thomas utters a determined '*arigatō*', underlining the word with a little bow and accentuating his typically gaping eyes. Excited, Mitsuko grabs Jun by the arm and, shaking him a little, says: 'Hey, he spoke Japanese!', and then finishes with a loud '*arigatō*!', while the elderly musician is already walking away.[26] In Jarmusch's world, one single word is enough to delude yourself into thinking you understand each other.

The fundamental instrument not only of communication, but of identity *tout court*, that an actor may in no way be robbed of, is his voice. And it is in this sense that one must interpret Jarmusch's aversion to dubbing and his disapproval of those great directors, such as Fellini, who exploited dubbing to choose the voice that best suited the face, as a tool to increase further the director's control or dominion of the film itself.[27]

The opinion of one of the most prominent dubbing directors of Italian films for the English-speaking market, Nick Alexander, resonates with Jarmusch's.[28] When asked how much is 'lost' and how much 'gained' in dubbing the voice of an actor, Alexander expressed his position quite pragmatically, eliminating any possible idealization of his profession: 'Nothing should be gained in the dubbing. It is a copy of the original and consequently a fake.'[29] For Alexander, a dramatic film in general adapts better to another language than a comic film, which is prone to losing a great deal in the dubbing because of the different performances and sense of humour. The aforementioned Italian adaptation and dubbing of *Night On Earth* that robbed it of its multilingualism and so distorted a good part of the film's originality, is clear proof of this.

Things change, however, when the 'actors' are not real: 'Strangely, a cartoon lends itself very nicely to dubbing in other languages and the performances may even be improved.'[30] In a cartoon or animated film, far more so than in a film with real actors, sound effects are used in an expressive or narrative sense and often acquire the same function as dialogue, which reopens the question of sound hierarchies within audiovisuals: words are, in most cases, considered 'privileged sounds' with respect to the other acoustic layers. Whereas part of the *image* in a shot may escape even the most vigilant eye – and the reasons may vary, such as the speed of editing (Oliver Stone), lack of focus (the Danish Dogme 95 films) and an overcrowded shot (Peter Greenaway) – when it comes to *sound* this appears to be 'forbidden': every word must be understood, in all circumstances. Alexander confirmed this tendency, particularly in the Hollywood tradition, and pointed out two of its origins:

> When he finished shooting *Titanic* (1997), director James Cameron worried about the clarity of the dialogue and so insisted that the actors re-voice their roles so that during the final mix he could choose which was better: the direct sound, or the dubbed. No wonder it took more than three months to mix the film! However, in just about any film shot with direct sound, there is always a small percentage of the dialogue that escapes the spectator. But the problem of understanding the dialogue is an old one that arose at two precise moments: the first, with the affirmation of the Actor's Studio that believed a heartfelt, internal performance to be far more important than clearly enunciated dialogue; the second came with the transfer of direct-sound films to the television format. In the first instance, a technical solution was found with the development of special filters and compressors that enhanced and pumped up the dialogue, even the most inaudible lines. In the second instance, the problem was solved by re-mixing the film destined for television, thus creating a TV version that

highlighted the dialogue, which was then often spoiled by TV sets with poor audio equipment.[31]

That verbocentrism is the dominant tendency in cinema is thus ascertained and historically documented by the technical evolutions in dubbing. Parallel to this line of thought, Jarmusch's aversion to dubbing and his preference for subtitles can be interpreted as a symptom of his critical attitude towards verbocentrism: to give up the *voice* of an actor through dubbing is a far greater sin than giving up some of the meaning of the words his voice expresses through subtitles. An opinion, however, not shared by Alexander: 'I think any director who believes wholeheartedly in the imagery of his work doesn't want it marred by subtitles.' Recognizing that this point will always be controversial – on one side those who insist that the dialogue must be understood at any price, on the other those who feel that a convincing story can also be told without the perfect intelligibility of the dialogue – Alexander concluded that: 'After all is said and done a film is a visual product with a visually told story, and its dialogue simply dressing.' These different approaches stimulate further discussion, which can certainly not be reduced to a univocal, restricted vision.

Voices:
Roberto Benigni

1

In the films of Jim Jarmusch foreign languages are often spoken, and not always subtitled. One of these is Italian, a language that you obviously represent. It is portrayed on two levels, one of poetry and innocence in *Down By Law*, and a more physical, carnal level in *Night On Earth*. With innocence and poetry in mind, I defined Bob in *Down By Law* as a 'poetic' character, in the sense that he often expresses himself through poetry to communicate with others, quoting – in Italian, of course – American poets such as Robert Frost and often referring to Walt Whitman. How much do you think poetry can help us communicate?

Well, since poets are usually the parents of a given language, to make myself understood I used the language spoken by Mum and Dad. By so doing, we try to be friends, protective, warm, close. In order that one feels we share a common bond. Poets, great poets, are adults and children at the same time, something akin to the character I played, who committed a murder no less, while also being the purest of children. To quote Dante, the purest language is spoken by a child suckling its mother's breast. So when a foreigner makes a mistake speaking another language, he immediately sounds like a child who is learning, and you can't help liking him for it. Later, while growing up, one needs to add that poetic spark to things, so to speak. Since I didn't know the English language and I love poetry very much, I would learn the verses of Whitman, Frost and other Americans by heart, so that I could communicate. In fact, some American critics said I pretended not to speak English, because every now and then I would quote whole verses by great American poets, leaving them

flabbergasted, convinced I spoke a very refined English, as someone
wrote, simply because I quoted these poets. It's like someone arriving
in Italy and speaking only in Montale's verses!

Or in tercets, or in hendecasyllables.

Yes, in tercets or even extremely difficult and modern Montale-like
hendecasyllables. Every now and then I would learn something by heart,
and when a question lent itself I answered by turning poetry into prose.
And then Jim picked up on my daily use of notepads, which, like a child,
I took with me wherever I went, asking, 'How do you say this, how do
you say that?', repeating it over and over until the cows came home.

That's right. One of the tragic moments in the film is when Bob loses his
notepad: 'I lost my book of English!'

He lost his tongue. He lost his map. He lost his way. It was terrifying: a
real nightmare. Being a lover of poetry, Jim has great respect for words.
In fact, when we first met in Salso Maggiore, we became friends by
quoting poets, respectively Italian and American. Our friendship was
born on poetical quotes, sometimes from French, a language we both
dabbled in. Our bond strengthened through poetry, and continued to do
so. He has great respect and gives an almost evangelical-like dignity to
all things foreign. He has a Franciscan love for foreigners, and all things
different, seeing them as a source of enrichment, and he makes you feel
very much at ease. He deeply loves everything alien to his culture, which
is extremely rare, but comes naturally to him: it's instinctive, and it is
why in his films Jim uses sound in such an extraordinary way. The mix
of sounds and languages is a real gift to his audience.

Indeed, he has directed actors in Japanese, Finnish, languages he doesn't
speak.

Exactly. In *Mystery Train*, for example, the style in which he uses his
actors is unique. There are some films by Max Ophüls – one of the
world's greatest directors, thanks to his particular use of the camera,
the maestro to Bertolucci, Kubrick, they all consider him as the greatest
manoeuvrer, his use of the camera almost poetic – in which he also
directed foreign actors, including for instance the Italian actress Isa
Miranda. However, every now and then – and allow me to say this
without being overheard hopefully – he lacked something when it came
to directing those same foreign actors. You can tell he was uncomfortable

because, not knowing a foreign language he didn't know which words to stress and whether or not the acting was good or bad. What makes Jim so extraordinary is that despite not speaking all these languages, he succeeds in doing it perfectly. All the foreign actors I've seen him work with, I have to say, act perfectly. Summing up, I believe that Jim is truly one of the most cultivated directors I have ever met, one of the most cultivated people. His knowledge of Italian literature, especially with regard to the latter half of the twentieth century, is quite extraordinary: he knows it all!

2

In Jarmusch's films it would appear that the distinction between so-called 'high' culture and 'street culture' doesn't exist, and that all the ingredients they consist of end up in one big melting pot. Do you think, especially with regard to words, that there is a distinction between 'high' culture and 'street culture'?

No, I don't think so. It's the same with music. There are composers like Stravinsky or Mahler who used saucepans, ladles, glasses, stones, tinker's tools, or even jazz, which has used anything. Music and words are very similar to each other; they're both sounds. The difference is that during his time Dante succeeded in doing so by calling his work *Comedìa*, comedy, precisely because he wanted to use the street style, which allowed him to reach everyone, and also to reach the most incommensurable heights. You can't reach the top without first starting at the bottom. You see, you reach heaven by first passing through hell, it's obligatory, don't you think? Racine went as far as to say that you couldn't use the word 'handkerchief' in a tragedy because it would have ruined the poetry. Dante not only managed to use the word 'handkerchief', but he went so far as to write, not only farce and comedy, even tragedy, talking about excrements and our most lurid parts, thus mixing all the styles. So I don't think there's a distinction in the language used. The difference between Dante and Petrarch, for example, is that Petrarch is always adult, whereas Dante, as I was saying earlier, succeeded in doing what only the greatest do: be an adult and a child at the same time.

Petrarch is extraordinary because he influenced European culture for 300 years, including Shakespeare, precisely because the language he uses is so sublime, but he's 'colder' in the way he didn't write lines like 'At once my lips all trembling kiss'd.' Petrarch lacks sensuality, and one needs to bring sensuality and tenderness together. Petrarch has tenderness, a maternal tenderness, not the sensual, erotic, deep-reaching tenderness, the kind that gets under your skin. Instead all the effort involved in modern poetry, modern music, modern words, even modern painting has been directed towards uniting all these materials. But to have done it in Dante's time was something incredible, also because the hardship of twenty years' work risked going up in smoke quite simply because it was written in *volgare*, the street language of that era. Dante's greatness is to have dedicated twenty years of his life, with fathomless knowledge, effort and endless suffering, literally living a very real hell, not a metaphorical one, and succeeding in coming back up again.

High and low have to live together, no doubt about it. And this is something that I always recognize in Jarmusch's films.

Of course, that's exactly what you find in Jim's aesthetics, the high and the low. He is very Dante-esque.

3

So clearly your first meeting with Jarmusch in Salso Maggiore was love at first sight. What happened when you first met Tom Waits and John Lurie?

Yes, it really was love at first sight with Jim. Friendship is as deep as love, is it not? Indeed, it has lasted our whole lives, we have never been able to do without it. And I feel the intimacy of the distance that separates us. The geographical distance made our friendship even more special. Now every time we speak it's like picking fresh fruit from the tree.

Actually, when I interviewed him, it was some time ago, I told him I still had to interview Benigni and he immediately said: 'We spoke today already.'

You see, you see. . .

He also does a great impression of you.

(Laughing) I know, I know.

And how about your first encounter with Tom Waits and John Lurie?

Well, they're both musicians. I knew who Tom Waits was but not John Lurie. The same thing happened when I first saw John: an unforgettable friendship was born. He is a kind of reptile, a kind of lizard, and in fact his first group was called The Lounge Lizards. His brother Evan did the soundtracks of my first three films, *Piccolo Diavolo*, *Johnny Stecchino* and *Il Mostro*. John's soundtrack for *Down By Law* is magnificent, unforgettable, and then there are Tom Waits's songs . . . They too are very Dante-esque! It was a real happening; it reminded me of the Dolce Stil Novo group of poets, you know Cavalcanti, Lapo Gianni . . . it was wonderful, my very first American friends.

Right. Like in Dante's famous poem: 'Guido, i' vorrei che tu e Lapo ed io . . .'.

Yes and for me especially. It was also the first time I went to another continent, where I heard a different language finally being expressed in such a sublime and wonderful way by musicians. You know, a musician's life is all about counterpoint. They're the kind of things you say that might sound rhetorical; when it feels you've known someone for ever, and no one's even been introduced. We were like people meeting again after a very long time. They taught me fake English, because I was always asking: 'How do you say this, how do you say that?'

Speaking of which, is the story about 'I have to flame' true?

Yes, absolutely, very true! I always said I had 'to flame' when I needed to take a pee in bars, and I kept on saying it until a few years ago; it was a long time before they told me I shouldn't say 'to flame'.

Erik Sanko, who played bass with The Lounge Lizards for a number of years, told me that still today when he tours with his band Skeleton Key, and they're on the road, they pull into a petrol station for a 'flame stop'![1]

That's hysterical! I'd love to take a trip inside Jarmusch's music again, because his films are truly musical, there's that thing about them, they push you to the edge. They're like Japanese haikus, they're like a sound. Even his film, *Broken Flowers*, is really made up of four Japanese haikus. He truly is one of the directors and people I love most in the world.

And he is not afraid of using silence.

Right, he uses silence the way some painters do, because he loves paintings. It's like the paintings of Vermeer, who managed to paint silence, and Jim is one of those people who manage to paint silence in the cinema.

Rome, June 2008

6 The Melting Pot of Words, the Way of Cultural Relativism

'Which is more musical, a truck passing by a factory
or a truck passing by a music school?'
John Cage, *Silence* (London, 1987), p. 41

'And let each truth be false to us which was not greeted by one laugh!'
Friedrich Nietzsche, *Thus Spoke Zarathustra*, trans. Adrian del Caro
(Cambridge, 2006), p. 169

'Indians, Niggers, Same Thing . . .'[1] (Old Consigliere, *Ghost Dog*)

The absence of a model and a scale of dominant values, in other words
the idea that there exists no cultural hierarchy, is a basic assumption in
all Jarmusch's work. He does not hesitate to grab with both hands, to
quote, to 'steal' and to be inspired by the most varied cultural and art -
istic universes, at times some quite distant from each other, without
the slightest concerns of 'hierarchal' nature. Hip hop, Schubert, Betty
Boop cartoons and William Blake: artistic expressions that on 'Planet
Jarmusch' all have the same ID and the same citizenship rights. There are
no *sans papiers* in his galaxy.

To confirm the fact that Jarmusch does not apply scales of value,
but is on the contrary very suspicious in general of classifications like
'high' and 'low' – especially if referring to art and human expression –
I would now like to focus on a constant characteristic of his cinema, in
which *language* once again plays a decisive role: the use of irony and
comedy, which are almost always intended by Jarmusch to be vehicles
for themes far more diversified and profound than a simple distraction

triggered by a quick line of dialogue. As has been observed by the Italian scholar Giulio Ferroni,

> Comedy was for centuries relegated to the 'lower' spheres, that could not be fully negated nor erased, but were only tolerated as being subordinate to 'authentic' values, labelled 'serious', 'true', 'high', 'noble', 'sublime', etc. Regarding the values that render man 'human', comedy has taken on the role of intermission, of momentary digression: a recreational break within a life overly burdened with commitments and difficulties, a chance to catch one's breath and then to resume with more enthusiasm the climb upwards, towards a full possession of 'seriousness'.[2]

Running through Jarmusch's filmography it is evident that irony is instead a constant, capable of spanning and connecting the most varied of genres, from the road movie to the western, from the gangster movie to the comedy. Quoting Ferroni, it has nothing to do with 'momentary digression' or 'intermission': the sphere of comedy is an established element of Jarmusch's art, with dignity being as equal in every way as seriousness, and just as fundamental. To reconfirm the basic principle of cultural relativism, something serious does not necessarily equate with nobility or truth, irony can be just as true and worthy of attention. No hierarchy rules these diverse categories of human expression. What interests Jarmusch more is their meeting and merging. To quote from *Hagakure*, Yamamoto Tsunetomo's samurai manual that inspires Ghost Dog's behaviour, 'Among the maxims on Lord Naoshige's wall there was this one: "Matters of great concern should be treated lightly." Master Ittei commented: "Matters of small concern should be treated seriously."'[3]

'I Scream, You Scream, We All Scream for Ice Cream!'[4]

How, why and in what circumstances you laugh depends on numerous factors: environmental, linguistic, cultural and personal. Such variety is difficult to coalesce and even harder to translate: it is by no means a given that a dialogue adaptation from one language to another will grasp the comedy and linguistic tone of the original, and have the spectators of different nationalities and cultures laughing their heads off.[5] Irony, the play on words, the taste for a cynical and at times vaguely surreal humour have been, in spite of this, a constant of Jarmusch's films since the beginning of his career. He seems to care little for the inevitable 'risk of untranslatability'. In fact, it is the linguistic nuances and the play on words that represent one of the recurring causes behind the irony of his films. In some more than others.

Starting with its title, *Down By Law* is the ideal example dealing with the subject of language and misunderstanding:[6]

> 'Down by law' is an expression with a long history and signifies the opposite of what it at first might seem: 'oppressed, crushed by the law'. Born in black culture, the complete expression was to be 'down by law with someone', meaning to be united with another person, to enjoy mutual trust, to give and receive help. If two men were in prison together and the two were 'down by law' with each other, the first to be released would look after the other's family, would take care of his wife and children, and so on. In the 1970s, the expression re-emerged in the Rap culture of New York's Afro-American ghettoes, used in particular by the young members of street gangs: if you weren't 'down by law' you'd do well to stay out of sight, otherwise pay the consequences . . . Today, the expression has lost a lot of its original connotations and is used to describe someone cool, someone who knows how to keep himself under control.[7]

The original meaning of the expression is the one that best describes the relation between the three characters of the film – Bob, Jack and Zack – as cellmates and then as fellow fugitives, each different from the other and yet united by a strange but undeniable mutual solidarity. The desire and the search for solidarity and for a common 'lingo' are among the principle themes of *Down By Law*, themes often reaffirmed thanks to the irony of speech, idioms and word games.

In the memorable prison revolt sequence, the three neo-jailbirds chant the ditty that is probably the better remembered among the word games that pepper the film: 'I scream, you scream, we all scream for ice cream!' What comes to the fore is Roberto Benigni's unmistakable Italian accent: 'I screama, you screama, we alla screama for ice creama!' which adds considerably to the already undeniable comedy of the little song. The frail but energetic Bob repeats it at least two or three times to his stunned listeners and cellmates, Jack and Zack, to make absolutely sure that they fully understand the semantic slide. For some mysterious reason, perhaps due to their amused amazement, the two decide to join in the game and so 'sing' along with him. As in an awkward, improvised ritual, the three dance around their cell shouting their heads off in an ever-growing crescendo, louder and louder. Slowly, one begins to hear an echo, their words multiplying, and their voices going from three to 30, 100, 300, more and more. The innocuous ditty has triggered the start of a revolt, more *spoken* than physical, quickly crushed by the guards' riot sticks clattering across the cell bars.

The brief, liberating protest is the prelude to the threesome's prison escape, one definitely not only *spoken* but spurred on by grammatical nuances. With an innocent but determined expression, Bob tells his two companions that he has found a way to escape. He opens the discussion with his usual question: 'How do you say in English when . . .?' As always, Jack responds gruffly: 'Escape!' Unperturbed, Bob explains to the two sceptics that breaking out is indeed possible. He knows what to do and is convinced that the escape can take place out in the exercise yard. The key is in a *preposition*. Bob responds to his companions' curt and incredulous reaction by stressing in a decisively cryptic way: 'Not *from* the yard, *to* the yard.' Thus said, no further words are deemed necessary to clarify *how* the plan will unfold. Jarmusch shows nothing of the jail-break, other than the three running away through what appears to be a sewage drain. The act of escaping is completely de-spectacularized: first they were in, then they were out, being hunted. As in real life, changes can be sudden and, above all, totally unexpected. Absurdly, Jarmusch might not have had the time to film the escape, one that I would like to define as *linguistic*, and in sharp contrast with the traditions of prison movies like *Papillon* or *Escape from Alcatraz*, a genre that Bob appears to be well acquainted with.[8] In fact, his first words following their successful breakout are: 'We escaped! Like in the American movies!'

Continuing with *Down By Law*, a considerable slice of Bob's linguistic curiosity, other than towards poetry, is directed towards proverbs, speech patterns and idioms. Having just entered the cell where Zack and Jack, because of their fight, are still glaring at each other, Bob consults his inseparable notebook and debuts with: 'If looks can kill I am dead now.' The fact that the phrase is grammatically wrong and pronounced with the customary funny accent does not matter. What does matter is that, thanks also to the immunity that a speech pattern can offer through its universally recognized validity, the visibly nervous newcomer succeeds in the somewhat difficult endeavour of making the two

seemingly violent heavies take their eyes off him: following Bob's opening phrase, met without comment or a greeting punch, the two do in fact
turn their collective penetrating glare elsewhere. Using a play on words,
a proverb or an idiomatic phrase that condense a truth shared by common sense, is a more or less naive search for a supportive reaction from
the person being spoken to. It is perhaps because of this that Bob, seeking comprehension in every way, often expresses himself through them.

To confirm the *linguistic* nature of Benigni's character, I would like
to make two more examples. Staying with the scene of his admission to
the cell, after both Jack and Zack have refused to shake his hand, Bob
once again tries his luck with the spoken word. He is not afraid of drifting into triviality. On the contrary, touching on the comic register he
deliberately looks for a form of human contact when, again quoting
from his faithful notebook, he says: 'Not enough room to swing a cat
. . . Cat, the animal . . .'. Jack and Zack do not respond, notwithstanding the fact that Bob's gesture of swinging a cat by its tail has powerful

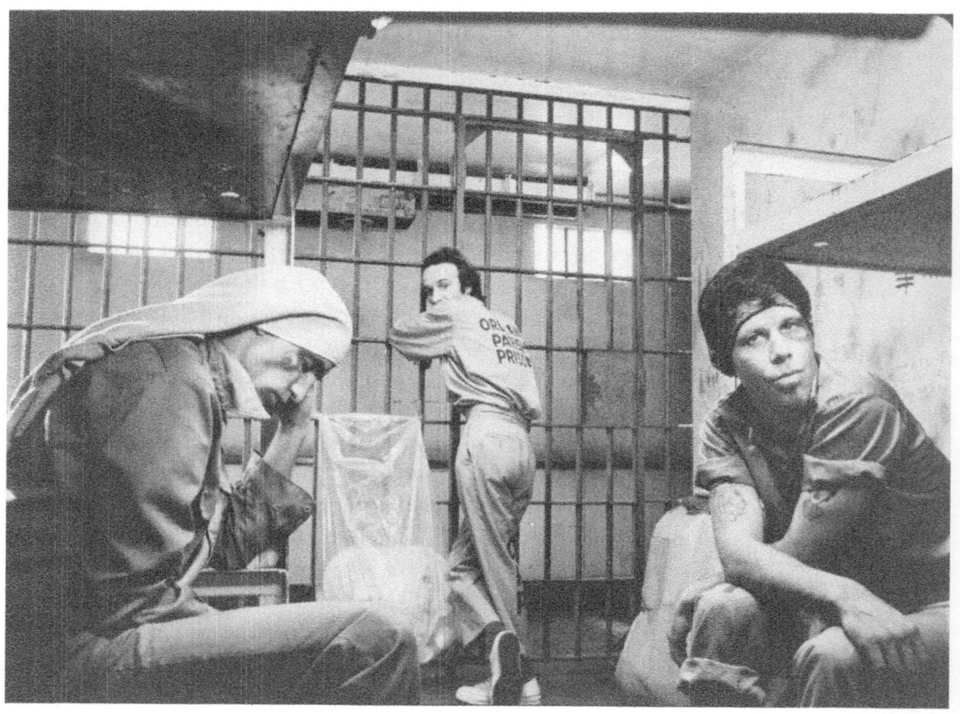

'If looks can kill
I am dead now',
Down By Law.

comic potential. Jarmusch appears to be saying that solidarity does not come that easily.

The second example comes from the significant end sequence of the film: on the road in front of the isolated house in the bayou that overnight becomes their love nest, Bob and his new-found girlfriend Nicoletta say goodbye to Jack and Zack, possibly for ever. Here Benigni produces a truly 'idiomatic performance'. The Italian with the ruffled hair shouts at the two Americans as they are leaving, but still clearly visible in the shot: 'Wish you were here! . . . Don't forget to write!' What strikes you here, particularly with regard to the first of the two idioms, is that it is very much a written expression, postcard-like, thus decidedly out of step with the scene. At first it might seem a banal example of Bob/Benigni's ignorance of the English language or a simple joke, but in my opinion it conceals a far more articulated idea instead: the phrase shouted by Bob in fact negates the distinction, generally meant as hierarchy, between the written word (synonymous with truth and reliability) and the spoken one (synonymous with volatility and absence of guarantees). Not for nothing does Bob stress that the two 'American friends' must not forget to write to him. Thus, even if decidedly veiled and hidden, it is possible once again to glimpse the principle of *relativism* so dear to Jarmusch: communication, whether it be verbal or written, comes to the same thing, has equal dignity, and so becomes a complex communicative material that avoids formal classifications and schematic evaluations.

'Faces and Names'[9]

Having established that for Jarmusch the ironic register implies the re-affirmation of the general principle of *relativism* – because in the cinema just as in life, both the serious and non-serious are always combined – one of the comic motors he prefers is the play on personal names. Not a device of little import, but one that hints at the person's very identity. The *name*, the presumed unassailable bastion that encompasses the character and sums up the essence of someone, because it is normally coupled with the verb 'to be', can instead be a point of discussion, a source of misunderstanding, can even become ridiculous or the brunt of hysterical gags. Jarmusch's particular passion for this play on names runs through his entire filmography to the point that it has become a recognized 'trademark'.

I would like to touch upon certain examples from *Stranger Than Paradise* to *Only Lovers Left Alive,* in some cases quoting passages from the screenplays.

Already in *Stranger Than Paradise,* the character of Willie/Bela (John Lurie) clearly personifies the link, and the contrast, between name and identity. Willie often stresses the fact that in no way does he want to be called by his real Hungarian name: his new American identity compels him to forget that part of himself. Even if, in Willie/Bela's case, irony plays a less important role, there is an exemplary scene in which a sort of bizarre Dante-esque 'law of retaliation' is applied: when Bela tries at last to be amusing with cousin Eva, and wants to tell her a joke, his memory lets him down. Sitting with her at Aunt Lotte's kitchen table Willie throws in the towel after a couple of false starts, forced to admit that he has forgotten the punchline. 'But it's good!' he promises Eva, who laughs nonetheless. The paradox is that in this case one laughs at the lack of the punchline, a paradox that brings to mind the condition of Willie/Bela: if the amputation of a slice of Willie's Hungarian identity is not exactly funny, the absence of the punchline is.

In *Down By Law,* the name game is far more direct and deliberately comical. The characters played respectively by Lurie and Waits are called Jack and Zack and, in addition to their rhyming names, are more alike than they would wish to admit. In the balance between the three characters, the two Americans play straight men to the Italian. It is inevitable that Bob/Benigni, struggling with the English language right from the moment he enters the film, is forced into a sort of incessant verbal combat to get their names right – without ever really succeeding. Here the underlying theme to the superficial gag is not so much about identity, as with Willie/Bela, but rather about the already mentioned search for solidarity, understanding and a common language that Bob wants more than anything else to establish with his two new 'American buddies'.

The gag on names in *Mystery Train* alludes instead to the more political theme of racial intolerance. As already touched upon, the white British champion of black rights, Johnny, is nicknamed 'Elvis' by the African American regulars at Shades because of his 1950s look. This does not go down too well with Johnny, who considers Elvis a symbol of white exploitation. In the ensuing dialogue, Johnny sits near the pool table with his friend Ed drowning his sorrows, and discussing Carl Perkins, one of the forgotten voices in the history of rock 'n' roll, notwithstanding the fact that he wrote an absolute classic like 'Blue Suede Shoes'. In the opinion of many, the song was skilfully ripped off and raised to planetary heights by Elvis Presley himself.

> Pool player 2: Hey! What's the matter with Elvis?
> Johnny: Don't call me Elvis! If you can't use my proper name
>   why don't you try Carl Perkins Junior, or something? I mean,
>   I don't call him *Sam and Dave*, do I?
> Pool player 1: Hey man, my name *is* Dave . . .
> Ed: His name *is* Dave . . . Look it's all right man, he's cool.
> He's cool.[10]

To avoid a fight by the skin of his teeth with the corpulent Dave, who is in no mood for word games, Johnny is forced to grin and bear it and reluctantly accept the hated nickname.

In *Night On Earth*, a highly explicit game on names takes place in the New York episode. Two totally different characters are seated in the rundown taxi: ex-clown Helmut Grokenberger,[11] an East German immigrant, and Yo-Yo, a chirpy and fiery Hispanic Brooklynite.

> Yo-Yo: What's your name man?
> Helmut: Helmut Grokenberger, you can read it. That's me.
> Yo-Yo: Helmet?!
> Helmut: Helmut.
> Yo-Yo: That's your name?! (laughs)
> Helmut: Ja.
> Yo-Yo: That's a fucked-up name to be naming your kid! Helmet.
>   'Cause in English it would be like something you wear on your
>   head, you know? A helmet! (laughs) In English that'd be like
>   calling your kid . . . lampshade! Some shit like that. Hey!
>   Lampshade, come here and clean up your room! (laughs)
> Helmut: So, what's your name?
> Yo-Yo: Yo-Yo.
> Helmut: Was?
> Yo-Yo: Yo-Yo, that's my name!
> Helmut: Ist doch kein Name . . . Yo-Yo?
> Yo-Yo: Yo-Yo!
> Helmut: Yo-Yo . . . (laughs) Das ist ein Spielzeug für Kinder,
>   weisst du? (mimics playing with a yo-yo).

Yo-Yo: It ain't got nothing to do with that. It's my name: Yo-Yo.
Helmut: It's a toy for kids: yo-yo.
Yo-Yo: It ain't got nothing to do with that, man!
Helmut: Okay. Your name: Yo-Yo; my name: Helmut. It's good.

In this funny dialogue, the potential fight is resolved by Jarmusch once again using the principle of *cultural relativism*, applied here in a quasi-literal manner: neither of the two may boast a hypothetical linguistic or cultural superiority. Whether dealing with a helmet or a child's toy, the two will not let the polysemy of a name ruin their evening. After this dialogue exchange, their journey will continue without further verbal blunders.

Another sequence that almost seems like an anthem to *cultural relativism* is the highly amusing dialogue on the name of Ghost Dog, in the film of the same name that deserves to be quoted in full. Louie, the mafioso and Ghost Dog's 'employer', is interrogated by the shabby Italian American 'cupola', hell-bent on tracking down and eliminating the killer with the mysterious name.

Sonny: Now, what the fuck is his name?
Louie: Ghost Dog.
Sonny: What?
Louie: Ghost Dog.
Mr Vargo: Ghost . . . Dog?
Old Consigliere: He said Ghost Dog!
Louie: He calls himself Ghost Dog. I don't know, a lot of these
    black guys today, these gangster-type guys, they all got names
    like that, they make up for themselves.
Mr Vargo: Is that true?
Sonny: Sure. He means like the rappers. The rappers, they all got
    names like that: Snoop Doggy Dogg, Ice Cube, Q-Tip, Method
    Man. My favourite was always Flavor Flav from Public Enemy.
    'He got the funky fresh fly flava. Live lyrics from the bank of
    reality. I kick da flyest dope manoeuvre technicality, to a dope
    track.' I love that guy!
Mr Vargo: I don't know anything about that, but it makes me
    think about Indians. They've got names like Red Cloud, Crazy
    Horse, Running Bear, Black Elk . . . (makes a sound like an elk)
Sonny: Yeah. That kind of shit.

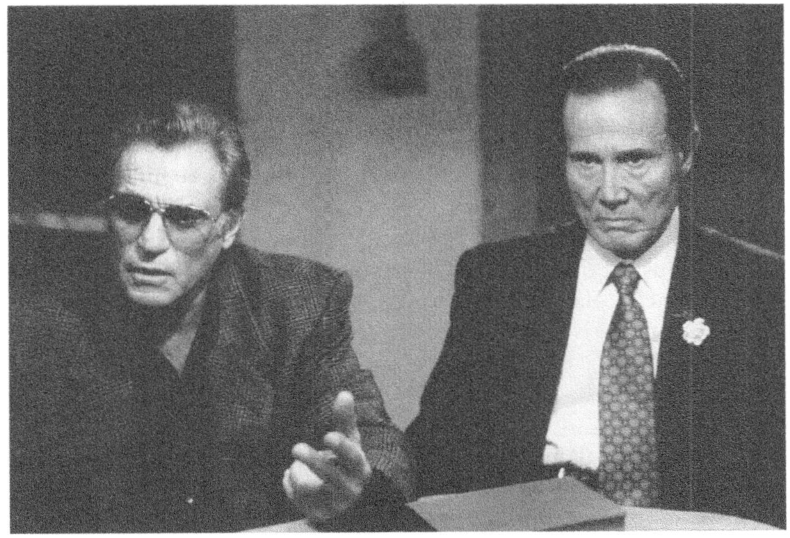

Old Consigliere: Indians, niggers, same thing.
Sonny: Johnny!
Johnny: Sonny? Mr Vargo?
Sonny: Go outside. Get Sammy the Snake, Joe Rags, Big Angie.
    Get 'em in here, will you?
Johnny: Right away.

Black gangsters, rappers, Native Americans, Italian American mafiosi. Jarmusch uses a varicoloured procession of names and pseudonyms through which, without shunning irony, he causes us to reflect on themes of identity, of tolerance, maintaining at its base the common denominator of *cultural relativism*.

In the more recent *Broken Flowers*, the running gag on the protagonist's name continues throughout the film from start to finish. Every time he is introduced, Don Johnston (Bill Murray) is forced to point out that his surname is Johnston with a 'T' because of the similarity with Don Johnson, the overly polished and suntanned icon of the 1980s, star of the highly successful TV series *Miami Vice*, considered by Jarmusch to be an example of anti-aesthetic.[12] Don is condemned to being continually associated with this glossy world and his tired resigned expression says a lot about how distant he is from it.

Unlike in Don's case, a name can sometimes adapt itself perfectly to the character. A fitting example of this is the girl (Alexis Dziena) with the exaggerated propensity for exhibitionism, the daughter of Laura (Sharon Stone), Don's first ex-girlfriend, whom he visits during his pilgrimage into the past. Soon after the usual Don Johnston misunderstanding, the teenage girl who opens the door reveals to him her name.

> Lolita: Well, come on in. So, my mom'll be home from work soon, so just sit down. Here. Make yourself comfortable. So, my name's Lola. Well, sometimes people call me 'Lo' but my really real name is Lolita.
> Don: Lolita?
> Lolita: Yeah.

With great nonchalance, Lolita then performs one of the rare full nudity scenes of Jarmusch's filmography, causing a terrified and very embarrassed Don to hightail it out of there.

An encounter with another girl will be less problematic, in fact quite tender, her name fitting the character perfectly.

> Don: What's your name?
> Sun: Sun. Sun Green.
> Don: Sun Green? Perfect.
> Sun: What's yours?
> Don: Don. Don Johnston.
> Sun: Really? Don Johnson?
> Don: Johnston. With a 'T.'

Sun Green (Pell James) is the young florist who, apart from her ability with floral compositions, proves to be quite a skilled nurse when taking care of Don's black eye, the result of what he calls a 'minor misunderstanding' with the brutal biker friends of ex-girlfriend Penny (Tilda Swinton). The thoughtful girl is the namesake of another Sun Green to whom Jarmusch probably wanted to refer in this scene: the adolescent girl who fights for Planet Earth in the saga *Greendale*, the environmental opus by friend Neil Young, composed of no less than a concept album, a film and a graphic novel, rigorously published on recycled paper.[13]

Both Lolita and Sun Green are reflections of their names, an idea elaborated in the more recent *The Limits of Control*. Here, for the first and only time in his filmography, Jarmusch did not use real names, but chose to go the way of the allegorical name that embodies a peculiar quality of the character. Thus, for example, the solitary killer played by Isaach de Bankolé is simply named 'Lone Man'; the character representing the world of music is 'Violin' (Louis Tosar); the platinum-haired allegory of the cinema personified by Tilda Swinton is 'Blonde'; and the minute personification of science is named 'Molecules' (Youki Kudoh). 'Nude' (Paz de la Huerta), who is vastly different from Lolita's adolescent exhibitionism in *Broken Flowers*, is a paradigmatic and adult example of full nudity, the allegory of desire who makes futile attempts to seduce the impassive Lone Man.

In all these cases of harmony and identification between characters and names, Jarmusch for once appears to distance himself from his usual orientation towards relativism by choosing absolute assumptions. And yet there is something in *The Limits of Control* that renders the mentioned allegorical names slightly less absolute than they appear: the characters never introduce themselves, a one-off in Jarmusch's cinema. In order to discover their names, the spectator has to wait and read the end credits, if he has the patience. If on one side the allegorical name is thus given enormous responsibility, seeing that it encompasses far more than a casual summons, a sign of recognition and identification of a person, on the other side such importance is at the same time negated, seeing that the allegorical name is never mentioned. This apparently contradictory approach thus expresses once again Jarmusch's tendency to relativize a hypothetical absolute value: that which, at first sight, would appear fundamental to understanding the nature of a character remains instead unexpressed and as a matter of fact annulled.

In Jarmusch's most recent film, *Only Lovers Left Alive*, one could talk of symbolic, literary and historical names rather than allegorical ones. The two main characters' names, Adam and Eve, are not only a quite obvious biblical symbol, they also stand for unconditional, immortal love. Love for each other, but also love for science, art, nature, poetry, cinema and culture in general: their only 'food', along with what they call 'the good stuff', type O negative blood. The fact that Adam and Eve have been wandering undercover through time and space for an indefinite number of centuries offers Jarmusch an extraordinary opportunity: a virtually infinite series of names. Every time they have to travel, they are forced to change identity and sometimes gender, at least on paper, demonstrating again how relative a name can be. Eve, for example, takes

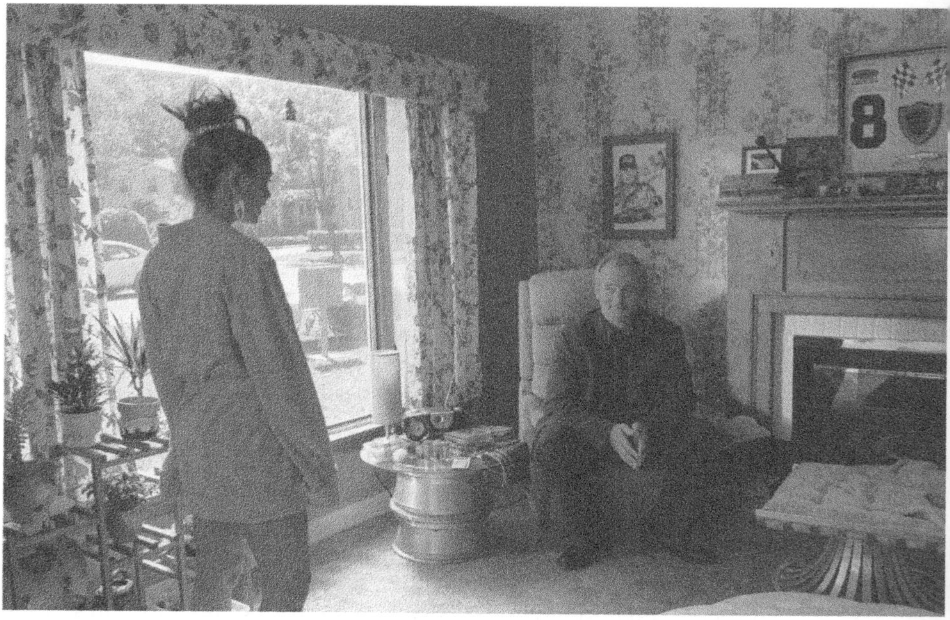

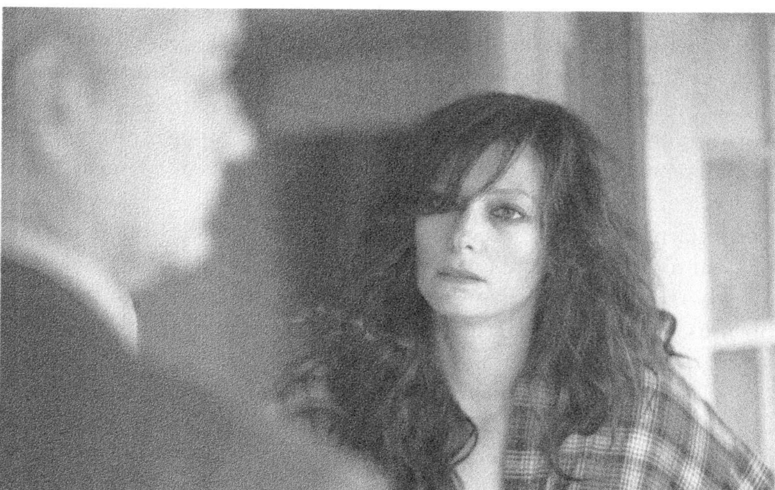

Alexis Dziena
as Lolita in
Broken Flowers.

Tilda Swinton
as Penny in
Broken Flowers.

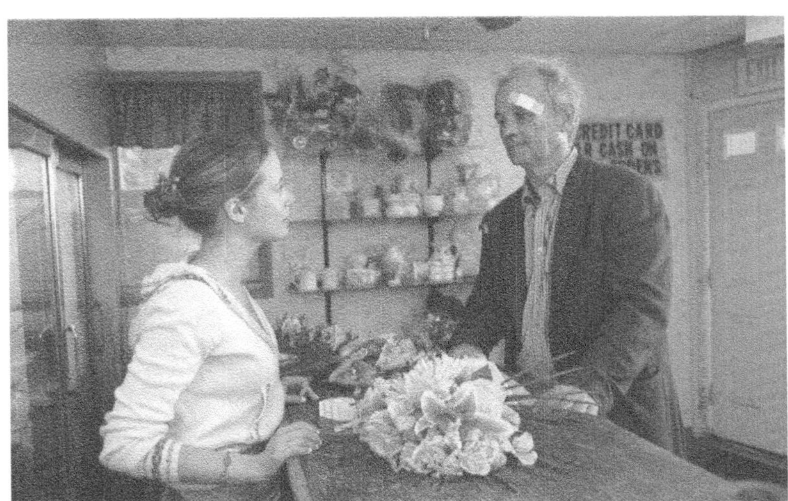

Molecules, *The
Limits of Control.*

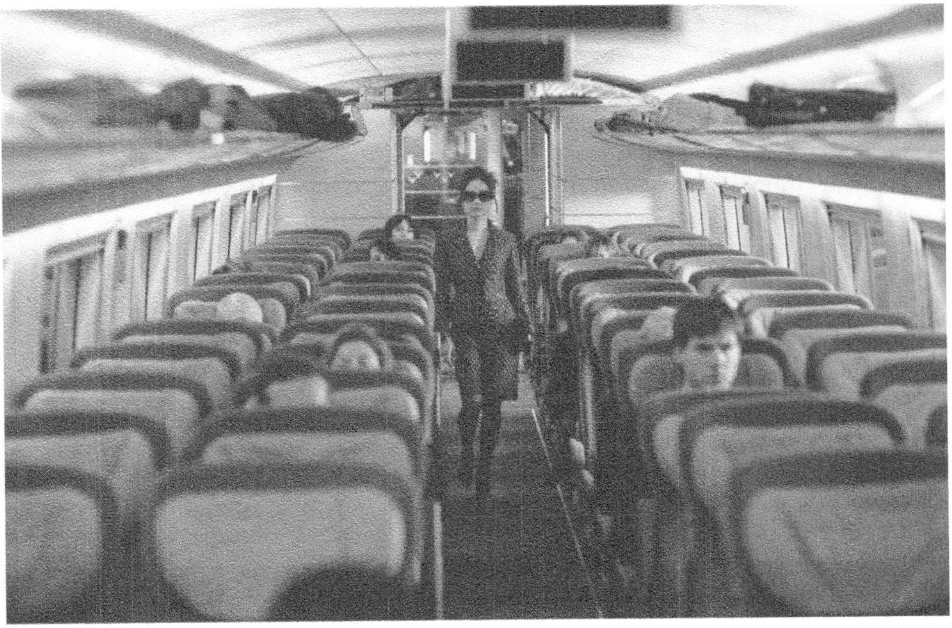

on the identities of Fibonacci (1170–1250), the Italian mathematician famous for the number sequence associated with his name, and of the literary character Daisy Buchanan from F. Scott Fitzgerald's *The Great Gatsby* (1925). Adam 'is' Stephen Dedalus – literary alter ego of James Joyce and character in his novels *A Portrait of the Artist as a Young Man* (1916) and *Ulysses* (1922) – and Dr Faust, the legendary figure that inspired countless artists over the centuries. It is probable that Jarmusch wanted to refer to one in particular: Christopher Marlowe and *The Tragical History of the Life and Death of Doctor Faustus* (published posthumously in 1604). Adam displays this highly symbolic name on his fake doctor badge when he goes to the hospital's lab to get new supplies of 'good stuff' from illegal blood-dealer Dr Watson (Jeffrey Wright). The namesake of the famous character in Sir Arthur Conan Doyle's *Sherlock Holmes* stories, frightened by the sudden, phantom-like appearance of his strange, pale 'customer', gives him a few more nicknames: Dr Strangelove and Dr Caligari, as if Jarmusch wanted to intersect literary and filmic references.

Finally, in *Only Lovers Left Alive*, there is one more character whose name is neither symbolic nor literary, but rather historical: Christopher Marlowe (John Hurt). In this case name and character coincide, something that rarely happens in Jarmusch's films.[14] To be even more historically accurate, Jarmusch made Adam and Eve regularly call the innovator of blank verse drama – and fellow vampire – by his real nickname, Kit. Making Christopher Marlowe a senior vampire can be seen as the strategy chosen by Jarmusch to question the accounts of the real Marlowe's mysterious alleged death in 1593 at only 29 years of age. As John Hurt put it in Cannes after the premiere of the film: 'Jim utterly believes in Christopher Marlowe. He believes that he wrote Shakespeare. He believes that he should be alive now. And I am.'[15]

Staying with the subject of literary identities, and taking a big leap back in Jarmusch's filmography, the last observations on names must include two characters whose names are an integral part of the film's entire narrative: William Blake and Nobody in *Dead Man*.

Nobody: What name were you given at birth, stupid white man?
William Blake: Blake. William Blake.
Nobody: Is this a lie? Or a white man's trick?
William Blake: No, I'm William Blake.
[Horse neighing]

Nobody: Then you are a dead man.
William Blake: I'm sorry. I d— I don't understand.
Nobody: Is your name really William Blake?
William Blake: Yes.

The Native American cannot believe that he is talking to the – dead –
great British poet and painter, whose homonymy with the unacquainted
bookkeeper from Cleveland is the essence of the rapport between the
two travelling companions and, above all, explains the deep respect that
Nobody immediately feels for Blake. If his name is William Blake, then
he must *be* William Blake. Nobody's concept of names is much like
the original archaic and outdated biblical one of the so-called Adamic
language, according to which the name of an entity is not only referring
to, but also identical with, the very entity itself. He has no doubt about
this. The young bookkeeper played by Johnny Depp is not of the same
opinion. Contrary to Nobody, Blake does not believe in the uniqueness

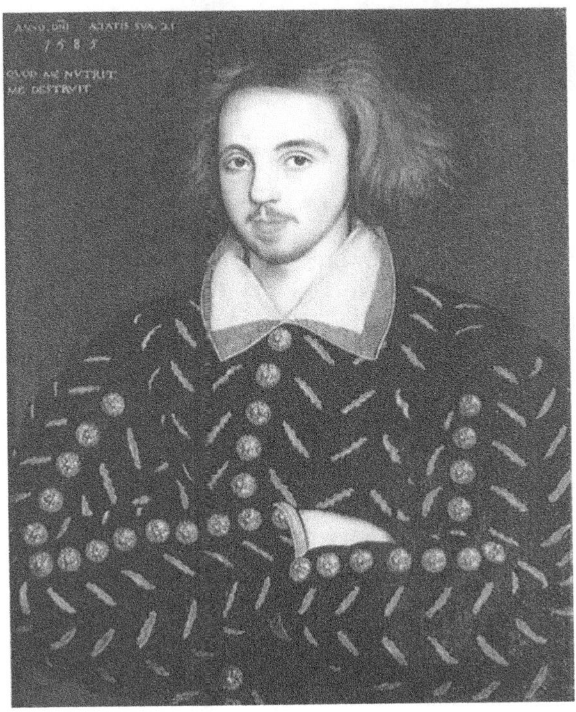

Putative portrait
of Christopher
Marlowe by
unknown artist
(1585).

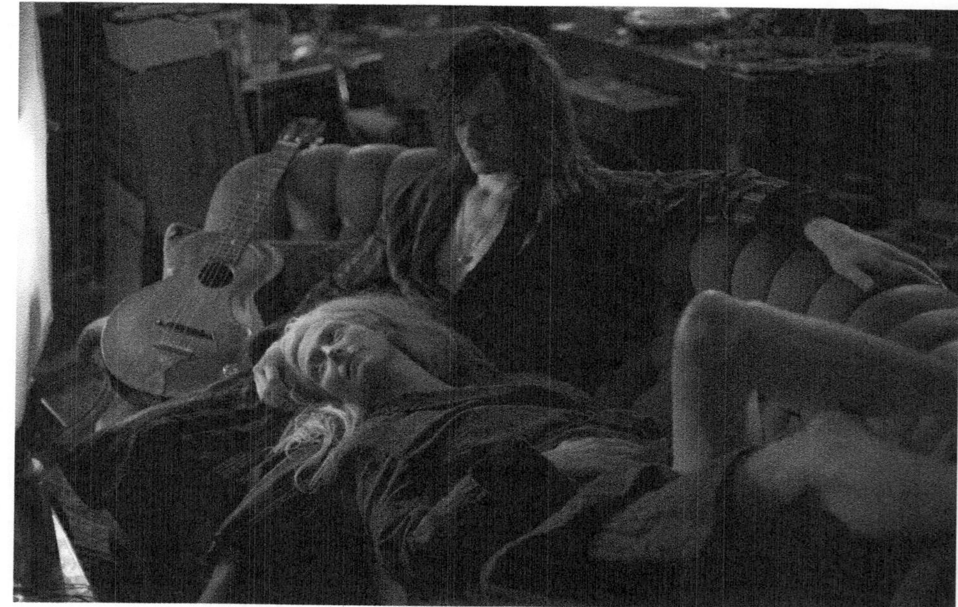

of a name, and accepts its multiplicity without reservation, as an expression of the far more modern linguistic principle of the arbitrariness of
the sign.

Adam and Eve,
*Only Lovers Left
Alive.*

> William Blake: What is your name?
> Nobody: My name is Nobody.
> William Blake: Excuse me?
> Nobody: My name is Xebeche: He Who Talks Loud, Saying
> Nothing.
> William Blake: He Who Talks . . . I thought you said your name
> was Nobody.
> Nobody: I prefer to be called Nobody.

The Native American's various names – Nobody, Xebeche, He Who Talks
Loud, Saying Nothing – do not surprise Blake, who just tries to understand which of the three is the correct one. These names conceal extremely
heterogeneous cultural references: from the revisionist spaghetti western
Il mio nome è Nessuno (My Name is Nobody) to Homer's *Odyssey*,
hinted at in the dialogue – 'Who are you travelin' with? I'm with Nobody'

– and to James Brown's funk classic 'Talkin' Loud and Sayin' Nothing'.[16] The literary and artistic references to William Blake, fundamental ingredients of Jarmusch's savoury cultural melting pot, should, of course, be mentioned in the same breath as the three above. Thanks to the play on names, the irony, the attention and the passion for words, Jarmusch confirms his propensity for *cultural relativism*, an approach that in some cases can put in doubt the very concept of origin.

Original Black Samurai Meets Dante

The *nom d'art* is an antique phenomenon as old as art itself. In music pseudonyms are surely an integral and inescapable part of both the rap and hip hop galaxies. In the world of rhymes and poetry it is practically par for the course to have at least one if not more pseudonyms. Generally, rappers declare their various names in their lyrics, often followed by a customary 'in the house'.

Drastically restricting the field to the hip hop collective that Jarmusch has worked with, the Wu-Tang Clan, it is quite extraordinary how many pseudonyms date back, for example, to Russell Tyrone Jones, who died prematurely in 2004:[17] ODB, the acronym for Ol' Dirty Bastard, is certainly the most famous, but at least another 30 names could be added to the list, including Dirt McGirt, Osirus, Dirt Dog, Ason Unique, Big Baby Jesus and Joe Bananas. Just as prolific is Robert Fitzgerald Diggs who founded the Clan in the early 1990s together with his cousins ODB and Gary Grice, aka GZA/Genius. Diggs is better known as RZA, but also answers to Prince Rakeem, Chief Abbott, Bobby Digital, the Rzarecta, Bobby Steels and the Scientist. This insistence on the variety of pseudonyms can be interpreted as a constant identity game, like some deliberate attempt to hide one's tracks. Or, reversing the discussion, the variety of names can be construed as a strategy to affirm the importance and uniqueness of one's identity, recognizable in the voice, in the music and in the style, regardless of the name chosen for the occasion. Both theories are plausible. There is a third, less psychological theory that could be dictated by far more pragmatic contractual and copyright demands coupled with the single pseudonyms. This is something not to be considered totally improbable, taking into account the strong entrepreneurial matrix that since the beginning has marked the Clan or, perhaps better, the 'dynasty' of music and business started in 1993 by the three cousins and the other six MCs:

infiltrating every major hip hop label by having their members sign solo contracts, while the group itself had its own unified pact . . . With their own semiotics and iconography, the cult of the Clan bled out into the world of comic books, fashion, film and books, in ways previously unknown to hip hop.[18]

Whether it is about video games, like *Wu-Tang: Shaolin Style* made for the Sony PlayStation, or about the clothing and accessories line Wu-Wear, right from the start the collective has aimed at creating a real 'Wu identity' that the fans could wear in every sense, metaphorically and otherwise.[19]

What is surprising is that such an identity, born and raised in the black community of New York's Staten Island, has little to do with the classic mythology of the African American origins tied to the infamous history of colonialism and slavery: for RZA it is not Africa that represents the cradle of his culture, it is Asia and the first man is the *Asiatic black man*. As Chad P., a follower of the Clan, told me in New York, it is whites who want to believe that the ancestors of today's black people came from Africa:

> Our heroes were the Shaolin monks! We all grew up the same way in the mid-1980s. On Saturday afternoon at three o'clock on Channel Five we were all watching the same kung fu movies. *Return to the 36th Chamber.* My favourite always was *Executioners From Shaolin.* The Wu-Tang is pure underground hip hop I can relate to, identify with, even wear. They are real life.[20]

The fact that even the concept of *origin* is relative and in no way static is made even clearer by the words of RZA in an interview given to a French magazine in 1999, to coincide with the release of *Ghost Dog: The Way of the Samurai*:

> I don't have this great passion for my African roots. As far as I'm concerned, Africa is the name given to a territory discovered by an explorer. To keep us happy, we're often told that Africa is the cradle of humanity, but to me the origins of humanity can be found in Asia just as easily as in Africa. I prefer to think that the first man was an Asian. When I was a kid, it wasn't Africa

that appealed to me, it was the Far East. The American culture
seemed static, frozen, whereas the Asian one was vibrant.
All the members of Wu-Tang watched the same Japanese
manga on TV.[21]

Speaking specifically of *Ghost Dog* and the apparent lack of 'anger,
rebellion and Rap message' – in a film revolving around a white mafioso
who is served by a black man until his death – RZA points out that
Jarmusch's story is simply a 'fairy tale' about a samurai. The connection
to Asiatic culture is deeply rooted in RZA's personal and musical history
and does not necessarily coincide with a strictly political black liberation
message: 'The first Rap group was called Grandmaster Flash. Where do
you think that name came from?' RZA is referring to the heroes of the one-
dollar kung fu and karate movies that were shown at low-budget theatres
in black ghettos and that he and his friends used to see. 'That's where my
culture comes from, and Hip Hop too.'[22]

Being on the same wavelength with Jarmusch and Ghost Dog –
whom RZA meets during a brief but incisive cameo in the film – seems
thus inevitable. What undoubtedly unites the three is the leitmotif of
cultural relativism by virtue of which RZA argues the very concept of
origin, a fact that could not help but charm Jarmusch, creator of the
black samurai killer character, his own personal variation on the theme
of the *Asiatic black man*. And just to muddy the waters of the cultural
universes of reference a little further, Jarmusch, who defines RZA's essential and minimalist music as 'poetically beautiful but slightly damaged',
rather fittingly refers to him as 'the Thelonius Monk of hip hop'.[23]

Remaining in the field of music and going from Asia to Africa,
this is the appropriate place to mention Ethiopian maestro Mulatu
Astatke again. An idea similar to the one described this far, as *the relativism of origin*, was in fact expressed by Astatke with regard to the
Derashe tribe of Ethiopia, whom he called *the scientists of sound*. In
his opinion, they are the ones who, centuries ago, invented and played
the diminished twelve-tone scale that bebop rendered so popular, overwhelming what is today taught in conservatoires and universities.
According to Astatke, we owe the origin of this scale so vital to the
future development of music and jazz improvisation not to Bach, not
to Debussy and not to Charlie Parker, but to an unknown tribe in
Southern Ethiopia.[24] Now, speaking of both RZA and Mulatu Astatke,
and extending the subject to include Jarmusch, the point is not so much

Ghost Dog and RZA, *Ghost Dog: The Way of the Samurai.*

that of wanting to exchange one continent for another, a primacy for another, an originality or an origin for another. What I wish to highlight is the link that, tied to *relativism*, unites all three: the fact that these same notions – nationality, primacy, origin, originality – are not considered static or frozen within cultural, historical and socially dominant models. Instead, they move within the infinitely vaster reign of possibilities and it is this that allows the three artists in question to maintain an open, fresh and genuine view, one that is certainly respectful of, but not submissive to, a presumed, pre-existing and lifeless hierarchy of ideas.

Approaching the end of this chapter and finally returning to the realm of *words*, the common denominator of this section of the book, I would like to quote a verbal game expressed in the dialogue of the already mentioned Paris episode in *Night On Earth*, which again alludes to the theme of origins.

It is past midnight in Paris and the taxi driver played by Isaach de Bankolé is struggling to put up with his very noisy and annoying passengers. The two African diplomats are drunk and over the moon about having pulled off some diplomatic coup, which makes them feel even more free from liability than the immunity their profession already guarantees them. So free in fact that they consider themselves authorized to make discriminatory, offensive and gratuitous remarks aimed at the young immigrant driver. The play on words is based on his country of origin and his somewhat dubious driving abilities. After various attempts at guessing the immigrant's origins, the two Cameroonian diplomats add insult to injury by coming up with a wide range of stereotypes of African nationalities. The taxi driver, who until then has been practically mute, finally loses his cool and shouts that he is from the Ivory Coast: 'Ivoirien! Je suis Ivoirien, de la Côte d'Ivoire!' After a moment's hesitation, a reaction to the immigrant's loud and somewhat unexpected outburst, the more brazen of the two diplomats, with the eye-popping expression of someone who has finally received an answer, responds: 'Ça explique tout! Il est Ivoirien . . . Il voit rien!! C'est pour ça qu'il ne sais conduire! Il voit rien!!' 'He can't see, which is why he can't drive', is the comment based on the diplomat's offensive pun. As far as the driver is concerned, this is the final straw: he floors the brake pedal and kicks the two out of his taxi. Thanks to the play on words based on the homophony of 'Ivoirien' and 'Il voit rien' the two diplomats try to associate the driver's name, in this case identified with the country of origin, with the presumed characteristic, namely that of 'not seeing'. In their own limited vision, the two try to recover that archaic and out-dated ideal of the Adamic language in which name and thing – in this case name and characteristic – are identical. Obviously, their endeavour fails: an 'Ivoirien' can see perfectly well. The name, corresponding here to the origin, is in a profoundly relative and arbitrary association with reality, and a cinematographic reality to boot.

Having established that 'Jarmusch's way' could without hesitation be defined as the 'way of cultural relativism', I would like to conclude with a theory, slightly paradoxical I admit, that Jarmusch illustrated during the 43rd London Film Festival (1999), and that still involves *words*.[25] After a funny parenthesis on sports, during which Jarmusch defined baseball as 'a very Zen-like game' and admitted to his total ignorance of cricket – 'I find it beautiful to watch and I like that they break for tea. That is very cool, but I don't understand' – the talk concentrated once again on words, poetic words in particular. Jarmusch explained: 'If you go into a bar in most places in America and even say the word poetry, you'll probably get beaten up.' With his typical propensity for cultural hodgepodge, and swinging the discussion towards Italy and its literary traditions, Jarmusch continued his reasoning: 'I think that Dante was hip-hop-culture because he wrote in vernacular Italian, and at the time that was unheard of; people wrote in Latin or Petrarch wrote in high Italian, and so Dante was talking street stuff.' Now, I do not want to propose adventurous links between the New York hip hop of the 1990s and the Florence of the thirteenth and fourteenth centuries, between the coarse lyrics of RZA and the Wu-Tang Clan and the hendecasyllabic verses of the *Divine Comedy*, yet, in a certain way, an analogy is possible.

The 'poetry of the street' or the 'vulgar', intended as languages more easily understood by the populace, are both literary and social categories that cross historic-temporal barriers. When cardinal and scholar Pietro Bembo wrote his famous *Prose della volgar lingua*, the first edition dated 1525, his objective was to find a model for written Italian, both for poetry and prose. The chosen poets were Petrarch and Boccaccio, and not Dante. 'Between Laura's bard and Dante, [Bembo] didn't hesitate to award the former, because to the nobility of the subject and the doctrine of the *Divine Comedy*, he did not see the use of an adequate style.'[26] According to Bembo, Dante's shortcoming was not being able to handle lofty themes like Paradise with a language considered noble enough. William Blake was also hindered and blasted by the critics of his time. Walt Whitman was criticized for his political ideas and for his 'debauchery'. One can say something similar about the often risqué, but not always trivial and unacceptable language of the rappers of the Wu-Tang Clan. The lyrics of ODB and RZA certainly do not stand out for their modesty, gentleness and refinement. Nevertheless, their language helps to highlight serious topics like discrimination, the use of weapons and violence within African American clans, identity and ignorance. To do this, they use the vernacular with which they grew up: slang, comedy, vulgarity, sex and – why not? – obscenities too.

The more immaterial aspects of the cinema – words, sounds, music – along with gentle instruments like irony and puns, helped Jarmusch create a film universe, in which dominant cultural models are irrelevant and where Bach and the Ramones, Dante and Ol' Dirty Bastard may potentially coexist. Even history, including the history of literature, is part of the varicoloured melting pot cooked by Jarmusch, in which if something has to be 'dominant' then it must be the idea of *relativism* and the absence of static hierarchies. As Luc Sante said: 'History is

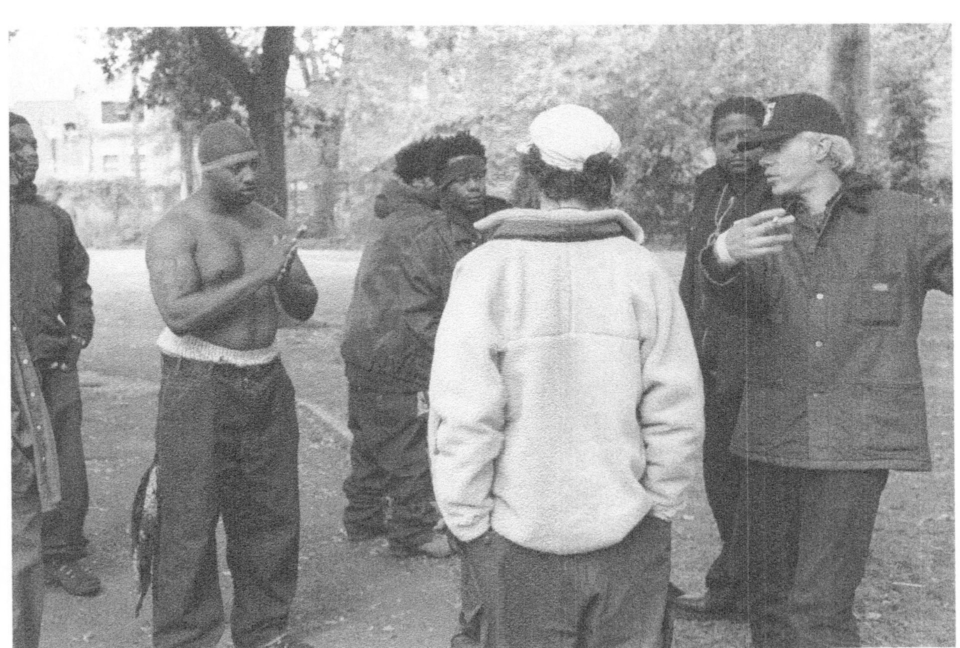

mythology, really. Another way of saying it is that the past is constantly in flux. It's a received idea, and may bear precious little resemblance to what actually transpired at the time.'[27]

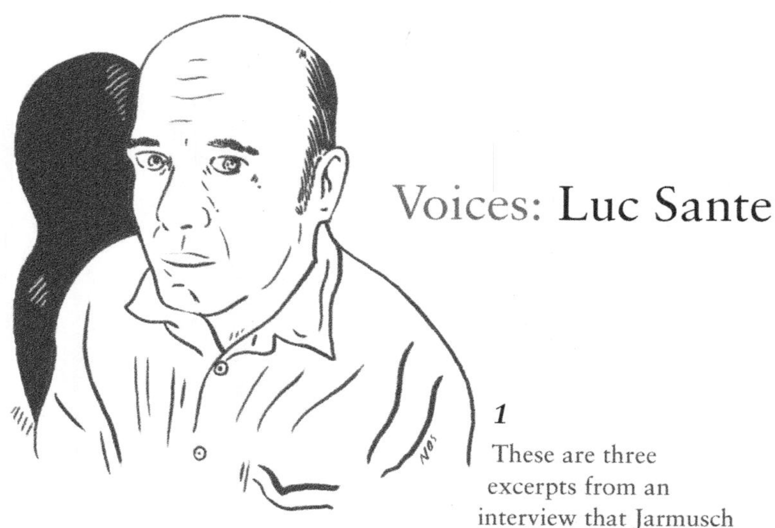

Voices: Luc Sante

1

These are three excerpts from an interview that Jarmusch did with the British film critic Geoff Andrew in 1999.

'Poetry is a really strong beautiful form to me and
   a lot of innovation in language comes from poetry.'
'I think of poets as outlaw visionaries in a way.'
'They are certainly not in it for the money.'

I think that the melting pot that Jarmusch is showing us in his films has a lot to do with his ability to mix and make coexist different 'languages', in a broad sense. Sometimes in a very subversive way, in my opinion, because there is no such thing as a so-called 'high' culture versus a 'low' one. What do you think about this?

After *Ghost Dog* came out I was in Paris and I picked up a copy of *Les Inrockuptibles*. In it there was an interview with Jim, in which he was saying that when we were young, we were always fighting to get respect for popular culture, which was being shunted to the side, not taken seriously by cultural arbiters. Today the situation is entirely the reverse. Pop culture is the only thing that people seem to pay attention to. You really want to get them to read the classics, John Donne and Milton, Shakespeare and Marlowe! It's a matter of remaining alive and alert to the entire spectrum. Every frame of Jim's movies exists along the entire continuum, it's never merely pop, and it's never merely high culture.

That straddling of the fence is true of all the great masters: Dante, Shakespeare. They spoke to a range of audiences, not to just one set of people.

I think that, for example in *Dead Man*, this idea is very clear. It is actually coexisting physically in the character of Johnny Depp, because he is William Blake but he is also the bookkeeper.

Right.

Another thing that relates to poetry is the interest that Jarmusch has for the *sound* of words, not necessarily connected to an actual meaning. One can enjoy a word simply for its *sound*.

Well, before Jim met Roberto [Benigni] and went to Italy we would have long conversations in fake Italian. One of Jim's pet phrases at the time would be 'mitragliatrice'!

Really?! Do you know what that means?

No, what does it mean?

Machine gun!

He must have gotten this out of a movie . . .

Well, the whole process of Roberto Benigni actually learning the language while shooting *Down By Law* must have been something incredible to witness.

Well, I wasn't personally there but I heard all about it. That was more than an influence, it actually made the script.

2

A lot of Jarmusch's films have a quite clear 'poetic structure'. It is possible to recognize rhymes, in scenes that literally come back, verses and stanzas, in the episodic structure. In *Dead Man* the black leader between the scenes in my opinion defines and creates a very magnetic rhythm, a sort of ultra short verse contained in one shot. He also created what I call 'poetic characters' who often express themselves through poetry. How much of the poetry student who published his poems in the *Columbia Review* in 1975 is still in Jim Jarmusch today?

Oh, a great deal. Really a great deal. He still writes poetry, literally, but it's been years since he has shown me any, he is very, very private about it. And I know he reads poetry all the time. He sends me these little postcards every once in a while and they often have quotes by Henri Michaux, a Belgian poet who was very influenced by Asian poetry.

One of the poems in the *Columbia Review*, 'Five Bagatelles', really makes me think of Japanese haiku.

Yes well, Jim published poetry in two issues of the *Columbia Review* and also in another magazine called *Bird Effort* that a friend of mine edited.[1] In the future these will be rare items, they probably are already. The biographers will seek out the collected published poetry of Jim Jarmusch. There is not very much of it but they're wonderful, I can remember many of them line by line. And he is very conscious of poetry, he really absorbs so much. We were both students of what was called the New York School – we studied with Kenneth Koch and David Shapiro. Both of us and Phil [Kline] and other friends who were in the same classes were very influenced by John Ashbery and Frank O'Hara and I think in a lot of ways especially maybe Ron Padgett. I think Jim's humour has a lot in common with that of Ron Padgett.

Whom I don't know, I must admit.

He's alive and well, and both Jim and I are friends with him and see him every once in a while.

3

You wrote the lyrics of the Del-Byzanteens song 'Lies to Live By' back in the early 1980s and told me that the line 'If I only have one life, let me live it as a lie' was 'diverted' from a commercial for a hair product: 'If I only have one life, let me live it as a blonde!' I really like all forms of linguistic and cultural contamination, and this is a very good example. Can you tell me what the creative process was like in the Del-Byzanteens days? The singer was Phil Kline, right?

Yeah, and Jim as well. Phil did not have a prepossessing voice but he is an incredible composer. He's great and also has been a friend of Jim since grammar school. They've known each other since they were seven or eight years old. Although Phil has never written the music for one of Jim's movies, he did write an entire score for one that Jim and I were writing

and never finished, *circa* 1983, *The Garden of Divorce*. He wrote all of
it before any of the script had been written. Phil was also the only real
musician in the Del-Byzanteens. Jim has a deep understanding of music,
but at the time he was just starting to play, and the same was true of
the bass player, Philippe [Hagen]. Everybody in the band had another
vocation: Jim was a filmmaker, Philippe was a graphic artist and the
original drummer, James Nares, was a painter. So Phil did pretty much
determine what was going on. It was not entirely a democratic process.

I understand. So let's say that in this creative process there was a leader,
who was Phil. And even though you were together making all the
decisions, he was the 'real musician', so to say.

Yes, exactly. So there were the usual conflicts, the way band dynamics
work. I think it's possible that even under the best of circumstances the
Del-Byzanteens would not have lasted that long. My own tastes at the
time were quite different from the band's. I didn't care so much for rock
'n' roll, and was much more interested in black music.

All quite far from the Del-Byzanteens sound.

Exactly. But it was still interesting. There was that business of using non
professionals, non musicians as musicians, which has very long and
deep roots, it goes back to avant-garde stuff in England in the 1960s –
and punk of course. And then you can see how that translated right
away in the way Jim started making movies. It hasn't been as true of
his last few movies, but at least in the first few, he was always casting
people who'd never been in a movie.

Yes, like for *Permanent Vacation*, Aloysius Parker, Chris Parker.

Yeah, I've been talking to him on the phone once a week these days.

Really? What is he doing?

He's writing a book, well, he can't really write . . .

How do you mean?

Well, he's not illiterate, but he's not a writer, so he's doing the research,
he's putting the book together and somebody else is executing it. It's a
biography of this character who was a boxing promoter in NYC in the
1930s to the '50s and knew everybody. He's the one who introduced
The Beatles to Muhammad Ali. Anyway, that's what he's doing.

Is he still living in New York?

He lives in New Jersey.

How old would he be now? He was very young when he did *Permanent Vacation*.

When Jim and I met him, he was a teenage graffiti artist, he graffitied our kitchen when we were living on 101st street, so I still think of him as a teenager, but he must be in his late forties. And as regards the casting of *Stranger Than Paradise*, John Lurie had made some movies, he had been in movies the way everybody was in everybody else's movies then, but he wasn't really an actor, and Richard Edson, I'm not sure he had ever been in a movie, although he's still a professional actor today.

He has a great face.

Yes, he does. And he's really an interesting guy too. He still plays drums and trumpet in bands in Los Angeles, and he's a photographer as well these days, and has interviewed many older funk and jazz musicians for magazines.

It's remarkable that all these people could be involved in something because they simply felt they had something to say and that virtuosity didn't really count.

That's certainly one part of it, yes it is.

The last question is just an open one, is there anything you want to say about Jim Jarmusch?

Let me think about this, I'm sure there's a million things to say, just finding one thing to say is hard . . . I admire Jim and his movies so much. I admire so much the fact that he has remained absolutely true to his vision and there is real consistency, within a frame of change of course, he has evolved and grown but he has remained consistent to the same vision since I have known him, which is more than 35 years.

And there is also this really extraordinary thing: the fact that he actually owns his negatives.

Yeah, that was the thing about Jim that I didn't know that I learned, which is that he is a really tough businessman. I had no idea.

And I don't think that for him it's so much about the money, it's about the actual property of his own vision, you do not sell that.

That's right. And in the world of the movies you really have to know how to fight. It's worse than in any of the other art forms.

New York, December 2003

7 Jarmusch, the Poet

'Dammit! I like poetry. Anyone got a problem with that?!'
Jim Jarmusch, interview with Geoff Andrew, 43rd London Film Festival,
15 November 1999

The poetic word is untranslatable. It is unique but this does not make
it elitist. The principal cause for its uniqueness, and therefore its untranslatability, is not one of 'literary snobbism' but is attributable to the
simple fact that the *sound* of the poetic word, and its place in the text,
assumes an added and impalpable sense, enriching it with layers of
unpredictable meaning, difficult to reproduce or translate into different
languages and cultures. The phonic wrapping of the poetic word is by
no means a colourless and arbitrary garment 'worn' by its content for
the sole purpose of comprehension: the *sound* of the poetic word is an
individual garment, made 'to measure', of which we can distinguish
the colours, the cut, the fibre and the style, that influences our perception of the word's content. This gives it its uniqueness. On the other
hand, the poetic word, like music, allows the reader or the listener a
wider range of subjective and interpretative projections: therefore, in spite
of it being unique, it is certainly not univocal.

Having made these premises, one can derive a better understanding
of Jarmusch's passion for the poetic word and why, right from the start,
it has often gate-crashed his films. A word that does not limit itself to
being a 'code' for the mere purpose of transmitting a content; a word
that leaves room for the imagination; a singular word, unique but not
'dominant' from the cultural point of view that, if anything, stimulates reflection; a word that converses with the image in an unusual

way; finally – and this is perhaps the most determinant fact – a deeply musical word.

In fact, it was these poetic forms that Jarmusch experimented with when starting out at New York's Columbia University where, as remembered by his friend Luc Sante, 'We formed half the Columbia Poetry Team.'[1] Before being accepted almost by surprise to the NYU Graduate Film School in 1976, literature was at the centre of his studies. His professors were leading names of the New York School of Poets like David Shapiro and Kenneth Koch. When in 1975 – the year of his English and Comparative Literature BA – several of his poems were published in Columbia's literature review, it seemed that James Jarmusch's aim at the time was to become a poet.[2]

'A Golden Rule'

'Five Bagatelles' is one of the poems published in the *Columbia Review*. A brief extract reveals one of Jarmusch's fundamental work principles not only as a writer but also as an artist in general:

> 4
> five Dutch sailors eating dinner
> a large loaf
> a firkin of butter
> a cag of brandy
> a dog enters the saloon

What immediately catches the eye is Jarmusch's use of vaguely archaic English words like 'firkin' and 'cag' that are certainly not part of today's vernacular. However, this archaic quality combines well with the freshness of the image of five sailors seated at a table: a poetic image told in five brief verses that could quite easily describe a scene taking place on an imaginary film set.

Jarmusch stated years later that, once back in New York after his final year at university in Paris and the numerous hours spent at the Cinémathèque Française, 'I was still writing, and my writing was becoming more cinematic in certain ways, more visually descriptive', which prompted the young literature student with a passion for music to take the next step: the cinema.[3] His five verses already show an undeniable proximity between poetry and prose, leaning more towards the latter. But one must not be overly amazed – the 'five Dutch sailors' were in fact mentioned for the first time in a prose passage and not in a poetic one: 'In the kitchen, *five Dutch sailors sat at breakfast, with a large loaf, a firkin of butter, and a cag of brandy,* the bung of which they often applied to their mouths with great perseverance and satisfaction.'[4] In this case the passage's archaic quality is more than appropriate because it comes from a mid-eighteenth-century work that Jarmusch might have read while at university: *The Adventures of Roderick Random* by Tobias Smollett (1721–1771), a Scottish author famous for his picaresque novels and satirical style. Since it appears highly improbable that the literal quote of Smollett's passage was mentioned by chance, the principle that this innocent 'robbery' confirms and ratifies was mentioned by Jarmusch in an article written in 2004, entitled 'My Golden Rules':

> RULE NO. 5: Nothing is original. Steal anything that resonates with inspiration or fuels your imagination. Devour old films, new films, music, books, paintings, photographs, poems, dreams, random conversations, architecture, bridges, street signs, trees, clouds, bodies of water, light and shadows. Only steal things that speak directly to your soul. If you do this, your work (and theft) will be authentic. Authenticity is invaluable; originality is non-existent. And don't bother concealing your thievery – celebrate it if you feel like it.[5]

It is in this sense that Jarmusch's literary 'youthful theft' should be intended, when referring to Smollet's classic, probably one of the first in a long series of analogous 'thefts' more or less hidden in the system of quotes and references so frequent in his films. The basic principle that Jarmusch puts into practice in the fourth of his 'bagatelles' is no more than the literary equivalent of sampling musical technique, the vital ingredient of hip hop, or of the variations on a theme technique at the base of jazz composition and improvisation, both sources of inspiration for Jarmusch, man and artist. With respect to a literary passage or a piece of music, the chance to use 'quotes' is greater and in cinema occurs at different levels: from the text to the music, from the scenic, architectural and general visual environments to the rhythmic-temporal structures. For a polyhedral and insatiable 'culture consumer' like Jarmusch it is only too easy to understand how the cinema overtook the other forms of expression, thanks also to the ideal terrain it offers in order to combine the various ingredients, audio and visual, stolen and not, that complete the film's final mix.

One could object that for his part, however, as owner of the negatives of nearly all his films, Jarmusch uses double standards should he be the victim of 'the theft' rather than the culprit. In reality, the ownership of the negatives is exploited by Jarmusch not merely to guarantee himself the right legally to pursue whoever uses extracts of his work without permission, but also in order to have complete freedom and artistic independence that the director must at all costs maintain at every level, from the film's creation to its production and finally to its distribution.[6] In this sense 'golden rules' numbers two and three are very much in your face, also meant by Jarmusch as advice to young directors:

> RULE NO. 2: Don't let the fuckers get ya. They can either help you, or not help you, but they can't stop you. People who finance films, distribute films, promote films and exhibit films are not filmmakers. They are not interested in letting filmmakers define and dictate the way they do their business, so filmmakers should have no interest in allowing them to dictate the way a film is made. Carry a gun if necessary. Also, avoid sycophants at all costs. There are always people around who only want to be involved in filmmaking to get rich, get famous, or get laid. Generally, they know as much about filmmaking as George W. Bush knows about hand-to-hand combat.

> RULE NO. 3: The production is there to serve the film. The film is not there to serve the production. Unfortunately, in the world of filmmaking this is almost universally backwards. The film is not being made to serve the budget, the schedule, or the résumés of those involved. Filmmakers who don't understand this should be hung from their ankles and asked why the sky appears to be upside down.[7]

Having established his status as the champion of authorial autonomy at any cost, Jarmusch is not afraid to highlight a director's sacrosanct freedom to steal, on the understanding that the 'theft' is driven by necessity and authentic inspiration. Being caught does not matter. In a poem entitled 'Split-Screen', published in 1990 by the German magazine

Literaturmagazin and of which I quote an extract, Jarmusch appears to steal from his own filmography by thematizing his 'linguistic obsessions':

> This reminds me of the Hungarian
> who moves to Los Angeles
> forgets how to speak Hungarian
> and never learns a word of English.[8]

One immediately thinks of the Hungarian characters in *Stranger Than Paradise* – Eva, Willie/Bela and Aunt Lotte – and their daily battle with language and identity. The idea of someone being left 'without language', as suggested in the poetic image created by Jarmusch in 'Split-Screen', is obviously more extreme and surreal with respect to the relationship the film's characters have with the two languages, Hungarian on one side and English on the other. But one of poetry's strong points is its ability to create by simple means surreal and extreme images that, as pointed out, are unique but not univocal. What is beyond doubt is Jarmusch's belief that poetry and cinema are two worlds that are connected and complementary and cannot do without each other.

In order to render this connection palpable and not relegate it to a merely theoretical sphere, Jarmusch utilizes particular strategies, for example, the creation of *poetic characters*.

Poetic Characters

To use the adjective *poetic* implies taking several risks. A frequent one is yielding to generic terms: vague sensibilities, the tendency to romanticize and sentimentalize, delicateness and kindness or a visionary and dreamy atmosphere. So, to avoid lexical misunderstandings, I would like to make it clear immediately that the characters I define here as *poetic* have a single principal characteristic that unites them: a *poetic character* always expresses himself – in addition to language, spoken and otherwise – by means of the *poetic word*. This said, the characters in question could not be more different from each other. In particular, I have chosen six that I would like to take a closer look at, allowing myself the right to put them in the following non-chronological order: Man With Money/Rammellzee from *Stranger Than Paradise*; the pair Nobody/Gary Farmer and William Blake/Johnny Depp from *Dead Man*; Ghost

Dog/Forest Whitaker from *Ghost Dog: The Way of the Samurai*; Bob/Roberto Benigni from *Down By Law*; and finally Christopher Marlowe/John Hurt from *Only Lovers Left Alive*.

Jarmusch decided to give sustained voice to characters who respond to this criterion, thus making the poetic word an omnipresent element of his filmography. Keeping in mind what I stated about the absence of hierarchies or dominant cultural models – fundamental to Jarmusch – the poetic word is characterized by the fact that its phonic and thus musical elements – such as timbre, rhythm and metre – are vehicles of significance comparable to the word's content. Just as in a traditional sonnet, likewise in a free verse composition – or a rap or a spoken word performance – the *sound* of the poetic word serves to transmit a supplementary meaning that is added to what the word 'signifies' or, to quote John Cage, 'It is not poetry by reason of its content or ambiguity, but by reason of its allowing musical elements (time, sound) to be introduced into the world of words.'[9]

Rammellzee

It is because of this vicinity of word and musical elements that the bizarre character played by Rammellzee in *Stranger Than Paradise* may be looked at as a *poetic character*. The Man With Money appears only once in the film, in the third and final episode shot in Florida. His role is as brief as it is fundamental to the delicate outcome of the story: because of a banal misunderstanding, the Man With Money hands a cash-filled envelope of dubious origin to the wrong person – Eva (Eszter Balint) – who by pure chance finds herself in the right place at the right moment and, above all, wearing the right hat. Seconds after Eva exits the scene with the ill-gotten gains in her pocket, a visibly confused and anxious girl (Sara Driver) appears wearing an identical hat, obviously aware that she has arrived too late for the very important appointment. Besides the cash-filled envelope, she also misses out on Rammellzee's brief and explosive monologue in which he bombards Eva, who just stands there without uttering a sound.

Yo' the freak right?
Got the hat on, man.
I see the dome piece on your top, man. Listen!

It is evident that the verbal style of the *poetic character* in this case identifies with that of the multiple character artist, Rammellzee, who was active as a writer, MC, break-dancer, visual artist, sculptor, pioneer of hip hop and theorist of Gothic Futurism.[10] His typical nasal voice led to him being given the ironic nickname of Gangsta-Duck and many believe that hugely successful rappers like the Beastie Boys and Cypress Hill were profoundly influenced by his style.[11] The hoarse verbal 'assault' to which he subjects clueless Eva is due to the girl turning up late, something he is very unhappy about because it means he will miss out on his 'sniff'. Rammellzee's words come across as a bizarre rap lullaby. The roughly 20-second monologue ends with the following strongly rhythmic words:

> You tell
> Rammell
> That I ain't down with this no more
> You cool?
> You clean?
> There you go
> Good-bye
> Peace!

This type of rhythmic, broken-up and richly alliterated talk obviously reveals much of the character's nervous and amphetamine nature. He even makes an explicit reference to himself – 'You tell Rammell' – and thus steps out of his fictional role. On other occasions Rammellzee demonstrated a particular talent in the style defined by David Toop as 'stream of consciousness rap'.[12] In the 12-inch single 'Beat Bop', released in 1983 on Tartown and produced by Jean-Michel Basquiat, who also designed its cover, Rammellzee gave a perfect example of *slanguage* while confronting the rapper K-Rob in a 'poetic battle' in which a boy and a gangster argue the pros and cons of going to school.[13] As Toop goes on to say: 'The language glides bafflingly in and out of hip hop cliché, social realism and pure nonsense – Rammellzee is the Screamin' Jay Hawkins of rap.'[14] And if on one side the surreal and nonsense element in his poetic word is undoubtedly alive, then on the other a more aggressive and militant concept of the word springs up, with a political and not only aesthetic role. The way in which the Man With Money verbally assaults Eva in *Stranger Than Paradise* does a

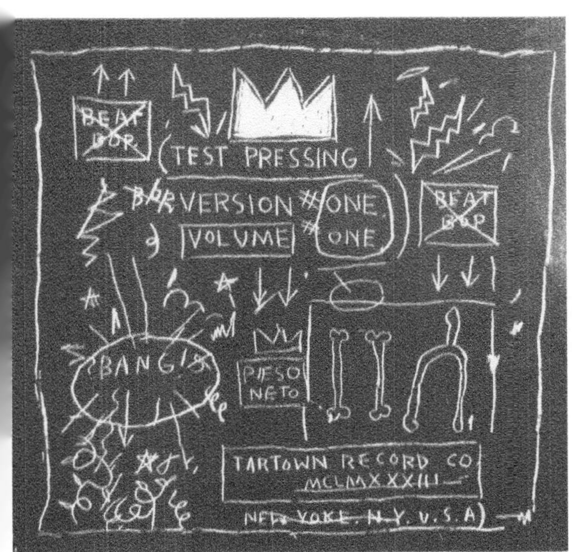

Cover of
Rammellzee, 'Beat
Bop', 12-inch single
(1983).

good job of representing the idea of the artist and theorist of 'armed letters', who looked upon the single letters of the alphabet as weapons that, torn from the page, take on sharp and multiple forms, understandable only to whoever enters into the style and philosophy of the *Ikonoclast Panzerism*, also theorized by Rammellzee. Furthermore, the act of spraying trains was fittingly called 'bombing' in the slang of the writers who, like him, were active on the New York Subway, roughly from the 1970s to the mid-'80s, an act of urban terrorism that did not create any victims but did open up holes in the city's budget.[15]

What makes Rammellzee a true *poetic character* – to whom Jarmusch offered a stage far more visible and lasting in *Stranger Than Paradise* than the 'rolling pages'[16] of the trains on which he wrote – is his ability to energize the word with a new, highly personal sound and significance. To say that the word, or rather the single letter, is a weapon is tantamount to saying that eloquence and, with it, education is a weapon in the hands of its possessor. Rammellzee's attempt to 'free' the letters of the alphabet to create his own cryptic code looks at a matter far more political than it might initially seem: what happens if you whites fail to decipher our 'armed letters'? How will you succeed in dominating us if you cannot even understand our lingo? The invented patter that leaves Eva literally speechless is Rammellzee's personal form of scat-talk, a stratagem already used by his black ancestors to baffle their redneck masters and then used in numerous musical forms over the next decades. To the purely aesthetic level one can thus add a supplementary, essentially militant slant. It is certainly no mystery that Jarmusch was fascinated by the Rammellzee character, with all the parallels and references to the broader artistic and political scenario of Afrofuturism to which his persona is necessarily connected.[17] Nonetheless, it is within the actual theme of the 'armed letters' where, in my opinion, a serious

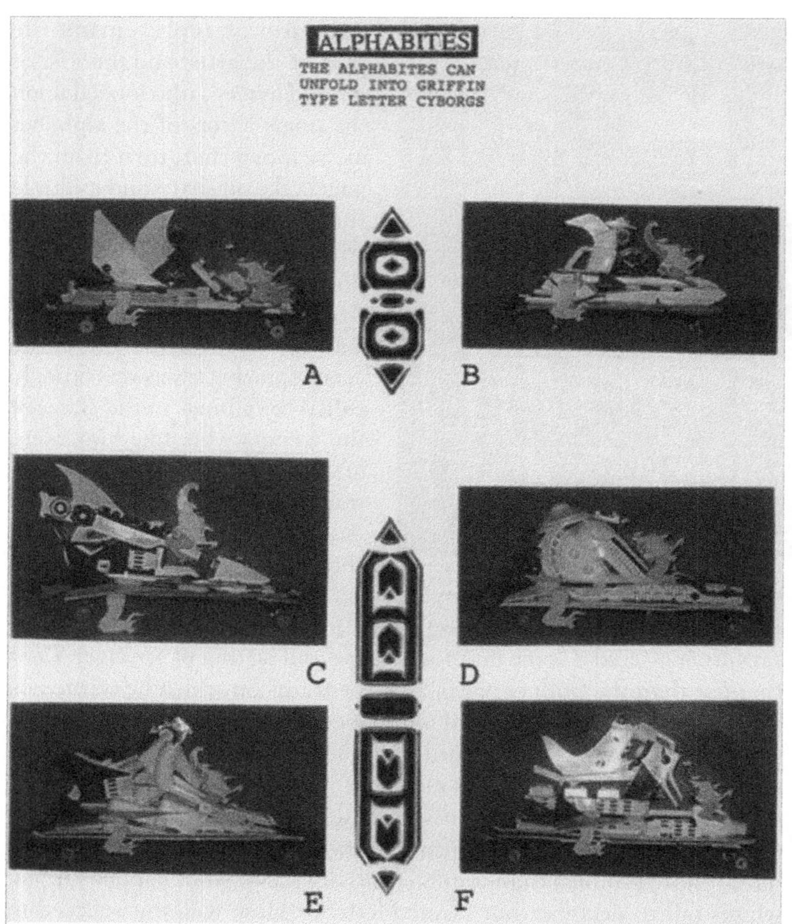

Armed letters, Rammellzee.

point of contact between the poetic character Rammellzee and his director can be found.

Nobody and William Blake

A loud echo of the word-as-weapon theory is clearly audible in *Dead Man*. Here Jarmusch created another pair of unmistakable poetic characters:

Nobody: William Blake, do you know how to use this weapon?
William Blake: Not really.
Nobody: That weapon will replace your tongue. You will learn
     to speak through it, and your poetry will now be written
     with blood.

Taking a ten-year leap forward in Jarmusch's filmography, the essence
of Rammellzee's discussion on the 'armed letters' jumps off the train,
takes on a hint of western mythology and reappears in the dialogue
between Nobody and bookkeeper William Blake: no more sharpened
letters, no more words travelling on the 'rolling pages', just bullets and
blood punctuating Blake's poetic route. Accompanying him on his
escape is the film's real *poetic character*: Nobody, the cultured Native
American.

In the case of *Dead Man*, an important premise once again involving the principle of cultural relativism should be made: the central
nucleus of the story is, in fact, based upon an explicit form of contamination between two different linguistic and literary worlds apparently
very distant from each other. As Jarmusch explained:

> Blake walked into the story on his own accord . . . I was carrying
> around a lot of notes on this film for years and just before I was
> about to write the script, I had been reading a lot about Native
> American thought and writing. To take a break from that, I
> picked up William Blake. I hadn't really read Blake for a number
> of years, and I was struck by how similar a lot of his thoughts
> were to those that I had just been reading about American
> Indians. For example, I picked up *Proverbs of Hell*, and one of
> the proverbs is: 'The eagle never lost so much time as when he
> submitted to learn from the crow.' Another one is: 'Expect poison
> from standing water.' These just struck me as so similar to what
> I was reading about the native tribes. So he just walked into my
> story at that point. I hadn't even thought about it until then.[18]

The aura of a slightly magical 'irrationality' that accompanies Blake's
entry into the story also infects Nobody, who is soon convinced that
Blake, the wounded young bookkeeper, is really the great English poet
who died in 1827: 'Is this a lie? Or a white man's trick? Is your name
really William Blake? Then you are a dead man.' The *poetic character*

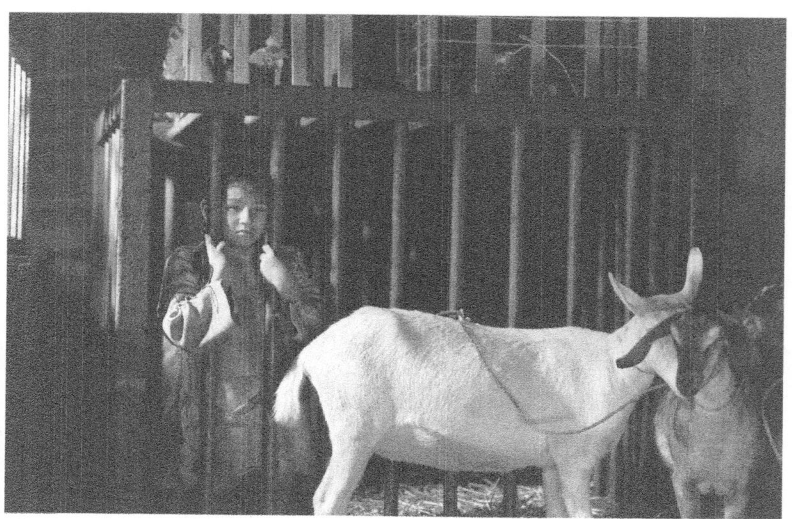

Nobody can calmly accept that his friend is a ghost, but what he cannot accept is why Blake does not appear to remember that he is the great poet and painter who fascinated him so greatly in his childhood. Nobody's story is a controversial one. The beauty of his character resides in his complexity, in his not revealing any similarity between himself and the stereotype image of Native Americans: Gary Farmer, the corpulent actor of the Cayuga Nation, behaves neither as a blood-thirsty, animalistic and fearsome primitive who is against industrial progress, nor as an equally stereotypical 'good savage', family man, reasonable, understanding, in harmony with himself and the cosmos. Nobody is simply a 'complex human being'.[19] He is familiar with the writer of the *Songs of Innocence* and the *Songs of Experience* because as a child he was abducted from his tribe by the palefaces and, after endless wanderings, sent off to England. There he received an education and learned all about William Blake, whose words of visionary power and revolutionary passion left the boy enchanted. Nobody quotes the famous poet at various times, as when he first encounters Blake's 'ghost'.

Every Night and every Morn
Some to Misery are Born
Every Morn and every Night
Some are Born to sweet delight

Some are Born to sweet delight
Some are Born to Endless Night

This extract from the celebrated 'Auguries of Innocence', published some 30 years after the poet's death, assumes a particular importance in the film.[20] It is thanks to one of its verses that the disorientated Blake can be accorded the title of *poetic character*, alongside Nobody: just before killing Sheriffs Lee and Marvin – an obvious tribute from Jarmusch to one of his favourite actors[21] – Blake expresses 'his' poetic word for the first time, completing the process of identification between himself and the departed poet.

Marshal Marvin: You William Blake?
William Blake: Yes, I am. Do you know my poetry?
(shoots marshals Marvin and Lee)
Some are born to endless night.

The 'autograph' that Blake leaves the hypocritical and racist missionary (Alfred Molina), who runs the riverside emporium, is a pen nailed into his hand, a highly symbolic, almost biblical gesture, which will be followed by the ritual and lethal bullet. Nobody's vehement words, said with relative nonchalance shortly before Blake kills the missionary, are

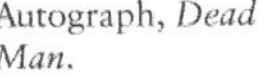

Autograph, *Dead Man*.

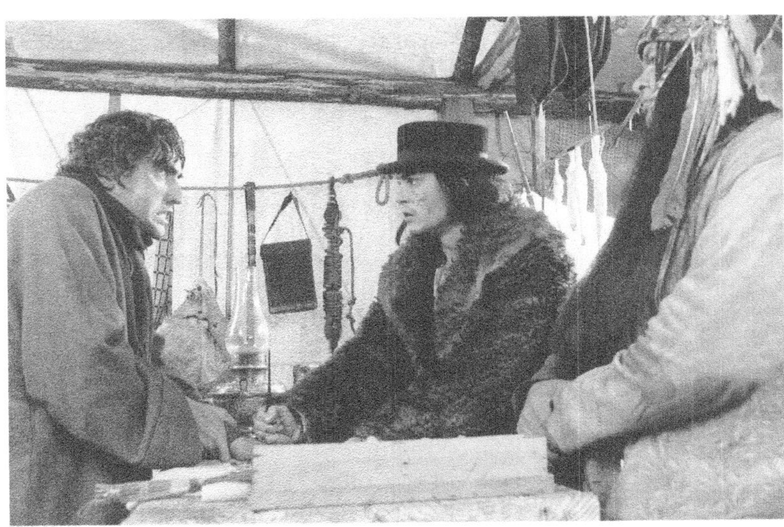

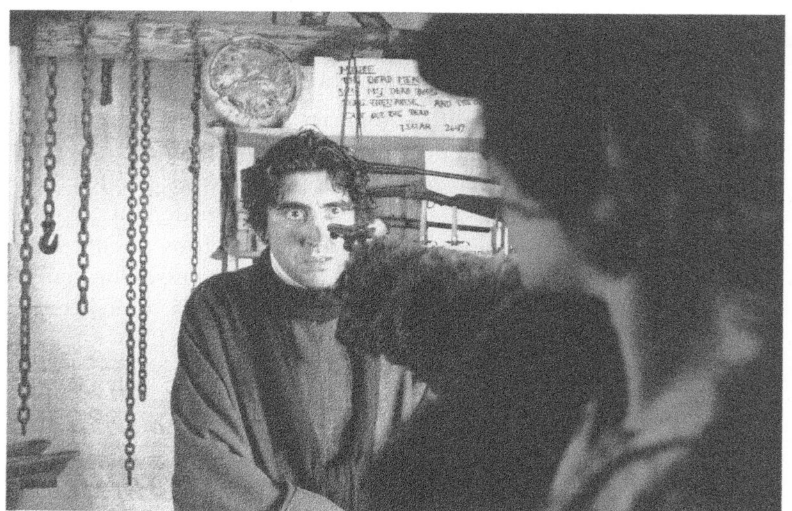

The outlaw-poet,
Dead Man.

taken from the poem *The Everlasting Gospel* and reflect the heavy criticism that the author directed at the ecclesiastical hierarchy of his times: 'The vision of Christ that thou dost see, is my Vision's greatest Enemy.'[22] This line is more realistic than it might seem, because from childhood Blake the poet claimed to have regular visions of angels and archangels who inspired him and encouraged him in his work. Blake, the film character in search of his own vision, appears to want to emulate his real-life namesake, despite having nothing to do with his mystic Christianity, but rather with the ritual vision quests of Native Americans. As Jarmusch explained:

> When Nobody leaves him alone after taking peyote, Blake is left to go on his own vision quest briefly, whether he knows it or not, because he is fasting – not because he wants to but because he doesn't know how to eat out there. That's a really important ceremony of most North American tribes – a vision quest where you're left to fast, usually for a three-day period.[23]

In this sense, Blake puts into effect a very real metamorphosis. At the end of the film he has taken on multiple identities and, apart from his tartan suit just visible beneath the animal skin he is wearing, there remains little of the unemployed bookkeeper: he is the dying 'killer of

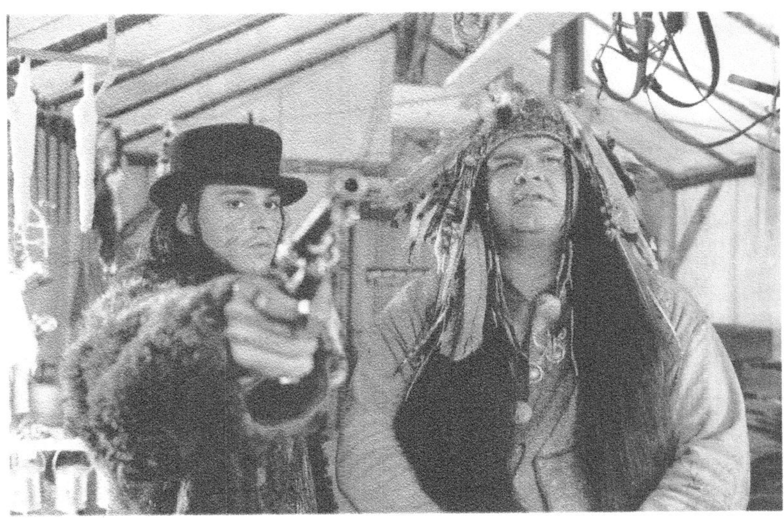

white men', but also the Native American, with the cedar-covered canoe, the ritual tobacco and the traditional headdress but, more than anything else, he has become the poet himself with whom he now shares, apart from the words, the silent and ecstatic vision. Nobody's initial prophecy, according to which the pistol will substitute for Blake's 'tongue', has been fully realized: his every gunshot results in a death. The *poetic character* embodied by Johnny Depp, 'the poet as an outlaw',[24] spews bullets even though the ensuing deaths are totally devoid of anything even remotely heroic, so typical of westerns. Death is painful, dirty, futile, mechanical and, on at least a couple of occasions, horrendous too: there is no possible ritual or redemption capable of rendering it 'pretty'.

Ghost Dog

The silent killer played by Forest Whitaker in *Ghost Dog: The Way of the Samurai* is a *poetic character* who, despite his appearance being diametrically opposed, has many traits in common with Johnny Depp's Blake. Starting with the title, it is clear that the cultural and literary universe referred to in the film – released in 1999, four years after *Dead Man* – is certainly not nineteenth-century England but rather the Far East, particularly the archaic Japan of the samurai, dropped anachronistically into the urban criminal undergrowth of the United States where the story takes place. And yet, notwithstanding the manifest environmental-temporal differences, the two characters are deeply linked to each other: both killers, though not by vocation; both taciturn, though out of necessity; both their journeys end with death; and mainly both share an indissoluble bond with the poetic word. If for Blake the very existence of his character is based in some way upon having the same name as the dead English poet, in Ghost Dog's case the poetic word directly influences his behaviour and his nature: the silent killer is the modern samurai who, in debt to the Italian American mafioso Louie (John Tormey) for saving his life when a kid, becomes his trusted retainer-killer basing his discipline and behavioural ethics on the antique Japanese code of *Hagakure*.[25]

This classic book deals with the teachings of ex-samurai-turned-Buddhist-monk Yamamoto Tsunetomo (1659–1719), noted down by his pupil Tsuramoto Tashiro between 1709 and 1716 after his master had spent ten years in solitude and self-denial. Just like the *Proverbs of Hell*, Yamamoto's maxims and thoughts became a source of inspiration for Jarmusch, who chose those that more suitably adapted to the story and better outlined Ghost Dog's character, the way he did for Blake and Nobody in the *Dead Man* screenplay. Nevertheless, as opposed to William Blake's work, that *Hagakure* should reach Jarmusch is not something to be taken for granted: 'From 1945 to 1952, the years of American occupation of Japan, the book was placed on the forbidden books list because it was considered responsible for having fanned the flames of militarism.'[26] The fact that *Hagakure* survived from the eighteenth century to today, handed down from generation to generation and safeguarded, has something almost miraculous about it: a story worth telling.

If 'obedience' holds such a prominent position among the samurai's greatest ambitions listed by Yamamoto – other than 'loyalty, modesty, filial compassion, kindness'[27] – it is quite amazing to think that this book survived to the modern day due to a serious act of disobedience. Without the insubordination of apprentice Tsuramoto – who, instead of obeying his teacher's deathbed wish and burning the book as promised,[28] circulated it to the samurai of northern Saga in Kyushu, with the title *Nabeshima Rongo* (The Words of Nabeshima) – Jarmusch would never have come across it and thus been inspired by it. Having escaped the flames, the book remained a secret code until 1906 when it was published for the first time with a new title, *Hagakure*. However, its wider distribution meant its wider exploitation, its text often given only a partial interpretation. The famous words, used also by Jarmusch in the initial sequence of the film – 'The Way of the Samurai is found in death' – should not necessarily be followed 'to the letter'.[29] In reality, the death referred to by Yamamoto can be interpreted in a more abstract and articulate way: the samurai 'dies' dedicating his life entirely to his lord, freely choosing to relinquish his own individuality and to live in absolute obedience. Furthermore, death must be the samurai's constant thought, to be meditated upon in perfect sync with each breath, with the object of relishing a greater joy of living (and serving one's master), and thus defeating the most human of all fears, death. Yamamoto himself put this teaching into practice. When his *daimyo*, his feudal lord, died, he too 'made the decision to die' but his 'sacrifice was the tonsure of the Buddhist monk . . . Becoming a monk is the equivalent in practice to death.'[30] In spite of these lucid words – perhaps motivated by the fact that the practice of ritual suicide had been outlawed since 1661[31] – it was the militarist and imperialist interpretation that held sway.

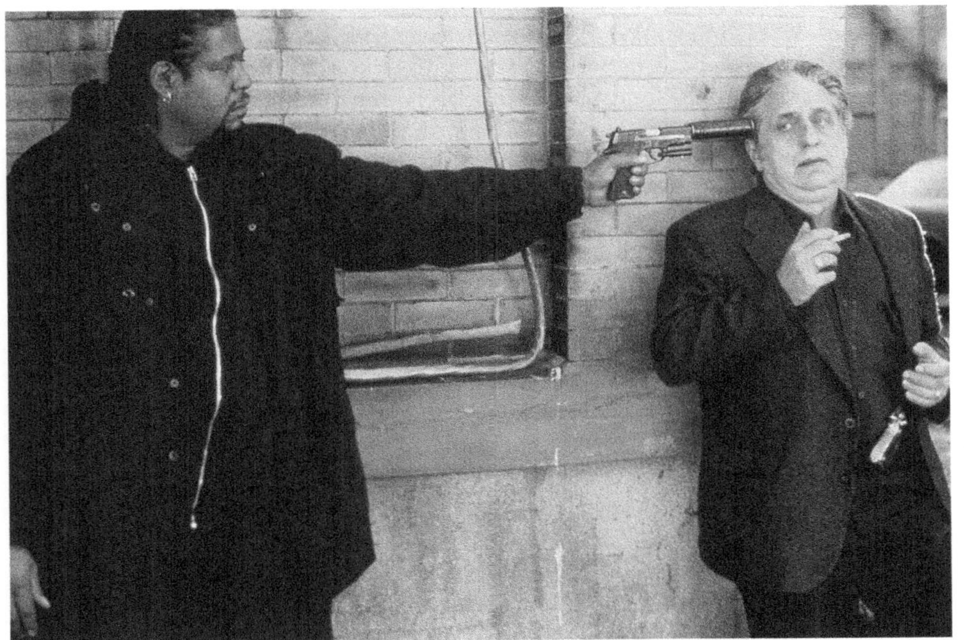

However, *Hagakure* was back in the limelight on 25 November 1970, at noon to be exact. Internationally acclaimed and prolific writer Yukio Mishima, aged 45 at the time, chose that day to commit ritual suicide with the sword, culminating with his decapitation by one of his acolytes at the Ichigaya barracks in Tokyo in front of a large contingent of soldiers.[32] Three years before his spectacular and meticulously planned 'last act', Mishima – a writer obsessed with time and the thought of death, and a fervent promoter of an archaic nationalism in defence of the Emperor and Japanese culture – had published *Hagakure Nyumon*: an introduction to Yamamoto's book, which he defined as 'The foundation from which my every written word is born.'[33] Naturally, this reignited international interest in *Hagakure*, the first English edition of which was published in 1979.[34] But it was not until November 1990, twenty years after Mishima's death, that this highly discussed book was gradually rediscovered and re-evaluated. And finally reached Jarmusch.

Going back to the film, in *Ghost Dog: The Way of the Samurai*, the text from the book manifests itself physically. Yamamoto's words are not 'just' an acoustic entity, spoken by the off-camera voice of Ghost Dog and – only once, at the end of the film – by little Pearline (Camille Winbush), Ghost Dog's book-loving young friend. They are also clearly visible on fifteen prompt cards, written white-on-black, which Jarmusch gives the spectator all the time to read from beginning to end. The text thus becomes a character with its own graphic body that is visible and legible to the audience, while being an irreplaceable travel companion for Ghost Dog. The role of the guide that in *Dead Man* belongs to Nobody, interpreter of the 'poetry written in blood' that directs the actions of Blake, in *Ghost Dog* is covered without mediation by the very text, both in card and book form. Symmetrically, at the start and the end of the film, Ghost Dog and then Pearline are shown reading *Hagakure*. The two passages chosen by Jarmusch are seemingly different and yet in reality very complementary:

The Way of the Samurai is found in death. Meditation on inevitable death should be performed daily. Every day when one's body and mind are at peace, one should meditate upon being ripped apart by arrows, rifles, spears and swords, being carried away by surging waves, being thrown into the midst of a great fire, being struck by lightning, being shaken to death by a great earthquake, falling from thousand-foot cliffs, dying of disease

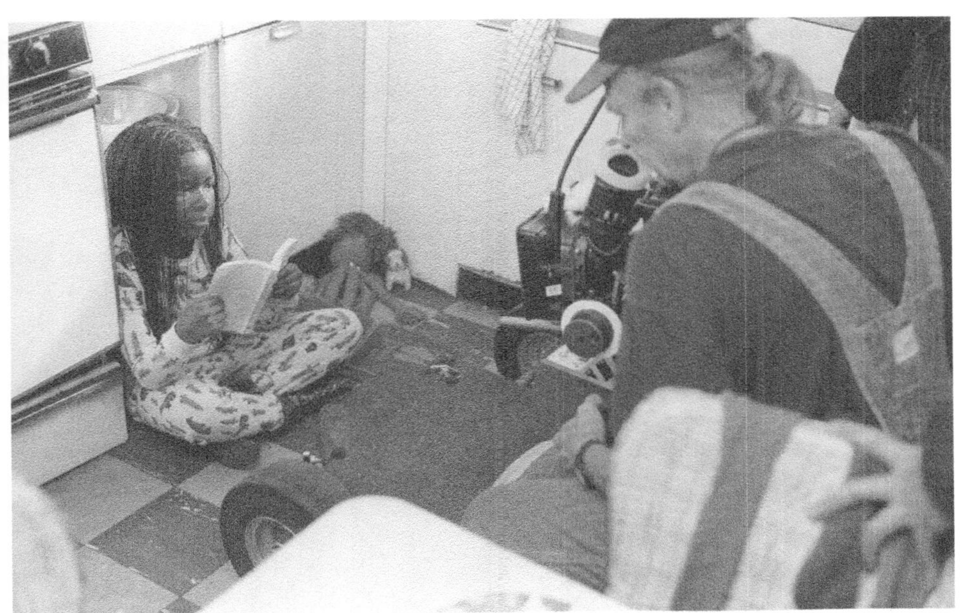

or committing *seppuku* at the death of one's master. And every day without fail one should consider oneself as dead. This is the substance of the Way of the Samurai.

Pearline is given the rather important task of reading the quote that ends the film: 'In the Kamigata area they have a sort of tiered lunchbox they use for a single day when flower viewing. Upon returning, they throw them away, trampling them underfoot. The end is important in all things.'

Following the death of the killer/reader Ghost Dog in the final showdown in perfect *High Noon* style, little Pearline thus becomes the new guardian of the Text.[35] In the last scene, while the little girl concentrates on reading, it becomes clear to the spectator that the centrality of the meditation on death with which Ghost Dog begins the story, and the importance of 'the end of all things', are not ideas that are distant from each other. With this conclusive image Jarmusch probably means to allude, and none too subtly, to the passage from generation to generation of a book that has been able to hang onto its validity – and readability – for many centuries, despite the fact that the samurai public to which it was originally targeted has been extinct for some time.

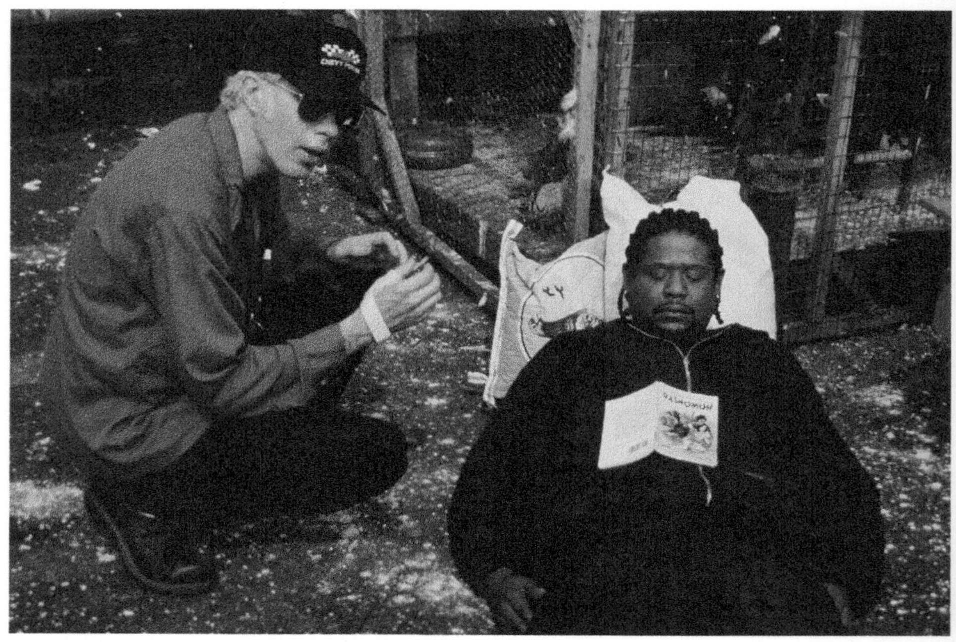

So why having survived fire, censorship and political exploitation is this anachronistic book still a good read today, to such a degree it inspired a director like Jarmusch to make it the pivot of his film? In my opinion, besides the general appeal that Japanese culture holds on many readers, one of the motives of its longevity is its fundamental *relativism*. This is expressed in the propinquity of daily, almost banal themes on one side, and universal reflections of a more spiritual and philosophical nature on the other: a variety of register that, as already amply observed, is at the base of all Jarmusch's filmography and his poetics. The considerations on whether or not to perfume one's hair before a fight, the debate on whether or not to clench one's teeth, or to dwell on the use of face powder, for example (the latter photographed for one of the title cards used by Jarmusch), are a little astonishing, but they also enrich the text with a healthy dose of irony and timeless 'humanity':

It is good to carry some powdered rouge in one's sleeve. It may happen that when one is sobering up or waking from sleep, a

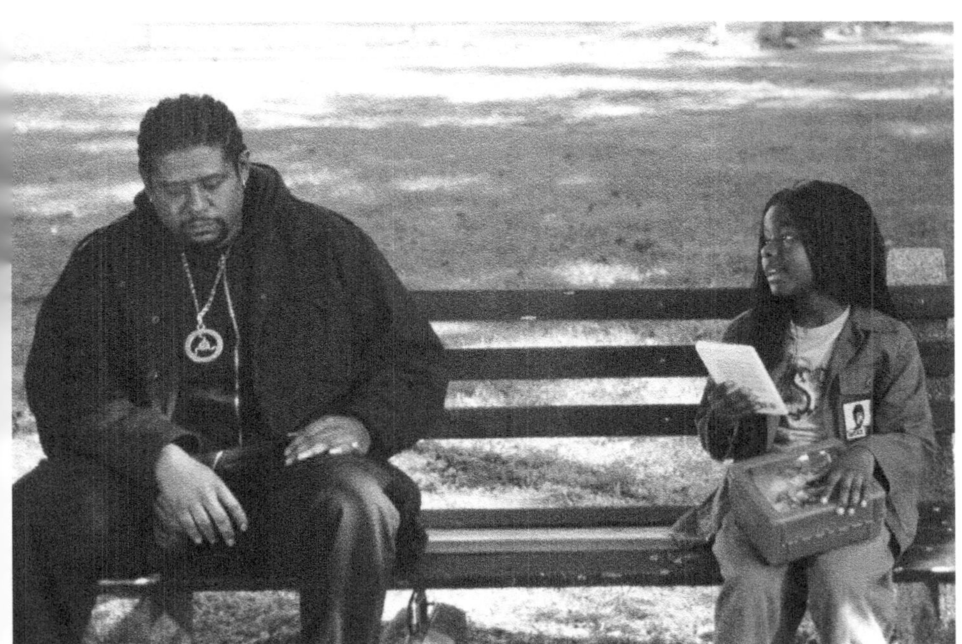

samurai's complexion may be poor. At such time it is good to take out and apply some powdered rouge.

Another of the poetic moments of daily routine worthy of note – even though Jarmusch did not use it in the film – again reveals the sincerity and humanity of the writer and has to do with Yamamoto's very personal tribute to sleep:

Human life is truly a short affair. It is better to live doing the things that you like. It is foolish to live within this dream of a world seeing unpleasantness and doing only things that you do not like. But it is important never to tell this to young people as it is something that would be harmful if incorrectly understood. Personally, I like to sleep. And I intend to appropriately confine myself more and more to my living quarters and pass my life away sleeping.[36]

Far better known than *Hagakure*, another Japanese classic emphasizes *Ghost Dog*'s narrative path, even though in this case without the help of literal quotations: *Rashomon* by Ryunosuke Akutagawa. The book contains a collection of short stories, two of which supplied the narrative base for Akira Kurosawa's 1950 film of the same title: *In a Grove* (*Yabu no naka*) supplied the characters and the plot, *Rashomon* the name and the setting.

In *Ghost Dog*, Akutagawa's book appears in several key moments, passed from character to character. The first to read it is Miss Louise Vargo (Tricia Vessey), the boss's spacy and introverted daughter, involuntary and unexpected eyewitness to the murder of her reckless lover Handsome Frank (Richard Portnow) who is gunned down with cold-blooded precision by Ghost Dog. Following the three silenced shots, the girl and the killer stare at each other in stunned silence for a moment, before Ghost Dog's attention is drawn to a copy of *Rashomon*, thrown on the floor moments earlier by a lethargic Louise, who has no idea that the book is about to save her life. Scared to death, she just manages to mumble, 'Did my father send you to do this? It's a good book. Ancient Japan was a pretty strange place. You can have it, I'm finished with it.' Ghost Dog picks up the book and exits as quietly as he came. Later, he passes the copy of *Rashomon* onto Pearline, a voracious reader of a wide variety of literature, whom he meets regularly in the park.[37] The killer willingly lends her the book and asks only that she give him her opinion after she has read it. Like any child would, Pearline takes him very seriously and, during the film's end sequence, keeps her promise: 'I especially liked the first story. It's one story, but each person sees a totally different story.' Ghost Dog's young friend is referring to *In a Grove*, Kurosawa's main inspiration, albeit loosely, to make his celebrated film winner of the Golden Lion at the 1951 Venice Film Festival.

Jarmusch's *Rashomon*-like approach is confirmed by the flashbacks in which Ghost Dog and Louie take it in turns to remember the armed punk's attack on the former. In his flashback, Ghost Dog remembers the aggressor aiming a gun at him in front of Louie, reluctant eyewitness to the violent attack on the still young African American.[38] Louie draws his powerful gun and shoots the punk, saving the life of Ghost Dog, who is lying on the ground bleeding. Louie remembers it differently: initially, his gun is aimed at Ghost Dog, and when the punk turns his gun on Louie, the mafioso blows him away. In Louie's memory, acting in self-defence robbed his actions of any heroism, and saving Ghost Dog's life was simply lucky 'collateral damage'. Totally opposing points of view, and yet neither is a lie because Jarmusch, as Kurosawa, questions

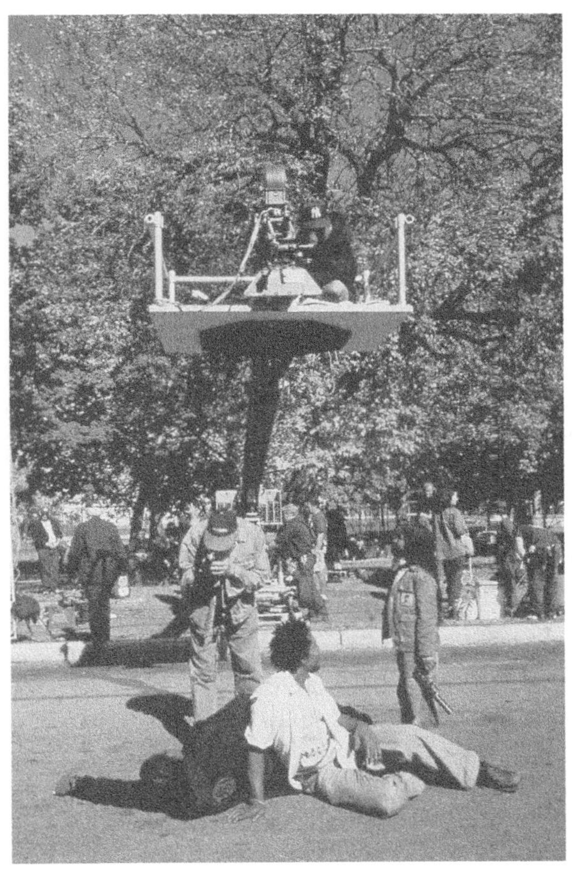

The 'fake' show-down, *Ghost Dog: The Way of the Samurai*.

reality. Memory is just as subject-ive as truth.

Like the memories of Ghost Dog and Louie, *Hagakure* and *Rashomon* seem to be in sharp contrast with each other. While the former is a code supposed to indicate *the* only way to go and *the* perfect and exemplary disci-pline never to be betrayed, the latter contradicts the very idea of an only way, maintaining instead the superiority of the subjective points of view. In reality, the place in which these two apparently distant texts meet is once again that *relativism* which Jarmusch appears incapable of doing with-out. *Hagakure* is in reality a code rich in contradictions and far less rigorous than it seems: the trib-ute to sleep or the opportunity to use cosmetics have the same 'right to citizenship' as the Sutra of the Heart or other teachings close to Zen philosophy or Buddhism. Is it perhaps because of this that Yamamoto made his apprentice promise to burn the manuscript? Did he perhaps find it intolerable that 'high' and 'low' are inevitably joined? At first glance, Kurosawa's *Rashomon* and Akutagawa's *In a Grove* might seem a classic whodunit, in which the various characters are called upon to give their own personal version of a bloody crime, specifically a crime of rape and murder. The ingredi-ents appear to be all there: victims, perpetrators, murder weapons and witnesses. And yet, what is fundamental to any 'mystery' is missing: the solution. It is not so much the *why* but the *how* that covers the main role and interests Jarmusch. 'Nothing makes any sense any more', Louie says to *poetic character* Ghost Dog, whom he has just fatally wounded in the final – fake – showdown. 'Fake' because the modern samurai, obviously looking to die, faces the last gunfight of his life with an intentionally empty gun. So can it be called a showdown? Or would it be more appropriate to call it a modern ritual suicide in which, instead of being decapitated like Mishima by fellow Tatenokai militia members, the unarmed samurai is filled with lead by his master Louie? Even the dying Ghost Dog, however, does not betray his literary vocation as a *poetic character*: before shutting his eyes for good, his final act is to give Louie the bloodstained copy of *Rashomon*. Louie takes the book and seeks refuge in the limousine where Miss Vargo awaits him. The glacial *femme fatale*, a hint of incredulity in her eyes, is quite adamant about the book being hers. She turns to Louie and, with the bossy but calm voice of someone who will brook no contradiction, orders: 'It takes place in ancient Japan. You ought to read it.'

The book is back. The circle is complete.

Bob/Benigni

Poetic character Bob/Benigni requires a major jump backwards in time. Thirteen years, to be precise.

Night-time in New Orleans. Zack (Tom Waits) – totally plastered after having been kicked out of the house by his girlfriend Laurette (Ellen Barkin) – is huddled against the half-closed door of an alcohol wholesaler's, muttering songs to an invisible audience. Like the first word on a white page, a man with tousled hair, his back to the camera, makes his first appearance entering the frame from left to right. His hands behind his back, similar to an elementary school teacher, he stops in front of Zack and without further ado, his booming, accented voice betraying the fact that he is not American, declares: 'It's a sad and beautiful world!' This is the opening line said by Roberto Benigni, the *poetic character* at the centre of *Down By Law*. He plays Bob, his quasi-autobiographical self, a role that will for the first time bring him fame beyond the borders of Italy.[39] At first Zack appreciates the words of this bizarre little character, but when the guy just stands there for a while without saying another word, the American loses his cool, muttering: 'Buzz off'. However, his voice is too slurred by alcohol to sound even remotely aggressive. Bob, his back still to the camera, does not understand and, like a baby learning to talk, calmly responds with: 'Thank you. Buzz off to you too.' Zack insists, his words accompanied by an appropriate gesture of the hand, and Bob finally gets the message. Only now does Bob turn, and we finally see his face as he pulls out his faithful notepad to write down the words, while speaking them out loud, 'Buzzza ... Offfa ...', before stepping out of the 'page' the same way he came.

Jarmusch's introduction of Bob, the film's pure soul and communicative motor, is brief but incisive and already reveals certain fundamental traits of this *poetic character*: optimism, curiosity and innocence. Bob's principal attribute is his notepad that, as seen, he produces at his very first appearance. This time there are no books or manuals to help find the way, as there are in *Ghost Dog*, or authors/alter egos to refer to as in *Dead Man*: Bob will write the book himself, as he struggles to learn this hitherto unknown language. As Jarmusch himself pointed out:

> He's not equipped with the language, the most elementary form of communication. Despite this, he's still able to communicate to these guys [Jack and Zack] the sense of optimism that he has. He's able to partially resurrect their spirits. They're basically dying until he comes.[40]

Besides being an incurable optimist, Bob is also a lover of American poetry, just like Roberto Benigni is in real life. He refers to two illustrious and quite different poets, quoting from memory Robert Frost and often mentioning Walt Whitman, and he certainly does not do it to appear cultured in the eyes of others. On the contrary, as far as Bob is concerned the poetic word is a key instrument with which to communicate, a necessary tool that can at times even *precede* natural language. This makes him the epitome of the *poetic character*, clearly without belittling the other characters met thus far. What makes Bob unique compared to Rammellzee, Blake/Nobody and Ghost Dog who, like him, express themselves through the poetic word, is his foreign accent – an Italian, or rather a Tuscan catapulted to New Orleans. His somewhat shaky linguistic abilities force him to live communication with his fellow man like a never-ending, fanciful obstacle course, and at times like an exhausting evolution. Bob reveals an irrepressible infantile curiosity when asking Zack and Jack again and again: 'How do you say in English?' And his recurring question, 'Do you like Walt Whitman?', becomes a running gag when, in the cell he shares with Jack and Zack, he talks of his 'brutal' murder, caused by the apparently innocuous and fatal throwing of a pool ball. Sarcastically, Jack asks him: 'Why did you do that . . .? Why did you kill a man, Bob . . . He didn't like Walt

Whitman?' Bob seems to take this provocation seriously and, with the naive tone of someone who has just discovered something that was obvious, responds: 'I never asked this man if he liked Walt Whitman.' As observed by critic Umberto Mosca:

> It is important that Bob be the character to present the name of Walt Whitman, the nineteenth-century poet and interpreter of the *melting pot* and the realization of the American dream that came about through the perfect integration of every man with the same natural environment, the same culture and the same institutions.[41]

Bob, both *poetic* and *natural character*, is the only one really to blend with nature, to relieve the dramatic situations – escape, hunger, cold – and to resolve the dangerous ones: it is he who saves the three men in a boat from drowning by realizing that the shaky little tub in which they are trying to cross the bayou has sprung a leak. Ironically, Bob is the only one who is unable to swim. Before their water-bound adventure, Jack, with his usual sarcasm, encourages Bob to wait for Mark Twain who will no doubt come and get him with a steamboat. The three fugitives shelter for one night in the hut in the middle of the woods (incredibly similar to the cell they just escaped from), where Bob gives an exhibition of his versatility by reciting – in Italian – several verses of Robert Frost's famous poem 'The Road Not Taken'. The almost rigorous verse of Frost, who often criticized the absence of rhyme by comparing it to 'playing tennis without the net',[42] has little to do with the revolutionary free verse of opera lover Whitman. Bob, with his funny accent and undying passion for literature, unites the two poetic concepts, abolishes the idea of hierarchy and uses every instrument that poetry permits in order to communicate.

The only person with whom he discusses poetry appears to be DJ Zack, who is amazed by Bob's literary culture and his ability to read and appreciate poems in a language different from its original. Frost's famous verses, which the diminutive Italian recites in the hut, already allude to where the paths diverge in the woods in the final sequence of the film.

> Two roads diverged in a wood, and I –
> I took the one less traveled by,
> And that has made all the difference.[43]

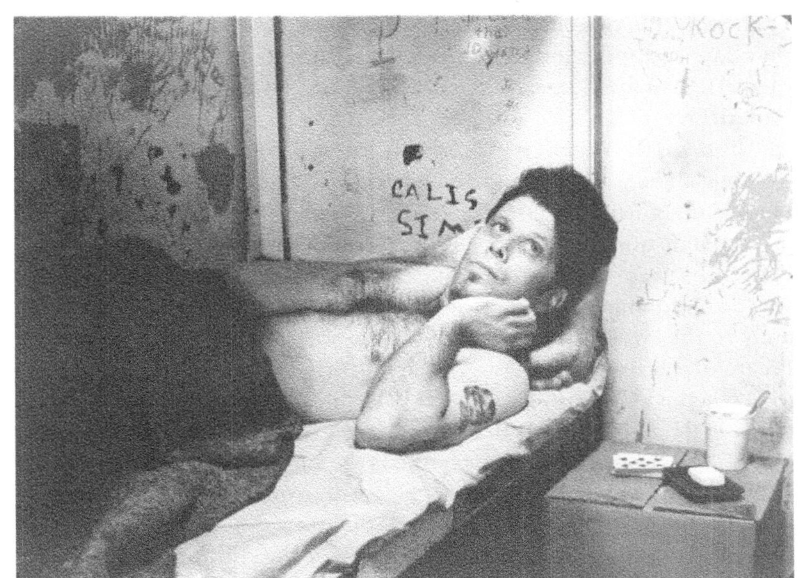

Tom Waits as
Zack 'Lee Baby
Simms' in *Down
By Law*.

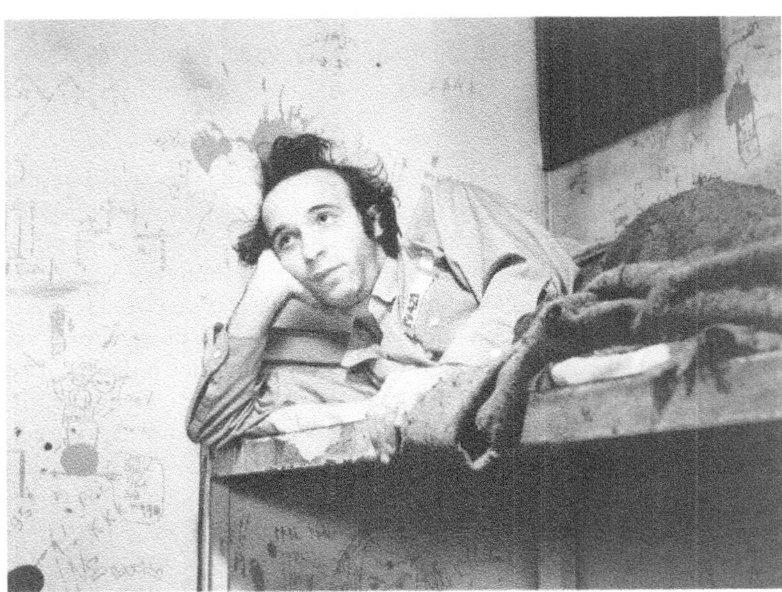

Roberto Benigni as
Bob, *Down By Law*.

By the time the two enemies/friends Zack and Jack separate definitively they have swapped clothes as if to affirm the interchangeability of their identities, or being two likenesses, albeit contrasting, of the same 'American type'.

Bob, on the other hand, ends his journey right there in the woods from which he was escaping, and where he is struck by love at first sight. He no longer needs to go on, to chase his naive American Dream made up of poetic quotes and film culture. 'Are you sure that you want to go? I stay!' he says, grinning at Jack and Zack, who stare at him in amazement, while as a foreigner in America he hugs Nicoletta and dances passionately to the swinging rhythm of 'It's Raining' with his new, all-Italian dream or, perhaps even better, with his 'princess'.

The device of using a fairy tale with a happy ending – a literary topos in its own right – is in fact what best suits the narrative structure of the film. A fairy tale of which Bob is the catalyst, willingly or unwillingly taking things forward, his struggle with words overcome by his agile body language, and whose 'direct and somatic actions express an unconventionality that links him with the jester or the child'.[44] Body, cinema and poetry are thus the voice of Bob/Benigni, the *poetic character* with the communicative nature and innocent sensibility, who, though he often mentions his hero Walt Whitman, never actually quotes his poetry.

Christopher Marlowe

'Trapped by a Thing Called Love' is a title that could very well describe the remarkable dance scene between Bob and Nicoletta just mentioned. Jarmusch chose to use this song – Denise LaSalle's 1971 hit – on another more recent and just as remarkable dance scene: vampires Adam and Eve's 'make up dance' in *Only Lovers Left Alive*. Having lived for centuries, the couple have a deep knowledge of music and all art forms, one of their biggest passions being poetry. In her Tangier hide-out, Eve keeps books everywhere and is able to read in all languages apparently by simply caressing the pages of her numerous volumes. During his long life Adam has personally met countless writers and poets, his knowledge going way beyond their works. Without hesitation he refers to Byron, who is definitely not one of his favourites, as 'a pompous ass'. Eve is not particularly fond of Byron either, making him – and a few others – responsible for Adam's depression and suicidal tendencies. 'I mainly blame Shelley, Byron and some of those French assholes

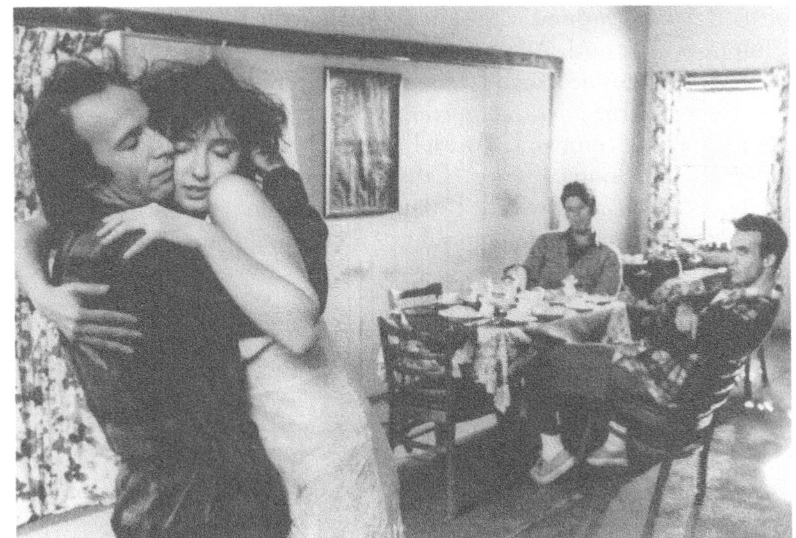

'It's Raining' by
Irma Thomas;
Bob and Nicoletta,
Down By Law.

'Trapped by a
Thing Called Love'
by Denise LaSalle;
Adam and Eve,
*Only Lovers
Left Alive*.

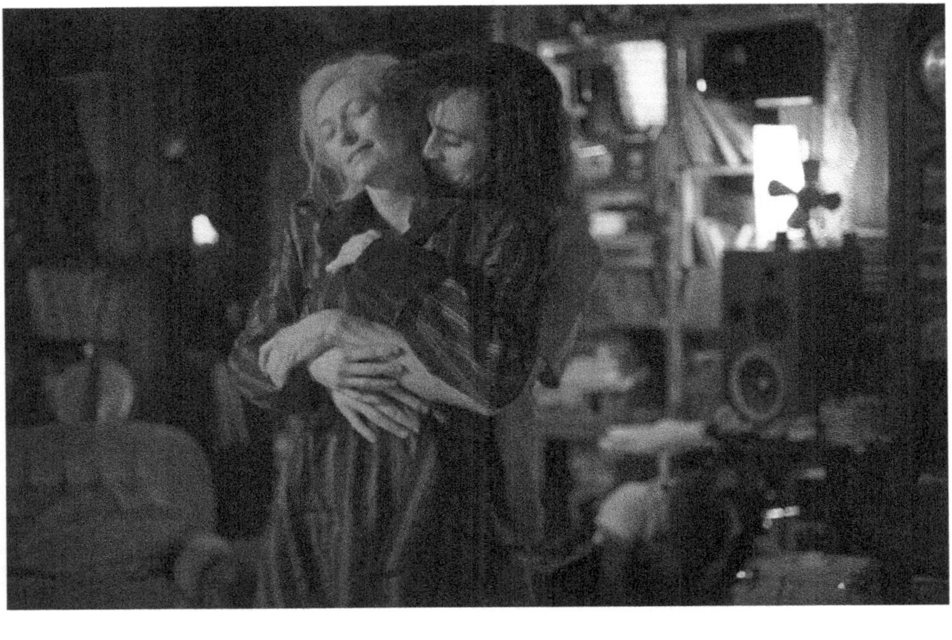

he used to hang around with', she confides to the one poet – and fellow vampire – that both Adam and Eve have an absolute adoration for: their very long-time friend Christopher Marlowe.

He is the true *poetic character* who 'infects' the couple of younger blood-drinking companions with his words. On two occasions first Eve and then Adam quote his poetry, thus becoming *poetic characters* themselves, even if only 'by reflex'. During Eve's nocturnal travels from Tangier to Detroit, on a comfortable 'Air Lumière' flight, she reads from a book of Marlowe's poetry:

> Love alters not with his brief hours and weeks,
> But bears it out even to the edge of doom.
> If this be error and upon me proved,
> I never writ, nor no man ever loved.[45]

Towards the end of the film, on Marlowe's deathbed, Adam quotes him again: 'What is this quintessence of dust?'[46]

By this moment in the film Jarmusch's point has been made clear: he is not at all convinced that William Shakespeare was the author of the numerous works, especially the sonnets, attributed to him. As Jarmusch said in Cannes in 2013:

> I think that one of the biggest scandals in literary history that some day may be divulged is that William Shakespeare didn't write anything. There are a lot of us, so-called anti-Stratfordians, who don't believe this. They included Orson Welles, Sigmund Freud, Emerson, John Gielgud . . . and now John Hurt! So there are different theories on who wrote these things, one of them is very possible. It is possible that Christopher Marlowe's death was faked.[47]

Marlowe is not the only 'real Shakespeare' that has been suggested at different moments in history, the authorship debate dating back at least to the nineteenth century.[48] As stated by Jarmusch the theories are many, including that of a collective of writers, even though in the film he is clearly inclined to follow the Marlowe track. Sitting next to Eve, the older poet describes her husband Adam as a 'suicidally romantic scoundrel' and regrets not having met him at the right time: 'Lord I wished that I'd met him before I wrote *Hamlet*. He would have provided the most perfect role model imaginable.' And it is precisely from *Hamlet* that a dying Marlowe delivers the line that makes him a true *poetic character*, the famous 'What a piece of work is a man'.

Confirming what Luc Sante said – 'History is mythology, really' – Jarmusch wants to instil the idea in his audience that different re-readings of the past are perfectly legitimate. His vampires, however, at least as long as they can get a hold of 'the good stuff', have a gift – perhaps a curse – not granted to humans, or zombies, as they would call us: the gift of immortality. Being eyewitnesses of historical and cultural events obviously changes their perspective on the present moment completely and allows them to carry secrets they share only with each other. Especially the idea of 'authorship relativism' is made clear by Jarmusch in two dialogue exchanges, the first about music and the second about poetry:

> Eve: I love your newest music, too. It made me think of when you gave that string quintet to Schubert, remember? And he presented it as his own.
> Adam: Yeah, but I had asked him to do that. And I only gave him the adagio. Just to put something out there.

The second dialogue excerpt is in the same idiom and perhaps more 'daring', especially in the definition that Marlowe gives of Shakespeare.

> Marlowe: Illiterate zombie philistine!
> Adam: The game paid off though, Kit. You still got the work out there . . .

Having the work 'out there', rather than a name, is thus what counts, an idea that brings back the observations I made about pseudonyms of artists in general and, for example, of the Wu-Tang Clan rappers in particular. Who 'owns' a work of art once it becomes a part of culture and is shared by a potentially infinite audience? Jarmusch seems to suggest that it does not really matter, or perhaps that the work 'owns itself' or is 'owned' by the public. When at the beginning of the film Eve meets Marlowe in his Tangier café and asks: 'How is the fabulous Christopher Marlowe tonight?' he quickly replies, almost frightened, 'I told you never to call me that name in public!' Revealing his true identity, thereby uncovering the 'game', is perhaps what will make him

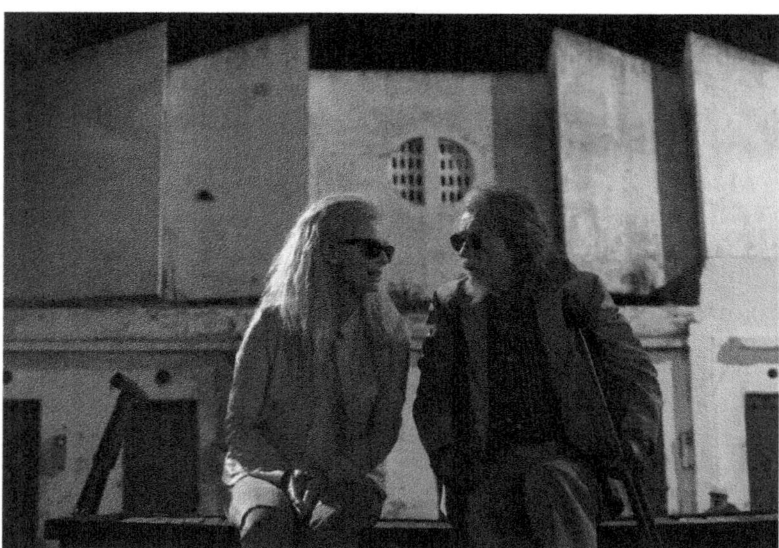

mortal. The work, no matter which name is to be read on the front cover, has a virtually never-ending life of its own.

Literary Approach: The Short Story

Jarmusch's passion for writers and literature is not only revealed by the creation of *poetic characters* but can also be recognized in the broader literary structure that he has chosen for his films.

In *Mystery Train*, Jarmusch wanted to highlight the film's literary setting right from the start. Jun and Mitsuko, the young Japanese couple, are on a musical pilgrimage from Yokohama to Memphis. On leaving the train, the two minute teenagers walk through the city carrying a large, flaming red suitcase. They start their urban wanderings with Mitsuko noticing the name of the street they are walking along, a name that contradicts its anonymous aspect. 'Chaucer Street!' she cries out with her very marked Japanese accent as she reads the street sign.[49] It is evident that Jarmusch did not want this 'detail' to be lost, ensuring that even the most distracted member of the audience not only sees but also hears the name of one of the fathers of English literature. His choice is by no means casual, considering that *The Canterbury Tales* is a clear point of reference for the film, and at the base of both is the idea of different stories coming together in a single place: the city of Memphis and the Arcade Hotel in *Mystery Train*, and the road to Canterbury in Chaucer's collection of stories.

This apparently anecdotal detail offers the chance to broaden the interpretation of the particular 'literary approach' of his films: being 'poetic' is not limited to single characters, but extends also to the very structure of the film itself, which is rich with rhetorical figures and stylistic traits, typical of literature. I am not referring just to the quotes from more or less famous written works, to their titles, to the characters caught in the act of reading – 'according to Godard *the* radical cinematic gesture', as remembered by Juan A. Suárez.[50] From a stylistic point of view, Jarmusch gladly uses rhyme, repetition and assonance, while on the side of the overall narrative structure he prefers brief, episodic forms – often broken up into 'chapters'[51] – even if joined by a common thread, be it spatial or temporal, such as the apparently insignificant parenthesis of a nocturnal taxi ride that takes place simultaneously in different cities and countries; or the recurring shots of a table where that moment of suspension so typical to the act of drinking coffee and smoking a cigarette is consumed.

Coffee and Cigarettes is clearly told in episodes, collected over a period of nigh on twenty years; in *Broken Flowers* the recurring theme

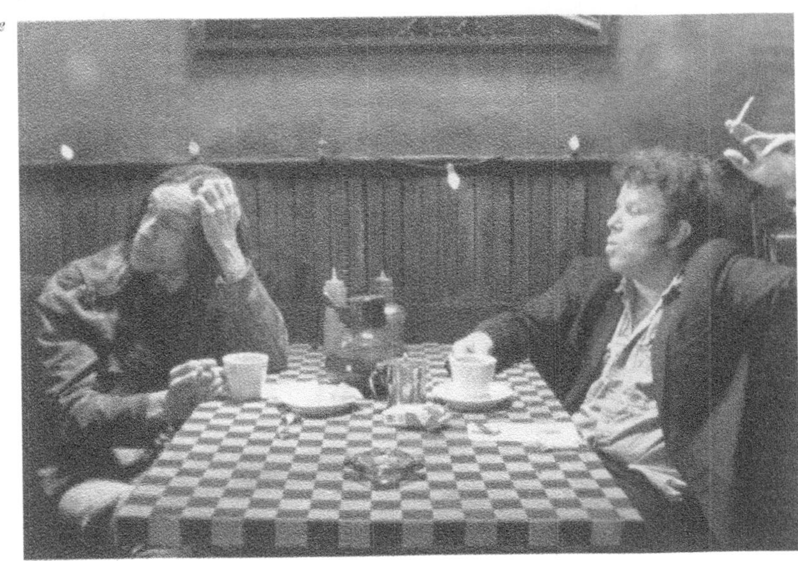

Short stories, *Coffee and Cigarettes*.

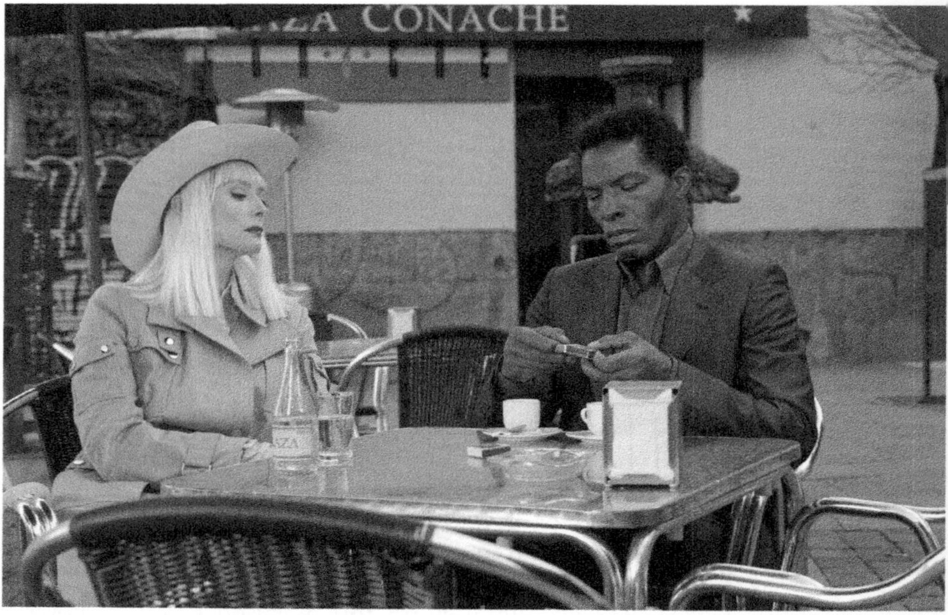

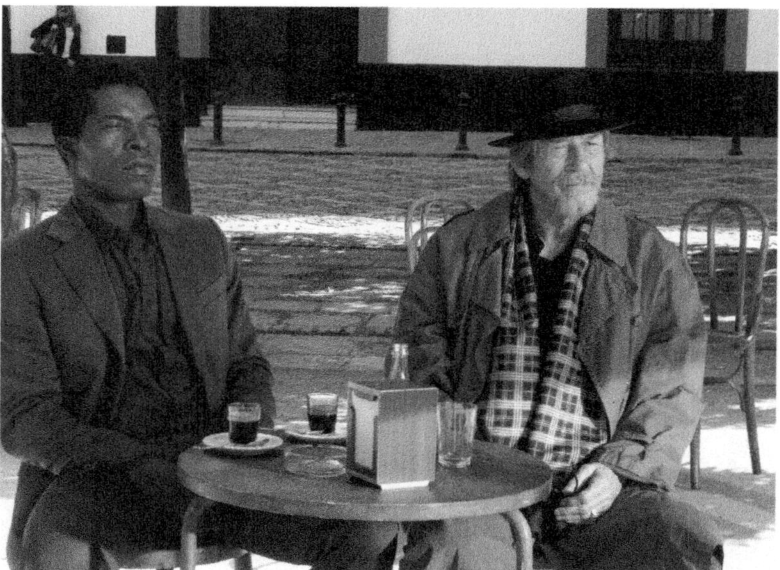

Allegorical names:
Blonde, *The Limits
of Control.*

Guitar, *The Limits
of Control.*

Allegorical names: Violin, *The Limits of Control.*

Lone Man, *The Limits of Control.*

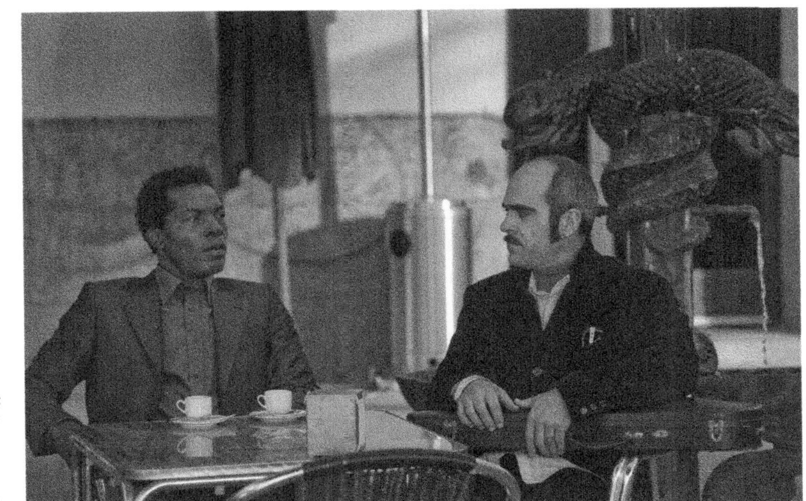

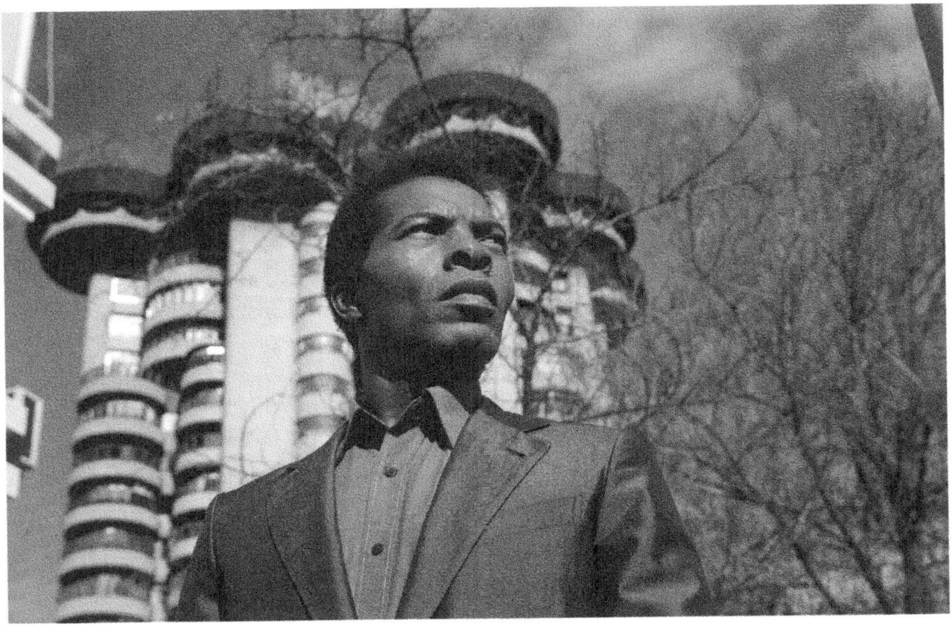

of Don turning up at an ex-lover's without warning gives the story a sort of regular beat, a pattern, in this case chronological, made up of 'short stories'; in *The Limits of Control*, Lone Man during his mysterious journey obsessively repeats the same gestures with the different characters he meets along the way, again with a structure that without hesitation may be defined as episodic;[52] and finally the short *Int. Trailer Night* was Jarmusch's contribution to the episodic film *Ten Minutes Older: The Trumpet* (2002), whose producer Nicolas McClintock managed to put together a stellar cast of fifteen directors – Werner Herzog, Jean-Luc Godard, Claire Denis, Bernardo Bertolucci, Spike Lee, Aki Kaurismäki, Wim Wenders, to mention just a few – asking each one in turn to come up with a ten-minute reflection on Time.

I would like to take a closer look at *Broken Flowers* and *The Limits of Control*, which could be defined as 'episodic road movies'. In *Broken Flowers*, Don's actions are always the same: setting off, turning up at an unknown address, giving flowers to an ex-lover from the past, trying to find out about his unknown hypothetical son and taking off again empty-handed. The episodic narrative format, repetitive and unsolved, nonetheless sustains the film very agilely. Instead, in *The Limits of Control*, in spite of structural similarities with *Broken Flowers*, the narrative course, also based on repetition, is anything but agile and ends up becoming almost exhausting by the end of the film. Why?

It is possible to come up with a hypothesis that must once again involve a literary figure. The characters chosen by Jarmusch to 'live' the structure of *The Limits of Control*, as observed with regards to their names, are all allegorical: Blonde (Tilda Swinton) is the allegory of the cinema, Molecules (Youki Kudoh) of science, Violin (Luis Tosar) of music, and so on. Nonetheless, these are not *poetic characters* in the way I have discussed thus far, rather characters who *in themselves* wish to represent the rhetorical figure as such – in this case the allegory – without necessarily expressing themselves through poetic language. The actions or, better still, the non-actions repeated by Lone Man and the allegorical characters met during his journey end up looking very artificial and the myriad details, including variations, are not enough to sustain the structure as a whole. The cold perfection of Christopher Doyle's cinematography completes the picture. Even if Jarmusch declared his intentions in the most evident way, the coldness coming off this cerebral narrative strategy is what in my opinion hampers the film:

The idea of the variations was there from the beginning, because the guy is doing the same things over and over: going to the café, waiting, going to some safe house, waiting, going to the Reina Sofía Museum in Madrid to see a single painting each time. It's an action film without action, a suspense film without the drama of suspense.[53]

In *Broken Flowers*, on the other hand, the same structure is inhabited by characters who are also not *poetical*, but who enjoy a real, pulsating and anything but allegorical humanity: the unshakeable amateur detective Winston (Jeffrey Wright), the solar Laura (Sharon Stone) and her exuberant teenage daughter Lolita (Alexis Dziena), the fragile and melancholic Dora (Frances Conroy) and the hardened Penny (Tilda Swinton), just to mention a few. Naturally, one might object that the vicissitudes of Don Johnston, the ex-Casanova searching for his nameless son, in themselves offer a more catchy narrative with respect to the monotony of Lone Man's enigmatic journey. And yet, the more unresolved of the two stories is the one told in *Broken Flowers*: we will not know if the son really exists, we will not know what is written in the letter/*coup de théâtre* that Don receives at the end of the film, that perhaps contains fundamental information for him (and for us). Instead, Lone Man will honour his contract by killing the American – the last allegorical character and the only truly negative one in the film – paradoxically played by the same Bill Murray who embodies the melancholic Don. And yet, on its own, the narrative structure of *The Limits of Control*, no matter how solid, is not enough to support the framework of a film that suffers not so much from a lack of a more or less articulate or resolved plot, but rather from the incompatibility between the schematic allegory personified by the characters and the degree of authenticity necessary for a story – invented or otherwise – to seem credible and genuine to an audience.

Thel and Plume

Instead, a film in which the allegorical register works quite well is *Dead Man*. William Blake, besides incarnating the poet and the bookkeeper, is the allegorical figure who represents the passage from life to death, his demise possibly the slowest in the history of cinema. The doubly lethal bullet, shot by Charlie Dickinson in the 25th minute, first rips through

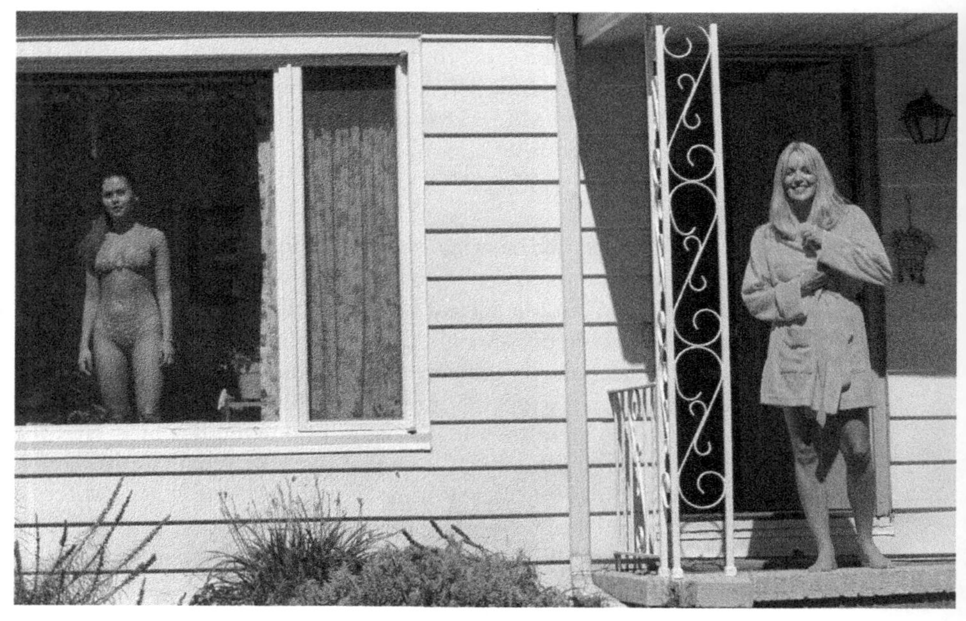

Lolita and Laura,
Broken Flowers.

Blake's one-night lover, Thel, killing her almost instantly, before burying itself in Blake's chest and taking practically the rest of the film to kill him off. The girl's name is filled with references well in keeping with the film's literary approach: the poem *The Book of Thel* was written by William Blake probably between 1788 and 1791 and is frequently interpreted as an allegoric equivalent to the *Songs of Innocence*. In the allegorical-literary economy of the film, the bullet that slowly kills Blake also immolates the innocence from which the young poet-bookkeeper slowly distances himself during the course of his journey. The death of his parents, being left by his fiancée, Dickinson's refusal to employ him, Charlie's awkward murder and the failure to save Thel's life are the initial stages of the journey that will inevitably end with Blake's death.

The film's opening words – 'It is preferable not to travel with a dead man' – add further literary points, as shown by Juan A. Suárez in his fascinating analysis when defining *Dead Man* as 'a meditation on death and dying influenced by the Belgian-born writer and painter Henri Michaux (1899–1983)'.[54] Among the numerous assonances that Suárez gleaned from Michaux's literary work and the film, there is one regarding the initial quote. The line, as Suárez goes on to explain, is

278 | words

taken from Michaux's collection of sketches, *Un certain Plume* (1931), their tone at times surreally comical, at times disturbing, or both. Plume is a man who seems to have made it his speciality to walk into dangerous or simply absurd situations, with a passivity and an 'agile clumsiness' that evoke Blake's character in *Dead Man*. In the fragment 'The Night of the Bulgarians', Plume is on a train ride at night, sharing the compartment with a friend and a group of Bulgarians. Not trusting the fellow travellers, primarily because of their muttering and constant moving around, Plume and his friend pull out their revolvers and kill them. As the journey continues, Plume and his killer-companion sit among the dead, trying to prevent their heads and bodies from toppling over in all directions, an image reminiscent of the dead priest in the Roman episode in *Night On Earth*.[55] The bodies, however, cool off quickly and Plume realizes that it will not be easy to hide the misdeed. The essence of the story, Michaux concludes, is that 'it's always preferable not to travel with a dead man. Especially when he has been the victim of a revolver bullet.'[56]

Having consolidated such an obvious truth – though both Michaux and, by reflection, Jarmusch felt it would be useful to reassert it – I

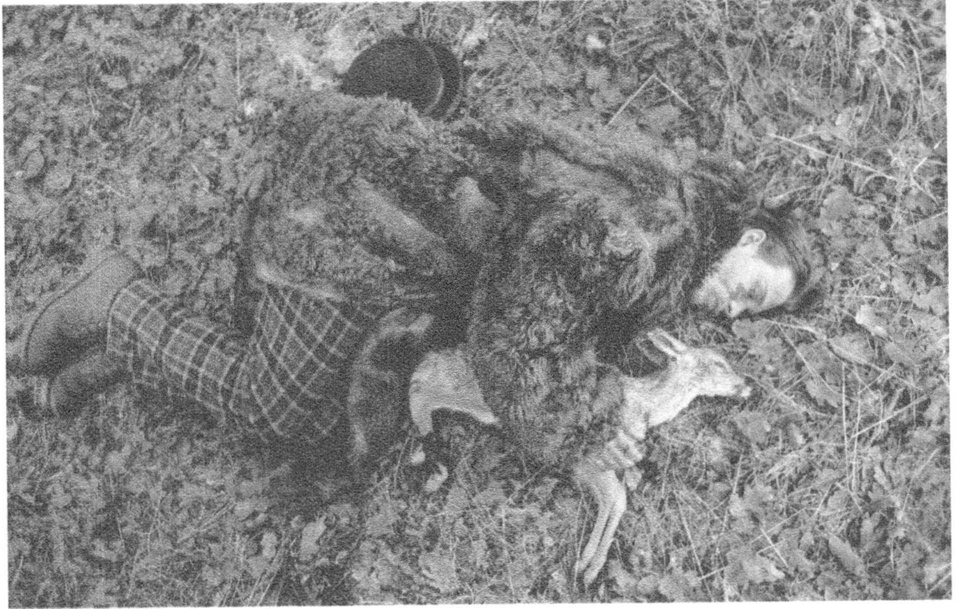

would like to conclude this panorama on the central role of the literary form by staying within the theme of travel: but I will risk stepping just outside the lines drawn by the filmography that has guided me this far.

Passing Stranger

'Passing Stranger', as well as being the incipit of one of Walt Whitman's most famous poems, 'To a Stranger',[57] is also the title of an audio and poetic experiment decidedly in keeping with the arguments discussed to this point. The complete title of the experiment is 'Passing Stranger – The East Village Poetry Walk', and this time the journey is anything other than allegorical: it is a real walk over two miles through the streets of New York's East Village during which the visitor is accompanied by an audio guide written and produced by Danish author, and adopted New Yorker, Pejk Malinovski.[58] The sonic walk begins at St Mark's Church, home of the Poetry Project since 1966, and is made up of a remarkable collection of anecdotes and highlights of the history of poetry and American literature, told by the voices of the poets who have populated those streets, many since the 1950s. The audio fabric is composed of archived historical recordings, for example, original readings by Allen Ginsberg and Kenneth Koch, comments made by poets like Ron Padgett and Anne Waldman, and key figures of that scene like Bob Holman, poet and 'proprietor'[59] of the Bowery Poetry Club, and Richard Hell, writer, musician and punk icon. The music is by John Zorn. Among the many voices it is impossible to miss the deep and phlegmatic tone of the narrator: Jim Jarmusch.

The common thread of poetry is thus well anchored, tied with a double knot to the life – not only cinematographic – of this long-time East Village inhabitant. A knot that, since his first feature film, *Permanent Vacation*, shot entirely in the Lower East Side, has to this very day never been untied. So it is no surprise that Allie had already made some palpable references in the film to Jarmusch's passion for books, even if with that pinch of sarcastic cynicism that would remain among the director's trademarks, also in the decades to come. After a bored Allie has read a long and rather violent extract from *Les chants de Maldoror* by Lautréamont to his girlfriend Leila, he says: 'I'm tired of this book, you can have it'. Leila responds that she has already read it and a moment later starts to rip out pages in order to make aeroplanes.

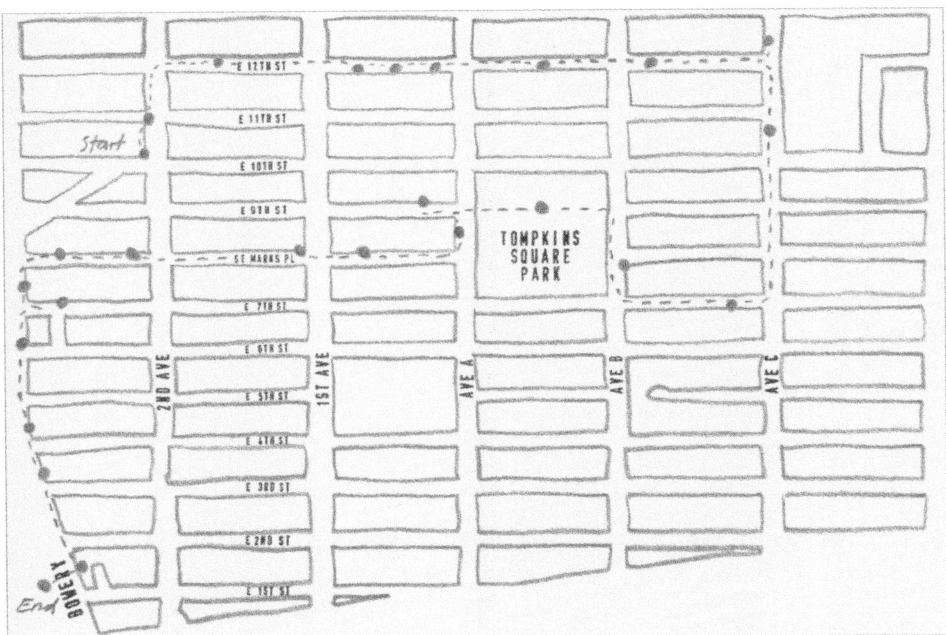

'Passing Stranger – The East Village Poetry Walk' map.

Books – perhaps Jarmusch is telling us – are certainly not sacred. Poetry often hides in the most unlikely of places: in a crack in a wall, in a look on someone's face, on a building's dirty facade, in a melody without lyrics.

noise

Voices:
Eszter Balint

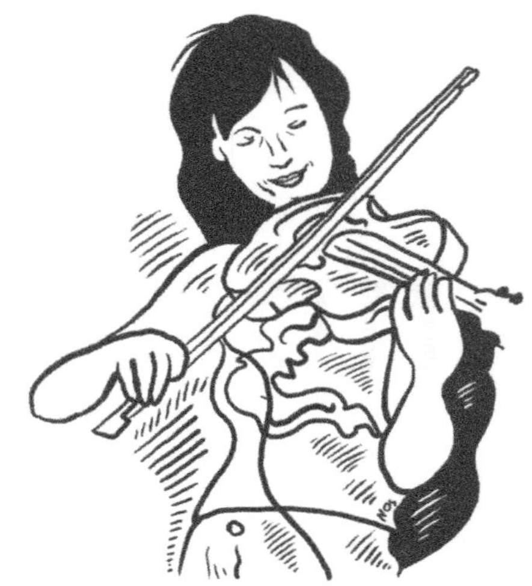

1

Especially when coming from a different linguistic area into a new environment, 'sounds' become very important in order to communicate. All sorts of sounds in my opinion: noises, words and music. Was this true for you when you first came to NYC from Hungary? How big was the importance of voice, noise and music within the Squat Theatre?

Well, I was an eleven-year-old kid from Hungary, by way of Paris, so to me New York was very noisy! But it was noisy in a wonderful way, in an exotically exciting way. So in that sense noise played a very big role in my youth and I think I can say that for Squat Theatre too. Kids are like sponges. They absorb fast. I had an intuitive desire to become one with this crazy noisy place. I quickly felt very much at home, even though it was all new and foreign. Squat Theatre and my parents were very influential in that regard of adapting and assimilating – there was this almost outspoken discomfort with and resistance to being confined to any one particular identity, nation, genre, art form, and we always felt like citizens of the world in some ways. When we came to New York in the late 1970s, this was a very homey place for such people. But I'm straying from your question about noise . . .

There were also concerts at the Squat Theatre and you were a DJ, right?

Yes. I think that was actually one of the most memorable experiences for me in my early years growing up in New York, all the music that I was surrounded by, and which was happening at Squat Theatre. Some of it was pretty amazing and groundbreaking stuff. I just breathed it

284

and drank it, it was part of daily life. Which is exceptional if you think about it, that this stuff was taking place in my home!

Which bands do you remember from that time?

It's such an endless list, there is actually an online resource that lists all the events through all those years of it being a club: the Squat Theatre Digital Archive. Anyway, I could mention The Lounge Lizards, DNA, Kid Creole and the Coconuts, Defunkt, James Chance, Sun Ra, tonnes of jazz and blues legends . . .

Well, James Chance, if we talk about noise, sounds just about perfect.

Yes, a lot of noise! And Sun Ra, too. I'm just listing the bands that were the 'house bands' basically, who played there on a fairly regular basis. I think I can say without sounding arrogant that it was one of the music venues at the time which really mattered. The website has a page specifically devoted to the music, and I must say that when I looked at it recently myself, I was astonished. It just hit me, looking at that list, with new perspective: gee, I guess I spent a big chunk of my childhood, and all of my teenagehood, in a pretty spectacularly happening place!

What about you being a DJ there? How old were you?

Is there a statute of limitations on getting arrested for a misdemeanour? I think it would be considered a misdemeanour. Anyway, I was really young . . . I probably shouldn't say. I had no business being a club DJ. Probably thirteen, maybe fourteen? It sounds crazy now. I was very precocious.

What kind of music did you like to play?

It was completely eclectic. There was no specific genre I'd strictly adhere to, but I was really into funk music at the time. Things like Funkadelic, Parliament and James Brown. Most people I was surrounded by and knew were into all that stuff too, so of course I was influenced, but I don't think it was just peer pressure, I really loved all that. There were some pretty wonderful records coming out at that time, but I would mix it up with classics. I was really into Motown for instance, so I'd mix up The Supremes with PIL and then throw on some Funkadelic and then some Clash and then some Chic. And some of those very early rap tracks. That kind of thing.

Did you play No Wave music at all?

Less of that, but the occasional James White and the Blacks track, yes. Though maybe they were too funky to be considered official No Wave fare . . . There wasn't so much No Wave on recordings at that time, we have to remember that.

Well of course those were the bands coming to play, so they were there anyway . . .

Exactly. And then every once in a while I'd throw in some classic thing that didn't make any sense in that context, like a Jimi Hendrix tune or something from the White Album. But most of it was what, at that time, would be considered music to dance to, I suppose.

I wish I could be in a little time machine and spend a night at the Squat Theatre.

Me too (laughing). Now it just seems so mythological. At the time I took it all for granted of course; sometimes it was wonderful fun and other times were difficult or even downright shitty. I had my own issues like anybody that age. I didn't look at my life as at this exceptional mythological event, I was just living it.

Does the location still exist?

No. The building was torn down. It is really too bad, I believe it was a landmark building which was supposed to be protected. It had a long and varied history. Now it's merely a ghost somewhere in the Chelsea Cineplex.

2

I read on your website that your recording debut was on an early rap track featuring Rammellzee, who has a brief cameo role in *Stranger Than Paradise*. Jim Jarmusch spotted you in a play and asked you to star in the film.

I *think* he saw me in a play. That might be slightly fictionalized . . . maybe you should ask Jim about that as I don't remember for sure. It is also possible that John Lurie recommended me.

Especially the music and film scenes, but in your specific case, also the underground theatre scene, at the time were very connected to each other.

Absolutely. They were inseparable. So in a way it doesn't really matter where exactly he saw me.

How natural was it and is it for you to switch from theatre, to music, to film? And what did *Stranger Than Paradise* mean in your career?

The first part, theatre to film, was very natural. I come from a theatre tradition, which was heavily influenced by a cinematic approach to acting. As I recall, there were two unwritten rules: 1) bring your very personal, individual presence, almost in a magnified way to the stage, and 2) never be false. Certainly, I didn't come from a traditional theatrical acting school, so that transition felt like a piece of cake. We used films as part of our plays, but the live actions had a cinematic quality as well. Cinema was part of the general aesthetic.

From there the transition to music, again, was fairly natural. I have had music in my life since I was a little kid. I started by studying classical violin as a child, and have taken some basic theory classes. And at Squat Theatre I was constantly exposed to music. For some reason I had a scam going within the theatre where I had this reputation of having impeccable musical taste, so I became the house DJ when the theatre was a club, and later I was basically asked to be the musical consultant on the shows. So music has always been there for me in some form or another, it wasn't an entirely abrupt change in direction. Becoming a songwriter is a bit of a different story. That is a relatively new direction, in that it feels more directly personal as a choice, it is not something I grew up doing or happened into through circumstances. So it does not necessarily have so much to do with my particular historical context. Other than inheriting and continuing in the general legacy of several generations of tortured artist types.

Songwriting for me comes first and foremost, I think, from my love of words, writing and poetry and just the general yearning to tell a story of some kind, maybe not a linear story, certainly not one with a neat beginning and end, but some glimpse or fragment of a story nonetheless. And music is a huge part of that of course; in a song the music can tell the story as much as the words, sometimes more so. This storytelling drive has always been there for me, but I don't know that it is necessarily part of any particular culture I grew up with. Now that I think of it, maybe the one direct influence I can trace from my past is that my songs often do have a cinematic quality to them, or at least so I've been told. I think my father's work in the theatre, as well as his writing, had quite a bit of that thing we call 'cinematic quality'. So maybe there

is a tradition there, which I have integrated. Not sure if it's nature or
nurture . . . I have never thought about it before.

And what about Stranger Than Paradise, what did it mean in your career?

It is a double-edged sword. It has been helpful, because it is expected of
everyone working in any creative field, especially in this country, and
especially in the not-particularly-tender music business, that you have a
story. An interesting story that identifies you immediately. That is how the
umpteenth songwriter to come along this year and present yet another
collection of songs is distinguished from the one who came along last year
or the myriad others who won't be heard at all. At first at least. So having
those credentials helped give me a story. That is one edge of the sword.
The other is that the film is not the whole story, it's not my only story,
and though it's a wonderful one, it can become quite a boring story, if
you have to retell it so often over decades. So it has been both a blessing
and a little bit of a curse. It's not much more complicated than that.

*Did it feel like a label that was put on you, and which at some point
you really wanted to get rid of?*

In some ways, yes. Like a sign that's kind of tattooed on your forehead,
which is your single identifier of who you are. And you can't even
answer a question about it with honesty anymore, because your face
just defaults to this frozen expression, the words lose their meaning
after a while . . . But it certainly helped too, and I'm not going to deny
that and whine about it. It probably could have helped me a lot more if
I didn't have such mixed feelings and even resistance to putting it to use.
But we're talking only about the 'legacy' of the film as it pertains to my,
well, let's call it current professional life – and not the film itself – just
to be clear. I have only fondness towards the movie itself and am
immensely proud of my association with it as part of my history.

*What do you think about the music in Stranger Than Paradise, how do
you think that that worked?*

I think it's gorgeous, it is simply a beautiful piece of music. I do think it
was influenced by that little Bartók phase in John's life, but he filtered
that influence so beautifully and of course in his own totally unique
way. I have not seen the movie in ages, but if I heard the music now I
would instantly recognize it. It is so haunting and memorable. I think
Jim has great taste in music.

In the book I argue that Eva is using the Screamin' Jay Hawkins song
'I Put A Spell On You' on one hand to gain her own American identity
and on the other hand literally to try to communicate to the – at first –
hostile male characters. Would you agree? And if yes or no, why?

The first part I'll come back to in a sec, but the second, wow, that never
occurred to me personally. See, that is what's so wonderful about music,
about a good song. It leaves so much room for the individual's imagination. It is possible that in a subconscious way the idea was there, but it
was never discussed and I was never aware of it. But hey, it works, so
why not, maybe that was in Jim's mind all along – I just never knew.
The song was her way of taming the boys.

As for the first part, yes, I think so. It was never discussed, and the
inclusion of this song really came strictly from Jim as I recall, he was very
definitive about wanting it. My interpretation of it was, at the risk of
stating the obvious, that it would be funny and effective to have this fresh
off the boat young immigrant girl be acquainted with something so quin-
tessentially American, which at the same time is not representative of the
most typical mainstream version of America. In fact her very American
cousin, who wants nothing to do with Hungary, isn't even familiar with
it. It gave her character a certain confidence, and like all good things, it
had an element of the utterly unexpected, taking something out of context, juxtaposing things in a surprising way and forcing us to listen with
fresh ears. I mean, Screamin' Jay's voice, his delivery couldn't be any more
in contrast to our first impression of her. So I think that almost provocative
contrast was the inspiration. This is probably a long-winded way of
rephrasing your idea about American identity – but in any case that was
my intuitive feeling about why Jim might have thought of it.

3

John Lurie told me a little about the time you were working on Bartók,
he called it a 'little class' in which you would listen to and write up the
music together.

I'm glad he remembers that, I remember it too. Well, it sometimes happens
that I lose touch with the violin for a period of time – in fact it happened
for nearly fifteen years once. Some time ago I needed something to
inspire me to play again and I picked up those little Bartók duets, which,
along with the Bartók quartets, if I remember correctly, were some of the

pieces we looked at with John back then. So I have just recently rediscovered those beautiful duets and practise with them sometimes.

Then it's a really good timing to ask you.

Absolutely!

Can you tell me something about your music now and about your collaboration with John Lurie and with Marc Ribot? I'm interested in how all these different influences that you had, and this 'Bartók class' was an example of that, flow into your music now.

I don't think there really is any direct connection that I can put into words, except that everybody absorbs their history and the things they've been exposed to one way or another. Everything that a person lives, that enters their consciousness or even unconsciousness comes out somehow. Now that I am looking at those little violin duets again I am more consciously aware of how brilliant the composition is but I can't say that it ever had any *direct* influence. What did have influence, I like to hope at least, is being exposed to a pretty vast collection of talented people, of different persuasions, early on in my life – and all with very high standards, high levels of commitment. Other than that, my ears just seem to gravitate towards a particular direction at this time, and I really don't know for sure or dwell on why it feels organic and it sounds good to me, though it can take a lot of work for me to get it to feel and sound just right, till it's just the right amount of tension between elements.

But the rest is just best left up to mystery. In some ways my songs are so super simple – well, that's not necessarily what the musicians who play them say – that I feel silly and pompous talking about brilliant compositions and composers and artists having any direct or even indirect influence. I make no claim to being an accomplished anything, much less an accomplished composer of any type or types of music. But maybe I'm starting to have a little bit of an inkling of what's a pretty good song. To me, I mean. I like to feel that I am not confined to anything in particular and that there is room to absorb all these different things, and let them come out how they will after the E. B. filter. At the same time there are certain sounds, grooves, chords, patterns, moods, I seem to fairly consistently gravitate towards in my writing – well, that's where my ears are at now.

All in all, it would be hard for me to point to any particular genre, or band, or musician, or period in my life, which has specifically influenced

me, it's more that a lot of these wonderful creative people I grew up with
and around had a certain attitude which I respond to and which has had
influence. I don't know exactly how to describe it, but it has something
to do with making music, 'doing art', very much in the context of the
bigger picture of fully living and absorbing and observing life.

I was also talking with John about how especially his film music makes
you travel to a million different places and you never have the feeling
that there is any kind of hierarchy, there is no 'high' music versus say
'folk' or 'pop'.

I am a firm believer of that. It's like Rod Stewart said, probably the best
thing he ever said, which is hearsay and I'm absolutely sure he never
even said it: 'There's only two kinds of music in the world: good music
and bad music.'

That's very true. I heard this quote, but someone told me it's Louie
Armstrong or Duke Ellington, I can't remember.

Yeah, so it's probably one of those myths, you know, which was said by
no one in particular.

And how did you collaborate on the music level with John Lurie?

I think I just helped him write out the music we were listening together,
as notation and ear training practice. I really wouldn't call it 'a collaboration'. Later, when the score was completed, I probably gave him a little
friendly jab about how that music really found its way in there – all in
good spirit of course. I have nothing but huge respect for his musical
talents and even for his particular choice of influences.

Yes, I see. You didn't work with The Lounge Lizards, did you?

No, not with the Lizards. But I did do some singing with John on the
Marvin Pontiac record. I am on three or four tunes, usually with a small
group of girls.

I remember a girls' chorus, they sound a little bit African.

That's right and there is one tune, which I think might just be me,
called 'Pancakes'.

And what about the collaboration with Marc Ribot? I know you've been
touring with his band Ceramic Dog.

I'm lucky enough to have been asked by Marc to participate in a few things over the years including a Serge Gainsbourg duet on a tribute album by Zorn, an appearance on his second Cubanos record, and more recently some guest performances with his band Ceramic Dog. It's a bit of a clichéd thing to say, but performing with him live is a pretty damn special experience – and of course at times intimidating as hell. It's a strange contradiction: it can feel almost effortless in some ways because that level of musicianship and the 100 per cent invested energy he gives – always! – can simply make you shape up, and give you the sense that it's carrying you along; on the other hand, he continually and deliberately – at least I think it's deliberate – creates situations where everyone is sure to be off guard. Especially me. So it took more courage to do it than I ever thought I could muster up. I learned a lot.

There is also a project of songs of his – or I should say it's more centred around his 'songwriting' than any previous projects of his that I'm aware of, and I was involved in the original recording of demos for this a number of years ago. We did a guerrilla session of rough tracks, and the project has been under lock and key since, as far as I know. Whether I'll end up being included in any way or not, I do hope this project or some version of his collection of songs see the light of day. They are original and moving and funny and should be heard.

New York, March 2005

8 Communicating at all Cost: Intelligent Noise

'I have too much trust in the efficiency, value, strength and suggestiveness of images to believe that they cannot be without music. I do however need to draw on noise.'
Michelangelo Antonioni (1961), *Fare un film è per me vivere: scritti sul cinema,* ed. Carlo di Carlo and Giorgio Tinazzi (Venice, 1994), p. 42.

Noise – sound effect in cinema – is an objective sound. The noise of a plate breaking, for example, does not change in intensity according to the mood or intention of the person who breaks it, but varies only according to certain physical characteristics (its speed of travel, the type of surface it hits, its weight and so on). The reason it was smashed to pieces is irrelevant. However, when associated with an image, an objective noise produces an 'added value' capable of augmenting the information linked to it. As Michel Chion explains:

> By added value I mean the expressive and informative value with which a sound enriches a given image so as to create the definite impression, in the immediate or remembered experience one has of it, that this information or expression 'naturally' comes from what is seen, and is already contained in the image itself.[1]

Clearly, in cinema the image in itself does not contain a sound, and neither does a sound contain a certain image, rather both travel along parallel tracks and the director decides what relationship will be forged between the two. The sound of the broken plate may thus express conflicting meanings according to the image it is associated with, and the same sound convey different emotions to the audience, ranging from joy, terror, a release of tension or revenge. Having said this, it is clear that objective noise, even if not linked to an image, conjures up different emotions and meanings depending on the listener. For example, someone who celebrates New Year's Eve by merrily breaking old plates will not associate that noise with the same emotions as a person fired on the spot from a restaurant for having broken the umpteenth dish. This does not mean that the noise will have a joyous and carefree inflection in the first instance and a sad and angry one in the second.

So although in nature there exists what might be called a self-standing *objective catalogue of noises*, filtered through the listener's subjective experience, one cannot claim that there is anything similar in cinema: noise is a malleable, subjective sound matter at the director's disposal, just like music or words. It should be said, though, that cinema generally tends to couple noises with images in a way that 'mimics' nature. For example, if a frame of a hand holding a gun is followed by a close-up of the smoking barrel with the sound of a gunshot between the two, the editing will create the perfect illusion of synchronicity in the 'audio-spectator' between what is seen, or rather believed to have been seen, and what is heard.[2]

Acoustic Ecology

Having made these premises, what the more alert audio-spectator will notice in Jarmusch's cinema is not limited to the degree of 'objectivity' or closeness to nature of a particular sound. Above all he will be aware of the conscious use and the consequent broadening of the expressive and narrative possibilities of noise within the general economy of the film, not merely in terms of its sound effects or the soundtrack. In Jarmusch's – and our – post-Cage sound world, the virtually limitless semantic spectrum of sound includes all audio materials. As avant-garde composer and multi-instrumentalist Elliot Sharp pointed out, 'There's a continuity between this world I construct and the world that I hear. It is not a separation at all. It's like one ecology of sound.'[3] The idea of an 'ecology of sound' is certainly in line with Jarmusch's overall *Weltanschauung*, both inside and outside cinema, and brings to mind one of the main concepts elaborated by Canadian composer and a true pioneer in the fields of Sound Studies and Environmental Sound R. Murray Schafer: acoustic ecology. The balance between sounds that

Schafer longs for – and that he sees endangered by a dominance of noise – calls to mind the lack of hierarchy, which is at the heart of Jarmusch's poetic universe, an idea confirmed by his treatment of sound. Indeed, the various types of sound matter – music, words and noise – do not compete or relate to each other hierarchically. Instead, they form an organic albeit constructed soundscape, in which Jarmusch seems to be on a constant quest for the balance between sounds as defined by Schafer. In his films words do not dominate, music does not accompany, noise is not necessarily confined to the background; rather all these kinds of sound matter are interconnected, sometimes performing different functions from their usual ones in cinema.

For the sake of completeness, I should add that the term 'soundscape' was also coined by the far-seeing Schafer, founder in the late 1960s of the World Soundscape Project:

> There is a word, landscape, describing all the things that you can see. We didn't have any word for listening to sounds that were near or far, human sounds, sounds of animals, sounds of machines.
> If you don't have a word to describe something, it doesn't exist. Which is strange but true. We had to invent a word in order to get people to listen to the landscape.[4]

Even though, today, the term 'soundscape' is often used – especially by composers – to describe certain electronic music compositions, Schafer clarified that this was not his original intention. The first studies were aimed at analysing the changes of acoustic environments across history, the types of sounds people were surrounded by, for example, in the Renaissance and how that soundscape would be different from today's: a social study including recordings made for an illustrative purpose rather than compositions. According to Schafer, 'The word has been used, and perhaps been overused by young composers.'[5] Regardless of how it is defined, this kind of attention given to soundscape, meant as the fabric of noises and sound effects of a given landscape, is on the same wavelength as Jarmusch's working method in cinema which, by his own admission, is somewhat obsessive. As he told me, the utmost accuracy should be devoted to sound details such as a particular motorbike model and the song of a certain species of woodpecker.[6] Under no circumstances should the pileated woodpecker (*Dryocopus pileatus*) be confused with the red-headed woodpecker (*Melanerpes erythrocephalus*),

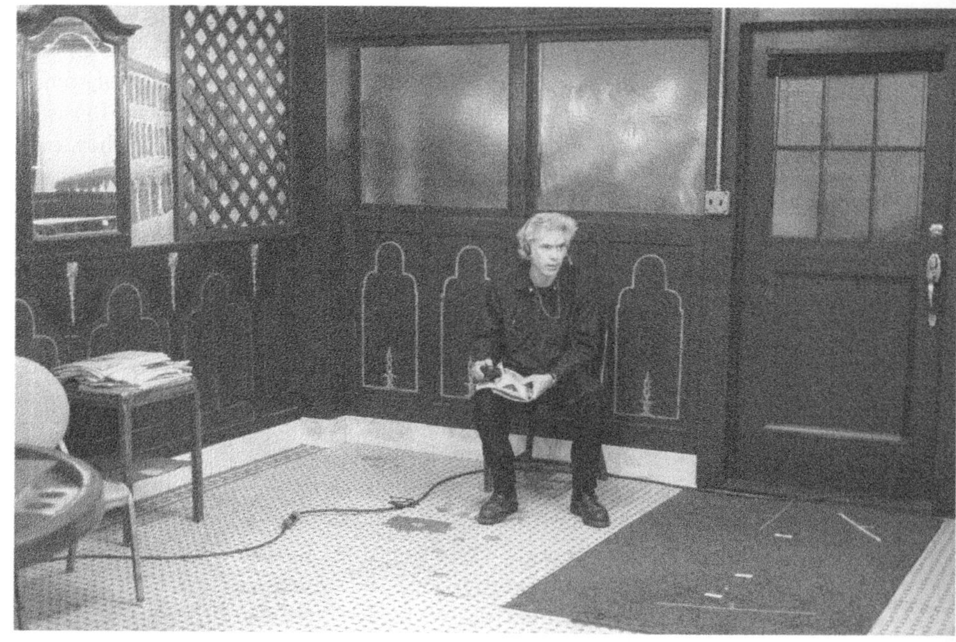

demands that often make life complicated for his sound department.[7] Given his obsession for sound nuances, Jarmusch would appear to want to recreate in the cinema that very same *objective catalogue of noises* that can be heard in nature's soundscapes. But this is only one aspect of the special attention Jarmusch devotes to noise and, one might argue, it is not the most surprising one given how 'meticulous' he generally is on his film set.[8] There are another two particular uses of noise that interest me more: the first enhances the narrative function of sound effects within the structure of the film, the second its expressive role.

Narrative Noise/Expressive Noise

As noted, Jarmusch has a predilection for episodic storytelling and multi-layered narratives, interwoven within the film's structure. *Mystery Train* is a case in point, since it is divided into three episodes, all sharing a unique feature: simultaneousness. Spectators only cotton on to this gradually as they pick up clues scattered throughout the film. These are not just random clues but also, significantly, audio clues: a gunshot; the voice of radio DJ Tom Waits introducing Elvis Presley's 'Blue Moon'; and a train whistling in the night.

The gunshot is heard in all three episodes, but we have to wait until the end of the third to discover which gun was fired, who pulled the trigger and in what circumstances. The culprit turns out to be a drunken and very clumsy Johnny who, while doing his utmost to commit suicide, accidentally shoots former brother-in-law Charlie in the leg when he tries to stop him. The train whistling and the song on the radio are also repeated and can be heard in different contexts and from various vantage points. 'It's 2.17 a.m.' announces DJ Tom Waits, his bewitching voice coming from the ubiquitous radios in the rooms of the Arcade Hotel where most of the film is set. Thus we discover that at exactly the same moment as Japanese teenagers Jun and Mitsuko are lying in bed, reconciled after their lovers' tiff, newly widowed Italian Luisa has just been paid an unexpected visit by the ghost of Elvis Presley. The train whistling in the night also gives a clue to both time and space, albeit more discreetly than the sharp sound of the gunshot and Elvis Presley's trademark voice in the repeatedly played song.

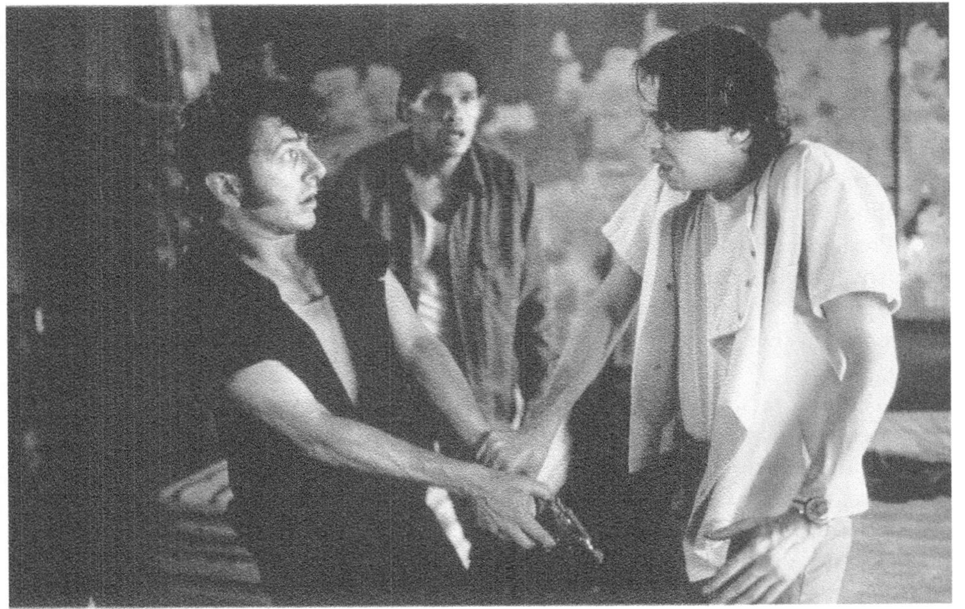

Narrative noise: the gunshot, *Mystery Train.*

All these audio clues contribute to outlining the film's narrative structure and help the audience understand that the three stories take place simultaneously. Within this all-encompassing time frame we are struck by the fact that each instance of sound matter has the same function, existing on the same level as the others outside any hierarchy: the sound effects – the gunshot and the whistling train; words – the DJ's silky voice; and finally music – 'Blue Moon'. All things audible contribute equally, providing a concrete example of *sound democracy* where Jarmusch has decided to do without the spoken word's usual monopoly. It is not only through words and their meaning that we understand what is unfolding before our eyes, but also thanks to an acoustic fabric where the voice is on the same level as music and noise. The entire structure of the film is based on a 'democratic' principle and the three stories, as Jarmusch observed, are 'just separate cars pulled by the same train'.[9] The train provides the set for the film's opening and closing scenes and is mentioned on several occasions on the soundtrack (in Rufus Thomas's 'Memphis Train' and in the two interpretations of 'Mystery Train' by Elvis Presley and Junior Parker). With its haunting whistling in the night it is also an irreplaceable element of the soundscape and it contributes, although almost subliminally, to the unfolding of the plot and the creation of the overall atmosphere.

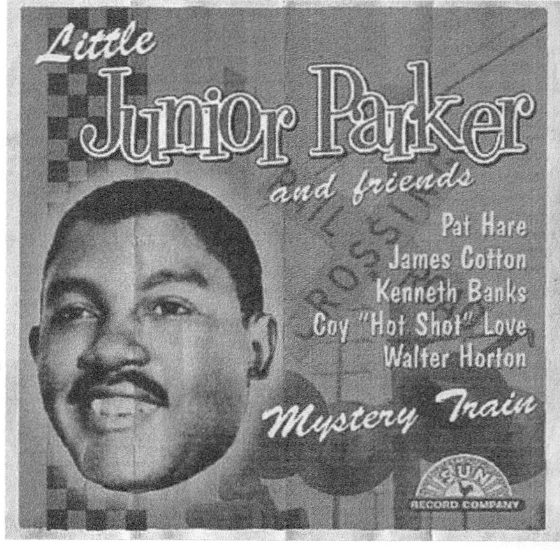

Little Junior Parker and Friends, *Mystery Train* (1974).

Noise can also facilitate communication, becoming a true instrument of expression at the director's fingertips. As expected, Jarmusch did not let this opportunity pass him by. A case in point is the succession of scenes in *Down By Law* in which the three heroes Bob, Jack and Zack escape from jail. What makes this jailbreak unusual, apart from Jarmusch not providing an explanation for it, is the fact that there are no visible pursuers. However, their absence is only apparent since we hear noises (but not voices) coming from those supposedly in hot pursuit, the prison break heralded by just the blaring of the siren and the constant barking of the dogs. Each member of the audience thus creates his own individual image of this faceless danger, which goes entirely against the grain of classical filmmaking, where this sequence would probably have been conceived along the more traditional lines of cross-cutting between pursuers and fugitives. When during the escape Jack and Zack abandon Bob by the river because he cannot swim, the fear in the small Italian's face held in the camera's unwavering gaze is there for all to see, his terror due not so much to the approaching dogs, which he has not seen and will not see, but more to the sound of their relentless bark-ing. Clearly, one of Bob's worst fears, besides being bitten, is not being able to translate 'hold back the dogs!' from his Tuscan dialect (*arreggi i cani*) into English. His literal translation, 'Arregg the dogs!', is a naive attempt doomed to fail, were it not for Zack's last minute, knight-in-shining-armour intervention. Not only does Bob escape being bitten, but also he no longer needs to strain his imagination in search of *le mot juste*.

The Invisible War

One of the many characteristics of noise is to be able to conjure up the invisible, something that in cinema can be used both expressively and narratively, and that Jarmusch has made conscious use of since the beginning of his career.

In *Stranger Than Paradise* the lengths of black leader separating the film's scenes are punctuated by John Lurie's music but often also by sound effects. They generally anticipate the next image, also function-ing as a suggestive acoustic thread linking the scenes of the sequence. Another example of sound playing a premonitory and allusive role is audible in a more recent film, *Broken Flowers*. Before the actual open-ing credits, as we see the logo of Focus Features (who co-produced the film with the French BAC Films), we clearly hear the unmistakable tap-ping of a typewriter. This sound plays a central role, since the film's story is triggered by the writing of an anonymous letter, its presence announced acoustically.

Jarmusch had already used a very original example of 'evocative' noise in his first feature film, *Permanent Vacation*. At the end of the scene in which Allie reads extracts from Lautréamont's *Les chants de Maldoror* to Leila as she starts making a paper aeroplane out of the book's pages, Allie moves to the window of the bare apartment and makes a theatrical announcement with his back to the camera:

> I'm gonna go back and see my mother. I haven't seen her in over a year. She's in an institution. But first I'm gonna go back to where I was born, the building that my mother and father lived in. It was blown up during the war. I'm gonna walk through the rubble there. And just look at it one more time. Looking at how the building is all bombed out.

When a sceptical Leila understandably asks him: 'Blown up by whom?!' Jarmusch zooms in on Allie, who finally decides to turn round and, with the face of someone stating the obvious, answers: 'The Chinese!' The reply catches us off guard, also because it is underlined by a crescendo of the slowed-down gamelan music in the background, which strangely synchs with Allie's dazed facial expression that is far too serious for us to believe that 'the war against the Chinese' was meant as a joke. The following sequence shows Allie walking through the 'bombed out' building, an impressive, abandoned edifice set against the green wilderness, an unexpected landscape for New York. It is here that Jarmusch creates what is literally an 'invisible war', relying crucially on sound effects. As Allie approaches the building, the roar of the first planes can be heard, followed by bombs exploding and machine guns firing. Though one might initially think that this imaginary war exists only in Allie's mind, this thought is dismissed when a war vet (Richard Boes) suddenly enters the scene and tells Allie he should run for cover since they are about to be bombed. Allie reassures him: 'These are not even planes, they're choppers. The Cong doesn't have choppers. You see? Those are American.' His reply has the desired effect and the veteran is reassured. Allie has succeeded in making him see the invisible. As for the audience, the issue of the elusive war between the Chinese and the Americans remains unresolved.

The idea of an invisible sound army is not exclusive to cinema. In his book *Sonic Warfare: Sound, Affect and the Ecology of Fear* (2010), Steve Goodman explored that place where sound and fear meet, on the border where sound vibrations can become true weapons: an 'ecology of fear' of sorts, miles away from R. Murray Schafer's 'acoustic ecology'.[10] Among the many examples quoted by Goodman, one in particular brings to mind the invisible war, or indeed the sound war, in *Permanent Vacation*:

'Ghost Army' was the nickname given to a division of the
U.S. Army, the Twenty-Third Special Troops, stationed in
Europe during World War II. They consisted of artists deployed
in the fabrication of camouflage and fake inflatable equipment,
and sound and radio engineers using equipment pioneered
at Bell Labs. The Ghost Army's aims were to trick the enemy
into reacting against the presence of a nonexistent phantom
army using sounds of troops, tanks, and landing craft,
allowing the actual troops to manoeuvre elsewhere . . . The
sonic deception involved the generation and distribution
of sounds to produce the sonic experience of the battlefield
in order to confuse, mislead, or distract the enemy. Blending
actual recordings and artificially generated noise, it was
targeted at the enemies' ears and listening devices. The less
effective the enemy's visual capabilities, the more powerful
sonic deception could be.[11]

In *Permanent Vacation* – at least for the audience – war is as acoustic and
invisible as the one staged by the Twenty-Third Special Troops. We will
never know whether the war helicopters that Allie 'shows' the stunned
and frightened war vet are inflatable or completely made up. What stays
emblazoned in the mind are the scenes of New York that Jarmusch
committed to celluloid: a truly post-nuclear scenario of rubble and
neglect filmed in June 1979, unthinkable in the Lower East Side today,
where the booming real estate expansion sounds far louder than the –
imaginary – Chinese bombs.

Flexible Noise

So far I have talked about bombs, explosions and 'acoustic' war. However,
noise does not necessarily mean a loud and discordant din. Although it
is often associated with an annoying sound blasting away at ear-splitting
volume, the idea of noise contains a wide array of registers: it can be
slight, almost imperceptible, bordering on silence.

In the post-Cage era it has become less and less important to find
a clear-cut, accurate definition of what noise actually should be, and
how it could differ from music. Adam Harper, in *Infinite Music* (2011),
amplified this matter by going so far as to say:

'Music' is only a word, after all, and indeed, not one whose definition has an equivalent in any language. In many non-Western cultures, what we would call music is simply an aspect of the general activities of life and not a differentiable concept of its own . . . At a further level, many artists have even thrived on the fact that the border between art and 'real life' itself is fluid, if truly there at all. This could be what the twentieth-century composer and theorist John Cage, one of the first to plumb the depths of the infinite possibilities of music, meant by the phrase he was so fond of repeating: 'everything we do is music.'[12]

Beyond the universal projection of this message what I would like to underline is simply that, recalling the words of Elliot Sharp, the supposed barriers between types of sound matter are perfectly fluid and flexible: a statement that before Cage was not nearly as obvious as it might appear today.

Word-Noise

Speaking of the three types of sound matter in cinema, I would now like to touch upon certain areas in the films of Jarmusch (and not only) in which noise 'infiltrates' the other two.

There are cases where noise spills over into the field of words, situations that can be fittingly defined as *interference* or *disturbance*. I have mentioned examples where Jarmusch plays down the role of words themselves, a technique defined as 'proliferation' by Michel Chion, where a kind of 'verbal overkill' interferes with communication, almost or completely cancelling it out. In *Mystery Train* there are two garrulous characters who are perfect examples of this: the Sun Studios guide and Dee Dee, Johnny's ex-girlfriend. The two women overwhelm anyone within range with a constant flow of words, thus leaving the person they are talking to quite speechless, interference being the culprit. Words and noise join in this concept of *interference*, becoming a single sound matter that is highly expressive even though not dialogical: the content of what is said slips into the background with regard to the function of *interference*, characteristic of noise, that the word adopts in the examples given.

The mix of these two sound matters has more extreme consequences than mere interference for logorrhoeic killer Conway Twill

(Michael Wincott), one of the three hit men chasing William Blake in *Dead Man*. His unstoppable chatter creates a constant *disturbance*, unbearable to the point that it will undermine any other form of communication: Cole Wilson (Lance Henriksen), the quieter and more sinister of the trio, tired of his colleague's senseless ranting, silences him once and for all with a single bullet. The lethal rifle shot is a highly expressive noise, its function immediately obvious to the audience despite Jarmusch having deliberately separated it from the image with a length of black leader, thus leaving spectators with only the audio effect. The following sequence confirms the expressive function of noise: sitting by the camp fire, Wilson reveals himself to be both killer and cannibal and, devoid of any etiquette, he smacks his lips and makes the most disgusting sucking sounds as he feasts on Twill's body, specifically his forearm. By paying special attention to these revolting sounds, or 'sounds of horror',[13] Jarmusch ensures that Wilson's violent and perverted nature becomes even more apparent to the audience.

However, one should not forget that there is nothing ghastly about these sounds *in themselves*. They become blood-curdling when juxtaposed with these particular images. The same gruesome sucking and chewing sounds made by Wilson and associated with other images could have a hilarious, comic effect: for example, imagine a scene in which a Chinese character, for whom a different set of table manners applies, has

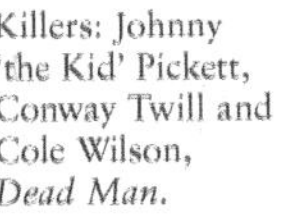

Killers: Johnny 'the Kid' Pickett, Conway Twill and Cole Wilson, *Dead Man*.

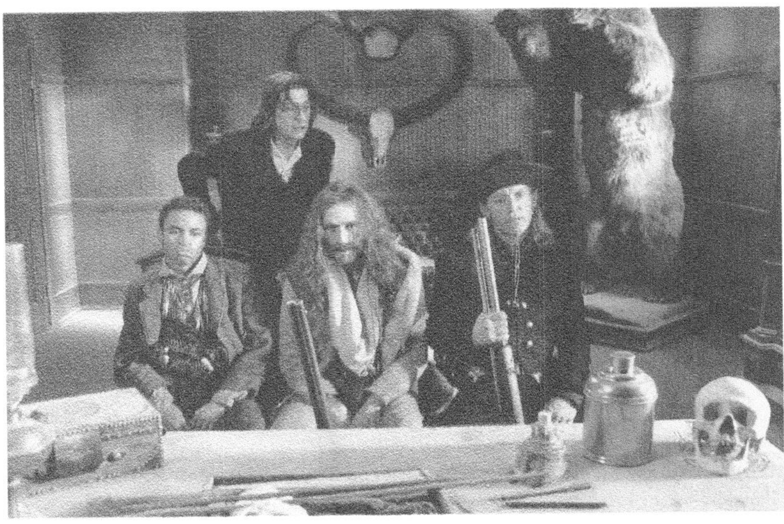

been invited to a gala dinner at a European royal palace and, to everyone's embarrassment eats his meal with great gusto making enough noise to wake the dead.

Moving briefly away from Jarmusch's filmography, I would like to quote another instance of 'word/noise', or rather 'word/murmuring', clearly audible in Wim Wenders's *Wings of Desire* (*Der Himmel über Berlin*, 1987). In the famous sequence shot in the National Library in Berlin, the two angels Damiel (Bruno Ganz) and Cassiel (Otto Sander) wander around unseen by people deep into their reading, a situation that one would normally associate with silence. Instead, the sequence's sound fabric is very rich and elaborate: the angels can actually hear what mortal human beings in the library are thinking. Their inner thoughts and readings, inevitably expressed through words, are layered and overlap, thus forming a fragmented yet at the same time unified mass of sound made up of disjointed sentences, whispers and words spoken in foreign languages that are all examples of 'proliferation', where murmured words take precedence over content. They are pure acoustic matter hovering in the library's open spaces.

The layers of voices floating around inside the library also evoke the history of Berlin, a city haunted by past conflict, its dead and what is no longer there.[14] The 'invisible war' that Jarmusch conjured up quite literally through the sound of bombs and machine-gun fire in *Permanent Vacation* comes to life in Wenders's library as a body of voices consisting largely of word-noise, but also – not a minor detail – of music. On top of the layered voices of the scene's audio track, in the exact moment in which the angels Damiel and Cassiel enter the picture, Wenders introduces the slow crescendo of Jürgen Knieper's choral work 'Die Kathedrale der Bücher' ('The Cathedral of Books'), its sacred atmosphere reminiscent of a modern-day requiem. The closely knit music and word-noise thus create the scene's timeless atmosphere. Their fusion into a deeply evocative, layered sound matter succeeds in crossing the boundaries of space and time, defined by the physical building of the library and by History itself.

Music-Noise

Noise is quite capable of physically infiltrating *music*, creating an even stronger link than that which Wenders demonstrated in the aforementioned sequence. Myriad voices have contributed to the rich and multifaceted dialogue between music and noise, in a cross-contamination of genres often considered to be far removed from each other. Very liberally and without digging too deeply, I would like to quote some of these voices, taking into account the variety of their languages and provenance, for example, those of Pierre Schaeffer and Pierre Henry, the initiators of *musique concrète* in France in the early 1950s.[15] They gave ample space to noise in their work, letting it seep 'concretely' into their compositions, partly consisting of tape recordings and manipulations of sounds from the previously mentioned *objective catalogue of noises*. In Germany, Helmut Lachenmann — a student of 'noise-oriented' composers Karlheinz Stockhausen and Luigi Nono — came up with the idea of *musique concrète instrumentale* in which music-noise is actually created by the instruments of a traditional orchestra, instead of being recorded, as was the case with his French predecessors. Also in Italy, many composers used noise and sound effects. In the field of cinema the most famous of the older generation is certainly Ennio Morricone, but fellow contemporary composers such as Salvatore Sciarrino and Giorgio Battistelli, each in his own way, also explored interaction with noise. Sciarrino mainly used extended vocal techniques and explored the borders between voice and noise, for example, in *Lohengrin*, in which the female narrator's voice whispers, swallows air, makes clicking noises and other labial sounds that are a far cry from traditional singing or acting.[16] Battistelli chose to incorporate the 'sounds of work' into the orchestra, as in his piece *Experimentum Mundi*, in which a group of sixteen craftsmen, including confectioners, cobblers, bricklayers, coopers and knife sharpeners, practise their craft generating a vast array of non-musical sounds.[17] The fact that the various music scenes are far less distant from each other than might at first appear becomes even more apparent if considered that in the very same years in which Sciarrino's and Battistelli's work was being performed, many of those who belonged to the so-called industrial music scene were also experimenting with noise. Some of the groups born in the 1980s played a crucial role in musical subcultures, influencing musicians for generations to come. In Germany, Einstürzende Neubauten founded by Blixa Bargeld and N. U. Unruh used pneumatic hammer drills, ordinary drills and other tools as instruments, advocating a spontaneous non-mediated, thundering and analogue use of noise, whereas the British band Coil, with its members John Balance and Peter 'Sleazy' Christopherson, in the same years were experimenting with samples and synthesizer-modified sounds, preferring a more electronic and alienating approach to noise.[18]

Concluding this brief overview and returning to Jarmusch's cinema, I would like to mention another strategy that allows noise to enrich the artist's musical vocabulary: creating a single sound matter made up of both, where, in a manner of speaking, music *becomes* noise.

This type of experimentation, which has its roots in the long history of electronic, contemporary and avant-garde music, can be traced back to pioneers like La Monte Young and, naturally, John Cage, and has often been referred to as drone music. In fact, the idea of a drawn-out, seemingly endless, anti-melodic sound supporting a whole composition, be it a note or a chord, in other words some kind of 'musical noise', is much older than the twentieth century. La Monte Young and Cage were in turn inspired by non-Western music cultures, like that of India. The musical concept of the drone itself is rooted in folk music, as with the bagpipes and other instruments designed to play prolonged, uninterrupted notes.

It is fascinating to think that efforts to bring music and noise closer together appear to be timeless, and continue to intrigue newer generations of musicians. I refer in particular to the doom scene, also known as drone doom or drone metal, just to waste a few more tags. American groups such as Earth and more recently the duo Sunn O))), composed of Stephen O'Malley and Greg Anderson, but also the Japanese group Boris, are generally considered by music critics as belonging to the drone doom scene because of the massive wall of sound they manage to create. One of Sunn O)))'s live performances was described as follows:

> The music was unbelievably loud – so loud, in fact, that the sound waves made your rib cage vibrate like a stereo cabinet and your teeth literally rattle in their sockets – but the effect was somehow more meditative than violent. The overall experience was not unlike listening to an Indian raga in the middle of an earthquake.[19]

Never-ending guitar chords, deafening volume and practically no melody are some of the genre's features that most likely caught Jarmusch's ear. Indeed, all three groups mentioned above contributed to the soundtrack of *The Limits of Control*. The fusion of music and noise into a single sound matter is what, according to Jarmusch, brings these groups closer to cinema, as he told DJ/pop star Moby in a radio interview:

I'm a big fan of those bands. To me that music is incredibly cinematic, atmospheric, when I listen to it and when I see them live. They are like landscapes . . . They are like painters with sound too, and it's electric and it's rock 'n' roll. I really dig slow music in general, whether it is Henry Purcell or Gustav Mahler or whether it's Sunn O))). I often make mix-tapes of just adagios of different things. I really love that, whatever genre it is I don't know . . .[20]

September 2010 provided the setting for an encounter between the director and the said bands, during the ATP (All Tomorrow's Parties) festival in the Kutsher's Country Club, Monticello, NY, which was largely programmed by Jarmusch himself.[21] Apart from Sunn O))) and Boris – who had just finished working on *The Limits of Control* and for the occasion collaborated on a project called *Altar* – the line-up also featured White Hills, a group claiming to belong to space rock – yes, yet another genre tag. While there is no need to agree on simplified definitions intended to capture a given style of music – an exercise which, it is worth repeating, is both laborious and somewhat pointless – it should be mentioned that White Hills collaborated in 2013 with Jarmusch on *Only Lovers Left Alive*, in which the band is filmed performing live.[22] Although their style is not based on exactly the same walls of sound that are typical of Sun O)))'s or Boris's live gigs, White Hills certainly have a soft spot for

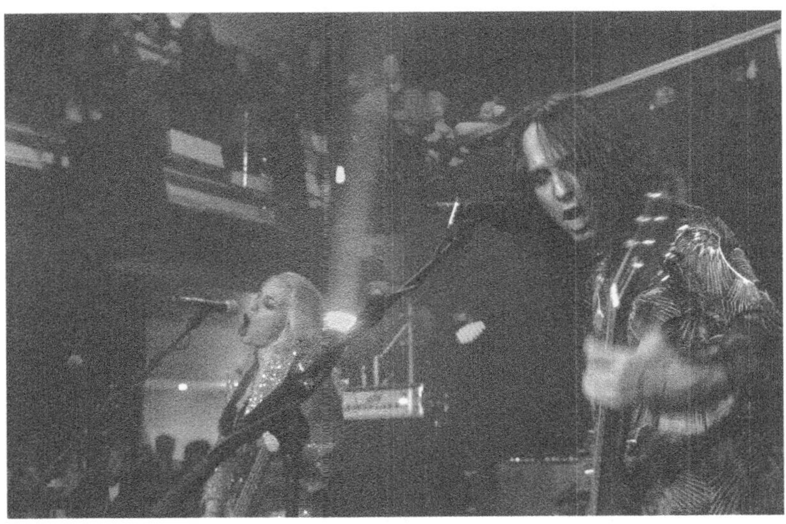

White Hills live in Cologne, 2013.

electric guitars, a passion they share with Jarmusch. His idea of a musical landscape regarding the songs of these groups evidently brings to mind the *soundscapes* that Murray Schafer spoke of, in which noises are part of the audio fabric just like any other sound matter.

A case in point is a sequence towards the end of *The Limits of Control*, where the walled-in compound in which the American is hiding is spotted by Lone Man, who is scanning the horizon with binoculars from a barren hill opposite the hideout. During the sequence a feeling of relentless and imminent danger escalates with the deep drone from the electric guitars of Sunn O))) and Boris.[23] Without apparent interruption, the guitars metamorphose into the helicopter's blades as it lands by the bunker's entrance, music and noise blending into a single matter, despite their alternating on the audio track. The point is not so much determining where the music ends and the noise begins, but the fact that, although each has its own distinct identity, its own disparity, they are made of the same sound material: in Jarmusch's *soundscape*, hypothetical sound hierarchies are not part of the scenery, and it would be a waste of effort to look for them.

In an interview in 2009 with musician and critic Alan Licht, Jarmusch reiterated that the borders between so-called genres remain fluid, and how fundamental a role music plays when he imagines and writes a film. Speaking with Licht of Boris and the band's collaboration with noise guitarist Keiji Haino, Jarmusch discovered a musical-cinematographical link that had escaped him. According to what Licht heard, the album *Hex; or Printing in the Infernal Method* by drone pioneers Earth 'was partially inspired by Neil Young's music for *Dead Man*'.[24]

Young's music allows a few concluding reflections on the three types of sound matter that are given ample space on the film's soundtrack CD, focusing in particular on noise. The thirteen tracks flow seamlessly one into the other almost as part of a single composition. *Music* is represented by no less than six guitar solos and one harmonium solo played by Neil Young; *words* are present through excerpts from the film's dialogue and original text by William Blake, read by Johnny Depp; finally, it is *noise* itself that blends the various sound matters together, taking on two different connotations, apparently far removed from each other. Blatantly anachronistic to the film's actual setting, running engines, car doors closing, distant trains and unidentifiable traffic are all noises that could

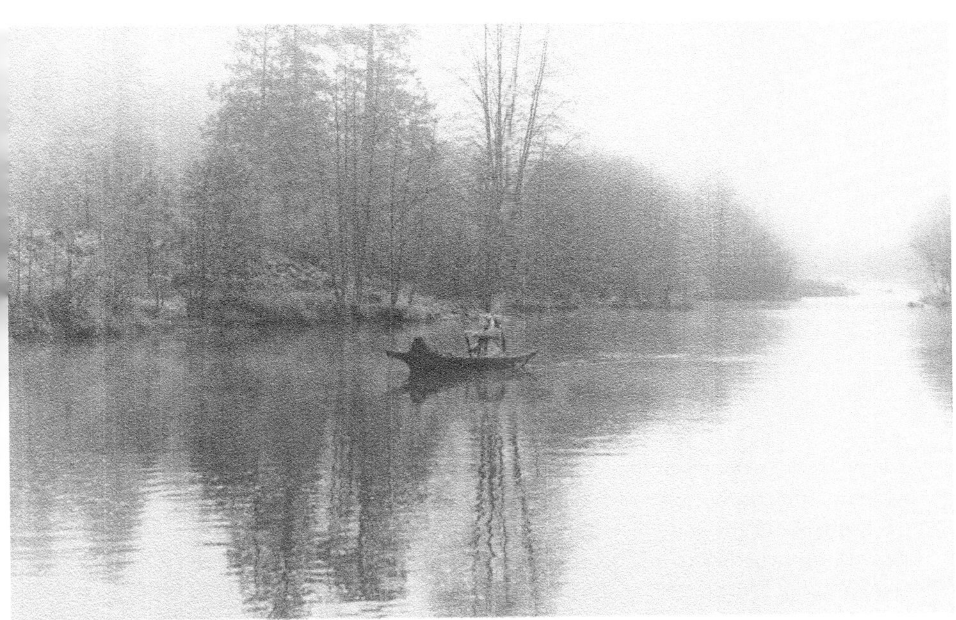

be described as *urban*. The sound of an approaching car or a door closing creates a sense of disorientation in the listener who sees the film's sequence in his mind's eye and, thanks to these *urban* noises, witnesses the scene as if displaced in a time different from the one inhabited on screen by Blake and Nobody. The second connotation that noise takes on is instead completely *natural*: we hear the blowing of the wind, the call of birds and insects, in a sound setting that at times brings to mind how artists like Luc Ferrari used the soundscapes of nature in *musique concrète* compositions.[25] The sound of the waves is particularly striking because it is virtually omnipresent, lasting, for example, over fourteen minutes on one of the tracks.[26] Here Neil Young's phrasing on the guitar appears to be an infinite loop, certainly hypnotic but at times a little tiring, with minor variations, reminiscent of waves rippling on a sea shore, all different and yet the same. The soundscapes created by the guitar blend in with natural sounds, demonstrating how music and noise can coexist perfectly well together. *Urban* and *natural* noise create a new sound fabric together with music and words, once again bearing witness to how the various types of sound matter are anti-hierarchical, versatile by nature and able to merge with each other.

Voices: Taylor Mead

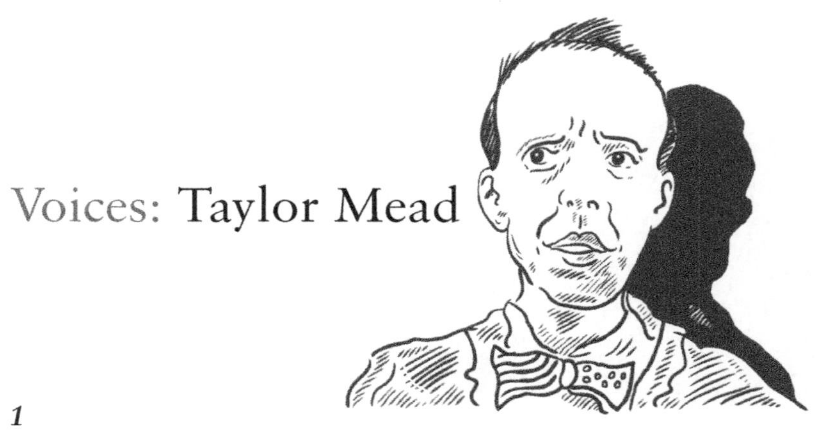

1

Music loses virtue when it accompanies. Nothing in life or art needs accompaniment, because each has its own centre (which is no centre). To bring about the state of no-accompaniment, there must underlie everything (whether words, pictures or what have you) a rhythmic structure.

. . . Accept music for what it is: a way of life devoted to sound and silence, the only common denominator of which two is rhythm (not as a pattern but as quantity, free to have or not to have accents, for example). This accepted, one may have back, paradoxically, that much of harmony, melody etc. one wishes to permit oneself.

It may seem artificial and forced (life often does) to clamp a rhythmic structure onto something that doesn't have it. It is of course artificial (so are the houses we live in; they don't however, keep us from falling in love).[1]

So that's really a long quote . . .

Was that John Cage?

Yes.

He's full of shit! No, I mean he's a purist. I better answer spontaneously to that. In a way I admire him because that's his thing. I don't criticize other composers for not struggling, working with movies, with paintings . . . I once tried to play the piano while Stan Brakhage's thing was going on, and he is a purist too. And he stopped me from playing the piano. Stan Brakhage's thing is just like Merce's [Cunningham] thing. I've known Merce for ever. I admire him tremendously, but I'd die to put music to everything he's done. I don't believe in that purist thing about the separation of the arts.

After this long quote the question I wanted to ask you is: Given that poetry can also be defined as a 'rhythmic word' or 'word as sound', can you tell me about the way music is involved in your poetry? I think especially about the way you used the little ghetto blaster during the poetry reading I saw at the Bowery Poetry Club in New York.

Well, both Merce and John Cage used chance, in fact they did combine sound because they have a dance in which people go between electronic poles on the stage, which make different sounds as they go by them, so this statement can be adulterated. Well, with me, I'm doing a great chance thing. I never know what music is coming up next!

Exactly, you use music totally randomly.

Well, both Merce and John Cage and William Burroughs and Allen Ginsberg and all the poets have gone into the realm of chance, so why not include music in that. Anyway, sometimes watching Merce's dance I really get very bored.

Okay, let's go on with the second question, this is a much shorter one. I'm sorry for the length of the first one.

No, that was a great question.

2

Can you give me your definition of silence? And do you think words are only important for their actual meaning or do you think that, so to say, the sound of a word has a meaning too?

You see, this is all purist stuff and I'm an impressionist as a painter, as a composer, as an actor and everything. So I would never separate it, you know? I mean, that's silly. That's the problem with the world: we're all separate!

And what about silence?

Silence . . . silence bores me. I automatically do silence, that's why I have my apartment in one of the busiest streets of New York. I have the back of the building, that's why they want my apartment. So I have

silence in general and I love it but then I turn on my wonderful radio
stations here in New York with music . . .

Yes, there was always music in the background when I called you.

But to me to capture silence and sit like a yogi for silence and meditate
. . . I once wrote: meditation is for people with happy childhoods.
And I had an extremely unhappy childhood. In fact at night here there
is a cacophony of all sorts of bad music and people yelling at each
other and I love it! It stimulates me. All the people here and all of this
new, popular music, drum machine music to me that's not music, that's
a machine.

3

Can you tell me how it was to work with Jim Jarmusch? He used
Mahler in your episode of *Coffee and Cigarettes* with Bill Rice, right?

Well, in a session while we were introducing the movie *Tarzan and Jane
Regained* by Andy Warhol at BAM [Brooklyn Academy of Music], which
is a great venue, someone asked me how it was working with Jim
Jarmusch. And I said, well with Andy Warhol and our films in the
1960s and even before Andy, whatever we shot was it. There was one
take, as they say in Hollywood. Well, I said, with Jim Jarmusch there
were three takes. So it was easy. I liked it.

Three takes is not very many.

That's very, very few!

So we have three short questions for three short takes. Is there anything
else that you would like to say?

Yes. Andy was easy to work with but he was cheap! He disinherited all
of us. He could have left ten or twenty of us a hundred grand each or
something and he left 500 million to people who love to fill out grant
applications.

And now you don't know if you can keep the apartment here on Ludlow
Street, right?

Well, I think I passed the last inspection.

That sounds great.

Knock on wood! (Knocks on the wooden table with his knuckles) And my middle name is Wood, so I can knock on my head.

New York, November 2003

Postscript: Taylor Mead died on 8 May 2013 in Colorado after suffering a stroke. He was 88 years old. Roughly one month before his death he had finally accepted a buy-out from his landlord and moved out of his tenement apartment.

9 Silence

'I like silent pictures and I always have. They are often so much more beautiful than sound pictures are. Perhaps they had to be.'
Akira Kurosawa quoted in *Rashomon: Akira Kurosawa, Director*, ed. Donald Richie (New Brunswick, NJ, 1996), p. 18

'There's a part of me, and I said it before and I kind of mean it even though I'm being flippant, that believes that cinema went downhill when they started talking in it.'
Tilda Swinton, interviewed by the author in Berlin, 12 February 2005

Silence on film is a recorded track just like any other. On a par with music, dialogue and other sound effects, silence must be recorded in order to be reproduced in a film. Taking into mind this simple technical observation, it is thus misguiding and only partially correct to think of silence as an acoustic 'void', a general absence of sound, as it is habitually defined. Naturally, John Cage was convinced of this when, at the 1957 Congress of Music Teachers National Association in Chicago, he made the following statement: 'There is no such thing as an empty space or an empty time. There is always something to see, something to hear. In fact, try as we may to make silence, we cannot.'[1] To confirm this affirmation, and also to render it slightly less theoretical and impalpable, Cage on that occasion spoke from his personal experience in the search of the perception of absolute silence: a futile search that nonetheless resulted in a very optimistic conclusion with regard to the future of music.

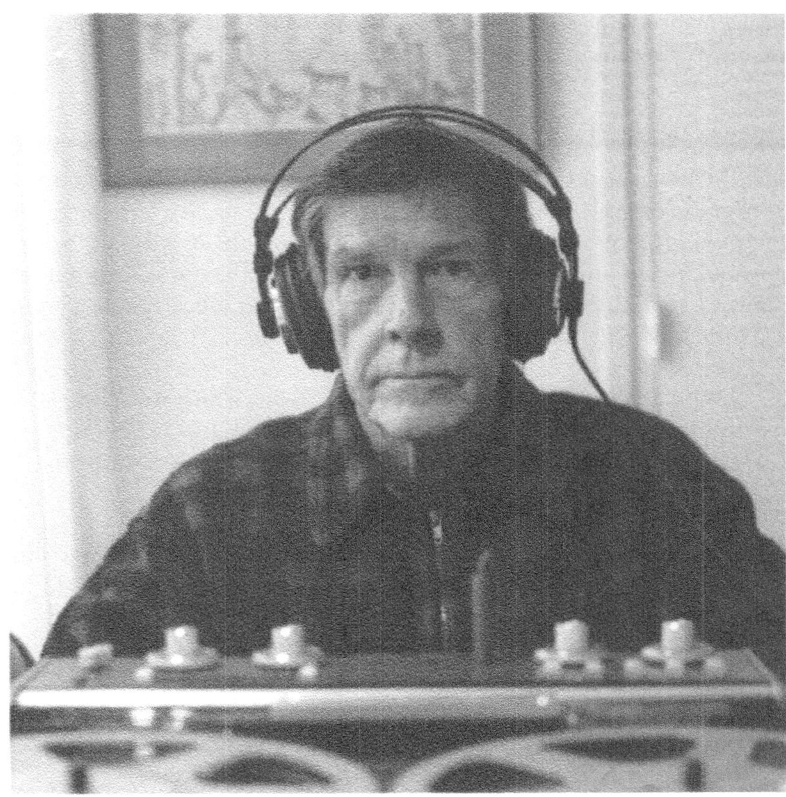

For certain engineering purposes, it is desirable to have as silent a
situation as possible. Such a room is called anechoic chamber, its
six walls made of special material, a room without echoes. I
entered one at Harvard University several years ago and heard two
sounds, one high and one low. When I described them to the engineer in charge, he informed me that the high one was my nervous
system in operation, the low one my blood in circulation. Until
I die there will be sounds. And they will continue following my
death. One need not fear about the future of music.[2]

Cage's optimistic and forward-projecting vision is a good premise with
which to open both this concluding chapter on 'silence' in relation to
Jarmusch's cinema, and a brief historical panorama on a few key

moments from the past that marked the passage from so-called silent –
or, as Michel Chion would say, 'deaf' – cinema to the Talkies.[3]

Deaf Cinema, Talking Cinema: 1895–

When Chion speaks of 'deaf' cinema, he is referring to the spectator's
perception of a silent film: 'It's not that the film's characters were mute,
but rather that the film was deaf to them', giving the moviegoer 'a deaf
person's viewpoint on the action depicted'.[4] In effect, it is a common,
almost banal ascertainment that the films of the pioneering days were
anything but 'silent'. Chion goes on to say:

> Could anyone rightly call this cinema silent, which was always
> accompanied by music from the outset – the Lumière Brothers'
> very first screening at the Grand Café in Paris – not to mention
> the sound effects created live in some movie houses?[5]

Chion's view is certainly acute, though the very first screening of a film
for a paying audience was, as considered by many historians, held in
Berlin and not Paris. As explained by Stephen Barber:

> Two near-forgotten brothers, Max and Emil Skladanowsky,
> had originated public film-projection by showing a program
> of their own films, on celluloid stock, to a paying audience at
> the Wintergarten Ballroom, in Berlin's Central Hotel, on
> 1 November 1895.[6]

Despite having beaten the Lumière Brothers to the punch by almost two
months with their achievements, the two German brothers of Polish origin were not destined to go down in history. Almost immediately after
their Berlin premiere they were overtaken 'in both technological and aesthetic domains, by their many rivals, so that they became stranded in
film-historical no-man's land'.[7] And yet that evening in the Wintergarten
Ballroom, thanks to the Bioskop (the manually operated dual-reel projector invented by Max and Emil Skladanowsky), the still somewhat
unsteady foundations for the future of cinema were laid, both visual and
acoustic. During the brief projections of 'physical spectacles, dances and
acrobatics' that lasted for about fifteen minutes in total the audience could
hear 'a loud music score, especially composed, capable of drowning

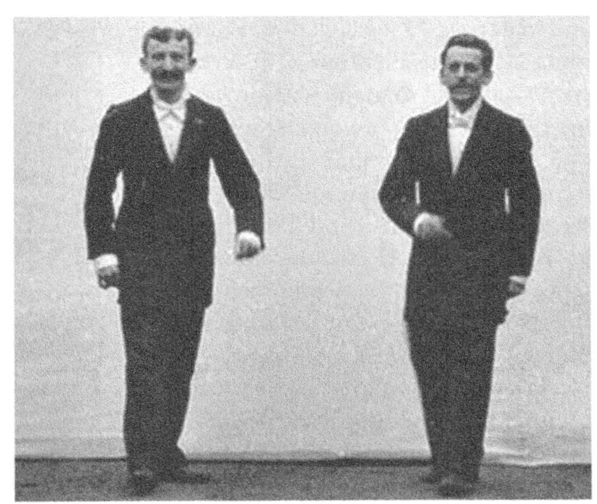

Max and Emil
Skladanowsky,
1895.

out the cacophony of the projector's operation'.[8] It should also be said that the first cinemas were far noisier places than those we are accustomed to today. Not very different from variety theatre and vaudeville audiences of that time, early moviegoers animatedly encouraged or contested the characters made of light moving about on the screen. There were commentators vocally interpreting or translating the title cards for the often illiterate audience. And neither were the cinemas plunged into total darkness as they are today: low lighting allowed the spectators to be not only more visible, but also encouraged them to be more audible. Especially in moments of technical impasse, when for example the projector would get stuck or the film snapped, the audience's exuberant involvement would raise the roof. The idea of a mute, silent, concentrated and collected cinema, akin to a vacuum-packed bubble, is nothing more than fantasy: image and sound were equals, an integral part of cinema right from its exciting first steps.

In 1926 the Vitaphone sound-on-disc technique brought even more sound into the cinema.[9] With this system a phonograph mechanically linked to the projector produced the film's sound, making a real mix of dialogue and music impossible.[10] Notwithstanding the initial extraordinary success that earned Warner Brothers almost $4 million in the United States alone, the Vitaphone system was not destined to last, as explained by Royal S. Brown in his rich study of film music, *Overtones and Undertones* (1994):

Vitaphone, purchased by Warner Brothers for its musical potential, died, to be replaced by sound-on-film technologies that facilitated the synchronizing of dialogue. Paradoxically, the technology that had been invented to promote film music all but killed off the art, except in the film musical.[11]

The possibility of mixing diverse sound materials – music, dialogue and sound effects – was thus the determining factor in sanctioning the technique of recording sound-on-film, which according to many had already been developed well before 1926. Nonetheless, I have no interest in trying to establish records and rankings based on, for example, the historic contrast between the Phonofilm system of sound-on-film, patented in 1919 by American inventor Lee de Forest on one side, and Theodore Case and Earl I. Sponable's Movietone on the other, perfected in 1925 and then adopted in 1926 by Fox Film Corporation for the production of newsreels, better known as Movietone News.[12] The point is rather to confirm that both awareness and experimentation in the field of acoustics have been present in cinema since its origins, though not in a univocal and linear way. Apropos of this, I agree with sound theorist Rick Altman when he affirms that 'film is not a unified object, nor cinema a homogeneous medium . . . its sound-based affinities with other media often challenging its apparent image-based unity'.[13] The need to identify a narrative responding to an idea of development and progressive technological innovation has actually produced attempts to project an image of the transition to sound far clearer and more linear than it was in reality, for example, focusing on 'the history of attempts to perfect sound cinema, the finances of Warner Brothers, or the heroic innovations of the first sound directors'.[14] The reality of this transition was characterized instead by accelerations, breakdowns and 'jurisdictional struggles', as Altman defines the

> constant battles over who should have jurisdiction over jobs and decisions. Who should play the disks in the theatre? The projectionist, a musician, an electrician, or a stagehand? . . . Should the needs of sound men or the desire of cinematographers have priority during a take?[15]

This last question is today still a difficult, if not impossible, one to answer univocally: a soundman, a director of photography, an actor and two directors would have a hard time coming up with the exact same response. Specific professional positions continue to have a variable importance, complicated to establish with precision. Also the definition of cinema itself, of audio-visual spectacle as a new typology not only of entertainment but also of a brand new collective experience, at its birth was by no means univocal. As Altman again explains, 'In the watershed year of 1908–09, for example, films were classified as a circus in Delaware and as an exhibition in Arkansas (until April, 1909, when they were reclassified as theater).'[16] Circus, exhibition, theatre. One of the first difficulties facing the new audio-visual spectacle was to shake off the tag of 'fairground phenomenon'. After an initial moment of rivalry, the theatre became a great ally: to free itself of the 'fairground logic', early cinema took its stories from what was considered elite culture – theatre, literature and opera.[17] Also the physical relocation of the cinematographic spectacle to theatres was all part of this vision of 'ennoblement', of which there still remains a clear trace in the American English definition, movie *theatre*. Naturally, the proximity to the theatre, both physical and thematic, brought the text and the performed word into particular focus: first through title cards (I think for example of Gabriele D'Annunzio's pompous and declamatory captions for the monumental *Cabiria* of 1914 directed by Giovanni Pastrone); and second through sound that finally gave voice to the film actor. All elements that appeared to endorse the dominance of the *word*.

An alternative evidently existed: the dominance of the *image*. This was the aesthetic choice by those who, like the Surrealists and numerous Russian directors and theorists, saw in the advent of sound the risk of a grave 'degradation' of cinema, its nature considered fundamentally visual. In 1928 Sergei Eisenstein, Vsevolod Pudovkin and Grigori Alexandrov begrudgingly admitted that 'The whole world is talking about the silent thing that learned to talk', acknowledging that the step to sound was by then an unstoppable process.[18] In their famous *Statement on the Sound-Film* the three directors, highly mistrustful of the new invention, presented non-synchronization between picture and image as the minimum condition for cinema not being subordinate to theatre.[19] Only the use of sound as an ulterior instrument at the service of montage could have guaranteed the genuineness of cinema as an art, perfectly capable of expressing itself:

> Sound, treated as a new montage element (as a factor divorced from the visual image), will inevitably introduce new means of enormous power to the expression and solution of the most complicated tasks that now oppress us with the impossibility of overcoming them by means of an imperfect film method working only with visual images.[20]

Having recognized the potential of this new acoustic editing, the common interpretation according to which 'the Russians' were opposed to sound *tout court* is thus too schematic and partial. What Eisenstein and his colleagues were really against was a cinema – silent and otherwise – whose objective was the non-critical and undiscerning imitation of reality.

Setting aside the supposed dominion of the word on one side and the image on the other, what I wish to highlight in the face of this brief exploration of the journey that took cinema from 'silence' to sound is the crucial transformation caused by the technical innovation of recording sound-on-film. No longer forced to resort to the real time 'soundtrack' made up of improvised live music, reading title cards out loud and sound effects reproduced in the movie theatre, the Talkie equipped with a soundtrack recorded on film went from being a cinematographic *spectacle* to a cinematographic *text*, in a word: film. Therefore if the cinematographic spectacle was *audio-visual* right from its origins, the film, intended as cinematographic text, became so only at the end of the 1920s.

Having said this, a fundamental fact must be clarified: the idea of a film/text as the finished product must not be looked upon as a point of arrival, like some static destination, but quite the opposite, a point of departure. Once it had acquired its 'body' – made up equally of image and sound – the film was able to start its journey in every direction imaginable, changing according to the circumstances into 'circus', 'exhibition', 'theatre', but also novel, poem, essay, symphony, song, painting or temporal fresco. This was possible, and continues to be so, thanks to that specific characteristic that makes cinema 'unique but not univocal': namely, the possibility to include materially in its own acoustic and luminous body multiple and miscellaneous artistic forms and expressions. In 1961, when talking to students in a lecture hall of Rome's Centro Sperimentale di Cinematografia, Michelangelo Antonioni said: 'There is no art from which the cinema cannot draw.'[21]

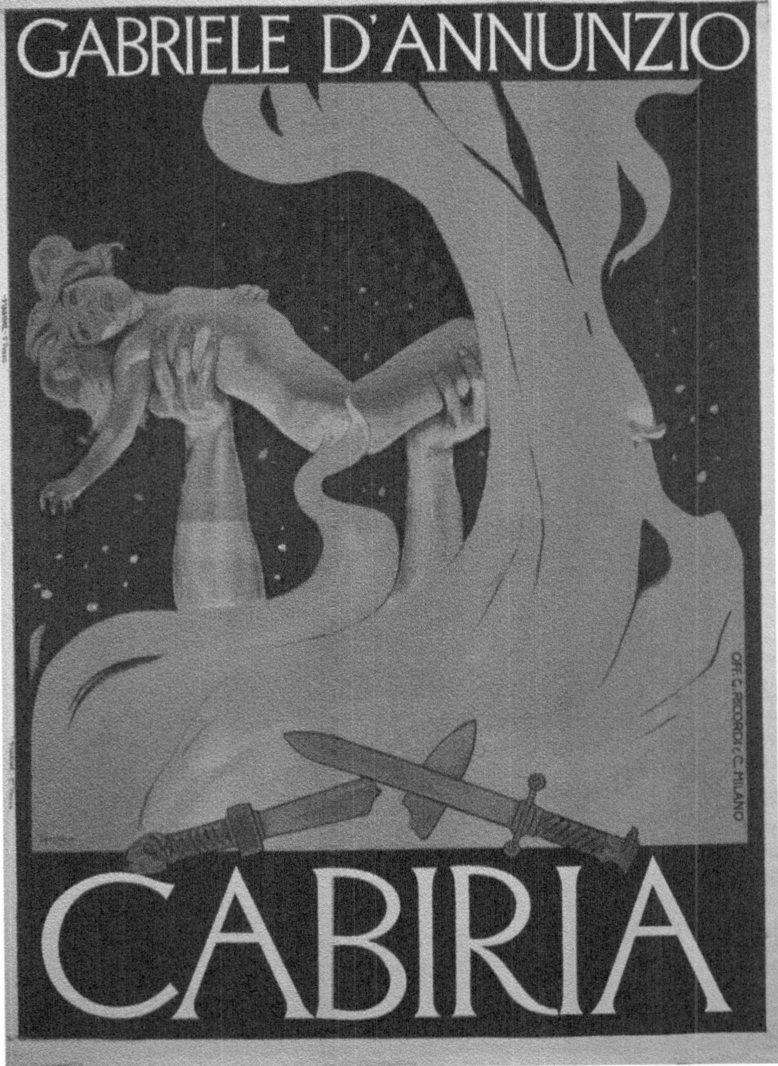

Cabiria, directed by Giovanni Pastrone and written by Gabriele D'Annunzio (1914).

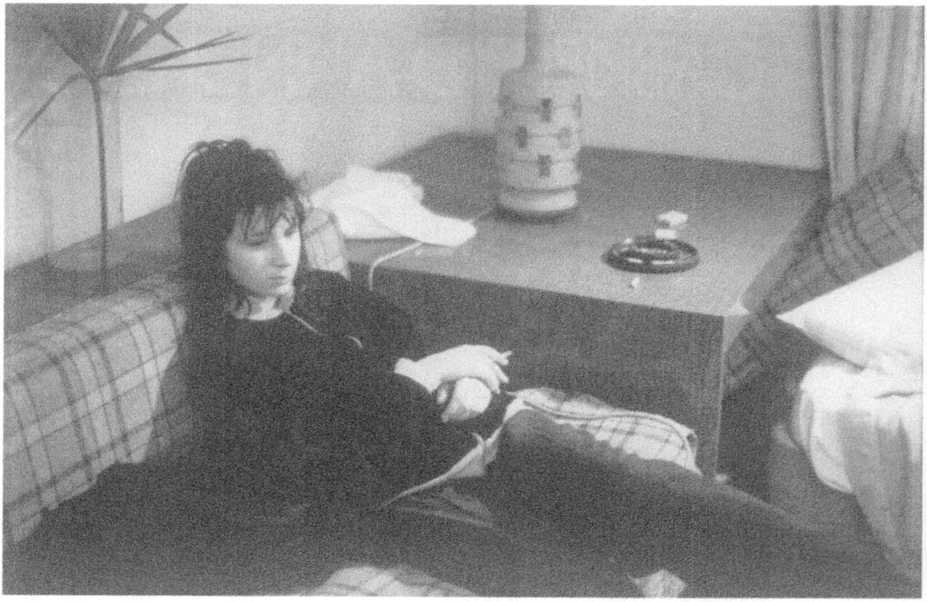

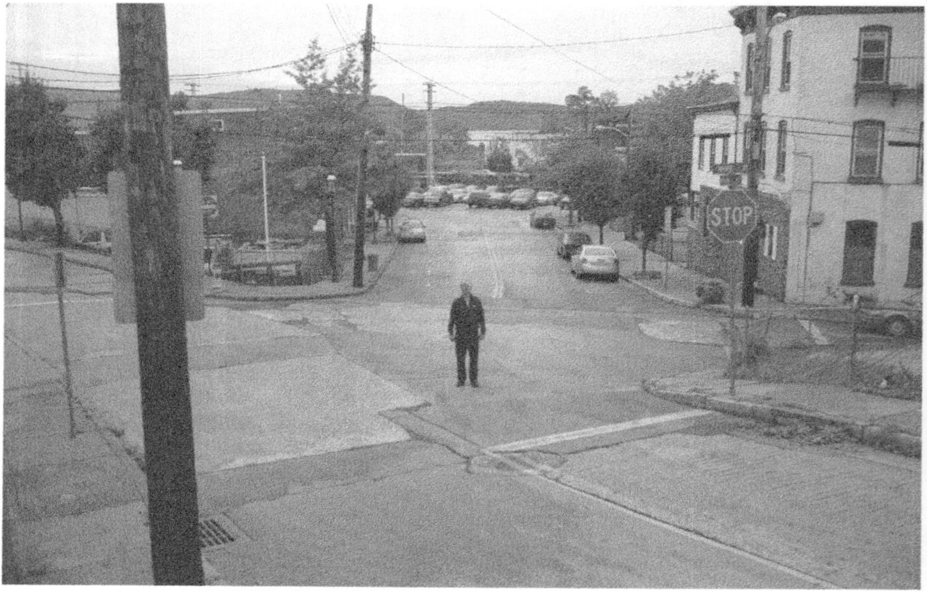

Measure Out Silence

It is certainly also this characteristic of 'inclusion' that set Jarmusch on the path to filmmaking, towards an art capable of 'encompassing' both literature and music. The more recent events confirm that the road to music was never really abandoned by Jarmusch, who has resumed playing and recording in the studio, while the road to poetry, though still an ongoing journey, is strictly a private matter, shared with just a handful of friends.

And yet, in my opinion, the *cinematographic text* – thus intended as an open, permeable and variable space – 'captured' his artistic purpose for yet another reason. Keeping in mind Cage's premise that silence in a strictly physical sense does not exist (at least until someone perceives it), the cinema offers the director the same possibility that music offers the composer: measure out silence. The formidable expressive capacity of silence is fully linked to *how* the artist, who chooses to use it in his work, measures it out. And Jarmusch has often made good use of this. His films are infused with silence, suspensions, apparent vacuums and taciturn characters: Allie, Eva, Zack, Jun, Blake, Ghost Dog, Don, Lone Man, Adam just to mention some of the leading ones. Scenes hinged on strong emotions like fear and love, often amply highlighted by the use of sound in traditional cinema, are instead dealt with by Jarmusch in an extremely silent manner: you only have to think of Ghost Dog's quasi-monosyllabic encounter with the mafia boss's wacky daughter, of Blake's amazement in the face of Charlie Dickinson's gunshots, or of Jun and Mitsuko's silent lovemaking in their room at the Aracade Hotel. Also Eva's drawn-out silences in *Stranger Than Paradise* and Don sitting in hypnotic-like stillness on his couch in *Broken Flowers* confirm this general tendency towards quietness.

But why is Jarmusch so interested in silence? If on one side it can be considered a simple and more than legitimate question of taste, on the other silence offers the director-musician the possibility to 'wake up' his audience because, denied a referent on the screen, spectators are 'forced' to use their own imagination. Naturally, this is as true of acoustic silence as it is of the *silence of the image*. An extreme case of a film 'without images' which illustrates well what I mean by *visual silence* is, for example, Derek Jarman's monochrome *Blue* (2003): not a frozen blue frame, but film that runs identically for 74 minutes, resonating as a suggestive and complex polyphony of music, words and

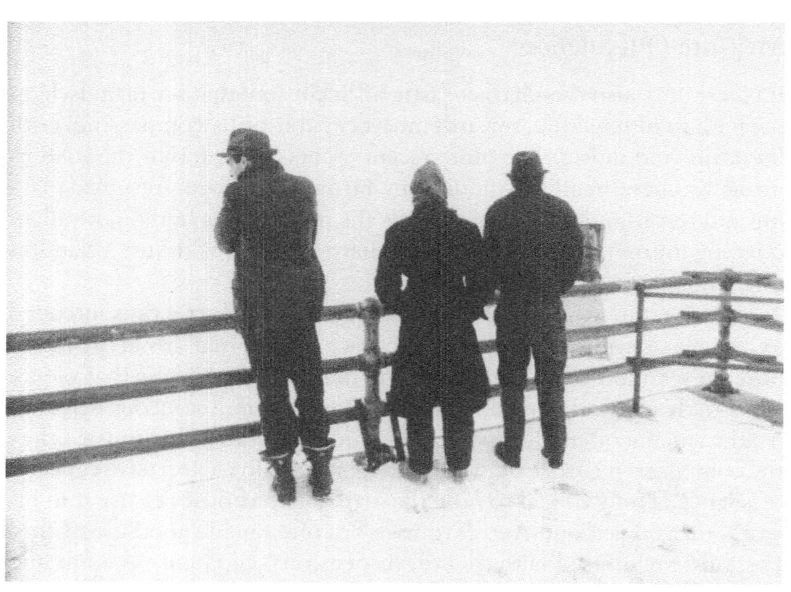

sound effects.[22] Whether faced with a monochrome image like that of *Blue*, an *invisible* one like that of Lake Erie in *Stranger Than Paradise*, or when plunged into acoustic silence, the public is somewhat left to themselves, but for an exact period of time established by the director or the composer. Anything can be projected onto this apparent emptiness with its well-defined arc of time, giving the spectator the chance to take an active part in the construction of the *cinematographic text*. The impatience that often greets prolonged silence is also an expression of the uneasiness or – if you prefer – the laziness overwhelming the spectators the moment in which, for a period of time unknown to them, they are asked to 'intervene'. How the spectator gets involved will depend very much on variables like character, humour, the time of day or night: either by slipping into a contemplative state or, more actively, trying to fill that momentary emptiness with personal sounds or images. In that moment of silence, or when faced with that absent image, the roles are reversed, and the audio-spectators suddenly find themselves directing and composing. As pointed out by Tom Waits, his opinion very much in harmony with Jarmusch, 'Silence is a huge part of music. It's essential. I'm always interested in what's not there and I like it when things are implied and things are left out.'[23]

Another musician dear to Jarmusch, Japanese composer Toru Takemitsu, who influenced him greatly and on whom I would like to end this section, described in a very suggestive way his relationship with silence, its expressive force something he often exploited, especially on his soundtracks:

> Within our Western musical notation the silences (rests) tend to be placed with statistical considerations. But that method ignores the basic utterance of music. It really has nothing to do with music. Just as one cannot plan his life, neither can he plan music.[24]

And if the claim of a composer who maintains he is unable to plan his own music might seem paradoxical, I on the other hand believe it to be a demonstration of unlimited faith in sound as an inexhaustible and unforeseeable source at the disposal of every artist and every man. Using words that put him on the same wavelength as a director whom I have amply quoted, Takemitsu clarified his idea even better: 'I wish to discard the concept of building sounds. In the world in which we live silence and unlimited sound exist. Painstakingly I wish to carve that sound with my own hands, finally to reach a single sound.'[25] It is hard not to hear the echo of Tarkovsky's words and the self-created image of the film director likened to a 'sculptor of time': faced with a 'block' of time he progressively eliminates the superfluous to reach finally the synthesis represented in the film. In the same way, Takemitsu wants to sculpt the single sounds from the sonorous and silent body of Nature. Time, sound and silence are therefore inseparable, a concept that the Japanese composer expressed with great clarity when talking of his collaboration with director Masaki Kobayashi:

> In *Kwaidan* (1964) I wanted to create an atmosphere of terror. But if the music is constantly saying 'Watch out! Be scared!' then all the tension is lost. It's like sneaking up behind someone to scare them. First you have to be silent.[26]

It is in the art of measuring out silence that Takemitsu has shown his great ability. In the documentary by Charlotte Zwerin, *Music for the Movies: Toru Takemitsu*, the Japanese maestro reveals one of his methods, as simple as they are efficient:

Takemitsu: Sometimes I'd want to cut the sound just a bit, even
a foot, to heighten the tension.
Kobayashi: He skips a beat, just one *ma* and then brings in the
sound. Instead of putting a sound where you'd expect it, he
shifts just a little.[27]

The concept of *ma* (間), as explained by film historian Donald
Richie, 'is very much like the idea of an emptiness, the old Chinese adage
that the sheet is not empty until you've made the first mark'.[28] The idea
that silence cannot exist without its opposite, in other words without
sound, contrasts with the general concept of silence as 'void' or 'absence'
to which I referred at the beginning of this chapter and which John Cage
considers highly debatable when he affirms that 'there is always something to hear'. It is no accident that the concept of *ma*, roughly interpreted
from Japanese as 'interval in time and in space', was born as a reference
to music. Therefore the space between sounds, the silence of which Tom
Waits speaks, is not an abstract and isolated entity; it exists thanks to
that sonorous sign that would appear to negate it: in short it would not
survive without its opposite. An idea that brings to mind the more
Western structural notion of binary opposition according to which, in
extreme synthesis, the brain pairs concepts that are opposite but complementary and indispensable to each other like, to mention just a few
classic examples, presence/absence, good/evil, high/low and so on.
Even if in his films Jarmusch measures out silence with different
objectives from those of Takemitsu – that are certainly more of a commen-
tary of the images meant to influence the audience[29] – it is undeniable
that both use silence in an active and very precise way. Jarmusch's objective is to create a general atmosphere that remains *within* the confines of
the film, and into which the spectator may decide whether or not to
immerse himself, the silent moments functioning as a 'white screen' onto
which he actively project parts of himself. His use of sounds and of the space
between them is not meant to be a comment or a button to press in order
to provoke some of the spectator reactions, such as fear, sadness, relief, hilar-
ity. What interests Jarmusch is rather the use of sound and silence as a
powerful instrument to create a 'state', a condition or, to use a conclusive
metaphor borrowed from Cage, to create his garden of images and sounds:

Cage has compared the silences in a passage . . . from *Music of
Changes* to the space between the objects in Japanese stone gardens.

Just as the stones are there so that we may be aware of the space between them, so the sounds are there in the music so that we may be aware of the silence that separates them.[30]

Silent-Sound Film: A Hypothesis

Having established that silence helps define sound and vice versa, it can sometimes assume functions that are instead normally attributed to an acoustic signal, such as sounding the alarm in the event of danger. In the town of Ystad, on Sweden's west coast, there still exists today a secular tradition the exact origins of which have long been forgotten, dating back to at least the seventeenth century. Every night of the year, from 9.15 p.m. until 1.00 a.m., at regular intervals of fifteen minutes, the watchman of the church of S. Maria stands atop the tower and blows his brass horn to inform the town that 'all is well'.[31] A note blown four times in the direction of the cardinal points reassures the population that there are no fires, no accidents and no other threats (the past will have included enemy attacks from the sea). According to tradition, in the event of a real emergency the watchman will not blow his horn: it is silence, and not a customary system like a siren or the ringing of bells, that will worry the population. The expressive and narrative force of silence can thus be compared to that of an acoustic signal, a fact that was already acknowledged some centuries ago, when the watchman's duty was clearly more essential and his role less 'folkloristic' than it is today. Silence has a versatile and flexible nature and may be the bearer of highly diverse messages, at times taking on functions normally entrusted to sound.

By going from the acoustic slant to the visual one it is possible to make similar observations with regard to the *silence of the image*. I refer, for example, to the darkness into which the spectator is plunged during those seconds of black leader that separate the scenes in *Stranger Than Paradise* and *Dead Man* and which create a brief reaction of amazement, reiterated after each cut between the silent image and the first shot of the following scene. In that moment of suspension between one scene and another, the reality of the film is entrusted entirely to the fragments of sound – music, sound effects or dialogue – that can be heard running on the black monochrome image, and trigger the spectator's fantasy. In *Dead Man*, for instance, during the journey undertaken by Blake and Nobody, there is a passage between two scenes, the first with the fugitives sitting around the campfire at night and the second with them riding through the forest the next morning, in which the 'silence of the image' lasts for a full six seconds – a minor eternity in terms of editing – creating a mix between spectator disorientation and expectation. The surprise effect that follows is thus provoked by the interposition of that six-second apparent void made up of sound and darkness which, like the Ystad watchman's silence, becomes highly expressive: the editing, rendered paradoxically visible thanks to that absence of images, produces a different awareness in spectators, perhaps even more profound with regard to what they are about to see.

The idea of the expressive versatility and flexibility of silence – both acoustic and visual – can adapt well to the aesthetics of silent film, in which not only the picture plays a central role, but also so does everything that is audible. It is exactly because the acoustic aspect of the pre-sound cinema is 'limited' that what is heard necessarily assumes more functions: in addition to covering the noise of the projector, the music played live must recount actions and emotions; the sound effects are exaggerated both in timbre and volume in order to be easily recognizable and so take on a supplementary narrative role; the written word is brief, to the point and at times poetic, while the spoken word read out loud by whoever is in the cinema (often translating the film's title cards) is a fundamental aid for audiences, foreign or illiterate, or both, who were quite numerous at the start of the twentieth century, especially in the United States. In short, if the typical over-acting, the exaggerated make-up, the often overly elaborate set designs and, in many cases, the editing broadened the narrative and expressive functions of the image, the same process of dilation occurred from the standpoint of sound.

By incorporating elements of pre-sound cinema in his films, Jarmusch has created a synthesis that, chasing a slightly paradoxical image, I would like to define as *Silent-Sound Film*. But what are the concrete strategies assimilable to silent film that Jarmusch uses – in a more or less unconscious way – in his work?

If at the base of silent film's aesthetic there exists an expansion of the expressive and narrative functions of both image and sound, provoked by the technical limitations of pioneer cinema, there are indeed many examples in Jarmusch's filmography in which one finds similar mechanisms. However, these mechanisms of expansion are in no way triggered by technical limitations but are, for want of a better word, auto-imposed: the battle against verbocentrism in favour of a more ample communicative approach that often goes beyond the simple verbal language; the assiduous use of foreign tongues and polyglotism; frequently resorting to the poetic word and literary structures with their ample interpretative and aesthetic horizons; the music never intended as mere accompaniment or as a button to cue audience emotions, but as an essential ingredient to create a *state*, a more vast and indeterminate atmosphere; silence as a stylistic signature; the narrative and expressive use of sound effects; cultural relativism and the consequent general enlargement of perspective; the absence of an acoustic hierarchy and the creation of a sound democracy. All these characteristics, amply dealt with in the earlier chapters, are some of the ingredients of Jim Jarmusch's *Silent-Sound Film* and very clearly determine its style.

Wanting to create an atmosphere *within* the film – meticulously planned in every detail, while leaving space for the spectator's fantasy, culture and inspiration – is an ulterior element that brings Jarmusch's cinema close to silent film. However, whereas the audience of the silent era was somewhat forced to imagine large chunks of the dialogue, intuit the vagaries of the plot and use the music and sound effects to complete the film in their own heads, Jarmusch's audience is instead often pushed into using its own imagination by the above-mentioned ingredients: relativization of verbal language, polyglotism, the poetic word, silence, absence of any hierarchy, and so on. The recounted escape in *Down By Law*, the imagined war in *Permanent Vacation*, the open endings in *Stranger Than Paradise* and *Broken Flowers*, and Lone Man's inexplicable access to the American's hideout in *The Limits of Control*, just to mention a handful of examples, require an imaginative effort from the audience that, in the last film, is given a little help:

American: How the fuck did you get in here?
Lone Man: I used my imagination.

Memory's inconsistency, or better, its subjectivity, is another tool used by Jarmusch to trigger the spectator's active vision. This is clearly expressed in the two separate flashbacks in *Ghost Dog: The Way of the Samurai* where Ghost Dog and Louie remember, each in his own way, the birth of their working relationship. A distracted vision might miss the 'subjective flashback' in a scene already rife with personal recollections. If the principle that memory is subjective carries any weight, then inevitably the audio-spectator cannot be passive when watching a film, but will create a new recollection each time at every screening and at every moment. The use of silence, either acoustic or visual, also confirms the idea of an active audio-vision and, creating an ulterior assonance with silent cinema, may reach a synthesis that contains both: *the silence of the text*.

The black suspensions that constellate *Stranger Than Paradise* and *Dead Man*, those long seconds of darkness and sound, become an acoustic equivalent to silent cinema's title cards, but deprived of the written word: black screens onto which everyone may project their fantasies and desires, depending on their sensibilities, language, culture, competence and – why not? – their mood at that particular moment. The space of the image's continuity is suspended and interrupted, the 'wordless title cards' creating an intermediary setting, made up prevalently of sound that on one side connects these two parallel – light and dark – visual tracks and on the other renders their physical separation visible.

Lastly, there is one more observation regarding the assonance with silent cinema. The 'involved' vision that Jarmusch more or less knowingly asks of the spectator, in my opinion, shows some analogies with the physically participated viewing of early twentieth-century nickelodeon spectators mentioned at the beginning of this chapter. The strongly corporeal dimension of the participation, typical of early cinema, was again fiercely expressed at the time of Jarmusch's film evolution in the New York of the late 1970s and early '80s, where the Super 8 films and then the videotapes of artists like Poe, Mitchell, Lurie, Nares and friends were shown at clubs during live concerts – looked upon as backdrops to the music, or vice versa depending on audience inclination. The Squat Theatre, just to name one of the venues, and the nickelodeons of the early twentieth century – crowded, sweaty places where moving images, live music and audience participation were structural ingredients – are thus perhaps less distant from each other than they might appear to be. The interaction not only aesthetical but also physical and linguistic with the screen and with the stage by a heterogeneous and international audience is a characteristic that undoubtedly belongs to both periods. In the case of the nickelodeons a substantial slice of the audience was made up of first-generation immigrants and so, regardless of social extraction, reflected the linguistic variety of North American cities at that time. In the case of the Super 8 films shown at the clubs – a scene certainly smaller in size compared to that of the five-cent movies so popular at the start of the century – the audience was made up in large part of those 'foreigners to the island' who crowded the downtown

scene frequented by Jarmusch, and in which the typical physical dimension of live music was connected to the cinema at the hip.

To hazard another historic parallel, the famous punk asynchrony of Amos Poe's *Blank Generation* can be ideally likened to the asynchrony celebrated by the Russian theorists and directors of the late 1920s. Even if in Poe's famous 'film-manifesto' of the downtown music scene objective technical limitations were to blame for the failed synchronization between sound and picture, the 'manifesto' thus having little programmatic about it, Poe's visionary initiative did not baulk in the face of a technical 'detail': 'I had no sound recording equipment, so I just was making silent films of punk bands like Blondie or the Ramones, Patti Smith or Richard Hell.'[32]

Thanks to the systematic use of Super 8, silent film slipped somewhat forcibly into the downtown music and film scene of the era, creating that blend of sound, picture, performance and direct audience participation that has had a profound influence on Jarmusch's work.

Therefore it is no big surprise that, in more recent times, Jarmusch has looked for a more physical contact with audiences by picking up a guitar and stepping back on stage to play live music, a little as he did at the time of Max's Kansas City, CBGB and other downtown venues. Music confirms its role as guarantor of the undeniable fact that the experience

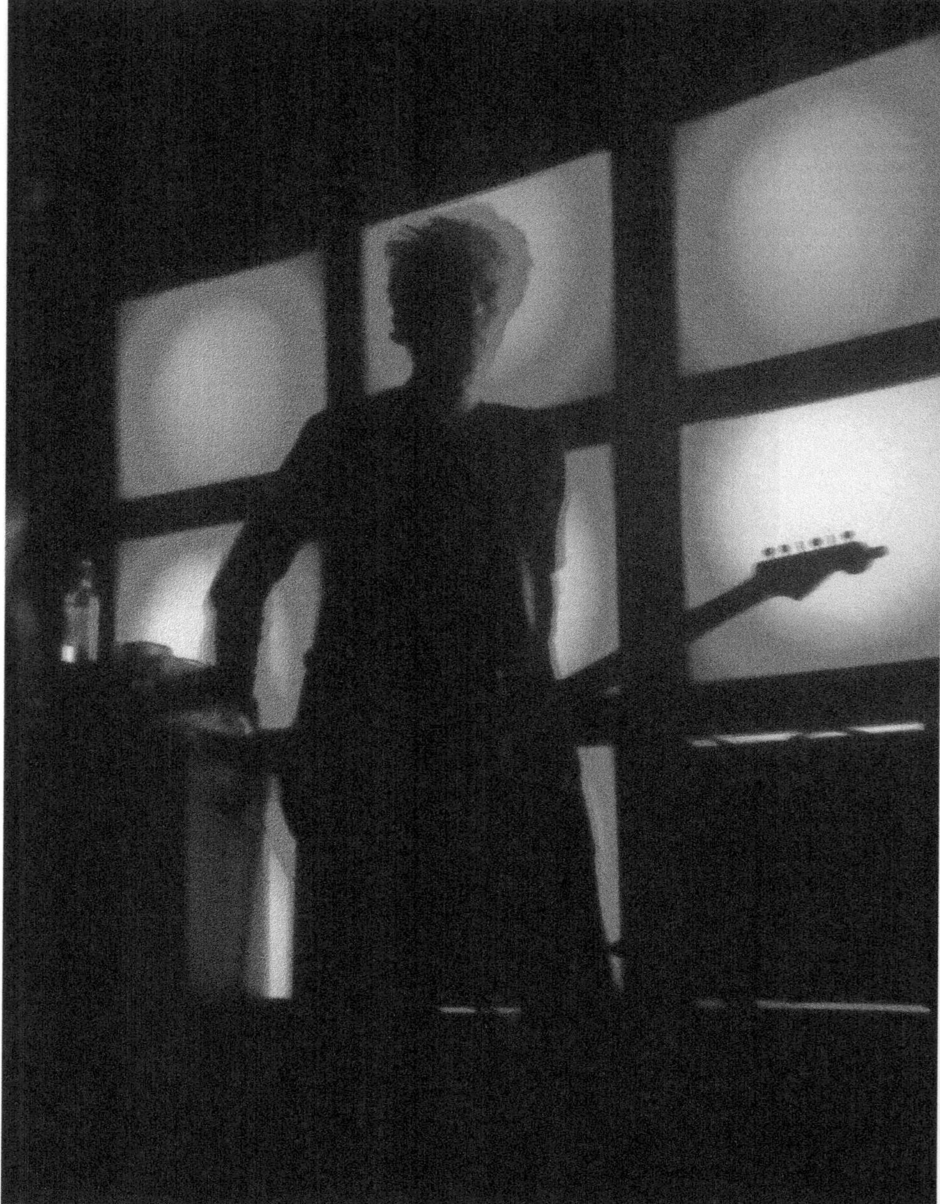

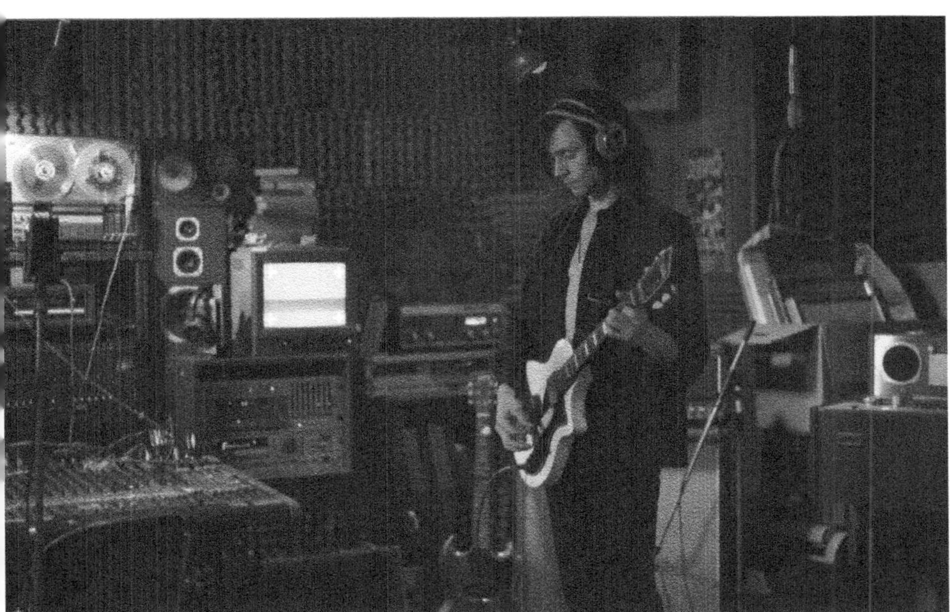

of performing live cannot be substituted with any surrogate technology, and thus – notwithstanding the very real crisis suffered by the recording industry – to quote Cage again: 'the future of music has nothing to fear' as long as there are musicians, bands, orchestras and listeners. On the other hand I do not mean to romanticize the notion of 'live' versus 'virtual'. It is a matter of balance, as Elliot Sharp sensibly points out:

> Now there is no place where people can assemble, it gets further and further away from the centre. And now, with the web, you do not have a centre. In a way it is more bloodless, but there is more instantaneous communication across geographical lines and across aesthetic lines because everything is accessible on the web. Maybe that devalues it. It's a question of balance. How does the value that is impacted by its accessibility, speed and lack of location balance the lack of blood and viscerality and smell? Smell to me is the thing that is always missing in digital art.[33]

In Jarmusch's world the invitation to use one's imagination and the lack of interest in a cinema classified as simple entertainment are largely tuned to acoustic frequencies made up of words, music and noise. In his most recent film, the vampire love story *Only Lovers Left Alive*, the fact that one of the two central figures is a musician is a crucial step on this path. Rather than have one of his numerous musician friends act, for the first time in his career Jarmusch asked an actor to play a musician. Apart from creating the role of Adam (Tom Hiddleston), Jarmusch also gave him a musical voice, by composing and performing the pieces of the vampire's repertoire.[34] The two natures of filmmaker and *musicien manqué* have succeeded in coming together – also physically – in this character.

The opening shot of the film shows a record player, its circular movement and the 7-inch single – Wanda Jackson's rockabilly classic 'Funnel of Love', in a slower version than the 1961 original – filmed from above.[35] The following shots of the main characters apparently sleeping or in a trance-like state – Adam in his Detroit hideout/recording studio and Eve in her Tangier bedroom – are also filmed from above and edited in alternation to the image of the record player. A striking detail immediately hits the audience. Despite the characters being motionless, they are anything but static: they spin around, like the record, creating a slight sense of dizziness in the spectator, the music literally propelling the camera movement and with it the entire progression of the film, the connection between sound and vision now complete. Jarmusch's *Silent-Sound Film* has thus closed a circle opened in the downtown clubs at the end of the 1970s, the coherent line of which he continued to draw on through the years, without any hurry. His meticulous attention and undying passion for sound material have accompanied him faithfully during the journey. 'Imagine the world without music. Man, just hand me a gun, will you?'[36]

Voices:
Ennio Morricone

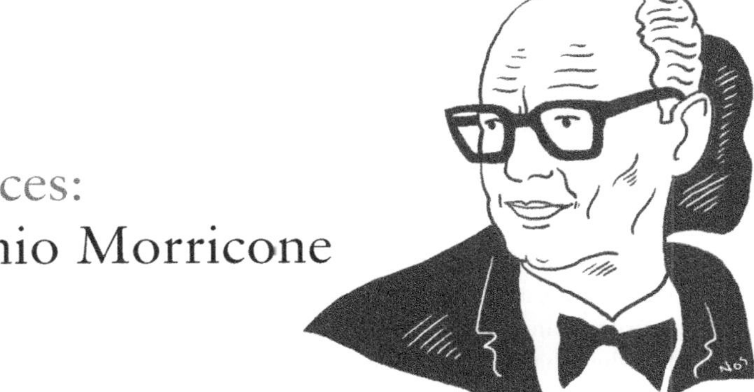

1

John Cage was one of the most innovative artists of the twentieth century. In 1937, with regard to improvisation and music written for percussions, he stated:

> Percussion music is a contemporary transition from keyboard-influenced music to the all-sound music of the future. Any sound is acceptable to the composer of percussion music; he explores the academically forbidden 'non-musical' field of sound insofar as is manually possible.
>
> Methods of writing percussion music have as their goal the rhythmic structure of a composition. As soon as those methods are crystallized into one or several widely accepted methods, the means will exist for group improvisation of unwritten but culturally important music. This has already taken place in Oriental cultures and in hot jazz.[1]

In some films – particularly in *Permanent Vacation* (1980) – Jarmusch and his steadfast composer John Lurie used free jazz improvisation. Given your long-standing experience as a contemporary musician, with the legendary Gruppo di Improvvisazione Nuova Consonanza, do you consider improvisation to be a valuable tool when composing a film score?

Yes, I do, because my personal experience confirms this point. In Elio Petri's *Un tranquillo posto di campagna* (1968) the result proved excellent: I composed 50 per cent of the film's original score, the rest was created with the Gruppo di Improvvisazione Nuova Consonanza. The problem was that improvised music cannot be repeated. Whenever we played a piece for a certain film sequence, which took us a long time, the music was never the same the second time round. So, after listening to our recording, we managed to turn our improvisation into something close to a written score. We would repeat those parts that seemed to work best, both for us and the director who was present. Elio Petri expressed his views, correctly so since he was the director. We mostly agreed with him because he was someone who had been around the block a few times. In other words, while also trying to improve them, we went back to repeat the pieces that had been improvised originally. I remember a piece that we played over and over again, one could practically say that it had been written, and Petri said: 'You see, at this point that thing there works.' So when that scene change came along, we repeated that same idea: it became a slightly less improvised improvisation.

Nonetheless, one can say that the genesis of the pieces originated from improvisation.

Yes, that's true. I remember that Walter Branchi started to improvise a piece, and the others quickly joined in; it worked very well and whatever came afterwards always took a turn in the right direction. Now with regard to the discussion on Cage and percussions: I think that the research on percussions is focused on the differentiation between the timbres. One can do everything with percussions. It is no coincidence that great percussionists, including pop music drummers – and I've recently heard some extraordinary ones, all Italians to boot – do not necessarily have to be musicians in the traditional sense. These musicians, the percussionists, go all out in their search for timbres, in their experimentation of sounds.

In fact Cage says that 'any sound is acceptable'.

Yes, indeed. I would not question Cage's discourse, his *Silence*. He is beyond any discussion. His message was so paradoxical that everyone must glean from it their own personal meaning. I was in Darmstadt at Cage's lectures and concert and . . . well, I was horrified. Then later I thought things over. Initially it wasn't easy. He turned on a radio, fiddled with the piano, turned pages, we waited five minutes, then he did something else, then quickly turned more pages, waited another five minutes, turned the radio on and off . . . the people were angry and rattled in Darmstadt. And I was a little shocked, too. Then I understood. I attended his lecture the following day: he decided each note by tossing a coin, heads one note, tails another, and he then wrote it down. Pure chance. All this is beyond argument, and the music he wrote can certainly be applied to film, as was Bach's *St Matthew Passion*. The problem of music in cinema is a very strange one.

Music is one of the few completely abstract art forms and, through sound, the composer tends to reproduce not so much the sounds of life, but the sounds of . . . of what? An emotion? Perhaps not; the emotions come at a later stage. Take a Bach fugue: it stirs up emotions, but wasn't composed on a blast of emotions. He wrote the theme, the countersubject and then elaborated on it, and yet . . . The fact is that music is perhaps the only true abstract art form that comes from an imprecise 'beyond'. Where does music come from? The air? The imagination? This possibility that music has of being abstract gives it an extraordinary power, though in cinema this can also become a weakness.

In cinema, the music may be interpreted differently by each individual, according to one's culture, not only musical. This is why in a film, we can adapt dozens of different music scores, all of which work anyway. Which is the best? There isn't one. This is owed to the quality and the possibility of abstraction that music has within itself, however, no sooner has it been applied to an image, this abstraction in part disappears and in part remains. Thus it lends itself to the interpretation of a clear and precise visual event, while at the same time that crucial halo of abstraction remains. For example, this allows an extremely sad piece by Mahler to be applied to both a dramatic scene, and to a joyous scene. This happens because if on one hand the dramatic music highlights the drama of the scene, on the other the same dramatic music over a joyous scene will imply something that no one knows, that might never happen, that might exist only in the soul of the individual viewer. This is an important miracle. My motto is EST – Energy, Space and Time. Energy, as the only way to transmit; Time is temporality, the duration; Space is the space that music has as opposed to all other sounds, the cleanliness of sound, speaking of which, we must take into account something else that we have yet to mention: the untrained ear can't register more than two different sounds at the same time. For example, if the two of us are talking and others are talking nearby we won't understand a thing, providing the volume is the same. If we shout, it'll be even worse, we'll never be on the same page. Music requires clarity, in other words its own space. We can't have one ear listening to the dialogue, the train passing, the guy shouting, the bombs exploding, and to the music, on top of all that.

In this respect, how do you deal with the other sounds, words, sound effects, noises? How do you take them into account?

I do take them into account, yes, but I want music to have its own autonomy in order to work. Not every word needs comment, the film as a *whole* needs comment. A film requires a 'sound frame'. This sound frame cannot take into account the fact that there is a swan, a girl with long hair, one leg against a wall, and a castle in the background . . . ! Music should not take such minor details into account. It should consider the scene as a whole. It is quite clear that the syncs, those moments in a scene in which sound and image meet, can indeed exist. But they must be so spontaneous, the music will be perceived as pre-existent, and the cuts natural. In the music of all the great composers of the past, there are sudden variations, cuts. From the introduction of the theme one comes to the passages. Then we have the second theme, as in the symphony or the sonata, and it develops from there et cetera, et cetera. Although we are clearly not dealing with exactly the same thing, all these cuts, passages and patterns have to exist in film music in order to maintain its coherence and unitary consistence. So the music must take into account what happens in the film, but the composer should pretend that his music predates the film. This might sound strange, but it goes back to what I was saying about the untrained ear not being able to hear more than two sounds at the same time. So, when I was told that the music I composed for Sergio Leone was better than the music I composed for others, I said it wasn't true at all. Leone allowed the music to be free of any sound for minutes at a time, whereas others leave twenty seconds of music together with explosions and galloping horses. It depends on the director's style.

In *Dead Man* Jim Jarmusch worked with the guitarist Neil Young. He took inspiration directly from the film's images to compose the score, improvising over a period of about three consecutive days. The result is a constant, organic musical flow, almost a single piece, in which one cannot discern a clear-cut distinction between tunes and/or songs, as is often the case in cinema. How do you view this type of experimentation in the relationship between director and musician?

Well, I would have to watch the film and listen to what he has done to give my opinion. But it's certainly legitimate. What instrument does he play?

Mainly the electric guitar.

Ah, good. That makes things much easier. Playing a single instrument, he maintains his style, his personality. Young may have watched the film for three days, may have improvised, but the end result is born from his capabilities, his technique, his imagination . . .

Jarmusch himself spoke of a kind of symbiosis between Young and the film.

But do you think that if Jarmusch had called another guitarist capable of improvising, the result would have been the same?

Absolutely not.

Right, it wouldn't. And do you think that if it hadn't been Young's music, someone else's guitar music wouldn't have worked?

It would have worked perfectly.

Another ten guitarists would have done just as well, maybe even better. There is never evidence to the contrary. It's exactly what I said at a conference in Spoleto, back in 1969. I suggested an experiment, which unfortunately nobody was able to fund: give the same film to ten different musicians and ask them to compose the score.

So this experiment was never carried out?

I took part in a similar experiment in Paris. A few months before our concert, Delerue, Legrand and I received a tape with a three minute 30 second film about Paris, for which we were supposed to compose the music. The film described Paris waking up at dawn. It showed the markets coming alive, some almost subliminal footage of the Pleyel concert hall. The film ended inside the Pleyel, while waiting for the orchestra to rehearse, while someone did the cleaning, while someone else positioned the music stands, then more footage of Paris, then back again to the hall. Anyway, Michel Legrand, Georges Delerue and I were charged with this experiment at the end of a concert given by the three of us. Michel Legrand's piece interpreted Paris as a huge metropolis, the sound quite extraordinary. Instead Delerue started with a harmonica and a barrel organ. It went very well, just as well as Legrand's piece. I did something completely different . . . Thank goodness! It would have been easy to do something similar to the other two. I started my piece before the beginning of the film, to show how one may serve a film in a different way, which is something akin to the experiment I suggested in Spoleto in 1969. My piece started with string instruments tuning up even before the beginning of the film. The tuning lasts three and a half minutes, the length of the film and beyond. The entire piece unfolds within this tuning. Then, at a certain point, the brass section starts playing a theme, oblivious to the tuning of the other instruments. I wrote the score with the film's finale already in mind, my piece ending just as it started. This was another idea, but which one was the best? Oh, I don't know. It depends on the director. If the director tells me: 'I want a film of epic proportions, with music of epic proportions!' I will give him music of epic proportions, and I'll give it my best shot. Then I might say to him: 'Now look, I would go for something a little softer here', like Delerue. If the director is happy with something abstract, I can suggest the piece that I wrote. But then again, another ten composers would have written something completely different.

2

Maestro, seeing that we mentioned the film, I would like to show you two short sequences from Jarmusch's *Dead Man*. The first is at the beginning of the film, the second almost at the end. Both have to do with travel, a classic theme in westerns, although *Dead Man* is not a typical western.

> 1. Opening scene: close-ups of William Blake (Johnny Depp) sitting in the train cross-cut with the rods of the train. Sound: train, sound effects, guitar music. TC 00:00:23 to TC 04:00:00
> 2. Scene in Native American village: William Blake enters the village. He is hallucinating and can barely walk; Nobody holds him and then goes to talk to the three elders inside a wooden structure, leaving Blake seated on the ground outside under a totem. Sound: some dialogue in Native language, sound effects, guitar music. TC 01:40:00 to TC 01:46:40

What struck me in the first sequence is how the music doesn't 'comment' on the close-ups of the main character, who is left 'in silence', but is instead layered upon the sound effects of the train's piston rods, defining and enriching the sense of a journey into the unknown that has just started. In the second sequence, I was struck by how the music helps to create and to perceive the delirious state of the character, who has almost reached the end of his terrestrial journey. What do you think of that?

Music has the huge potential of giving itself to the images, it's incredibly flexible. Therefore I say that the music in this case suits the environment quite nicely. It sounds like fairly sophisticated country music, not melodic, a little rhythmic, with a country-like colour. So I think it's right. But it's impromptu. It could have been any music. It wasn't written for this scene so, considering its versatility, in the first sequence the director experimented by removing the sound of the train and replacing it with the guitar, avoiding the expressivity that the music might have given the close-ups or anything else so abstractly interesting. But when I say that music is easily adaptable to images, I'm also saying that that music can be wrong, yet it can adapt, because it has this quality of expressive flexibility towards an image. Very often music adapts itself to the images, and the result is born of chance; it's not something that the director controls. This is one of those cases. It's right to experiment, but I don't think it's particularly interesting in this case. And when I say that music is flexible, I mean that another twenty, a hundred different scores could have been used, not just the score one presumes I could have composed. This score wasn't even written for that image. Someone is playing the guitar almost absentmindedly, with open strings; it's fake country, not classical, with a country timbre, and that is what deludes us. We can even accept the delusion if we play the role of the spectator and not critic. We can play along and not care. But if we must express an opinion, the experiment is a little on the weak side.

In this particular case the guitarist, Neil Young, isolated himself from the director for a few days and came up with this music watching a rough cut. So there is certainly an element of chance here.

He improvised.

Exactly. Even though as far as I know the music stayed where he played it.

Where you'll find a certain poetic value is towards the end of the second sequence, just before the main character enters that sort of Indian structure, which then closes. At that point, there appears to be a musical idea, but I'm not even sure of this, because we are so accustomed to something being wrong, that it becomes the most fortunate point of the error, so we enjoy it when compared to what preceded it. You don't agree, do you?

Let's say I am in absolute agreement about the element of chance. But as a spectator and listener, I feel that the effect reached by the music is to create something together with the picture. I feel this above all in the Native American village sequence, where in my opinion the music and image together create an atmosphere of mystery and uncertainty around the dying protagonist.

Yes, what you heard is a little more than nothing, and that little more than nothing is just as you describe, because the fact of hearing the guitar over the train's pistons has even less to do with a musical idea. Instead, I would prefer to hear the sound of the train, alternating the close-up, where I would willingly hear the guitar. I would consider it more interesting and more expressive to do exactly the opposite of what the director did. The human element of an instrument would thus become an expression of the traveller's desire to reach his destination, and I wouldn't want to hear the train during the close-ups – in other words, the opposite. Maybe that way he would have conveyed a more interesting message. I don't like it as it stands.

It's a perfectly legitimate opinion.

Well, yes, there is a little more than nothing, and thus you found it. It's much better like this than without music. It would be nice if the role of the train were on the train, and not on the close-ups and that one heard the sound as such, more poetical, more interesting. Instead, this musician plays both the banjo and the guitar like a cowboy without a clue. Do you have the film music on CD?

Yes.

You try doing the experiment: place the guitar over the character's face . . . Ah, but you don't have the sound of the train. One should hear the train when we see it, and the guitar, or the banjo – I think there is some banjo, probably a large one – on the close-ups. You could try this, but if you don't have the sound of the train you won't get the right result.

If I may be so bold, Maestro, how would you have done it?

By asking me this question, you push me into a creative corner. Well, I could answer you . . . In fact, I will. I would have omitted the sound of the train altogether. I would have tried to use a small orchestra, with a few instruments, guitars, banjos, double-bass, percussions, and I would

have composed not country music, but a close timbre relative that plays
continuously over the images, with rhythmic elements in some of the
instruments, that convey the rhythm of the train. It could even be interesting to take the sound of a real train, an old train, and play around
with its rhythm, using these few instruments, or even just one, a banjo.
Over the whole sequence. Then, if we want to try the same experiment
as the director, but with a single composition, running from start to
finish, maybe one could end on the close-ups, and leave the sound, but
without the train. Instead, when we see the close-ups of the locomotive's
wheels, leave the sound of the train and vice versa. In other words, the
rhythm of the train becomes MUSIC, which is a reality, but it becomes
another type of reality because it enters the realm of music, that
'beyond' we talked of earlier. This is what I would have tried to do.

3

Today, the demands of film production, especially in the United States,
are often hectic and sometimes penalize the composer's field of action. In
your opinion, what are the ideal working conditions for a film composer?

It's difficult to say because there are many ideal and satisfying ways to
collaborate. One is when the director says: 'I don't know what to tell
you, just go ahead and do as you like', thus making the composer more
responsible. Obviously he will have to account for what he does, even
before recording the music. It's an ideal setup, but it gives the composer
huge responsibility. A director has often told me, 'Go ahead and do
as you like, I don't know what to tell you.' So I get to work, compose
the piece, and report to him before recording, by either playing it on
the piano or describing it to him in plain words, because sometimes
the piano just doesn't help. Usually the director understands one thing,
then, when he listens to it, he hears something he wasn't expecting.
Obviously music can't be expressed in words, at most I can describe
the idea that inspires it. Another ideal setup, among the many possible
options, is the complete opposite of what I mentioned above, which is
to follow the director's instructions to the letter, while at the same time
coupling it with your own imagination. Give the director what he
expects, while imposing your own very personal and very evident stamp
as a composer. And that is the balancing act that every film composer is
up against. The two scenarios are thus at opposite ends of the spectrum,
but perhaps they come together because in both cases the composer

expresses his personality. It is this that cannot be denied those involved in a creative pursuit such as writing film music. I no longer accept work that doesn't let me contribute something personal, something of mine.

Is it important for you that the director has a clear idea of what he wants?

Musically speaking, the director never has a clear idea. Or rather, he might very well have clear ideas, but they will be about things he's heard before, and so will suggest ideas he already has in mind, ideas written by somebody else. The composer may go ahead and repeat those things, but I for one would no longer enjoy myself. However you look at it, these two conflicting scenarios exist.

I answered the second question on *Dead Man* as if the director had shown me the way, and said: 'This is what I would like', and I replied that I would do it like this, respecting the sound of the train, respecting the sound of the country guitar music. Then I would have suggested that the train – and he would certainly not have expected it – should be the rhythm of the entire sequence and the instruments should supply, not only the melody, but a sound, a country timbre over the train. This would have been my solution had the director given me instructions. Instead, had he said to me: 'Do as you like.' I don't know, I would have to give it some thought.

But the idea could be to not have any music, just the sound of the train, starting low, and then getting louder and louder on the close-ups, at which point you could perhaps add slightly more strident chords, especially in the second sequence. And perhaps during the second sequence the sound of the train could continue even if we don't see it, why not . . . if we want that sound to acquire a deeper meaning.

In the second sequence, perhaps have a human voice, primitive, a woman's voice, distant, adding itself to the sound of the train, which we can no longer see, but exists now only in the traveller's memory . . . This could be an expressive addition. However, there are directors who don't want 'expressive', and Jarmusch, whom I don't know personally, could be one of them, one of those who don't want anything expressed. In my opinion if he was looking to express nothing, he's even used too much music.

It's true that Jarmusch has an aesthetic sense of this type. You hit the nail on the head with regard to his expressing very little.

Perhaps he's the kind of director who doesn't want anything overly expressed, who wants a film to be as objective and detached as possible. There are also directors who don't like, are even jealous of, the expressiveness that music adds to their film.[2] The impression is almost one of him wanting to humiliate the music.

It's strange you think that, because music has always had an enormous importance for him, and Neil Young's contribution, as Jarmusch has often stated, has been fundamental.

Of course. What little room he gives him to play is fundamental. It's better that nothing. There is some music. Unwittingly though, he has humiliated the musician, because he doesn't let him play, interrupts him, disturbs him. There's no musical discourse, it's a tentative approach. But be careful; I have to admit that I have only seen two sequences of the film. It is possible that after giving us two cents' worth of music he goes on to give us four, then ten, and in the end 100. My judgement is based only on what I saw: ten minutes of music, divided in two parts.

In fact, there is a guitar theme that comes back again and again throughout the whole film, but is only hinted at during the Native American village sequence in *Dead Man*.

Touché! I admit I've neither seen it nor heard it.

Rome, January 2006

Voices:
Jim Jarmusch

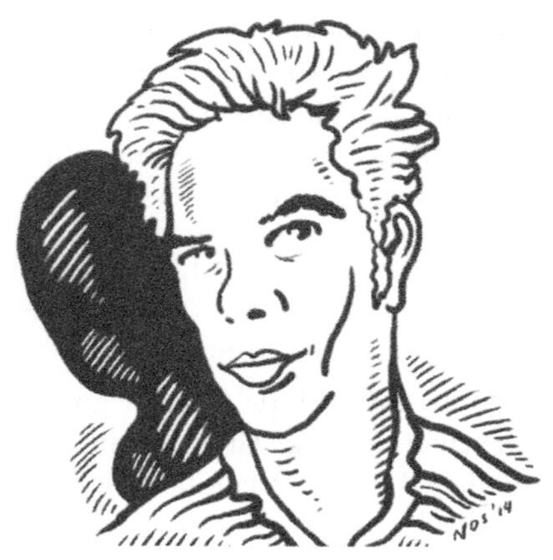

1 – *words*

I would like to begin with a quote by Michelangelo Antonioni. I will read it both in Italian and English.

> *Voci che siano soltanto voci. Non parole ma suoni.*
> *Che producano un effetto in chi le ascolta*
> *non per quello che dicono ma per quello che sono:*
> *rumori, suoni. L'homo presapiens doveva parlare così.*

> Voices that are only voices. Not words but sounds.
> Producing an effect in who is listening
> Not for what they mean but for what they are:
> Noises, sounds. Homo Presapiens must have spoken this way.[1]

I am very interested in words and languages. When you use foreign languages in your films, in my opinion, you often treat them as sounds. For example, in *Dead Man* and in *Down By Law* a lot of the foreign language is not translated. It can resemble poetry, where a word carries an additional meaning that has only to do with its sound and there is a 'lack of information', so to say. Can you tell me what you think about this?

Well, I like to often have languages in the films that aren't translated and that the characters in the film are not understanding, so I don't translate them for the audience. They become musical somehow, close to what Antonioni I think was saying. They convey emotion and parts of characters with the absence of understanding the meaning of the words. I got my courage to direct in languages I didn't understand when

346

I went to Japan for the first time. I collected a lot of videotapes of films by Mizoguchi and Ozu but they weren't subtitled, so I would watch these films back in New York without understanding the words at all, but studying the sound of their voices and the emotions conveyed by their sounds, the way they spoke. Of course I missed certain plot elements, but I still understood completely the emotional tone of what was going on. That gave me a lot of courage to direct actors in Japanese or Finnish, for example, that I don't really understand, although I wrote the dialogue first in English and then worked with translators. So I knew what the actors were saying while directing them, but I didn't know the exact language they were speaking. There's a brief part in *Dead Man* where you hear characters speaking in some native languages. I like that very much because the character of Johnny Depp is left out of everything, it becomes quite mysterious and it's not translated, so we are left in the position of that character who is hearing the language sort of as music.

I also read that it was partly thought of as a 'gift' for the very few people who would be able to understand it, because unfortunately there are very few people left who speak those languages.

Yeah, it was. And even getting the actors to speak it was difficult, 'cause there weren't too many people who speak those languages.

I spoke with Gary Farmer and he told me that he was really studying and practising a lot, especially for the native Makah language.

Yeah, which has a lot of clicking sounds we don't even use our vocal apparatuses for, you know? But they do.

In *Ghost Dog*, the two best friends actually don't speak the same language.

Right, but they somehow know what each other is saying. I love language and the ways in which people use words to say things. I love actors' voices, and that's why I hate dubbing. I don't like to have a different voice, then why would I want to work with that actor? I mean, dubbing Tom Waits's voice seems ridiculous! Why would you do that? I also don't like looping and I try to use direct sound, the sound recorded on the set, as much as I possibly can. I only loop if I have a real technical problem, when I have to replay something, but even that I find very painful because the actors are not in the same moment they were when they delivered the line. It's all such a delicate thing to me, I don't like to mess it up that way. I really freak out when I hear a lot of things in their original language but still dubbed later, and you could tell it's dubbed.

Well, in Italy there is an old tradition of dubbing. With the big film boom in the '60s many directors did it because they wanted to shoot really fast and would then dub the film later.

I know. Some people used it to their advantage. Fellini once was asking me why I hated dubbing so much and I said: 'Well, because I cast those actors for their physical presence *and* their voice.' He said: 'Yes but I can choose one face and another voice and have even more control.' And he did that very masterfully but he had a different approach that's very opposite to the way I think.

2 – *noise*

I think that in your films there is what I call 'sound democracy'. I mean that you consider all sounds – noise, music, words, silence – equally important. Most of the films we see mainly concentrate on words, as if the only task of the sound department is to make the dialogue as clearly understandable as possible. Films are generally focused on dialogue because humans are. We communicate mostly through verbal language after all. This is perhaps a rhetorical question, but do you think that communication happens only through words?

No, definitely not. There's a quote I love from Nicholas Ray. Comparing dialogue, or communication in a film to piano playing, he said: 'The dialogue is just the left hand, the melody is in the eyes.'

And that brings me again to looking at films in languages I didn't understand and studying how people communicate. I'm sort of obsessed with this, when you watch people on the street, in the Subway, in a restaurant, you can feel so much by the moments between their dialogue, and how they react physically or how much eye contact they make. You can really tell how someone is feeling that way. Sometimes the words are forced and will come from your brain and you construct them, but some-times a truer sense is in those other things: how people move, the way they look and how they physically react to a situation.

Or in the silences. I think that in a lot of your films one can see that you are really much more interested in what comes before or after a crux. It's more about those spaces in between.

Yeah. Absolutely. It can be much more revealing and also it gives
more power to when people do speak, because you have a dynamic.
It's like musicians, if you play every note then all the notes are equally
uninteresting, but if you leave spaces between of course that gives
emotional resonance. That's very important to me, but also all the
little background sounds are very important to me and although
I try to keep my films very quiet, in a certain way, I also try very
much to use backgrounds as landscapes, as colours, as little things
that deepen the texture of the atmosphere around the characters. So
whether you hear birds or a distant train or traffic, all these things
have a musical sense that adds something very resonant to the film.
I'm very particular about those sounds when I'm mixing. I've worked
with really great sound designers Bob Hein and Chic Ciccolini mostly,
and I also work with Dominique Tavella always in my mixing and they
understand my sensibility about all those details. They are cumulative
and they affect your emotional reaction to the film without them being
somehow flags or big signs that tell you: this means something! They
just affect you.

And maybe sometimes they can even help you tell the story.
They do, of course.

I'm thinking of the sound of the gunshot in *Mystery Train*, for example.
Yeah, right. People spend so much time on photography, which is of
course important, but the image is only half of a film unless it's silent. The
other half is the sound; it's extremely important and I think a lot of filmmakers concentrate on the picture more than the sound, but to me they
are equal. All these things in the film, like colour or furniture or wardrobe
that the characters wear or just the objects, they're all extremely important to me visually, but so are the background sounds or what does the
door sound like closing . . . One thing that really annoys me in films is
when you see people wearing sneakers or basketball shoes, but they use
the same foleys as though they're wearing hard shoes. It happens so often
and it just drives me crazy! Don't they understand that that's not the
sound coming from those shoes? You know, this kind of thing drives
me nuts. But all these details are all extremely important.

When you are working on a film would you consider that roughly half
of the time is for the images and half for the sound?

Well, most of the time is editing the picture and then you're working on the sound or someone is preparing it at the same time. It's in the mix when you make all the choices. But I spend a lot of time with the sound designers while they're preparing it. I like to audition certain sounds, they'll play five different possibilities for the sound of a car door and I'll pick the one that I think feels right, I'm very particular. In *Ghost Dog*, for example, there was a shot of a very particular bird, a pileated wood-pecker and at first Chic Ciccolini, the sound designer, had the sound of a red-headed woodpecker . . . I sort of study birds so I told him: 'Chic, that's the wrong bird.' 'Whattcha talkin' about!?' he yelled, 'It's a wood-pecker!' I said: 'No, no Chic, it's the wrong woodpecker. There will be ornithologists who will know.' So he had to go to the ornithological library to get the correct bird sound and he had to change it. Things like that. If a vintage English motorcycle goes by I don't want to hear the sound of a Harley, they have a different sound. So I don't want to be untruthful with sounds, and you know everything in a film is a lie, it's all created and constructed but I want it to feel right.

Well, there are good lies and bad lies.

Yeah, it's all for the purpose of the story. But I don't want some vintage bike enthusiast to come say: 'Uh, uh, that was a Suzuki on the Triumph'.

3 – *music*

The so-called punk/No Wave scene of the Lower East Side was impor-tant in your first years in New York. I read in an interview you did in Buenos Aires in 2001 that, I quote:

> If the Ramones had not existed, I would not have made any film . . .
> They took me to believe, around 1979, that I was able to make my
> films . . . Rock in the 1970s was recitals on enormous stages with a
> group of dinosaurs playing interminable guitar solos. Punk eliminated
> that and remained with the essence of rock, something similar to what
> independent cinema did with cinema in general.

I noticed that in the DJ culture of today, especially in the hip hop culture, in a way something similar is happening. Quite a while ago I was at a screening organized by DJ Spooky here in New York. It was a music documentary entitled *Mutiny: Asians Storm British Music*, by Vivek Bald.

Ah, I saw that.

You did?

Yes, 'cause I know Spooky and he invited me to a screening. Wow, it was a few years ago.

Exactly. So we both saw it.

Yeah that's interesting.

Quite a coincidence. Anyway, in the film there were a lot of bands – Fundamental, Asian Dub Foundation, Talvin Singh – and one of the Asian Dub Foundation members said something like: 'The moment that I understood that it wasn't necessary to be actually able to play an instrument to make music my life changed. I was finally *able*.' Obviously the Ramones are not Asian Dub Foundation or the Wu-Tang Clan, but do you think there is something in common? And did you consider yourself 'punk' when you first started making films?

Well, I don't know exactly what the label means but I definitely was inspired by that music scene for the reasons that you read in the quote. It was almost like the musical equivalent of what Dogme 95 proposed in the mid-1990s: stripping everything down to what is essential; and whatever you call it, that punk rock scene was doing that. So, in the same way as the guy from Asian Dub Foundation said, people were not so concerned with being virtuoso musicians, but they wanted to say something, to express something. And that affected me very deeply in terms of filmmaking. The group of people around the New Cinema, Amos [Poe], Eric Mitchell, Vivienne Dick, James Nares and all of those people were just making films because they wanted to use the form. That was really happening all around me. Hip hop culture was starting at the same time, with DJ Kool Herc in the late 1970s. He brought sound systems to the Bronx from Jamaica, where his parents came from. So that was a very similar thing: we don't need to be professionals and we don't need to have managers and recording contracts. We can make music out in the park! That comes really directly from Jamaican sound systems, so all those things interconnected also with so-called punk rock and graffiti. Graffiti artists weren't trying to put their names in a museum. They wanted them on a train that would go all through the city and maybe they'd meet more girls that way. The same way as musicians. That may be more important in a certain way of inspiration, all those things happened at the same time

and there was a period in the early 1980s where all those scenes
converged: you could hang out with graffiti artists and hip hop people
and punk rockers all together. Now it seems to have segregated itself
back out again. At the time I knew all those people, plus Fab 5 Freddy,
Rammellzee and Futura 2000.

Can you tell me something more about Rammellzee?

Yeah, well he's a strange genius who lives in his own world and just is
a really amazing mind and artist, but completely outside of any kind of
mainstream. Rammellzee started a lot of hip hop slang that now is used
all over the world, like using the word 'word', I think Rammellzee
started that. Saying 'word', 'cause he was reducing everything using a
word, which was the word 'word'. It's really fascinating and it spread
all over – I mean, it's sort of passé now, but it entered the language.
And other things of Rammellzee's just infected a lot of people, but he's
very strange, he never really tried to do anything for real commercial
reasons, so he remains really underground. He's a kind of heroic figure
to me still. [Rammellzee died on 27 June 2010, aged 49.]

And the word 'word' brings us back to language again . . .

Yeah, and reducing everything to the most simple thing like that is really
incredible. The word 'word' can mean so many things, depending on
how you say it. When someone says 'word?' like 'I agree' or 'I don't
understand', but it's just one word! Anyway, Rammellzee has always
connected a lot of things from the past and the future together in his
work. He has this theory of 'neo-Gothic Panzerism' and he makes these
robot models and puppets that take inspiration from ancient samurai
armour and from futuristic robots and he's always mixing all these
things together. His imagination is so wild and unrestricted and yet he's
interested in form, there is something formal about him also, he's a very
rare inspiration. But, you know, there are a lot of geniuses in hip hop
culture and graffiti culture. One of my favourite graffiti artists of the
twentieth century is PHASE 2, but there were so many, like Dondi [White]
and so many other brilliant graffiti writers.

I love that they call themselves *writers* too, which is interesting.
But I love all these things because they all were swirling around and
they weren't based on trying to get rich or famous, or maybe famous
by putting your name on a train, famous to that culture, but not famous
in the mainstream culture.

I was always thinking about the *sound* of words but actually in that sense we're also really talking about the *shape* and the *form*, as well as the *movement* of words.

Yeah, exactly. That's another variation. Having a word travel around on a train all over the city rather than an image, that's interesting too.

And then that word obviously produces a sound as well, and the circle keeps rolling.

Yeah, it's all connected. But going back to music, it annoys me too in films. I hate it when they use it to emotionally cue the audience and the more Hollywood films I watch the more it sounds like they just all used the same score. It isn't the same, but it might as well be. The world of music is so varied, why is it so limited in film scores? I really don't understand that, when you could get music from anywhere!

Can you tell me something about the score for *Broken Flowers*?

Well, there isn't really a score, it's all pre-existing music, most of it comes from Mulatu Astatke from Ethiopia. That's music that I discovered just as a lover of music, maybe six or seven years ago. I started collecting all the recordings I could find by Mulatu Astatke and that led me to other Ethiopian pop music and traditional music and, I don't know, I just wanted to get it in the film somehow. It seemed like I didn't know quite how to get it in but then I decided to make Jeffrey Wright's character of Ethiopian origin so that there would be some connection to this weird Ethiopian funk music from the late 1960s in a film that takes place in American suburbs now. I found one way to connect it and I wove it into the film.

It works very well.

I hope so. It's hard for me to see because I'm too close. I heard the music so much before that I never really quite know how those things work, but I love having music as part of the fabric of the film. Sometimes it even becomes a character in the film, for example, I think of Neil Young's score for *Dead Man* almost as being another character in the movie. Or in a different way when RZA made music for *Ghost Dog* that music became like landscape to me. I always thought of RZA's music as very atmospheric and creating this incredible backdrop for the vocals to lay over. I just love his musicality, it is really unusual, but you know it's always different. I've been so lucky to work with Neil and RZA and Tom Waits and John Lurie and the musicians that John brought, Naná Vasconcelos and Marc Ribot, just incredible people.

In your films sometimes music is really like another character. As a viewer/ listener I don't feel that you are telling me – like in most Hollywood films – 'Now, feel sad. Now, be happy.'

Right. I know. It's so lazy and condescending. So I try to avoid it.

You leave a lot of space to silence, which is really important, too. We're not always talking, there is not always a dialogue going on, there is not always music.

Yeah. I love trains in the middle of the night, when you hear it in the distance, it sounds so haunting and beautiful to me. I love hearing trains at night far away . . .

Have you travelled a lot on trains?

I have travelled on trains yeah, not a lot but I've taken some train trips. I love the sound of the train moving too, but it also makes me sleepy, there is something very lulling about it.

The opening scene in *Dead Man* is Blake's train ride. You combined the sound of the train moving on his close-ups and Neil Young's guitar when you cut to the rods of the train.

Yeah. We also threw some sounds in there that no one will ever hear: there's even a little bit of Jimi Hendrix mixed into the wheels of the train! But it's mixed so far back and distorted that you would never recognize it. I love doing that too, mixing ten sounds together so that you don't notice that they're made of different elements. Sometimes that can be really beautiful as long as it's not overdone or it doesn't pop out. Something to feel and not notice, almost subliminally.

Are you throwing in subliminal messages?

Sometimes, occasionally . . . Quite a few actually mixed in *Dead Man*. There's a great one no one will ever hear except me and the sound editor that I put in: there's a bar scene in *Dead Man* and I don't know if you're familiar with the old Popeye cartoons? It was a cartoon developed by Max and Dave Fleischer, who did all the Betty Boop cartoons . . .

Sure. I was a big fan of Betty Boop when I was small, even now actually.

Me too. Well, there's a character in Popeye named Wimpy who was always saying 'I will gladly pay you Tuesday for a hamburger today', and we mixed that into the bar, where there's a lot of people talking, but no one will ever, ever find it. It is just for my own amusement, I wanted to get Wimpy in there. There's a part where I can hear it but no one would ever hear it.

Actually, talking about these 'hidden sounds' and little bits of music: in *Permanent Vacation*, when Allie is in the cinema, we hear Morricone in the distance, the famous melody from *The Good, the Bad and the Ugly*, isn't it?

Yeah, that's right.

But it's not the film that is showing there.

Well, but maybe it's a double bill and we only see the poster of the other one . . . I've tried to rationalize that! (Laughs)

Okay.

That was a beautiful thing that opened a lot of people up when Morricone worked with Leone. They would use the music in conjunction with things happening, like *The Good, the Bad and the Ugly* they're shooting a hat that's in the air and the music cues are mixed together, it all becomes one thing. Of course, Morricone has done so many amazing things for all kinds of different films. He finds these beautiful textures. Another great master of scores is Toru Takemitsu, who worked a lot with Kurosawa. He is also the great classical modernist composer of Japan, but he died some years ago. I knew him and he was also very interested in mycology, and he learned from John Cage . . . I'm an amateur mycologist myself.

Isn't a mushroom the biggest living organism?

Yeah, the largest living organism on earth is a mushroom. Because the caps that we see on the ground are not a single organism, they're connected to mycelium underground and the mycelium is the organism. There is a large one in Michigan. The diameter is something like 60 miles, it's a honey mushroom. I forget the Latin name . . . I think it's called *Armillaria mellea*, but anyway it's the largest organism. The DNA of mushrooms is much closer to animal DNA than to plants', although they are neither . . . they are very strange.

But going back to music just one thing. Films are structurally like music because they move before you at their own speed, their own pace, like a piece of music, that's very different than reading a book or looking at a painting, so there's this big connection already with music and cinema, they're related just in movement.

Do you know that book by Tarkovsky, *Sculpting in Time?*

I never read that book but I'm a big fan of Tarkovsky.

He says that the director is a 'sculptor of time', somebody who basically carves away the time that is superfluous, whose job is to look for the right quality of time when making a film. I think the same can apply to music.

Exactly, they're all intimately connected from the beginning.

One last thing I wanted to ask you, that brings us back to the musicality of language. When I spoke with Luc Sante he told me there is a word in Italian that you all loved when you were first going to Italy: *Mitragliatrice!*

Mitragliatrice! Yeah, I wrote one poem in Italian just to amuse Roberto [Benigni], something like:

> *Attenzione ragazze*
> *Tre belle attrici*
> *Con mitragliatrici*
> *Io muoio*
> *Senza accappatoio*[2]

'Jim you are a poet in Italian!' He liked it. *Accappatoio* sounds Japanese to me. I love that word.

You know what it means, right?

Yeah. *Io muoio senza accappatoio*, I die wearing no bathrobe.

New York, February 2006

References

Introduction

1 Lindzee Smith, 'Men Looking at Other Men', *Bomb Magazine*, 2 (Winter 1982). The article is available at www.bombsite.com, accessed 12 September 2014.
2 Alex Simon, 'Jim Jarmusch: Ghost Story', *Venice Magazine* (March 2000). During the months spent in Berlin, thanks to a DAAD scholarship, Jarmusch came up with the initial idea for *Mystery Train* (1989). The interview is available at www.thehollywoodinterview.blogspot.de.
3 See Jarmusch's public interview with critic Geoff Andrew held on 15 November 1999 during the 43rd London Film Festival, and partly published in *The Guardian*: www.guardian.co.uk. The complete interview is published in Ludvig Hertzberg, ed., *Jim Jarmusch Interviews* (Jackson, MS, 2001), pp. 176–96.
4 To which one can add a handful of shorts and the documentary *Year of the Horse* (1997).
5 I am thinking of directors like Hal Hartley, Richard Linklater, Sofia Coppola and Kevin Smith. In the same press conference German producer Reinhard Brundig (Pandora Film) specified that *Only Lovers Left Alive* was financed thanks to a European co-production between Germany, the United Kingdom (Jeremy Thomas came on board in 2010), France and Cyprus. Jarmusch had to surrender the rights of the film, which is the first feature film of his career (with the exception of the documentary *Year of the Horse*) for which he does not own the negative.
6 Jim Jarmusch (April 1989), from the CD booklet of *Mystery Train*, a film by Jim Jarmusch, music by John Lurie (Barking Lady Music, 1989).
7 *Sex, Lies and Videotape*, produced by Outlaw and distributed by the Weinstein brothers' Miramax, with a budget of just over $1 million, grossed about $25 million at the U.S. box office alone. Many Hollywood executives started to think that such high profits would be the norm from

then on and began the hunt for new 'indie hits', especially at festivals like Sundance and its European counterparts. They succeeded with films like Kevin Smith's *Clerks* (1994) and Quentin Tarantino's *Pulp Fiction* (1994), but basically killed off the original spirit of the indie phenomenon.

8　Umberto Mosca, *Jim Jarmusch*, 1st updated edn (Milan, 2006), p. 68; Jonathan Rosenbaum, *Dead Man* (London, 2000), p. 14; and Juan A. Suárez, *Jim Jarmusch* (Urbana and Chicago, IL, 2007), p. 72. The plot of Jarmusch's *Dead Man* (1995) has many similarities with Wurlitzer's unpublished script *Zebulon*, from the name of the protagonist Zebulon Shook. Wurlitzer wrote it in the 1970s for Sam Pekinpah, who died before they could shoot the film. More than ten years on from the release of *Dead Man*, Wurlitzer finally published his version of the story as a novel: *The Drop Edge of Yonder* (New York, 2008). See Joe O'Brien, 'On the Drift: Rudy Wurlitzer and the Road to Nowhere', *Arthur*, 29 (May 2008); also available online at www.arthurmag.com.

9　Bob Fisher, 'Cinematography in Black and White: Frederick Elmes on Jim Jarmusch's *Coffee and Cigarettes*', *MovieMaker* (3 February 2007). The article is also available online at www.moviemaker.com.

10　From Jarmusch's interview with Geoff Andrew on 15 November 1999, 43rd London Film Festival, partly published in *The Guardian*, reproduced in Hertzberg, ed., *Jim Jarmusch Interviews*, p. 184.

11　Roman Mauer, *Jim Jarmusch: Filme zum anderen Amerika* (Mainz, 2006), pp. 184–5.

12　The film grossed a little more than $1 million in the United States, with an estimated budget of roughly $9 million. Jonathan Rosenbaum, 'Acid Western', *Chicago Reader* (27 June 1996). The article is available online: www.chicagoreader.com.

13　The film was backed by Pandora Filmproduktion of Cologne and JVC Entertainment Networks of Tokyo. The version presented at Cannes ran for 134 minutes. Jarmusch re-edited the film for its theatrical release, reducing it to 121 minutes. On the *Dead Man* distribution controversy, see Andrew Pulver, 'Indie Reservation', *The Guardian* (31 March 2000). The article is available online: www.guardian.co.uk.

14　Larry Johnson met Young during the time of Woodstock in 1969 and collaborated with him for several decades until his death on 21 January 2010. He produced or co-produced numerous films on Young including *Rust Never Sleeps* (1978), *Neil Young: Silver and Gold* (2000), *Greendale* (2003). He ran Shakey Pictures (the name taken from Bernard Shakey, Neil Young's pseudonym).The track for which Jarmusch shot a video is *Big Time*. The album *Broken Arrow* was released in 1996 on Reprise Records.

15　Marjorie Baumgarten, 'Like a Hurricane', *Austin Chronicle* (10 November 1997). The interview was reprinted in Hertzberg, ed., *Jim Jarmusch Interviews*, p. 167.

16 It grossed almost $14 million in the United States alone, and a little less than $33 million in the rest of the world.

17 Elmes worked with Jarmusch on *Night On Earth*, *Coffee and Cigarettes* and *Broken Flowers*. In the interview 'A Sad and Beautiful World' for *Cinema Gotham* (22 November 2002), Jarmusch mentioned *La Ricotta* (1963), the Pasolini episode for *Ro.Go.Pa.G*, as a source of inspiration for *Ten Minutes Older*. The protagonist Stracci (Mario Cipriani) is an extra on the set of a film about the Passion of Christ. During the break he takes his lunchbox back to his family to feed them. In Jarmusch's short the 'plot' is far more spartan and during the break the actress does little more than talk on her mobile phone inside her trailer.

18 Geoffrey Macnab, 'Swinton, Fassbender and Wasikowska Line Up for Jarmusch's Vampire Story', *Screendaily* (16 May 2011).

19 Logan Hill, 'No Limits: The Exotic Stylings of Jim Jarmusch's Latest Film: A Cultural Primer', *New York Magazine* (26 April 2009).

20 Doyle has photographed most of Wong Kar-wai's films, from *Days of Being Wild* (1991) to *2046* (2004), and at the Cannes Film Festival in 2000 was awarded Best Photography for *In the Mood for Love*.

21 In the United States the film grossed a little over $400,000. The total gross including the foreign market did not reach $2 million.

22 Transcript of the press conference following the premiere of *Only Lovers Left Alive* at the Cannes Film Festival, 25 May 2013.

23 Yann Lardeau, 'Un pont entre New York et l'Europe: entretien avec Jim Jarmusch', *Cahiers du Cinéma*, 366 (December 1984), p. 33.

24 Francesco Casetti and Federico Di Chio, *Analisi del Film* (Milan, 1998), p. 267.

25 Michel Chion, *Audio Vision: Sound on Screen* (New York, 1994), p. 179.

26 Amy Thiltges, 'The Semiotics of Alienation and Emptiness in the Films of Jim Jarmusch', *Organdy Quarterly*, 5 (December 2002), and Markus Widmer, *What Makes the Films of David Lynch and Jim Jarmusch Postmodern?* (Aberdeen, 1998), p. 4. 'The second aspect of Jarmusch's work which is evidently postmodern is the recurring theme of cultural identity, alienation and displacement.'

1 Flashback: New York Stories

1 Amos Poe is referring to the song 'Smalltown' by Lou Reed and John Cale, from the album *Songs for Drella* (Sire, 1990).

2 Transcript from Céline Danhier's documentary *Blank City* (2010).

3 Ibid. See also Tom Jarmusch's article 'Scotch and Kodak; After Hours: A Look at Rafic' in Clayton Patterson, ed., *Captured: A Film/Video History of the Lower East Side* (New York, 2005), p. 121.

4 Except for Shirley Clarke, none of the filmmakers Jarmusch mentioned
   was born in New York.

5 Jarmusch was born in Akron, Ohio, on 22 January 1953 and grew up in
   Silver Lake, a small residential community of fewer than 3,000 people,
   close to Cuyahoga Falls, near Akron.

6 *The Velvet Underground, Live at Max's Kansas City* was released in 1972
   on Rhino Records. The album saw the light of day thanks to the hard
   work of unshakeable fan and Warhol superstar Brigid Polk who, on 23
   August 1970, decided to immortalize the concert with her portable tape
   recorder. Her one-and-a-half-hour tape represented the heart of the
   record, arguably one of the first authorized bootleg albums in music
   history.

7 Rosma Scuteri, *New York Anni Ottanta: l'arte in presa diretta* (Rome,
   1999), pp. 8 and 10.

8 The film was shot between 1981 and 1982 but not released until the
   following year.

9 *Unmade Beds* (1976) and *The Foreigner* (1978) by Amos Poe; *Rome '78*
   (1978) by James Nares; *Underground USA* (1980) by Eric Mitchell. A vivid
   account of the graffiti scene of the period can be found in Patti Astor's
   self-published memoir, *The FUN Gallery . . . The True Story* (2012), see
   www.thefungallery.com.

10 As documented in *Style Wars* (1983), the classic film on graffiti writing by
   Tony Silver and co-produced by Henry Chalfont, in which a very young
   Dondi appears.

11 Transcript from Danhier's *Blank City*.

12 As Jarmusch said at a public event at the Museum of the Moving Image
   in New York on 23 April 2009. A podcast of the event is available online:
   www.movingimagesource.us/dialogues/all.

13 Renato de Maria, 'Lampi dalla No Wave', in Franco Bolelli and Riccardo
   Bertoncelli, *Almanacco Musica*, 2 (Winter 1979), p. 65.

14 Harris Smith, 'No New Cinema: Punk and No Wave Underground Film,
   1976–1984', in *Captured*, ed. Patterson, p. 173.

15 Transcript from Danhier's *Blank City*.

16 Ibid.

17 Jim Jarmusch, 'Jarmusch's Guilty Pleasures', *Film Comment*, XXVIII/3
   (May–June 1992), p. 35.

18 I interviewed Amos Poe in New York in December 2003.

19 Guido Chiesa, *La New Wave: l'ultimo cinema newyorkese* (Turin, 1985),
   p. 11.

20 Michel Chion, *Audio-Vision: Sound on Screen* (New York, 1994), p. xxvi.

21 Apart from Eric Mitchell, it also included Patti Astor, the artist Duncan
   Hannah and Debbie Harry.

22 I interviewed James Nares in New York in March 2005.

23 Produced by the bbc, the thirteen-part series was broadcast in the United States by pbs.

24 Lydia Lunch appeared in *The Black Box* (1978), *The Offenders* (1979; its cast also included musicians like John and Evan Lurie, shown between one concert and another at Max's Kansas City), *The Trap Door* (1980) and *Vortex* (1982), B's first feature film in 16mm.

25 Beth B. was among the guests of the Festival 'Life is Live # 6: Contort Yourself. Musik, Film und Performance im New York der Postpunk Ära' curated by Christian Höller and Christoph Gurk (Hau Theater, Berlin, 4–5 June 2011).

26 The cast of *Kidnapped* included Mitchell himself, Patti Astor and Anya Phillips. Mudd Club co-founder Steve Mass played the businessman. Mitchell used period music, such as Devo's hit cover of 'Satisfaction'.

27 The body of Sid Vicious's girlfriend Nancy Spungen had been found at the Chelsea Hotel not long before, on 12 October 1978.

28 Marc Masters, *No Wave* (London, 2007), p. 150.

29 A. O. Scott, 'That '80s Moment When Nothing and (Almost) Everything Mattered', *New York Times* (5 April 2011).

30 In 2012 the Hunter College Art Galleries in New York presented the *Times Square Show Revisited*, an in-depth look at the landmark 1980 exhibition organized by Colab. More information can be found online: www.timessquareshowrevisited.com.

31 Cassandra Stark, 'The Jim Jarmusch Interview', *Underground Film Bulletin*, 4 (September 1985), pp. 12–21. The *Bulletin* issues 1 to 9 were self-published by Orion Jeriko, also known as Nick Zedd (among other aliases), from 1984 to 1990 in New York. Stark's interview can now be found in Ludvig Hertzberg, ed., *Jim Jarmusch Interviews* (Jackson, ms, 2001), p. 48; Jonatan Rosenbaum, public interview with Jim Jarmusch at the Walker Art Center, Minneapolis, 4 February 1994, in *Jim Jarmusch Interviews*, ed. Hertzberg, p. 113.

32 Vera Dika, *The (Moving) Pictures Generation* (New York, 2012), p. 98.

33 Masters, *No Wave*; the quote can also be found online as Marc Masters, 'no! The Origins of No Wave', www.pitchfork.com, 15 January 2008.

34 Ralph Aue and Wolfgang Stukenbrock interviewed Jarmusch in 1980 and 1981 in Mannheim and Berlin. The compiled text of the interviews is now published in *Jim Jarmusch Interviews*, ed. Hertzberg, pp. 3–11. This quote is on p. 6.

35 Peter Belsito, ed., *Notes from the Pop Underground* (Berkeley, ca, 1985), p. 70.

2 Jarmusch, The Musician

1 Allie Parker finds inspiration not only from his music idol Charlie Parker, and bebop, but also conjures up another rebel icon – James Dean, who utters the same words in Nicholas Ray's *Knock on Any Door* (1949).

2 Ira A. Robbins, ed., *The Trouser Press Record Guide: The Ultimate Guide to Alternative Music*, 4th edn (December 1991), p. 180.

3 'Girl's Imagination' had a second life featuring in two different compilations released respectively in 1999 and 2001: *Pspyched!* ('Spiked') on the British label Beggars Banquet, and *Anti NY* on Gomma from Munich. The song 'My Hands are Yellow (From the Job that I Do)', from the debut EP, was re-released by British label Soul Jazz on the excellent compilation *New York Noise, Vol. 2* (2005).

4 I interviewed Phil Kline and Luc Sante in New York in December 2003.

5 Jarmusch's quote comes from the documentary *'Eskimo Lounge Music': Del Byzanteens Live at Hurrah* by Merrill Aldighieri (1980–2008), produced independently by the director and purchasable on her website, www.artclips.free.fr.

6 The interview is no longer available online.

7 Richard K. Ferncase, *Outsider Features: American Independent Films of the 1980s* (Westport, CT, and London, 1996), p. 6.

8 Ronnie Pede, '*Stranger Than Paradise*/Speurtocht naar een identiteit', *Film en Televisie*, 329 (October, 1984), p. 16.

9 Chris Campion, 'East Meets West', in *Jim Jarmusch Interviews*, ed. Ludvig Hertzberg (Jackson, MS, 2001), p. 202.

10 Yann Lardeau, 'Un pont entre New York et l'Europe', *Cahiers du Cinéma*, 366 (December 1984), p. 32.

11 Nicholas Saada, 'Entretien avec Jim Jarmusch', *Cahiers du Cinéma*, 498 (January 1996), p. 29. More recently, at the public event held at Rome's Auditorium, Parco della Musica, on 6 May 2007, during the Viaggio nel Cinema Americano series of interviews with American directors, programmed and hosted by Antonio Monda and Mario Sesti, Jarmusch confirmed the importance of Ray's lesson and how indispensable it is to work with actors separately on a determined scene, because each actor will look at it differently, and so it would be 'pointless and misguiding' to explain the scene collectively.

12 Peter Belsito, ed., *Notes from the Pop Underground* (Berkeley, CA, 1985), p. 59.

13 See the 'Wim and Music' section at www.wim-wenders.com. Actually, Wenders himself attributed the same quote to the Velvet Underground. Wim Wenders, *Stanotte vorrei parlare con l'angelo: scritti, 1968–1988*, 3rd edn (Milan, 1991), p. 183.

14 The boat was found by young production assistant Jarmusch, his presence
    on set especially requested by Ray.
15 Joyce Roodnat, 'Jim's grijze kinderen: Portret van de regisseur van
    Stranger Than Paradise', *Skoop*, XXI/1 (February 1985), p. 35.
16 I interviewed John Lurie in New York in March 2005.
17 See Sara Driver interview in Céline Danhier's documentary, *Blank City*
    (2010).
18 Wim Wenders, 'Der Mann an der Moviola', in Rolf Aurich and Stefan
    Reineke, eds, *Jim Jarmusch* (Berlin, 2001), p. 8.
19 Domenico De Gaetano, *Emozione e ragione: il cinema di Guido Chiesa*
    (Turin, 2000), p. 25.
20 Ibid.
21 The schedule of upcoming Unsilent Night events in New York and around
    the world can be found at www.unsilentnight.com.
22 Luc Sante, *Low Life: Lures and Snares of Old New York* (New York, 1991).
23 The full text of the lyrics of 'Lies to Live By':

    I found out the truth the hard way
    I got mistaken for an ashtray
    The truth will out and out it threw me
    Now I'm a mystery to those who knew me

    Truth is ashes – lies are golden
    Lies are clean when the truth is holding
    The truth's a wound but a lie's the gun
    Truth's the blues but lies have fun

    If you believe your own inventions
    Then others won't judge your intentions
    But if you want the power and the glory
    Just make up a seductive story

    If I only have one life
    Let me live it as a lie

24 I interviewed Luc Sante in December 2003.
25 Philippe Hagen's quote comes from the documentary *Eskimo Lounge
    Music* (2011) by Merrill Aldighieri.
26 See Phil Kline interview.
27 *Circus Mort*, released on Labor Records in 1981.
28 The title of Danhier's film is an obvious allusion to *Blank Generation*,
    the Amos Poe film inspired by the song/manifesto by Richard Hell and
    the Voidoids. Director, actor, writer, painter, underground icon – Nick

Zedd was the author of the *Cinema of Transgression Manifesto*
published anonymously in 1985 and editor of *Underground Film
Bulletin* (1984–90). Among his films are *The Wild World of Lydia
Lunch* (1983), *Police State* (1987), *War is Menstrual Envy* (1992), *Tom
Thumb in the Land of the Giants* (1999), and *I was a Quality of Life
Violation* (2004). He directed *The Adventures of Electra Elf and Fluffer*
(2002–8), a low-cost sci-fi satire starring Reverend Jen and featuring
the 'flying' Chihuahua Reverend Jen Jr. In March 2011 he relocated to
Mexico City and in 2013 published *The Extremist Manifesto*. He is much
admired by Jarmusch, who in 1996 said of him: 'Nick Zedd's films are
legendary. He is a truly seminal figure in the New York underground.
Now we have his first book [*Totem of the Depraved*] and I recommend
it to anyone interested in the rough underside of our overly processed
culture.'

29 I interviewed Céline Danhier during the 60th Berlinale, where *Blank City*
premiered in February 2010.

30 Andy Beta, 'James Chance', www.pitchfork.com, 1 April 2003. The
Contortions' first gig was at Max's Kansas City in December 1979.

31 DNA was one of the four bands chosen by Brian Eno for the celebrated *No
New York* compilation released on Antilles records in 1979. Shortly after
the recording, Crutchfield left the band. The line-up thereafter was Arto
Lindsay (guitar), Ikue Mori (drums) and Tim Wright (bass). They decided
to dissolve DNA in 1982.

32 Robin Crutchfield, 'Darker Days as I Recall Them', www.nowave.pair.com,
June 2001.

33 The compilation *New York Noise: Dance Music from the New York
Underground, 1978–1982*, released by the British label Soul Jazz Records
in 2003, is a must-listen for those who want to deepen their knowledge of
the period. Thanks to the success of volume 1, Soul Jazz Records quickly
released volume 2, in which Jarmusch and the Del-Byzanteens appear with
'My Hands are Yellow (From the Job that I Do)'. In 2006 volume 3 was
released; it includes a song by Robin Crutchfield's band Dark Day, 'Hands
in the Dark'.

34 On the radio show *Soundtrack*, aired on 13 August 2010 on New York's
WNYC.

35 My conversations with Morricone took place in Rome on 21 June 2001
and 8 January 2006.

36 At the time of shooting, Richard Edson was still the drummer
of Sonic Youth. He then left the band to join up with KONK who,
together with bands like Liquid Liquid, contributed to creating the
liaison between the 'No Wave/post punk' and 'disco-funk/proto-hip
hop' scenes, just to mention a few more labels, for whatever their
convolutions are worth.

37 Jarmusch chose to reset the rock star's masculinity and presented an effeminate Iggy Pop to the spectator, dressed as a woman and member of an improbable trio of criminals adrift on the prairie, as ferocious as they were freaky. The other members of the trio were Billy Bob Thornton as Big George Drakoulious and Jared Harris as Benmont Tench.

38 Jarmusch again collaborated with The White Stripes, signing the 'First Nations Remix' of their piece 'Blue Orchid' on xl Recordings and Third Man Records (2005). Michel Gondry signed the vinyl flip side 'Michel Gondry Remix'. As he told me before its release, in 2006 Jarmusch also shot the video for 'Steady As She Goes', the first piece by The Raconteurs, the group that Jack White formed with Brendan Benson, Jack Lawrence and Patrick Keeler. The White Stripes broke up in 2011, after an almost fifteen-year-long career.

39 The tracks by Bad Rabbit on the cd of the original soundtrack of *The Limits of Control*, released on Lakeshore Records on 28 April 2009, are: 'Intro', 'Sea Green Sea', 'Dawn'; the tracks on the Bad Rabbit ep, released on 12 May 2009, referred to by Jarmusch, are 'Dusk' and 'Blue Green Sea'.

40 Transcript of the interview with Moby for wnyc already quoted.

41 Logan Hill, 'No Limits: The Exotic Stylings of Jim Jarmusch's Latest Film: A Cultural Primer', www.nymag.com, 26 April 2009.

42 The character of the girl, in the film simply called Nude (Paz de la Huerta), is herself a literal reference to the character of Mami Hanada (Mariko Ogawa) in the surreal and anarchic cult gangster movie *Branded To Kill* (1967) by Seijun Suzuki. The film – a flop that provoked the immediate dismissal of its visionary director by the Nikkatsu studios – was also openly referred to by Jarmusch in *Ghost Dog: The Way of the Samurai* (1999) in the sequence in which the mafia boss Sonny Valerio (Cliff Gorman) is killed by a bullet in the forehead, shot upwards through the drain of the bathroom sink.

43 Hill, 'No Limits'.

44 John Schafer, 'New Sounds: Jozef van Wissem and Jim Jarmusch', Episode 3256, www.wnyc.org, 11 October 2011.

45 The first was released on Important Records (28 February 2012), the second, which also includes the voice of Tilda Swinton on the track 'More She Burns the More Beautiful She Glows', was released on Sacred Bones (13 November 2012).

46 The track is called 'Concerning the Beautiful Human Form after Death'.

47 Jozef van Wissem, *It is Time for You to Return*, released on Crammed Discs on 11 November 2014. Lebanese vocalist and songwriter Yasmine Hamdan, who also performed in *Only Lovers Left Alive*, is featured on the same track as Jarmusch.

48 The concert, part of the Open House and Sunday Sessions at ps1 in New York, was held on 18 November 2012.

49 Greg Eggebeen, 'Jim Jarmusch Taught Me All About Sunglasses Etiquette'. The article was released online on Noisey-Music by *Vice* (18 November 2012): http://noisey.vice.com/blog.

50 The hideout/recording studio indoor scenes were filmed in Cologne.

51 Guitarist Marc Ribot told me about the Chet Atkins in Berlin in October 2013, adding that the early Gibson 'is of course an early folk/country music classic but was also, with a pick-up added, the set-up that I believe Bruce Langhorne used on some great early Dylan stuff'.

52 Clint Holloway, 'Jim Jarmusch and Tilda Swinton on *Only Lovers Left Alive*, Creating their Own Vampire Mythology and Why Hollywood Film Music is Boring', www.indiewire.com, 11 October 2013.

53 Tesla's city of birth, Smiljan, is now in Croatia. The inventor's nationality is often grounds for argument between Serbia and Croatia. At the time of his birth in 1856 the city was part of the Austro-Hungarian empire, and in 1897 he became an American citizen. In spite of his numerous achievements and awards, Tesla died in neglect in 1943 at the Hotel New Yorker, where he had spent the last years of his life.

54 Information on the project is available at www.operaprojects.org.

55 Alexandra Wolfe, 'Theater Director Robert Wilson on Nikola Tesla's Elegance', *Wall Street Journal* (25 July 2014). Asked about his current obsessions, Wilson answered: 'Nikola Tesla. I'm making an opera about his work with Jim Jarmusch and Phil Kline. I have been fascinated by Tesla since I was a student – his ideas about electricity and light and the elegance in his dress.'

56 Alan Licht, 'Invisible Jukebox: Jim Jarmusch', *The Wire*, 309 (November 2009).

Voices: John Lurie

1 This is how Steve Piccolo, with whom I spoke in Berlin in 2005, recalls the genesis of The Lounge Lizards: 'This is the real story although at this point it sounds like a legend or myth but it's true: John was at Hurrah's standing at the bar talking with Jim Fourrat, the owner. I don't know who was playing on stage, I think a Rockabilly band of some kind. John said to Fourrat: "This is awful I hate it", and Fourrat said: "Well you can't do any better . . . ?", or something like that, and John bet him $100 that in a week we'll do something. Fourrat said: "Okay, you're on." So in a week we had to put together a band.'

2 *The Family of Man* (1955) by Edward Steichen struck a chord with the collective imagination. The more than 500 photographs were selected from roughly 2 million, taken by 273 photographers, professional and amateur, from 68 countries, and exhibited for the first time at MOMA, New York, on 24 January 1955. Entered in UNESCO's Memory of the

World register in 2003, it is now on permanent display at Clervaux Castle, Luxembourg. See www.steichencollections.lu.

3 John Lurie, Gamelan and Minimal Music

1 Marc Ribot was guitarist with The Lounge Lizards between 1984 and 1989. He also played guitar, banjo and trumpet on the original score of *Down By Law*, guitar and banjo on *Mystery Train*. I interviewed him in New York in December 2003.

2 Erik Sanko played bass with The Lounge Lizards between 1984 and 2000. He collaborated again with Lurie on the music for his *Fishing with John* TV series (1991) and for *Get Shorty* (1995) by Barry Sonnenfeld. I interviewed him in January 2006.

3 Andrey Tarkovsky, *Sculpting in Time: Reflections on the Cinema*, translated from the Russian by Kitty Hunter-Blair, 12th printing (Austin, TX, 2010), pp. 113 and 117.

4 I think of composers like Terry Riley, Steve Reich, Philip Glass.

5 From 'Minimal Music', in Alberto Basso, *Dizionario enciclopedico universale della musica e dei musicisti: il lessico*, vol. III (Turin, 1984), p. 145.

6 Actually, the Doppler effect causes a decrease in pitch and not an increase, as in the song's melodic line.

7 As Jarmusch said at the Pinewood Dialogues public event at the Museum of the Moving Image in New York on 23 April 2009: 'Richard Hell and the Voidoids wrote a song about him called "The Kid with the Replaceable Head".' It was issued on the album *Destiny Street* (Red Star Records, 1982). See www.movingimagesource.us/dialogues/all.

8 Ludvig Hertzberg, ed., *Jim Jarmusch Interviews* (Jackson, MS, 2001), p. 7.

9 David Toop, *Oceans of Sound* (London, 1995), chapter 1; and Juan A. Suárez, *Jim Jarmusch* (Urbana and Chicago, IL, 2007), p. 24.

10 Jarmusch's collaboration with Screamin' Jay Hawkins will be dealt with in the next chapter, in the section 'Bebop Meets Voodoo Jive'.

11 Jill B. Jaffe, viola; Mary L. Powell and Key Sterne, violins; Eugene Moye, cello.

12 Bartók's interest in ethnic music took him in 1913 to the Biskra Oasis in North Africa and, following his American exile in 1940, got him the chair in Ethnomusicology at New York's Columbia University.

13 Byrne, together with Ryuichi Sakamoto and Cong Su, won the Academy Award for the music of this popular film. With nine awards in all, including best film, direction and screenplay, the film confirmed Bertolucci's international success. Producer Jeremy Thomas did not rely on any major company to realize the ambitious project.

14 Jonathan Romney and Adrian Wootton, eds, *Celluloid Jukebox: Popular Music and the Movies since the 50s* (London, 1995), p. 129.

15 Ibid., p. 136.
16 Ibid.
17 See www.ejn.it/mus/lindsay.htm, accessed 22 April 2004.
18 *The Lounge Lizards* was released in 1981 on Editions EG.
19 In the 'Renée' episode.
20 Umberto Mosca, *Jim Jarmusch*, 1st updated edn (Milan, 2006), p. 48.
21 Roberto Benigni's real-life partner.
22 Jarmusch uses the same technique again in an almost identical way in the second episode, 'A Ghost', during the lateral tracking shot that shadows young Luisa (Nicoletta Braschi), whose husband has died suddenly, traipsing around Memphis.
23 It is enough to think of the entire opening sequence of *Down By Law* and its lateral tracking shots filmed from the car, or Eva's first walk in New York at the start of *Stranger Than Paradise*.
24 There are various reasons to explain this change, expressed very clearly by Lurie himself in the interview that opens this chapter.
25 John Lurie, *A Fine Example of Art* (New York, 2008), p. 155. *I am a Bear. You are an Asshole. God is God.* is the title of the work from 2005.

Voices: Marc Ribot

1 Rammellzee unfortunately passed away at age 49 on 27 June 2010.

4 Memphis Hip Hop, Mestizos and Samurai

1 Fred Jung, *My Conversation with Pharoah Sanders*, www.allaboutjazz.com, 15 October 2007.
2 For the quote 'switch on the soundtrack': Silvia Morini, 'La vision iperrealista, il paesaggio nel cinema di Jim Jarmusch', MA thesis, Sapienza University of Rome (1999). J. Hoberman, *Vulgar Modernism: Writing on Movies and Other Media* (Philadelphia, PA, 1991), p. 321.
3 Eva's referring to Hawkins (1929–2000) as a 'wild man' perhaps alludes to his memorable live shows, famous for their theatrics and eccentricity that made him a forerunner of so-called 'shock rock'. Apart from the extrovert clothing, from leopard skins to multicoloured leather outfits, he would usually appear onstage with a small skull, Henry, for which he would light a cigarette. He confessed to practising voodoo, and often began concerts by appearing from a coffin. When Jarmusch and Hawkins first met, the latter's career was not exactly flourishing. On the contrary, Hawkins was living in a trailer in New Jersey with no phone when Jarmusch came looking for him the first time. It is thanks to Jarmusch's use of 'I Put a Spell on You' and to the acting role as concierge in *Mystery Train* five years later that Hawkins was rediscovered.

4 Jeremy Clarke, 'Sixteen Coaches Long', *Films and Filming*, 422 (December 1989); and also Luc Sante, 'Mystery Man', *Interview* (November 1989), now in Ludvig Hertzberg, ed., *Jim Jarmusch Interviews* (Jackson, MS, 2001), p. 93.

5 Greil Marcus, *Mystery Train*, 5th edn (London, 2000), p. 193.

6 The name of Tom Waits's DJ role in *Stranger Than Paradise*.

7 Marcus, *Mystery Train*, p. xiv.

8 Jarmusch more recently paid tribute to Stax in a brief dialogue exchange between Adam and Eve during one of their car rides at night in *Only Lovers Left Alive*.

    Adam: Do you wanna see the Motown Museum? Although there's not much to look at from the outside . . .

    Eve: I'm more of a Stax girl myself.

9 Jim Jarmusch, 'My Golden Rules', *MovieMaker Magazine*, 53 (22 January 2004).

10 Katharina Dockhorn, 'Meine Filme haben keine besondere Botschaft: Gespräch mit *Ghost Dog* Regisseur Jim Jarmusch', *epd Film*, 2 (February 2000).

11 Jonathan Rosenbaum, 'Independence Day', *The Guardian* (27 August 2004).

12 Tod Lippy, 'Interview with Jim Jarmusch'; reprinted in Juan A. Suárez, *Jim Jarmusch* (Urbana and Chicago, IL, 2007), p. 169. In line with the hip hop approach, according to which the original and the copy are relative concepts, in 2000 a CD was released with the title: *Ghost Dog: The Way of the Samurai: The Album,* produced by RZA himself, featuring a series of artists affiliated to the Wu-Tang Clan that has little to do with the film's original score, released in 1999 by JVC, which has since become a rare and costly collector's item. Reading the online credits of the plagiarized 2000 version one discovers that it is simply 'inspired' by the film, probably to avoid legal matters, contrary to the legitimate CD's cover clearly stating 'Music from the motion picture'. See www.discogs.com.

13 Suárez, *Jim Jarmusch*, p. 127.

14 Nils Meyer, 'Ghost Dog: The Way of the Samurai (1999)', in Rolf Aurich and Stefan Reinecke, eds, *Jim Jarmusch* (Berlin, 2001), p. 262.

15 'Martha Cooper Interview', *Huck*, 7 (October 2007), available at www.huckmagazine.com. Perhaps her most famous book, published with Henry Chalfont, is *Subway Art* (London and New York, 1984).

16 Zephyr published Dondi's obituary and biography on 8 October 1998; it is available at www.graffiti.org, accessed 14 November 2014.

17 Rammellzee considered Dondi his mentor and had a small but incisive role in *Stranger Than Paradise* in a memorable scene with Eszter Balint. Unfortunately, he died on 27 June 2010, aged only 49.

18 It is possible that Jarmusch, an expert on French film, wanted to pay homage to one of the pioneers of technical experimentation in modern

cinema, Jean Vigo, who in 1930 had used a similar aerial shot to open his social documentary *A propos de Nice*. Vigo, who died of tuberculosis aged only 29, is greatly admired by cinephiles thanks also to *Zéro de conduite* (1933) and *L'Atalante* (1934).

19 As illustrated by Jarmusch during a public event held in Rome on 6 May 2007 at the Auditorium, Parco della Musica, for the 'Viaggio nel Cinema Americano' series of interviews with American directors, programmed and hosted by Antonio Monda and Mario Sesti.

20 Traditional composition arranged by Mulatu Astatke.

21 Focus Features was founded in 2002 from the merging of small independent production companies, usa Film, Universal Focus and Good Machine, and is today a division of Universal Pictures. Since Miramax, bought by Disney in 2005 and sold again in 2010, left the *auteur film* sector, Focus Features has enjoyed huge successes, such as Sofia Coppola's *Lost in Translation* (2003) and Ang Lee's *Brokeback Mountain* (2005).

22 Ann Powers, 'Tom Waits on Tour: Anything but Old Hat', *Los Angeles Times* (19 June 2008).

23 Quote from Neil Young's classic 'Cortez the Killer' on the 1975 album *Zuma*, which is based on the stories and legends of the conquest of Mexico during the first half of the sixteenth century. The song 'Pocahontas' released on the album *Rust Never Sleeps* (1979) gives an even more graphic idea of the violence of the massacres of Native tribes by European settlers; both albums were released on Reprise Records.

24 Sasha Frere-Jones, 'A Paler Shade of White', *New Yorker* (22 October 2007).

25 Klaus Walter, 'Alter Mann und weisser Neger: Strategisches Music Placement in den Filmen von Jim Jarmusch', in *Jim Jarmusch*, ed. Aurich and Reinecke, pp. 145–64; Norman Mailer, 'The White Negro: Superficial Reflections on the Hipster', *Dissent* (Fall 1957).

26 'At the start, Elvis sounded black to those who heard him; when they called him the Hillybilly Cat, they meant the White Negro'. Marcus, *Mystery Train*, p. 169.

27 Walter, 'Alter Mann und weisser Neger', p. 157.

28 Tom Breihan, 'Filmmaker Jim Jarmusch talks atp', *Pitchfork* (20 August 2010), www.pitchfork.com.

29 Chris Campion, 'East Meets West', *Dazed and Confused*, 64 (April 2000), reprinted in Hertzberg, ed., *Jim Jarmusch*, p. 207.

30 Jay S. Jacobs, *Wild Years: la vita e il mito di Tom Waits / Wild Years: The Music and the Myth of Tom Waits*, 1st Italian edn, trans. Alberto Nerazzini (Rome, 2004), pp. 172–3.

31 The co-production companies of *Down By Law* included Island Pictures, active from 1982 to 1998, as a subsidiary of Island Records.

32 Marc Ribot continued to collaborate with Waits for years, becoming one of the 'trademarks' of his sound. Other than *Rain Dogs* (1985), I would

like to mention *Frank's Wild Years* (1987), *Mule Variations* (1999), *Real Gone* (2004) and *Bad as Me* (2011).

33 The Sundance Film Festival website published a short account entitled *Jim Jarmusch On: The Music for Dead Man* in 1997. It is no longer available online.

34 Andrey Tarkovsky, *Sculpting in Time: Reflections on the Cinema*, translated from the Russian by Kitty Hunter-Blair, 12th printing (Austin, TX, 2010), p. 118.

35 Blake's journey has been defined in many ways: a 'definitive journey in which the only direction is death', Umberto Mosca, *Jim Jarmusch*, 1st updated edn (Milan, 2006), p. 93; 'the journey of a corpse', Suzanne Greuner, 'Dead Man', *epd Film*, XIII/1 (January, 1996); and 'close circuit journey, made up of "agglutinations" of characters who meet, shoot at each other and separate again' in the perceptive review by Marcello Garofalo, 'Dead Man', *Segnocinema*, 81 (September–October 1996), p. 93.

36 Silvia Bizio, Jim Jarmusch interview, 'Jarmusch cavalca nel lontano West', *La Repubblica* (30 April 1996), quoted by Garofalo in 'Dead Man', p. 93.

37 Among Jarmusch's future projects is another 'rockumentary' a musician friend asked him to shoot, Iggy Pop. This is how Jarmusch described it to *Rolling Stone* in 2010: 'It's something Iggy asked me to do because he knew I'm a huge fan of The Stooges, so he said: "Would you be interested in making a film particularly about The Stooges?" and I said: "Hell yes." So it's not an overview of Iggy Pop or his life or his career – of course The Stooges are so important in the history of music and certainly Iggy is the engine of it. We're going to work on it over a few years and try to make something visually interesting and not a cliché of a bunch of talking heads of old guys looking back. So we're gathering a lot of archival stuff and I have eight hours of Iggy on camera talking about everything that has anything to do with the Stooges.' At the 2014 Cannes Film Market, Jarmusch secured backing for the film which will be financed by New Element Global, Independent and ICM.

38 See interview with Young and Jarmusch included as special feature on the DVD version of the film.

39 As is underlined in the main credits, along with the recommendation to turn the volume up all the way before watching it.

40 See interview with Young and Jarmusch on the DVD.

41 Editor Jay Rabinowitz was nominated for an Eddie, for Best Edited Documentary Film, by American Cinema Editors (ACE).

Voices: Masatoshi Nagase

1 Jonatan Rosenbaum, public interview with Jim Jarmusch at the Walker Art Center, Minneapolis, 4 February 1994, printed in *Jim Jarmusch*

Interviews, ed. Ludvig Hertzberg (Jackson, MS, 2001), p. 125; Danny Plotnick, 'Jim Jarmusch Interview', *Village Noize*, VI/16, pp. 18–21, 48, reprinted in *Jim Jarmusch Interviews*, ed. Herzberg, p. 144; Geoff Andrew, public interview with Jim Jarmusch held on 15 November 1999 at the 43rd London Film Festival and partly published in *The Guardian*, printed in *Jim Jarmusch Interviews*, ed. Hertzberg, p. 185.

5 The Battle against Verbocentrism

1   Michel Chion, *Audio-Vision: Sound on Screen* (New York, 1994), pp. 5–6.
2   Ibid., p. 171.
3   Ibid., p. 177.
4   Geoffrey Macnab, 'Swinton, Fassbender and Wasikowska Line Up for Jarmusch's Vampire Story', *Screendaily* (16 May 2011).
5   The conversation took place in Berlin on 12 February 2005.
6   Chion, *Audio-Vision*, p. 180.
7   Umberto Mosca, *Jim Jarmusch*, 1st updated edn (Milan, 2006), p. 36.
8   The phone conversation with Gary Farmer took place on 10 December 2003.
9   Joshua Klein, 'Jim Jarmusch Interview', www.avclub.com, 15 March 2000. However, at the film's New York release a technical problem caused a glitch with the said subtitles, as Jarmusch explained in an interview with *Esopus Magazine* founder Tod Lippy, who asked: 'When the film came out in New York, weren't the subtitles for De Bankolé's French dialogue left out?' – 'Yeah, that was a big mistake.' Tod Lippy, ed., *Projections 11: New York Film-makers on New York Film-making, Interview with Jim Jarmusch* (London, 2000), pp. 264–5. The interview was also published in Juan A. Suárez, *Jim Jarmusch* (Urbana and Chicago, IL, 2007), pp. 169–70. The event was also reported in *Variety* by K. D. Shirkani: 'Errant "Dog" to Retrieve Auds' (20 March 2000) and can be found online: www.variety.com.
10   Peter Belsito, ed., *Notes from the Pop Underground* (Berkeley, CA, 1985), p. 69. A similar affirmation was made five years earlier by Jarmusch in his interview with Ralph Eue and Wolfgang Stukenbrock, 'Gespräche mit Jim Jarmusch', *Filmkritik*, XXV:10/298 (October 1981), pp. 453–60, now in Ludvig Hertzberg, ed., *Jim Jarmusch Interviews* (Jackson, MS, 2001), p. 5.
11   Director Lizzie Borden succeeded in a similar task with *Born in Flames* (1983), her feminist low-budget science fiction movie shot in New York in a semi-documentary style. In the film, a self-appointed women's army bombards the antenna that at the time still stood on one of the World Trade Center's Twin Towers, creating a disturbing *premonitory image* of the 9/11 attacks. This is how Borden recalls the experience: 'Literally the WTC transmission tower controlled everything and we went all the way to

the top and then walked out onto the roof with what looked like a bomb . . . and nobody stopped us! I had a $200 budget so I found this guy who built a model, then blew glitter through a tube and by slowing it down it looked like debris.' Transcript from Céline Danhier's documentary *Blank City* (2010).

12   Cord Riechelmann, 'Der Wille, richtig zu denken und zu leben', *taz. die tageszeitung* (14 May 2011). The article was published following the conference entitled 'The Limits of Hegel', which Slavoj Žižek held at the Volksbühne in Berlin on 12 May 2011.

13   The entire cinema sequence is very interesting from an acoustic point of view: the screened kung fu film is literally invisible to us, the audience, because Jarmusch frames only Eva and her three male companions, Billy, Willie and Eddie, watching the film, its audio taken from two different TV films recorded by Jarmusch, creating a sound collage, as he told Peter Belsito in *Notes from the Pop Underground*, p. 70.

14   Jonathan Rosenbaum, 'A Gun Up Your Ass: An Interview with Jim Jarmusch', *Cinéaste*, XXII/2 (June 1996), p. 23.

15   Todd J. Tubutis, in his Master of Arts thesis at the University of British Columbia's Department of Anthropology entitled 'Filming a Makah Village for Jim Jarmusch's *Dead Man*' (July 1998), deals with the question in great detail, referring also to ethnographic films by Franz Boas and Edward S. Curtis that inspired Jarmusch. The complete text can be downloaded at https://circle.ubc.ca.

16   Tag Gallagher, *John Ford: The Man and his Films* (Berkeley and Los Angeles, CA, 1986); Tag Gallagher, 'Angels Gambol where they Will', *Film Comment* (September–October 1993), reprinted in Jim Kitses and Gregg Rickman, eds, *The Western Reader* (New York, 1998), p. 274.

17   John Ford's famous cavalry trilogy, *Fort Apache* (1948), *She Wore a Yellow Ribbon* (1949) and *Rio Grande* (1950), was probably the first attempt made to rehabilitate the Native Americans, as John A. Price observed in *Native Studies: American and Canadian Indians* (Madison, WI, 1978), p. 206.

18   Ibid.

19   Rosenbaum, 'A Gun Up Your Ass', p. 21.

20   The phone conversation with Gary Farmer took place on 10 December 2003.

21   Ibid.

22   Rosenbaum, 'A Gun Up Your Ass', p. 21.

23   Ibid.

24   Peter von Bagh and Mika Kaurismäki, 'In Between Things', original title 'Asioiden välissä', *Filmihullu*, 5–6 (1987), pp. 63–6, reprinted in Hertzberg, ed., *Jim Jarmusch Interviews*, pp. 77–8.

25   Peter Keogh, 'Home and Away: An Interview with Jim Jarmusch', *Sight and Sound*, II/4 (August 1992), p. 9.

26 Rufus Thomas, who rather ironically labelled himself 'the oldest
   adolescent in the world', died in 2001 at the age of 84.
27 See my interview with Jim Jarmusch (1 February 2006).
28 Nick Alexander dubbed dozens of Italian films for the English-speaking
   market, such as Marco Ferreri's *Dillinger is Dead* (1969), Dario Argento's
   Deep Red (1975), Bernardo Bertolucci's *Stealing Beauty* (1996) and
   Giuseppe Tornatore's *The Legend of 1900* (1998).
29 I interviewed Nick Alexander in Rome on 8 May 2001, three years before
   his premature death in 2004.
30 Ibid. One example Alexander mentioned is Walt Disney's *The Aristocats*,
   the Italian version of which, in his opinion, is decidedly better than the
   English.
31 Ibid.

Voices: Roberto Benigni

1 Other than with The Lounge Lizards, Erik Sanko has also recorded and
   played live with John Cale, Yoko Ono, Gavin Friday and James Chance
   and the Contortions. His group Skeleton Key has recorded eight albums;
   the most recent, *Gravity is the Enemy*, was released in 2012 on Arctic Rodeo
   Recordings. Often defining himself as an 'ex-in-the-closet-puppeteer',
   Sanko, with the visual artist and set designer Jessica Grindstaff, founded
   the Phantom Limb Company in 2007. Since then it has produced, among
   others, *The Fortune Teller, Dear Mme. and 69°S*, the latter two in
   collaboration with the Kronos Quartet.

6 The Melting Pot of Words, the Way of Cultural Relativism

1 Jim Jarmusch, *Ghost Dog: The Way of the Samurai* (1999).
2 Giulio Ferroni, *Il comico nelle teorie contemporanee* (Rome, 1974), p. 9.
3 Jarmusch, *Ghost Dog*.
4 The well-known ditty used by Jarmusch in *Down By Law* (1986) comes
   from the homonymous song 'I Scream, You Scream, We All Scream for
   Ice Cream' (1927) by Howard Johnson, Billy Moll and Robert A. K. King,
   first recorded by Fred Waring and the Pennsylvanians, and then again in
   1928 by Harry Reser's Syncopators. Reser, the banjo virtuoso, was leader
   of an all-banjo orchestra, the Clicquot Club Eskimos.
5 This concept was made very clear by dubbing director Nick Alexander
   during our conversation in May 2001: 'In general, I believe that a
   dramatic film adapts better to another language than a comic film,
   not only because of the various performances but also thanks to the
   adaptation itself. The sense of humour of the original version won't
   necessarily correspond to that of the country seeing the dubbed version.

Unfortunately, the original comic performance is prone to losing a great deal in the dubbing process.'

6 'Down By Law' is also the title of a track by Fab 5 Freddy, featured in Charlie Ahearn's *Wild Style* (1983) and available on *Wild Style Original Soundtrack* (Rhino Records, 1994).

7 Luca Gasparini, 'Down by Law', *Buscadero*, 66 (January 1987), p. 52. Gasparini edited numerous films and documentaries by Guido Chiesa, who was Jarmusch's assistant director on *Down By Law*.

8 Franklin J. Schaffner's *Papillon* (1973) with Steve McQueen and Don Siegel's *Escape from Alcatraz* (1979) with Clint Eastwood are among the classic u.s. prison escape films. However, on the subject of escape films *Down By Law* also distances itself from the classic auteur film of the genre, Robert Bresson's *A Man Escaped* (*Un condamné à mort s'est échappé*, 1957) in which the preparation for the escape of a French Resistance fighter who has been condemned to death is illustrated in every minute detail.

9 Lou Reed and John Cale, *Songs for Drella*, Sire Records (1990). 'Drella', taken from the combination of Dracula and Cinderella, was one of the nicknames given to Andy Warhol, to whom this tribute album is dedicated.

10 The two pool players are tenor Charles Ponder and Stax pianist Marvell Thomas, who plays Dave. As the son of Rufus Thomas and brother of Carla Thomas, Marvell belongs to one of Memphis's most famous musical families.

11 A small tribute by Jarmusch to Otto Grokenberger, the German producer who played a crucial role in the lengthy making of *Stranger Than Paradise* and who is also credited as executive producer in the successive *Down By Law*.

12 Peter Keogh, 'Home and Away', *Sight and Sound*, II/4 (August 1992), p. 9.

13 The album is Neil Young's ninth made with trusty Crazy Horse, released on Warner Brothers on 19 August 2003. The film, written and directed by Young, was greeted with mixed reviews, and stars Sarah White as the young environmental activist Sun Green. Finally, the graphic novel *Neil Young's Greendale*, written by Joshua Dysart, illustrated by Cliff Chiang and coloured by Dave Stewart, was published in 2010.

14 The only exceptions to the rule are the *Coffee and Cigarettes* episodes, in which most characters play themselves.

15 The interview was published on 25 May 2013 and can be found online at www.youtube.com.

16 Directed by Tonino Valerii in collaboration with Sergio Leone, *My Name is Nobody* (*Il mio nome è Nessuno*, 1973), is the story of another male duo: tramp Nobody (Terence Hill) and the old bounty hunter Jack Beauregard (Henry Fonda). The film's score was composed by Ennio Morricone. Οὖτις ἐμοὶ γ' ὄνομα – Outis emoi g' onoma – My name is Nobody (*Odyssey*, 9:366); with this name the cunning Ulysses introduces himself to the terrible

Cyclops Polyphemus, who promises to eat him last, after his friends. But after Ulysses/Nobody has poked the flaming stake into the giant's one and only eye, and Polyphemus shouts that 'Nobody' has blinded him, none of the other giants comes to his aid, thinking that the Cyclops is drunk. *Talkin' Loud And Sayin' Nothing*, recorded by James Brown in 1970, was not released until two years later on the album *There It Is* (Polydor). Written by Brown and Bobby Bird, the piece is a classic example of original funk.

17   The official cause of Russell Jones/ODB's death, on 13 November 2004, two days before his 36th birthday, was accidental drug overdose caused by a lethal mix of cocaine and the prescription painkiller Tramadol.

18   Tal Rosenberg and Jeff Weiss, *C.R.E.W (Cash Rules Everything Wu)*. The quoted text was published in the abstract of the talk presented at the 'Cash Rules of Hip Hop' section of the 2011 Pop Conference, organized by the EMP Museum and held from 25–27 February at UCLA (University of California, Los Angeles). It is available online at www.passionweiss.com, 31 March 2011. Ignoring their given names and innumerable added pseudonyms, the nine members of the clan are: RZA, GZA/Genius, Ol' Dirty Bastard, Method Man, Ghostface Killah, Raekwon, Inspectah Deck, U-God and Masta Killa. Wu-Tang affiliate Cappadonna became an official member in 2007, as confirmed by RZA in a press conference on 2 October 2014; see 'RZA Reveals Cappadonna's Status in Wu-Tang Clan', www.hiphopdx.com, 7 October 2014.

19   Mitchell 'Divine' Diggs, CEO of the Wu-Tang Corporation, as well as being RZA's brother, and Oli 'Power' Grant, childhood friend of some of the Clan's original nine members, are the two commercial brains behind the group, and keep very much to the background with respect to the others. The launch of Wu-Brand, the 'haute couture' section of Wu-Wear, is among the more recent developments. The underwear line, labelled Ol' Dirty Bastard, is one of the unlucky projects that failed to make it.

20   I met Chad P. in New York at a Wu-Tang Clan concert in October 2003.

21   Tewfik Hakem, 'Wu au cinéma', *Les Inrockuptibles*, 215 (6–12 October 1999), p. 23.

22   To keep celebrating this culture RZA more recently contributed a track for a trailer of Wong Kar-wai's *The Grandmaster* (2013), based on the life of Yip Man, the legendary master of kung fu icon Bruce Lee.

23   '*Ghost Dog* – Intervista a RZA, Forest Whitaker e Jim Jarmusch', http://groovisionary-x.blogspot.com, 23 December 2011.

24   I interviewed Mulatu Astatke in Berlin on 30 October 2009. In the song 'Darashe', the digital bonus track on *Mulatu Steps Ahead*, released on Strut/Alive on 26 March 2010, Astatke offers a fusion of traditional Darashe music and jazz, the ensuing result being extraordinary in my opinion.

25   The public interview conducted by Geoff Andrew took place on 15 November 1999 and was published in *The Guardian*, where a shortened

version can still be read online: www.guardian.co.uk. It was also published
in Ludvig Hertzberg, ed., *Jim Jarmusch Interviews* (Jackson, MS, 2001),
pp. 179–80.
26 Emilio Cecchi and Natalino Sapegno, eds, *Storia della letteratura italiana:
Il Cinquecento*, vol. IV (Milan, 1966), p. 171.
27 Luc Sante's quote comes from the documentary *'Eskimo Lounge Music' –
Del Byzanteens Live at Hurrah* by Merrill Aldighieri, produced independently by the director and purchasable on her website: http://artclips.free.fr.

Voices: Luc Sante

1 Robert and John Dayton, eds, *Bird Effort 3/4 for John Hall Wheelock*
(New York, 1977). The poem by Jarmusch included in the magazine is
'The Flat Hand'.

7 Jarmusch, the Poet

1 Luc Sante, 'Mystery Train', *Interview* (November 1989), reprinted in
Ludvig Herzberg, ed., *Jim Jarmusch Interviews* (Jackson, MS, 2001), p. 88.
2 'Five Bagatelles' and 'Nature Mort' were published in *Columbia Review*,
LIV/1 (Winter 1975), pp. 29–30. At the time, Luc Sante was the magazine's
associate editor.
3 Lawrence Van Gelder, '*Stranger Than Paradise*: Its Story Could be a
Movie', *New York Times* (21 October 1984), p. 23.
4 Tobias George Smollett, *The Adventures of Roderick Random*, vol. II, 6th
edn (London, 1763), p. 36, italics mine.
5 Jim Jarmusch, 'Jim Jarmusch's Golden Rules', *MovieMaker Magazine*,
53 (22 January 2004).
6 Actually it was Jarmusch who was sued some years ago for plagiarism
regarding *Broken Flowers*. In March 2006 Reed Martin, writer, freelance
journalist and lecturer in film marketing at NYU, accused Jarmusch of
stealing the idea for *Broken Flowers* from a screenplay of his, and
demanded $40 million in damages, equal to the film's approximate take
at the box office. Jarmusch, who is known for never reading the screenplays sent to him, declared that Martin had 'absolutely no merit', adding
that: 'I had never had any contact with him or his work. I'd never even
heard of him. I still haven't seen the work he claims I copied. Anyone
who is familiar with my films and my writing process will know that this
claim is ridiculous.' On 28 September 2007, a Los Angeles federal court
returned a verdict in favour of Jim Jarmusch, and on 10 October 2007
U.S. District Court Judge Ronald S. W. Lew dismissed the case. See
'Stolen Flowers? The Controversy' at www.jim-jarmusch.net, July 2006.
7 Jarmusch, 'Jim Jarmusch's Golden Rules'.

8 Jim Jarmusch, 'Split-Screen', *Literaturmagazin*, XXVI (1990), p. 75. In the same volume also by Jarmusch are the poems 'The Trees are Crying' and 'Flexible Girls of Tokyo', published both in the original English version and in German, translated by Karin Graf.

9 Richard Kostelanetz, ed., *John Cage: Writer* (New York, 2000), p. 76.

10 To learn more about the universe of Rammellzee I suggest the article by Greg Tate, 'Rammellzee: The Ikonoklast Samurai', *The Wire*, 242 (April 2004).

11 Ibid.

12 David Toop, *Rap Attack #3*, 3rd edn (London, 2000), p. 122.

13 Following the success of 'Beat Bop' K-Rob's voice will again join Rammellzee's twenty years later on the album 'Bi-Conicals of the Rammellzee' (Gomma, 2004).

14 Toop, *Rap Attack #3*, p. 123.

15 Until writing-proof trains were imported from Japan, as observed by Greg Tate in the quoted article from *The Wire*.

16 Tom Breihaan, 'R.I.P. Hip-Hop Visionary Rammellzee', www.pitchfork.com, 30 June 2010.

17 Besides Rammellzee I can also mention some of the fundamental names among the exponents of Afrofuturism, principally Sun Ra and George Clinton's Parliament-Funkadelic.

18 Steven Rea, 'Interview with Jim Jarmusch: How William Blake Got Himself into a Picture', *Philadelphia Inquirer* (12 May 1996). The article is available at www.directors.ocatch.com.

19 Jonathan Rosenbaum, 'A Gun Up Your Ass: An Interview with Jim Jarmusch', *Cinéaste*, XXII/2 (June 1996), p. 21.

20 The poem 'Auguries of Innocence' was probably written between 1800 and 1803, and published in 1866 in the second collection of ten poems known as *The Pickering Manuscript*.

21 Jim Jarmusch, 'Jim Jarmusch's Guilty Pleasures', *Film Comment*, XXVIII/3 (May–June 1992), pp. 35–6. 'One actor I'm a big fan of is Lee Marvin . . . A secret organization exists called The Sons of Lee Marvin – it includes myself, Tom Waits, John Lurie and Richard Boes. We're initiating Nick Cave in it too.' Unfortunately, Richard Boes died on 21 February 2009.

22 William Blake wrote 'The Everlasting Gospel' probably between 1810 and 1812, even though the edition by J. Bronowski (1958) dates it as *c.* 1818. There is no definitive version approved by Blake, who left the poem unfinished.

23 Jonathan Rosenbaum, *Dead Man* (London, 2000), p. 70.

24 Jacob Levich, 'Western Auguries: Jim Jarmusch's *Dead Man*', *Film Comment*, XXXII/3 (May–June 1996), p. 39.

25 As pointed out by Luigi Soletta, the two Chinese ideograms for *Hagakure* are 'leaf' and 'hide', so it could be translated as 'in the shadow of leaves'

or 'hidden by leaves'. Yamamoto Tsunetomo, *Hagakure: il codice segreto dei samurai*, trans. Luigi Soletta (Turin, 2001), p. xiii. This edition contains a selection of 360 tales and aphorisms chosen from 1,343 of the original eleven volumes.

26 Ibid., pp. xv–xvi.
27 Ibid., p. xi.
28 Ibid., p. ix.
29 Ibid., p. xv.
30 Ibid., pp. 22 and 108.
31 Ibid., p. xiii.
32 To investigate the meaning of ritual suicide for Mishima, meant as life 'choreographed towards death' – the premonition of which is the Ankoku Butoh dance created by Tatsumi Hijikata, Mishima's great friend who together with Kazuo Ohno was one of the founding fathers of Butoh – I suggest reading Stephen Barber's brief and illuminating essay 'Mishima: Death-Fragments' (2007), available online in 'Collected Short Texts, 1990–2015', www.stephenkbarber.wordpress.com.
33 Tsunetomo, *Hagakure*, p. xvi. In 1966 Mishima had already staged his own suicide in the film *Rite of Love and Death* based on his own short story 'Patriotism'. Following Mishima's real death in 1970 every copy of the 30-minute film was destroyed, but the negative was saved. The film was restored 35 years later and can now be seen online at www.ubu.com, accessed 2 November 2014.
34 Yamamoto Tsunetomo, *Hagakure: The Book of the Samurai*, trans. William Scott Wilson [1979] (Tokyo, 2002). This is the edition used by Jarmusch.
35 As is made clear by Jarmusch in the dialogue:
    Ghost Dog: What is this, Louie? High Noon? Is this the final shootout scene?
    Louie: I guess it is.
36 Tsunetomo, *Hagakure*, pp 77–8.
37 The books that the girl pulls out of her schoolbag are: *The Wind in the Willows* by Kenneth Grahame, *The Souls of Black Folks* by W. E. Burghardt Dubois, *Frankenstein* by Mary Shelley and an improbable illustrated two-dime paperback with a catchy title and colourful cover, *Night Nurse* – a touch of irony typical to Jarmusch, which for a moment rocks the integrity of a highly moral character like Ghost Dog.
38 Played by Damon Whitaker, Forest's younger brother.
39 In 1986 – the year *Down By Law* was released – Benigni had not yet won the Academy Awards for *Life is Beautiful*, which in 1999 cemented his international success. In 1986 Tim Holmes of *Rolling Stone* explained how John Lurie had predicted Benigni's u.s. success: 'To American audiences, Benigni will seem like a real wild card, but *Down By Law* has the

potential to make him a big star here. "You can't imagine what a star he is in Italy," Lurie says. "I can think of an equivalent star, and that's the pope. When Roberto came to pick me up at the airport, all the people that handle the baggage stopped what they were doing and crowded around him."' Tim Holmes, 'Too Cool for Words: Jim Jarmusch Prefers to Let his Pictures Do the Talking', *Rolling Stone* (6 November 1986).
40 Ibid.
41 Umberto Mosca, *Jim Jarmusch*, 1st updated edn (Milan, 2006), p. 41.
42 Robert Frost, *Promises to Keep: Poems, Gedichte*, 6th reprint (Ebenhausen and Munich, 2008), p. 152.
43 These are the last lines of 'The Road Not Taken', from the collection of poems *Mountain Interval*. Now in Edward Connery Lathem, ed., *The Poetry of Robert Frost* (New York, 1974), p. 105.
44 Roman Mauer, *Jim Jarmusch: Filme zum anderen Amerika* (Mainz, 2006), pp. 94–5.
45 These are the four final lines of William Shakespeare's Sonnet 116.
46 William Shakespeare, *Hamlet*, Act II, Scene 2.
47 The interview was published on 25 May 2013 and can be found online at www.youtube.com.
48 One of the first publications on the subject was Delia Bacon's *The Philosophy of the Plays of Shakespeare Unfolded* (London, 1857).
49 The street sign was created for the film. See Hertzberg, ed., *Jim Jarmusch Interviews*, p. 127.
50 Juan A. Suárez, *Jim Jarmusch* (Urbana and Chicago, IL, 2007), p. 100.
51 *Stranger Than Paradise*, *Down By Law* and *Mystery Train* being clear examples of this approach.
52 The title *The Limits of Control* was inspired by the book of the same title by William S. Burroughs, originally published in *Semiotext(e): Schizo-Culture*, III/2 (1978), pp. 38–42, and reprinted in *Word Virus: The William S. Burroughs Reader* (New York, 2000). In Holly George-Warren, ed., *Rolling Stone Book of the Beats* (New York, 2000), Jarmusch wrote: 'Burroughs is the true godfather of outlaw artists. He was always hovering in the shadows, always suspicious of human nature and authority. Burroughs made us look for what masks the truth. He was always suspicious about movies, saying the truth can't possibly be found in twenty-four frames a second. In the greatest sense, Burroughs made me think about what's supposedly permissible in art.'
53 Logan Hill, 'No Limits: The Exotic Stylings of Jim Jarmusch's Latest Film: A Cultural Primer', *New York* (26 April 2009).
54 Suárez, *Jim Jarmusch*, p. 106.
55 Ibid., p. 107.
56 Henri Michaux, *Selected Writings* (New York, 1968), p. 101.

57 Walt Whitman, *Leaves of Grass* (New York, 1960), p. 122.
58 The audio guide was made with the support of the Poetry Foundation and officially presented to the public on 15 April 2012 at the Bowery Poetry Club. It is available for free online at www.eastvillagepoetrywalk.org.
59 For Holman's own definition of the word 'proprietor', see www.eastvillagepoetrywalk.org.

8 Communicating at all Cost: Intelligent Noise

1 Michel Chion, *Audio-Vision: Sound on Screen* (New York, 1994), p. 5.
2 Clearly, this does not apply to experimental and avant-garde cinema.
3 I met Elliot Sharp on 5 November 2005 during the Berlin Jazz Festival, where Sharp played as a special guest with former bass player of the first Lounge Lizards line-up, Steve Piccolo, and with Japanese electronic composer Gak Sato.
4 Tim Caspar Boehme, 'Das grosse Ohrensäubern', www.taz.de, 3 January 2011. This unpublished excerpt is quoted from the original transcript of Tim Caspar Boehme's interview with R. Murray Schafer, about the publication of the updated and revised German edition of his seminal work, *The Tuning of the World* (1977).
5 Ibid.
6 See my interview with Jim Jarmusch (February 2006).
7 Among Jarmusch's oldest collaborators I would like to mention Drew Kunin, who was responsible for the sound mixing of all his films from *Stranger Than Paradise* to date. Chic Ciccolini III, sound designer and Dominick Tavella, re-recording mixer, have also been part of the team of sound technicians who for years have collaborated with Jarmusch.
8 During an interview in April 2001 with Guido Chiesa, production assistant for *Stranger Than Paradise* and first director's assistant in *Down By Law*, I asked him to define Jarmusch on a film set using three adjectives. He replied: 'Meticulous, calm, concentrated. His film set reflects these aspects of his personality.'
9 Jim Jarmusch, NYC (April 1989), from the CD booklet of *Mystery Train*, a film by Jim Jarmusch, music by John Lurie (Barking Lady Music, New York, 1989).
10 Speaking with Schafer in Berlin after his presentation of the German updated edition of *The Tuning of the World* on 10 December 2010, I asked him if he had ever heard of sound being used in such a way, for example, as 'sound bombs', or Long Range Acoustic Devices, which shoot decibels on demonstrators, causing irreversible damage to their hearing. Schafer had never heard of this and reacted in shock when he learned of this aberration in the use of sound. 'This is horrible', he said.

11 Steve Goodman, *Sonic Warfare: Sound, Affect and the Ecology of Fear* (Cambridge, MA, and London, 2010), pp. 41–2. As well as having taught Music Culture at the School of Sciences, Media and Cultural Studies at the University of East London, Goodman is also the founder of the Hyperdub label and produces electronic music under the name Kode9.

12 Adam Harper, *Infinite Music: Imagining the Next Millennium of Human Music Making* (Winchester, 2011), p. 34.

13 Chion, *Audio-Vision*, pp. 21–4.

14 Stephen Barber, *The Walls of Berlin: Art: Film* (Chicago, IL, 2010), pp. 31–2.

15 Already in the 1940s Pierre Schaeffer started experimenting with electro-acoustic music at RTF – Radiodiffusion-Télévision-Française. In 1951 the Groupe de Recherche de Musique Concrète was born, with Pierre Henry among its members.

16 Salvatore Sciarrino, *Lohengrin: azione invisibile per solista, strumenti e voci*. First performed at the Piccola Scala di Milano on 15 January 1983.

17 Giorgio Battistelli, *Experimentum Mundi: opera di musica immaginistica per 16 artigiani, coro femminile, voce recitante e percussioni*. First performed in Rome at the Teatro Olimpico on 15 May 1981.

18 Unfortunately, both founders of Coil died in the 2000s – John Balance in 2004 and Peter Christopherson in 2010.

19 John Wray, 'Heady Metal', *New York Times Magazine* (28 May 2006). The article is also online at www.nytimes.com.

20 Transcript of Moby's interview with Jim Jarmusch for the *Soundcheck* programme, broadcast on WNYC on 13 August 2010.

21 Founded in 1999 by Barry Hogan, ATP is a record label and it organizes festivals, concerts and events around the world. ATP festivals are held in unconventional, often intimate settings and always different artists are in charge of the programming.

22 ATP also organized '*Only Lovers Left Alive* concerts', with live performances by all the musicians on the soundtrack: White Hills, Jozef van Wissem, Yasmine Hamdan, Zola Jesus and Sqürl. Concerts were held in Cologne and Berlin on 10 and 12 December 2013.

23 The track is 'Blood Swamp (TLOC Edit)', from the CD soundtrack published on Lakeshore Records (2009).

24 'Jim Jarmusch Unedited', *The Wire*, 309 (November 2009).

25 Luc Ferrari actually used almost exclusively sounds from nature, with very little interference from other types of sound matter. His *Presque rien* (INA-GRM, 1995) has become a classic of *musique concrète*, containing the famous *Presque rien No. 1 – le lever du jour au bord de la mer*, recorded between 1967 and 1970 on a beach in Yugoslavia, based entirely on field recordings condensed into a track that lasts almost 21 minutes.

26 Number 11.

Voices: Taylor Mead

1 John Cage, 'A Few Ideas about Music and Film', *Film Music Notes* (January–February 1951), reprinted in *John Cage: Writer*, ed. Richard Kostelanetz (New York, 2000), pp. 63–4.

9 Silence

1 John Cage, *Silence* (London, 1987), p. 8. First published in Britain in 1968.
2 Ibid., p. 8.
3 Michel Chion, *The Voice in Cinema*, ed. and trans. Claudia Gorbman (New York, 1999), p. 8.
4 Ibid.
5 Ibid., pp. 7–8.
6 Stephen Barber, 'The Skladanowsky Brothers: The Devil Knows', *Senses of Cinema*, 56 (October 2010). The essay can be found online at www.sensesofcinema.com.
7 Ibid.
8 Ibid.; Albert Narath, *Max Skladanowsky* (West Berlin, 1970), p. 23; Joachim Castan, *Max Skladanowsky, oder der Beginn einer deutschen Filmgeschichte* (Stuttgart, 1995), p. 57.
9 The famous 1926–7 biennium in the United States saw the release of two full-length feature films that are officially considered to be the start of the Talkies, thanks to the Vitaphone sound-on-disc technique: respectively *Don Juan* (6 August 1926) and *The Jazz Singer* (6 October 1927), both directed by Alan Crosland.
10 Chion, *The Voice in Cinema*, pp. 156–7.
11 Royal S. Brown, *Overtones and Undertones: Reading Film Music* (Berkeley and Los Angeles, CA, 1994), p. 57.
12 Among the most famous stories featured by Movietone News: Charles Lindbergh's Atlantic crossing and the *Hindenburg* disaster.
13 Rick Altman, ed., *Sound Theory, Sound Practice* (London and New York, 1992), p. 122.
14 Ibid., pp. 124–5.
15 Ibid.
16 Ibid., p. 124.
17 In 1908, for example, in order to 'dignify' cinema's bad reputation, the brothers Lafitte and the actors/directors André Calmettes and Charles Le Bargy founded the French production company Film d'Art. Among its most famous productions were *L'Assasinat du duc de Guise* (1908), *Le Retour d'Ulysse* (1909), *Les Misérables* (1913). Film d'Art remained in activity until the beginning of the 1920s.

18 Elisabeth Weis and John Belton, eds, *Film Sound: Theory And Practice* (New York, 1985), p. 83. The title of the celebrated 1928 manifesto by Eisenstein, Pudovkin and Aleksandrov is 'Buduš ee zvukovoj fil'my. Zajavka' ('Statement on Sound-Film').

19 Ibid., pp. 83–4.

20 Ibid., pp. 84–5.

21 Michelangelo Antonioni, *Fare un film è per me vivere: scritti sul cinema*, ed. Carlo di Carlo and Giorgio Tinazzi (Venice, 1994), p. 42

22 *Blue* is the last film by Derek Jarman (1942–1994), who was almost totally blind at the time of his death on 19 February 1994, eight years after being diagnosed HIV-positive. The film's sound texture is made up of the voices of Nigel Terry, John Quentin, Tilda Swinton and Jarman himself reading passages from his diary; music composed by Simon Fisher Turner and performed by numerous musicians including Peter Christopherson and John Balance of Coil, Momus and Brian Eno; and sound effects and soundscapes pitilessly describing the locations where Jarman spent the last period of his life, particularly St Bartholomew's Hospital in London.

23 George Varga, 'Tom Waits Interview', *Union Tribune* (3 October 2004).

24 Toru Takemitsu (1930–1996) was one of Japan's principal modern composers and music theorists. Composer of more than 100 film scores, including his memorable collaboration with Akira Kurosawa on *Ran* (1985) in which the use of silence is fundamental. Toru Takemitsu, *Confronting Silence: Selected Writings*, trans. and ed. Yoshiko Kakudo and Glenn Glasow (Berkeley, CA, 1995), p. 5.

25 Ibid., p. 6.

26 The quotes are taken from Charlotte Zwerin's documentary *Music for the Movies: Toru Takemitsu* (1994).

27 Ibid.

28 Ibid.

29 As Takemitsu himself confirmed regarding his work on the score for *Kwaidan* directed by Kobayashi.

30 Wilfried Mellers, *Music in a New Found Land: Themes and Developments in the History of American Music* [1964] (Piscataway, NJ, 2010), pp. 182–3.

31 St Maria Kyrka is Ystad's oldest building, dating back to the thirteenth century. The watchman's tower is from the seventeenth century.

32 See my interview with Amos Poe (December 2003).

33 I met Elliot Sharp on 5 November 2005 during the Berlin Jazz Festival.

34 Together with Sqürl and Jozef van Wissem.

35 Wanda Jackson's 'Funnel of Love' was released on the flipside of the single 'Right or Wrong' on Capitol Records (1961). More recently, the 'Queen of Rockabilly' collaborated with Jack White, who produced 'It Ain't Over Yet' on Nonesuch/Third Man (2011). For the soundtrack CD of *Only*

Lovers Left Alive Jarmusch collaborated with Madeline Follin, but the voice that is heard in the film is Jackson's.

36 Quote taken from the Q&A session after the screening of *Mystery Train* at the All Tomorrow's Parties festival held at Kutsher's Country Club in Monticello, NY, 11–13 September 2009; it is available online at www.criterion.com, 24 September 2009.

Voices: Ennio Morricone

1 John Cage, *Silence* (Middletown, CT, 1961), p. 5. Original note by John Cage: 'The following text was delivered as a talk at a meeting of a Seattle arts society organized by Bonnie Bird in 1937. It was printed in the brochure accompanying George Avakian's recording of my twenty-five-year retrospective concert at Town Hall, New York, in 1958.'
2 Ennio Morricone is probably referring here to Federico Fellini, who made his 'jealous' attitude towards music very clear in the brilliant radio conversation he had with his most faithful composer, Nino Rota, in 1979; an audio recording is available online: 'Fellini: "La musica? Solo al cinema" – Dialogo con Nino Rota', 6 October 2011, www.trovacinema.repubblica.it.

Voices: Jim Jarmusch

1 Michelangelo Antonioni, *A volte si fissa un punto . . .* (Catania, 1992).
2 This can be loosely and literally translated as: 'Watch out, girls / Three beautiful actresses / With machine guns / I die / Wearing no bathrobe'.

Profiles of Interviewees

1 Amos Poe

Born 1949. Director, writer, producer, actor. Inspiration for Jim Jarmusch, who often declared that Poe's *The Foreigner* (1978) was the film that made him decide to become a filmmaker. Poe used a $5,000 car loan to produce the film. In 1975, together with musician Ivan Kral, Poe directed, produced and edited *The Blank Generation*, which chronicled early performances of musicians such as Richard Hell, Patti Smith, Blondie, Ramones, Talking Heads and Television, among others. Poe cites Jean-Luc Godard, John Cassavetes and Andy Warhol as his primary artistic influences. *Unmade Beds* (1976) was Poe's homage to the French Nouvelle Vague. *Subway Riders* (1981) was his first film in colour and starred himself, John Lurie and Cookie Mueller, among others. More recently he has moved from film to canvas, working on his ROBOT series of monochrome paintings. His first solo exhibition was held in Spring 2013 at the Microscope Gallery in New York.

2 Phil Kline

Born 1953. Composer, sound artist, ex-lead singer and guitarist in the Del-Byzanteens, the early 1980s band he had with Jim Jarmusch. Friends from childhood, Kline and Jarmusch grew up in the suburbs of Akron, Ohio. Together with Jarmusch and Luc Sante, Kline attended Columbia University, while being an active member of the 'downtown scene'. He was part of Glenn Branca's guitar ensemble and collaborated with Nan Goldin on the soundtrack for her celebrated slide show, *The Ballad of Sexual Dependency*. Among Kline's many projects and recordings: *Zippo Songs*, based on the poems that American GIs inscribed on their Zippo lighters in Vietnam, and 'Unsilent Night', the boombox composition that debuted on the sidewalks of Greenwich Village in 1992 and is now a cult holiday tradition. Kline uses different musical forms, his compositions going from experimental electronics, to songs, to chamber, choral, theatre and

orchestral music. Among his projects 'in the making': an opera announced
as *Untitled Tesla Project*, together with Jim Jarmusch and Robert Wilson.

3 John Lurie

Born 1952. Composer, saxophonist, actor, director, painter, leader and founder
of The Lounge Lizards. He recorded 22 albums and composed scores for more
than twenty films, including all Jarmusch's films shot in the 1980s until
Mystery Train. He starred in *Permanent Vacation*, *Stranger Than Paradise*
and *Down By Law*. He wrote, directed and starred in the cult series *Fishing
with John* (1991) in which Lurie, who has no expert knowledge of fishing,
goes on fishing expeditions with his friends. They include Jim Jarmusch, Tom
Waits and Dennis Hopper. More recently Lurie turned his focus to painting.
His first solo exhibition was held in 2004 at Anton Kern Gallery in New York.
His works, dense with cynical humour and intertwined with the written word,
have been exhibited in the u.s., Europe and Japan. The MOMA in New York
has acquired his work for their permanent collection. He published *Learn to
Draw* and *A Fine Example of Art*.

4 Marc Ribot

Born 1954. Guitarist, composer. He is considered among the most eclectic and
versatile guitarists of his generation, exploring everything from the pioneering
jazz of Albert Ayler to the Cuban *son* of Arsenio Rodríguez. Ribot's teacher and
mentor was Haitian classical guitarist and composer Frantz Casseus. Musicians
he collaborated with regularly include John Zorn, John Lurie/The Lounge
Lizards, Tom Waits, T Bone Burnett, Elvis Costello; he also played as a side
musician for Wilson Pickett, Rufus Thomas, Chuck Berry and many more.
Presently Ribot has various individual bands: Ceramic Dog, Los Cubanos
Postizos, Marc Ribot Trio, Caged Funk. In 2003 he published *Scelsi Morning*,
inspired by Italian composer Giacinto Scelsi, which he performed at the
Salzburger Festspiele with the Ensemble Dissonanzen, and in 2009 he curated
the Century of Songs Festivals, a section of the Ruhr Triennale in Germany.
He has composed several film scores and played on Lurie's compositions for
Down By Law and *Mystery Train* by Jim Jarmusch.

5 Masatoshi Nagase

Born 1966. Actor, musician, photographer. Nagase's acting debut was in Shinji
Somai's 1983 yakuza film *P. P. Rider* (*Shonben raida*). His international career
was triggered by his role as rockabilly teenager Jun in Jim Jarmusch's *Mystery
Train*. In 1995 Nagase starred in the Icelandic road movie *Cold Fever* directed
by Fridrik Thor Fridriksson and produced by Jim Stark, who also produced

Jarmusch's *Down By Law, Mystery Train, Night On Earth* and *Coffee and Cigarettes*. Nagase has built a remarkable body of work as a character actor, for example, starring in the Maiku 'Mike' Hama detective films created by Kaizo Hayashi and Daisuke Tengan. Nagase released several albums of his own: on *Vending Machine* (1996) he collaborated with Joe Strummer, Iggy Pop and Ian Dury. He is also active as a photographer; his first solo exhibition, *Between Time Changes*, was held in spring 2013 at the Impossible Project Space in Tokyo.

6 Roberto Benigni

Born 1952. Actor, director, screenwriter. Roberto Benigni has often worked with Jim Jarmusch, starring in *Down By Law, Coffee and Cigarettes* and *Night On Earth*. His informal, satirical and often provocative style, especially on political topics, made him among the most popular public figures in Italy. In 1999 he won a triple Academy Award (Best Actor, Best Foreign Language Film, Best Soundtrack to Nicola Piovani) for *Life is Beautiful* (1997), written with Vincenzo Cerami, extending his fame to the u.s. and the rest of the world. A passionate lover of poetry, with an extraordinary improvisatory ability, Benigni has brought Dante Alighieri's *Divine Comedy* to public squares and theatres in Italy and abroad. In 2007 more than 10 million spectators watched his explanations and recitation by memory of the 'Fifth Song of Hell' broadcast on Italian public television. His deep knowledge of world literature has earned him many awards and honorary degrees from universities worldwide.

7 Luc Sante

Born 1954. Writer, critic, professor of writing and photography at Bard University. Sante's parents emigrated from Belgium to New Jersey in 1959. Author of *Low Life: Lures and Snares of Old New York* (1991), which earned him the role of historical consultant for Martin Scorsese's *Gangs of New York* (2002), Sante regularly contributes to the *New York Review of Books, New York Times Magazine* and many others. Among other titles by Sante are *Folk Photography* (2009), *Kill All Your Darlings: Pieces, 1990–2005* (2007), *Walker Evans* (2001) and *The Factory of Facts* (1998). In 1997 he was awarded a Grammy for the liner notes for the *Anthology of American Folk Music*. He collaborated with Jim Jarmusch on the never-released film *The Garden of Divorce* and is the author of some of the Del-Byzanteens' lyrics.

8 Eszter Balint

Born 1966. Actress, violinist, songwriter, dj, singer. Daughter of Stephan Balint, founder of the historical Squat Theatre that relocated from Budapest to New York City in the early 1970s, Balint got in touch with the 'downtown scene' at a very early age: she was sixteen when Jim Jarmusch chose her to star as Eva in *Stranger Than Paradise*. Currently busy principally with music, Balint has released two records of her own – *Flicker* (1999) and *Mud* (2004) – and has in 2015 completed a third, as yet untitled, recording. She collaborated with Marc Ribot, who is also featured on this most recent work, and John Lurie, among others. She sang on *Muy Divertido!* (2000), the second record of Ribot's band Los Cubanos Postizos, and duetted with him on the song 'Un poison violent, c'est ça l'amour', originally by Serge Gainsbourg. With Lurie she sang on *Marvin Pontiac's Greatest Hits* (1999), the first and only record by Lurie's dreamed-up African alter ego, who, according to legend, died in a road accident in 1977. More recently, Balint toured with Ribot's trio Ceramic Dog as a singer and violinist.

9 Taylor Mead

Born 1924, died 2013. Poet laureate of Andy Warhol's Factory, actor, composer. Besides Warhol, he worked with John Cassavetes, John Schlesinger, Jean-Luc Godard and others. When asked about his filmography, Mead estimated having acted in about 130 films, some of them shot in just one take. They include *Tarzan and Jane Regained . . . Sort of* (1963), *Taylor Mead's Ass* (1964) and *Lonesome Cowboys* (1967–8) by Warhol. In 2003 he acted in *Coffee and Cigarettes* (episode 'Champagne', with Bill Rice) by Jim Jarmusch. A long-time Lower East Side resident, Mead was very active at the Bowery Poetry Club where for years he performed his weekly one-man show, *Happy Hour with Taylor Mead*. His last poetry book is *A Simple Country Girl* (2005).

For the film critic J. Hoberman, Taylor Mead was 'the first underground movie star'. The film historian P. Adams Sitney called one of his earliest films, *The Flower Thief* (1960), 'the purest expression of the Beat sensibility in cinema'.

10 Ennio Morricone

Born 1928. Composer, conductor, trumpet player. A student of composer Goffredo Petrassi at S. Cecilia conservatory in Rome, Ennio Morricone received his composition degree in 1954. Music arranger for theatre, radio and television, in 1961 he wrote his first film score. The prolific collaboration with Sergio Leone – including *A Fistful of Dollars* (1964), *The Good, the Bad and the Ugly* (1966) and *Once Upon a Time in the West* (1968) – brought him international fame. In the mid-1960s Morricone entered the improvisation ensemble Gruppo di Improvvisazione Nuova Consonanza. Throughout his long career he has always continued to compose and record absolute music along with applied compositions for the cinema, his impressive body of work counting about 450 film scores and more than 100 other pieces. Directors he has collaborated with include: Gillo Pontecorvo, Pier Paolo Pasolini, Bernardo Bertolucci, Giuseppe Tornatore, Brian De Palma, Roman Polanski, Margarethe Von Trotta, Pedro Almodovar and Roland Joffé.

Musical Filmography

Permanent Vacation, 1980, colour, 77 mins

Screenplay/Story: Jim Jarmusch, **Cinematography:** James A. Lebovitz (Photographic Director), Thomas DiCillo (Cinematographer), **Sound:** Kevin Dowd, **Music:** John Lurie, Jim Jarmusch, **All Saxes:** John Lurie, **Music/Songs:** Earl Bostic, 'Up There in Orbit', **Editing:** Jim Jarmusch, **Principal Cast:** Chris Parker (Aloysius Parker, 'Allie'), Leila Gastil (Leila), John Lurie (Sax Player), Richard Boes (War Veteran), Sara Driver (Nurse), Jane Fire (Nurse), Ruth Bolton (Mother), Evelyn Smith (Patient), Maria Duval (Latin Girl), Frankie Faison (Man in Lobby), Eric Mitchell (Car Fence), Chris Hameon (French Traveller)
Production Company: Cinesthesia Inc., **Producer:** Jim Jarmusch

Stranger Than Paradise, aka The New World, 1982, black and white, 30 mins

Screenplay/Story: Based on an idea by Jim Jarmusch and John Lurie, **Cinematography:** Tom DiCillo, **Sound:** Greg Curry, **Music:** John Lurie, **Viola:** Aaron Picht, **Sax:** John Lurie, **Music/Songs:** Screamin' Jay Hawkins, 'I Put a Spell on You', **Editing:** Jim Jarmusch
Cast: Eszter Balint (Eva), John Lurie (Willie), Richard Edson (Eddie)
Production Company: Cinesthesia Inc., **Producer:** Jim Jarmusch

Stranger Than Paradise, 1984, black and white, 89 mins

Screenplay/Story: Jim Jarmusch, John Lurie, **Cinematography:** Tom DiCillo
Sound: Greg Curry (part 1), Drew Kunin (parts 2 and 3), **Music:** John Lurie, played by The Paradise Quartet, **Viola:** Jill B. Jaffe, **Violins:** Mary L. Rowell

and Kay Stern, **Cello:** Eugene Moye, **Music/Songs:** Screamin' Jay Hawkins,
'I Put a Spell on You', **Editing:** Jim Jarmusch, Melody London
Principal Cast: Eszter Balint (Eva), John Lurie (Willie), Richard Edson
(Eddie), Cecillia Stark (Aunt Lotte), Danny Rosen (Billy), Rammellzee (Man
with Money), Rockets Redglare (Poker Player), Sara Driver (Girl with Hat)
Production Company: Grokenberger Film Produktion (Munich), Cinesthesia
Inc. (New York), **Co-production:** ZDF – Das Kleine Fernsehspiel, Christoph
Holch, with special help from Paul Bartel, **Executive Producer:** Otto
Grockenberger

Down By Law, 1986, black and white, 107 mins

Screenplay/Story: Jim Jarmusch, **Cinematography:** Robby Müller, **Sound:**
Drew Kunin, **Music:** John Lurie. **Acoustic Bass:** Tony Garnier, **Banjo:** Marc
Ribot, **Cello:** Eugene J. Moye, **Drums:** Doug Browne, **Guitar:** Arto Lindsay,
Percussion: E. J. Rodriguez, Naná Vasconcelos, **Trombone:** Curtis Fowlkes,
Trumpet, Songs: Tom Waits, 'Jockey Full of Bourbon'; 'Tango Till They're
Sore' from the album *Rain Dogs*; Irma Thomas 'It's Raining' (Naomi Neville),
Editing: Melody London
Principal Cast: Tom Waits (Zack), John Lurie (Jack), Roberto Benigni
(Roberto), Nicoletta Braschi (Nicoletta), Ellen Barkin (Laurette), Billie Neal
(Bobbie), Rockets Redglare (Gig), Vernel Bagneris (Preston)
Production Company: Island Pictures, Black Snake Inc., Grockenberger
Film Produktion, **Producer:** Alan Kleinberg, **Co-producers:** Tom Rothman,
Jim Stark, **Executive Producers:** Otto Grockenberger, Cary Brokaw,
Russel Schwartz

Coffee and Cigarettes, 1986, black and white, 6 mins

Screenplay/Story: Jim Jarmusch with Roberto Benigni and Steven Wright,
Cinematography: Tom DiCillo, **Sound:** William (Billy) Sarokin, **Editing:**
Melody London
Cast: Roberto Benigni (Bob), Steven Wright (Steven)
Production Company: Black Snake, **Producer:** Jim Stark

Coffee and Cigarettes (Memphis Version), 1989, black and white, 8 mins

Screenplay/Story: Jim Jarmusch, **Cinematography:** Robby Müller, **Sound:**
Drew Kunin, **Editing:** Melody London
Cast: Joie Lee (Customer 1), Cinqué Lee (Customer 2), Steve Buscemi (Waiter)
Production Company: Black Snake, **Producer:** Rudd Simmons, Jim Stark,
Co-producer: Demetra MacBride

Mystery Train, 1989, colour, 113 mins

Screenplay/Story: Jim Jarmusch, **Cinematography:** Robby Müller, **Sound:** Drew Kunin, **Music:** John Lurie, **Guitar, Harmonica:** John Lurie, **Banjo:** Marc Ribot, **Bass:** Tony Garnier, **Drums:** Douglas B. Bowne, **Music/Songs:** Elvis Presley, 'Mystery Train' (Junior Parker, Sam Phillips); 'Blue Moon' (Richard Rodgers); Junior Parker, 'Mystery Train' (Junior Parker, Sam Phillips); Otis Redding, 'Pain in my Heart' (Naomi Neville); Roy Orbison, 'Domino' (Samuel Phillips); Rufus Thomas, 'The Memphis Train' (Mack Rice, Rufus Thomas, Willie Sparks); Bobbie 'Blue' Bland, 'Get Your Money Where You Spend Your Time' (Chester Burnett); The Bar-Kays, 'Soul Finger' (Jimmy King, James Alexander, Thalon Jones, Ben Cauley, Ronnie Caldwell, Carl Cunningham), **Editing:** Melody London
Principal Cast: 'Far From Yokohama': Masatoshi Nagase (Jun), Youki Kudoh (Mitsuko), Screamin' Jay Hawkins (Night Clerk), Cinqué Lee (Bellboy), Rufus Thomas (Man in Station), Jodie Markell (Sun Studio Guide); **'A Ghost':** Nicoletta Braschi (Luisa), Elizabeth Bracco (Dee Dee), Tom Noonan (Man in Diner), Stephen Jones (The Ghost); **'Lost in Space':** Joe Strummer (Johnny aka Elvis), Rick Aviles (Will Robinson), Steve Buscemi (Charlie), Rockets Redglare (Liquor Store Clerk), Tom Waits (Radio DJ)
Production Company: JVC Entertainment, Mystery Train Inc., **Producer:** Jim Stark, **Executive Producer:** Kunijiro Hirata, Hideaki Suda, **Associate Producer:** Demetra MacBride

Night On Earth, 1991, colour, 129 mins

Screenplay/Story: Jim Jarmusch, **Cinematography:** Frederick Elmes, **Sound:** Drew Kunin, **Music:** Tom Waits, **Horn:** Ralph Carney, **Cello:** Matthew Brubeck, **Guitar:** Joe Gore, **Bass:** Clark Suprynowitz, **Accordion:** Josef Brinckmann, **Percussion:** Mule Patterson, **Keyboards:** Francis Thumm, **Songs:** Tom Waits, 'Back in The Good Old World, Good Old World' (Tom Waits, Kathleen Brennan), Davie Allan and the Arrows, 'Cycle Delic' (Dave Allan), Blue Cheer, 'Summertime Blues' (Eddie Cochran, Jerry Capehart), **Editing:** Jay Rabinowitz
Principal Cast: 'Los Angeles': Gena Rowlands (Victoria Snelling), Winona Ryder (Corky); **'New York':** Armin Mueller-Stahl (Helmut Grokenberger), Giancarlo Esposito (Yo-Yo), Rosie Perez (Angela); **'Paris':** Isaach de Bankolé (Cab Driver), Béatrice Dalle (Blind Woman), Pascal N'Zonzi, (Passenger #1), Emile Abossolo M'bo (Passenger #2); **'Rome':** Roberto Benigni (Cab Driver), Paolo Bonacelli (Priest); **'Helsinki':** Matti Pellonpää (Mika), Kari Väänänen (Man #1), Sakari Kuosmanen (Man #2), Tomi Salmela (Man #3)
Production Company: JVC Entertainment, Victor Musical Industries, Pyramide Productions, Le Studio Canal+, Pandora Film, Channel 4 Productions, Locus

Solus Productions, **Producer:** Jim Jarmusch, **Executive Producer:** Jim Stark, **Co-producer:** Demetra J. MacBride, **Co-executive Producers:** Masahiro Inbe, Noboru Takayama

Coffee and Cigarettes (Somewhere in California), 1993, black and white, 12 mins

Screenplay/Story: Jim Jarmusch, **Cinematography:** Frederick Elmes, **Sound:** Steve Balliet, **Music:** See *Coffee and Cigarettes* (2003), **Editing:** Terry Katz, Jim Jarmusch
Cast: Iggy Pop (Himself), Tom Waits (Himself)
Production Company: Cinesthesia Inc., **Producers:** Demetra J. MacBride, Birgit Staudt

Dead Man, 1995, black and white, 121 mins

Screenplay/Story: Jim Jarmusch, **Cinematography:** Robby Müller,
Sound: Drew Kunin, **Music:** composed and performed by Neil Young,
Editing: Jay Rabinowitz
Principal Cast: Johnny Depp (William Blake), Gary Farmer (Nobody), Lance Henriksen (Cole Wilson), Michael Wincott (Conway Twill), Eugene Byrd (Johnny 'The Kid' Pickett), Robert Mitchum (John Dickinson), Gabriel Byrne (Charlie Dickinson), John Hurt (John Scholfield), Mili Avital (Thel Russell), Crispin Glover (Train Fireman), Iggy Pop (Salvatore 'Sally' Jenko), Billy Bob Thornton (Big George Drakoulious), Jared Harris (Benmont Tench), Alfred Molina (Trading Post Missionary), Michelle Thrush (Nobody's Girlfriend)
Production Company: 12 Gauge Productions, JVC Entertainment, Miramax Films, Newmarket Capital Group, LP, Pandora Film, **Producer:** Demetra J. MacBride, **Co-producer:** Karen Koch, **Production Executive:** Michael Boehme (Camera Film)

Year of the Horse, 1997, colour and black and white, 106 mins

Cinematography: Jim Jarmusch, Larry A. Johnson (Super 8), Steve Onuska, Arthur Rosato, **Sound:** John Hausmann, **Music:** Neil Young, **Guitar/Vocals:** Neil Young, **Guitar/Keyboards/Vocals:** Frank 'Poncho' Sampedro, **Bass/Vocals:** Billy Talbot, **Drums/Vocals:** Ralph Molina, **Songs:** Neil Young, 'Fuckin' Up, Slip Away', 'Barstool Blues', 'Stupid Girl', 'Big Time', 'Tonight's the Night', 'Sedan Delivery', 'Like a Hurricane', 'Music Arcade', 'My Girl' (William Robinson Jr, Ronald White), **Editing:** Jay Rabinowitz
Production Company: Shakey Pictures, **Producer:** Larry A. Johnson, **Executive Producers:** Elliot Rabinowitz, Bernard Shakey (Neil Young)

Ghost Dog: The Way of the Samurai, 1999, colour, 116 mins

Screenplay: Jim Jarmusch, **Story Consultant:** Sara Driver, **Cinematography:** Robby Müller, **Sound:** Drew Kunin, **Music:** RZA, **Music/Songs:** Ghostface Killah, Cappadonna, Raekwon, 'Ice-Cream Instrumental Mix' (R. Diggs, C. Woods); Wu-Tang Clan, 'Fast Shadow' (RZA); RZA, 'Raise Your Sword (Samurai Showdown)'; Killah Priest, 'From Then Till Now' (Walter Reed, Ernest Aye, D. Black, J. Barry, W. Warwick); Willie Williams, 'Armagideon Time' (Willie Williams, Clement Dodd); Andrew Cyrille, Jimmy Lyons, 'Nuba One'; Public Enemy, 'Cold Lampin With Flavor' (Flavor Flav, Hank Schocklee, Eric Sandler); William Loose, 'Dangerous Fun', **Editing:** Jay Rabinowitz
Principal Cast: Forest Whitaker (Ghost Dog), John Tormey (Louie), Isaach de Bankolé (Raymond), Cliff Gorman (Sonny Valerio), Henry Silva (Ray Vargo), Camille Winbush (Pearline), Victor Argo (Vinny), Frank Minucci (Big Angie), Richard Portnow (Handsome Frank), Tricia Vessey (Louise Vargo), Gene Ruffini (Old Consigliere), Damon Whitaker (Young Ghost Dog), Gary Farmer (Nobody), RZA (Samurai in Camouflage)
Production Company: Plywood Productions, JVC, Le Studio Canal+, Bac Films, Pandora Film, ARD/Degeto Film, **Producer:** Richard Guay, Jim Jarmusch, **Co-producer/Unit Production Manager:** Diana Schmidt, **Post-production Supervisor:** Jim Jarmusch

Int. Trailer. Night, 2002, black and white, 10 mins

Screenplay/Story: Jim Jarmusch, **Cinematography:** Frederick Elmes, **Sound:** Drew Kunin, **Music:** Johann Sebastian Bach, 'Goldberg' Variations (Aria and Variation #15), performed by Glenn Gould, **Editing:** Jay Rabinowitz
Principal Cast: Chloë Sevigny (Actress)
Production Company: Atom Films, Emotion Pictures, Odyssey Films, Film Förderunganstalt (FFA), JVC Entertainment, Kuzui Enterprises, London Matador Pictures, Road Movies, WGBH Boston, **Producer:** Cecilia Kate Roque, **Associate Producer:** Stacey Ellen Smith

Coffee and Cigarettes, 2003, black and white, 95 mins

Screenplay/Story: Jim Jarmusch, **Cinematography:** Tom DiCillo, Robby Müller, Frederick Elmes, Ellen Kuras, **Sound:** Drew Kunin, Wiliam Sarokin, Steve Balliet, **Music/Songs:** Richard Berry & The Pharaohs, 'Louie Louie'; C-Side, Tom Waits, 'Saw Sage' (T. Waits/R. Waters/D. Devore/Tom Nunn/ B. Hopkin), 'Lonesome Road' (Doug Wood); Jerry Byrd, 'Serenade to Nalani', 'Paauau Waltz' (John U. Iosepa), 'Hanalei Moon' (Robert Nelson); Modern Jazz Quartet, 'Baden-Baden' (Milt Jackson, Raymond M. Brown); Tommy James and the Shondells, 'Crimson and Clover' (Tommy James, Peter Lucia);

The Skatalites, 'Nimblefoot Ska' (Clement Dodd); Roland Alphonso, Carol McLaughlin, 'Set Back (Just Cool)' (Clement Dodd); Roland Alphonso and the Soul Vendors, 'Streets of Gold' (Clement Dodd); Eric 'Monty' Morris, 'Enna Bella' (Eric 'Monty' Morris, Clement Dodd); Fretwork, 'Fantazias for the Viols' (Henry Purcell); The Stooges, 'Down on the Street' (J. Osterberg/ R. Asheton/S. Asheton/D. Alexander); Funkadelic, 'A Joyful Process' (George Clinton Jr, Bernard G. Worrell); 'Nappy Dugout' (George Clinton Jr/Cordell Mosson/Garry Shider); Janet Baker and the New Philharmonia Orchestra, 'Ich Bin der Welt Abhanden Gekommen' (I Have Lost Track of the World) (Gustav Mahler); Iggy Pop 'Louie Louie' (Richard Berry), **Editing:** Jim Jarmusch, Melody London, Jay Rabinowitz, Terry Katz
Principal Cast: 'Strange to Meet You': Roberto Benigni (Roberto), Steven Wright (Steven); **'Twins':** Joie Lee (Good Twin), Cinqué Lee (Evil Twin), Steve Buscemi (Waiter); **'Somewhere in California':** Iggy Pop (Iggy), Tom Waits (Tom); **'Those Things'll Kill Ya':** Joe Rigano (Joe), Vinny Vella (Vinny), Vinny Vella Jr (Vinny Jr); **'Renée',** Renée French (Renée), E. J. Rodriguez (Waiter); **'No Problem':** Alex Descas (Alex), Isaach De Bankolé (Isaach); **'Cousins':** Cate Blanchett (Cate/Shelly); **'Jack Shows Meg His Tesla Coil':** Jack White (Jack), Meg White (Meg); **'Cousins?':** Alfred Molina (Alfred), Steve Coogan (Steve); **'Delirium':** GZA (GZA), RZA (RZA), Bill Murray (Bill Murray); **'Champagne':** Bill Rice (Bill), Taylor Mead (Taylor)
Production Company: Smokescreen (released by United Artists), **Producers:** Joana Vincente, Jason Kiliot, Jim Stark, Demetra MacBride, Birgit Staudt, Rudd Simmons, **Associate Producer:** Rachel Dengiz

Broken Flowers, 2005, colour, 106 mins

Screenplay/Story: Jim Jarmusch, inspired by an idea from Bill Raden and Sara Driver, **Story Adviser:** Sara Driver, **Cinematography:** Frederick Elmes, **Sound:** Drew Kunin, **Music:** Mulatu Astatke, **Music/Songs:** The Greenhornes with Holly Golightly, 'There is an End' (Craig James Fox); Jackie Mittoo, 'El Bang Bang'; The Tennors, 'Ride Your Donkey' (Albert George Murphy); Oxford Camerata, *Requiem* Op. 46 ('Pie Jesu') (Gabriel Fauré); Mulatu Astatke, 'Yekermo Sew', 'Yegelle Tezeta', 'Mascaram Seteba', 'Gubelye' (Traditional); Mulatu Astatke and his Ethiopian Quintet, 'Playboy Cha-Cha' (Oscar Garcia); Marvin Gaye, 'I Want You' (Leon Ware, Arthur Rose); The Brian Jonestown Massacre, 'Not If You were the Last Dandy on Earth' (Matt Hollywood); The Allman Brothers Band, 'Dreams I'll Never See' (Gregg Allman); Fretwork, *Aire* ('Pavan' A 5 in C minor) (William Lawes); Sleep, 'Dopesmoker' (Al Cisneros, Matt Pike, Chris Haikus); Holly Golightly, 'Tell Me Now so I Know' (Ray Davies); Mulatu Astatke and his Ethiopian Quintet, 'Alone in the Crowd' (Gilbert Snapper); Dengue Fever, 'Ethanopium' (Mulatu Astatke), The Greenhornes, 'Unnatural Habitat' (Keeler and Curley), **Editing:** Jay Rabinowitz

Principal Cast: Bill Murray (Don Johnston), Julie Delpy (Sherry), Jeffrey Wright (Winston), Alexis Dziena (Lolita), Sharon Stone (Laura), Frances Conroy (Dora), Christopher McDonald (Ron), Chloë Sevigny (Carmen's Assistant), Jessica Lange (Carmen), Tilda Swinton (Penny), Pell James (Sun Green), Mark Webber (The Kid)
Production Company: Five Roses, Focus Features, Bac Films, **Producers:** Jon Kilik, Stacey Smith, **Co-producer/Unit Production Manager:** Ann Ruark

The Limits of Control, 2009, colour, 116 mins

Screenplay/Story: Jim Jarmusch, **Cinematography:** Christopher Doyle, **Sound:** Drew Kunin, **Music:** Boris, **Additional Music**: Jim Jarmusch, Carter Logan, Shane Stoneback, **Music/Songs:** Boris, 'Feedbacker'; Boris with Michio Kurihara, 'Fuzzy Reactor'; Mstislav Rostropovich and the Melos Quartet, 'Adagio' from String Quintet in C, D956 (Franz Schubert); Boris, '   '; Sunn O))) & Boris, 'N. L. T.'; Bill Doggett, 'Moon Dust'; LCD Soundsystem, 'Daft Punk is Playing at My House' (James Murphy); Boris, 'Farewell'; The Black Angels, 'You on the Run'; Manuel El Sevillano, 'Por Compasión: Malagueñas' (Traditional); Sunn O))) & Boris, 'Blood Swamp'; La Macarena, 'Saeta' (Traditional); Talegón de Córdoba, Jorge Rodriguez Padilla, 'El Que Se Tenga Por Grande – "Dulce Pena" Arrangement' (Traditional); Earth and Bill Frisell, 'Omens and Portents 1: The Driver' (Dylan Carlson); Carmen Linares, 'El Que Se Tenga Por Grande' (Traditional), **Editing:** Jay Rabinowitz
Principal Cast: Isaach de Bankolé (Lone Man), Alex Descas (Creole), Jean-François Stévenin (French), Luis Tosar (Violin), Paz de la Huerta (Nude), Tilda Swinton (Blonde), Youki Kudoh (Molecules), John Hurt (Guitar), Gael García Bernal (Mexican), Hiam Abbass (Driver), Bill Murray (American), La Truco (Flamenco Dancer), Talegón de Córdoba (Flamenco Singer), Jorge Rodriguez Padilla (Flamenco Guitarist)
Production Company: PointBlank, EF Entertainment Farm, Focus Features, **Producers:** Stacey Smith, Gretchen McGowan, **Executive Producer:** Jon Kilik, **Associate Producer:** for PointBlank Films: Carter Logan

Only Lovers Left Alive, 2013, colour, 123 mins

Screenplay/Story: Jim Jarmusch, **Cinematography:** Yorick Le Saux, **Sound:** Drew Kunin (Detroit), John Midgley, Robert Hein, **Music:** Jozef van Wissem, **Additional Music:** Squürl, **Music/Songs:** Wanda Jackson, 'Funnel of Love' (Charlie McCoy, Kent Westberry); Kasbah Rockers, 'Harissa' (Pat Jabbar, Abdelaziz Lamari); Charles Yang, 'Caprice' no. 5 in A minor (Niccolò Paganini); Y.A.S., 'Gamil' (Mirwais Ahmadzaï, Yasmine Hamdan, Abdelouab Abrit); Charlie Feathers, 'Can't Hardly Stand It' (Joe Chastain, Charlie

Feathers, Jerry Huffman); Denise LaSalle, 'Trapped by a Thing Called Love' (Denise Ora Craig); Hot Blood, 'Soul Dracula' (M. Armbruster, P. Duc); White Hills, 'Under Skin or by Name' (Dave W., Ego Sensation); Black Rebel Motorcycle Club, 'Red Eyes And Tears' (Robert Turner as Robert Been, Peter Hayes, Nick Jago); Bill Laswell, 'Little Village'; Yasmine Hamdan, 'Hal',
Editing: Affonso Gonçalves
Principal Cast: Tom Hiddleston (Adam), Tilda Swinton (Eve), John Hurt (Marlowe), Mia Wasikowska (Ava), Anton Yelchin (Ian), Jeffrey Wright (Dr Watson), Slimane Dazi (Bilal)
Production Company: Recorded Picture Company (RPC), Pandora Filmproduktion, Snow Wolf Production, **Co-production:** ARD Degeto Film, Lago Film, Neue Road Movies, Le Pacte, Sanderfin, **Producers:** Jeremy Thomas, Reinhard Brundig, **Executive Producers:** Christos V. Konstantakopoulos, Jean Labadie, Bart Walker, Peter Watson, Stacey E. Smith, **Associate Producers:** Viola Fügen, Alainée Kent, Richard Mansell, **Co-producers:** Carter Logan, Marco Mehlitz, Gian-Piero Ringel, Christine Strobl

Acknowledgements

I am grateful to many people for their substantial help and precious advice throughout the writing of this book, in particularly Michael Leaman, Stephen Barber, Jörg Boehme and Steve Chapin.

This book would not have existed without the invaluable commitment and collaboration of Robert Brodie Booth, who translated it brilliantly from Italian and made the extensive revision process we went through together unimaginably light and pleasant.

At Exoskeleton in New York my deep gratitude goes to Jim Jarmusch for allowing me to have access to the collection of stills and to Carter Logan for his help and mediation.

At Reaktion in London I would like to thank Vivian Costantinopoulos, Maria Kilcoyne, Aimee Selby and Susannah Jayes especially, along with the entire publishing team, and at the University of Chicago Press, Ryo Yamaguchi.

Many people made crucial contributions of various kinds at different stages of the process. A massive thank you to: all the interviewees – especially Ennio Morricone and Jim Jarmusch; Gary Farmer, James Nares, Elliot Sharp, Steve Piccolo, Tilda Swinton, Chad P., Enrica Fico Antonioni, Nicoletta Braschi, Cristiana Caimmi, Myriam Trevisan, Guido Chiesa, Tom Waits, Tresa Redburn, Wim Lunsing, Akira Okano, Yoko Kim Kondo, Myia Yoshida, Andrea Grosso, Nick Pope, Steve Course, Alex Lay, Jessica Grindstaff, Erik Sanko, Rozalia Jovanovic, Jesse Richards, Marie Dahl, Gustaf Ljunggren, Susanne Schott, Daniel Spitzer, Simone Arndt, Bob Holman, Ludvig Hertzberg, Peter Hofknecht, Francesca Romana Ciardi, Giuseppe Goffredo, Alessio Elia, Ugo Piazza and Maria Piazza Renzi, Rita, Maria, Kiki, Frank and Ciro Scotti, Brigitte Boehme, Marcello and Marina Siniscalco, Nick and Irena Alexander, Judit Kurtág, Danny Zapata, Ben Porter Lewis, Silvia Morini, Natascia Pennacchietti, Giandomenico Curi, Marco de Marco, Massimiliano Busti, Mauro Zanda, Simone Caputo, Kristín Björk Kristjánsdóttir, Roberto Nanni and Nick Zedd.

Numerous friends and colleagues supported me in the most disparate ways – but with similar enthusiasm – throughout the years. You know who you are. However, I would like to mention: Pieter Steenhauer, Benedetta Bosco, Katja Noordam, May Noordam Croes, Marc Baronner, Tik Ho Ong, Saskia de Zee, Albert Meijvogel, Eveleena Dann, Kirk Bradley Peterkin, Sarah Silvagni, Sebastiano Bazzini, Garon Peterson, Gisella Sorrentino, Peter D'Elia, Giovanni Guardi, Fabio Gatti, Filippo D'Antoni, Eva Hoeppner, Jana Gross, Gerda Koch, Dorothea Horedt, Peter Baumgärtel, Guido Möbius, Elettra de Salvo, Francesco Stella, Alessandro Cipriani, Alessia Ganga, Giusi Valentini, Annika Krump, Marianne Kapfer, Chico de Luigi, Franziska Wagner, Martin Langer, Ariane Faber Velasco, Gabriele Avanzinelli, Annamaria Cattaneo, Cecil Thuillier, Muriel Koevoet, Rocco de Rosa, Stefano Consiglio, Enrico Cerasuolo, Dagmar Werther, Tatiana Bazzichelli, Stefano Maria Bianchi, Jane Alexander, Tatjana Mesar, Marzio Marzot, Irmela Heimbächer and Arnild Lun.

Finally, for their boundless patience, love and inspiration I am especially and forever grateful to my family: Giovanni Piazza, Christel Strohn, Laura Piazza and Tim Caspar Boehme.

Permissions

Michelangelo Antonioni, *A volte si fissa un punto . . .* (Catania, 1992) quoted with permission of Enrica Fico Antonioni.

Amiri Baraka, 'In the Funk World', in *Digging: The Afro-American Soul of American Classical Music* (University of California Press: Berkeley and Los Angeles, CA, 2010), reprinted by permission of University of California Press Books.

The Del-Byzanteens, 'Lies to Live By', quoted with permission of Luc Sante.

Transcripts of interviews with Eszter Balint, Jim Jarmusch, Phil Kline, John Lurie, Taylor Mead, Ennio Morricone, Masatoshi Nagase, Amos Poe, Marc Ribot and Luc Sante printed with permission of the interviewees. Transcript of interview with Roberto Benigni printed with permission of Melampo Cinematografica s.r.l.

Photo Acknowledgements

The author and publishers wish to express their thanks to the below sources of illustrative material and/or permission to reproduce it.

The author would like to express her deep gratitude to all those who contributed to the visual materials that enrich the book either by providing images or by granting permission to reproduce them. In particular I would like to thank Carter Logan in New York, but also Archivio Iconografico del Verbano Cusio Ossola (www.archiviodelverbanocusioossola.com), Julia Riedel at Deutsche Kinemathek, Amos Poe and Nesrin Wolf (who was most helpful with the picture material for the illustration on p. 123). Finally, a very special thank you to Niels Olaf Schroeder, whose other illustrations and artwork can be found at www.niels-schroeder.de.

Photographic credits for the Jim Jarmusch films: *Permanent Vacation* © 1980 Cinesthesia Productions Inc.; *Stranger Than Paradise* © 1984 Cinesthesia Productions Inc.; *Down By Law* © 1986 Black Snake Inc.; *Mystery Train* © 1989 Mystery Train Inc., photos by Masayoshi Sukita, *Night on Earth* © 1991 Locus Solus Inc., photos by Mark Higashino; *Dead Man* © 1995 12 Gauge Productions Inc., photos by Christine Parry; *Ghost Dog* © 1999 Plywood Productions Inc., photos by Abbot Genser; *Coffee And Cigarettes* © 2003 Smokescreen Inc.; *Broken Flowers* © 2004 Dead Flowers Inc., photos by David Lee; *The Limits of Control* © 2009 PointBlank Films Inc.; *Only Lovers Left Alive* © 2013 Bad Blood Films Inc.

Photographic credits for other images: Deutsche Kinemathek: pp. 68, 69, 70; Malte Göbel: p. 86; Lucas Heinz: pp. 84, 307; Cassandra Jenkins: p. 113; Marion Kalter: p. 315; courtesy John Lurie: p. 123; courtesy Pierre Michoud / Aaton: p. 11 top; courtesy James Nares: p. 78; Fernando Natalici: pp. 41, 43

top; Sara Piazza: pp. 155, 332; courtesy Luc Sante: pp. 62, 63, 75; courtesy
Niels Olaf Schroeder: pp. 22, 50, 92, 126, 170, 207, 236, 284, 310, 335, 346.

Index

Printed and bound by CPI Group (UK) Ltd, Croydon, CR0 4YY

13/05/2026

14878670-0002